Events Management

Contemporary events management is a diverse and challenging field. This introductory textbook fully explores the multidisciplinary nature of events management and provides the student with all the practical skills and professional knowledge they need in order to succeed in the events industry. It introduces every core functional area of events management, such as marketing, finance, project management, strategy, operations, event design and human resources, in a vast array of different event settings from sport to political events.

This new edition has been updated to include:

- New and updated content on developments in technology, risk management and event volunteering.
- New and updated case studies that include emerging economies.
- New industry voices by international practitioners.

Every topic is brought to life through vivid case studies, personal biographies and examples of best practice from the real world of events management. Written by a team of authors with many years' experience of working in the events industry, *Events Management: An Introduction* is the essential course text for any events management programme.

Charles Bladen is Senior Lecturer in Marketing and Events Management at GSM London, UK.

James Kennell is Principal Lecturer and Programme Leader for Events, Tourism and Hospitality in the Department of Marketing, Events and Tourism at the University of Greenwich, UK.

Emma Abson is Senior Lecturer on the Events Management courses at Sheffield Hallam University, UK.

Nick Wilde is an expert in sports marketing and sporting events management, with research interests in international sports marketing, which he has taught in many overseas institutions.

"The second edition of *Events Management* represents a step forward in recognising events as professional projects and will aid the continuing professionalisation of the events industry. The new edition has been well updated with event case studies which are truly international and which will enhance a student's ability to make the connection between theory and practice / real world learning."

Allan Jepson, *University of Hertfordshire, UK.*

"The updated edition of *Events Management: An Introduction* continues to be a comprehensive and accessible textbook. The second edition covers the principals of events management plus key industry trends and developments in technology, the role of emerging economies and the importance of strategic event evaluation. The book retains all the key features of the original with updated case studies, making this the go-to study companion for event management students."

Emma Nolan, *University of Chichester, UK.*

Events Management

An Introduction

Second Edition

Charles Bladen, James Kennell, Emma Abson and Nick Wilde

Routledge
Taylor & Francis Group

LONDON AND NEW YORK

Second edition published 2018
by Routledge
2 Park Square, Milton Park, Abingdon, Oxon, OX14 4RN

and by Routledge
711 Third Avenue, New York, NY 10017

Routledge is an imprint of the Taylor & Francis Group, an informa business

First edition published by Routledge 2012.

British Library Cataloguing-in-Publication Data
A catalogue record for this book is available from the British Library

Library of Congress Cataloging-in-Publication Data
Names: Bladen, Charles, author. | Kennell, James, author. | Abson, Emma, author. | Wilde, Nick, author.
Title: Events management : an introduction / Charles Bladen, James Kennell, Emma Abson and Nick Wilde.
Description: Second Edition. | New York : Routledge, 2018. | "Chapter 6" 2018 Robert Wilson"—T.p. verso. | Includes bibliographical references and index.
Identifiers: LCCN 2017021006 (print) | LCCN 2017033541 (ebook) | ISBN 9781315695204 (Master ebook) | ISBN 9781317442257 (Web pdf) | ISBN 9781317442240 (epub3) | ISBN 9781317442233 (Mobipocket) | ISBN 9781138907041 (Hardback : alk. paper) | ISBN 9781138907058 (Paperback : alk. paper) | ISBN 9781315695204 (Ebook)
Subjects: LCSH: Special events—Management.
Classification: LCC GT3405 (ebook) | LCC GT3405. B63 2018 (print) | DDC 394.2068—dc23
LC record available at https://lccn.loc.gov/2017021006

ISBN: 978-1-138-90704-1 (hbk)
ISBN: 978-1-138-90705-8 (pbk)
ISBN: 978-1-315-69520-4 (ebk)

Typeset in Sabon and Frutiger
by Keystroke, Neville Lodge, Tettenhall, Wolverhampton

Visit the companion website:
http://www.routledge.com/cw/bladen

Printed and bound by CPI Group (UK) Ltd, Croydon, CR0 4YY

Contents

Contents

Contents

Contents

Images

Figures

Tables

Tables

Case studies

Case studies

Acknowledgements

Charles Bladen: For Kim, Sol, Owen and Freya and Barbara.

James Kennell: For Lyra, Aphra and Evelyn.

Emma Abson: I'd like to thank my family and friends for their support during this project.

Nick Wilde: To all of my friends, family and colleagues around the world who have supported me in my career, with a special mention for my brother Phil Holden, as well as Rory Miller, Orlando Salvestrini, Fernando de Tomaso, Omar Larrosa, Alan Dennington and Trevor Williams. Finally to Ellie Ghassemi, the love of my life, you are my inspiration and I love you with all of my heart.

Guided tour

A visual tour of *Events Management: An introduction*

Pedagogical features

Events Management: An introduction offers a variety of ways to help lecturers introduce this exciting discipline, and to engage students and help them understand key concepts and issues.

CHAPTER AIMS

Each chapter opens with a series of key learning outcomes that students will be able to attain after reading the chapter. They serve to ensure more focused learning and teaching.

1.2 Aims of the second edition

By the end ~~pter~~ the student will be able to:

~~aracteristics of events;~~
~~n and history of events;~~
● describe ~~e of the contemporary events industry;~~
~~ationships between the events industry and the education sector; and~~
● explain ~~ok in order to develop their knowledge of event management.~~

FIGURES, TABLES AND IMAGES

The text uses a rich mix of figures, tables and images to represent important concepts and issues, creating an inviting visual design.

CASE STUDIES

International case studies are included in each chapter, illustrating the chapter topic area through a focused presentation of events management on the ground. Case studies are supplemented by study activities asking students to engage actively with the material. See *List of case studies* for full details.

CASE STUDY 1.1

Good ~~Food~~ & Wine Show Gauteng, South ~~rica~~

~~ican~~ annual food event of its kind, The Good Food & Wine ~~the~~ latest food and beverage products, innovations, lifestyle ~~d~~ appliances. The events have been held at various South African ~~ng~~ Johannesburg, with more recent event extensions in Cape Town ~~s~~ ~~an~~.

The prosperity of economy and image experienced by South Africa in the post-Mandela era has arguably been tarnished by what many regard as misgovernment, leading in particular to a devalued currency and falling wine sales. This festival has therefore been heralded as one of the important avenues by which these deficits might be corrected.

The core concepts of the show include themes, such as 'Eat Well, Live Well', 'Fresh', 'lifestyle' and 'baking'. The live theatre includes sessions on wine and

STUDY ACTIVITIES

The book fosters an active learning approach through discussion points and activities interspersed throughout each chapter. These can be used as the basis for class discussion, or developed into essay questions or research projects.

Study activity

1 In you   inion, to what extent is events management a profession? Use
  eviden   pport your answer.
         e present approach of defining the attributes of the events
         rofession resemble the various approaches presented in
2 How fe suggest event professionalism can be more effectively
  man

INDUSTRY VOICES

Voices come from a range of companies and organisations, from sponsorship consultants to security advisers, communication executives to mega-event programmers.

Industry voice

Joanna Griffith

" I   the British Council as an events officer, just after they had
  sta   anning the launch of a series of seminars to commemorate the
  40   iversary of world-famous playwright William Shakespeare's
  de   being interviewed, the initial plan was that the event, based
        re's play Twelfth Night, was to take place on the twelfth day
        stmas. However, by the time I commenced employment, the event
had been rescheduled for performance on its original date, 2 February, at its
original venue, Middle Temple, in London.

As a fairly recent graduate of Events Management, I was so excited to join the British Council team and the launch of the 'Shakespeare Lives Seminar Series' on such a significant date and venue.

CHAPTER SUMMARIES

A concise overview of each chapter – perfect to consolidate learning, or as a useful tool for student revision.

4.8 Summary

This chapte   ghlighted the importance of events operations. Throughout the chapter, it
                    that every event is different and individually complex, so there is no set
has been ma   s. The legislation relating to health, safety and risk changes regularly
                    t event managers keep abreast of the current legalities and regulations.
formula for   focused on two key operational aspects of events: the consideration of
                    licences, permits and contracts involved when managing an event; and
        d it is   ding logistical planning for customers and on-site at venues.
                    of event operations to decide which resources, skills and equipment will be
required is an essential part of the events management process and needs to be considered

FURTHER READING

Each chapter concludes with a list of key scholarly books and articles that will provide additional treatment of the theories and concepts covered. Students will find this list particularly helpful for developing and researching papers and other assignments.

Further reading

Allen, J., Ha   Jago, L. K. and Veal, A. J. (eds) (2000) *Events beyond 2000: Setting the*
                       gs of the Conference on Evaluation, Research and Education, Sydney
  Agenda: Australian Centre for Event Management, University of Technology,
  July 200   ers on event operations, including the Abbott and Abbott paper on
                       t and control. These proceedings also cover many fundamental issues
  Includ   ment studies and are thoroughly recommended.
                       Corporate Manslaughter Law: No Place to Hide, *Personnel Today,* 17
                       able at: www.personneltoday.com/articles/2008/03/17/44774/corporate-
manslaughter-law-no-place-to-hide.html. Accessed 28 December 2010. An interesting
article that offers a useful checklist for event managers operating within the regulations of
the Corporate Manslaughter and Corporate Homicide Act 2007.
BSI ISO20121 Sustainability in Event Management Available at: www.bsigroup.com/en-GB/
iso-20121-sustainable-events-management/. Full details on the ISO20121 standard can be
found here.

Companion Website

 http://www.routledge.com/cw/bladen

The second edition of *Events Management: An introduction* will also include an updated, comprehensive companion website of online resources for both students and lecturers. These include:

Student Resources

- Annotated further reading for each chapter to provide an accessible gateway to in-depth information on key issues highlighted.
- Various tools used by events management professionals to provide further insight into the realities of the industry.
- Multiple Choice Questions for each chapter for students to test their understanding.
- Further discussion questions for each chapter, which can be set as assessment tasks or used to prompt seminar or in-class discussions.

Lecturer Resources

- PowerPoint presentations for each chapter to provide lecturers with a ready-made foundation for their lecture preparation. The files can be downloaded and annotated.

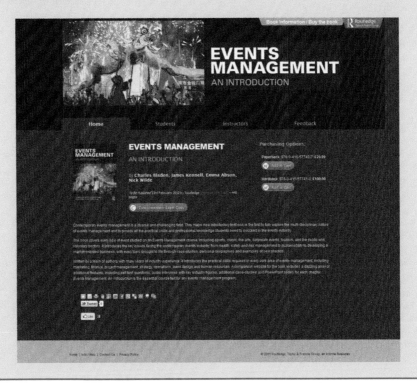

Chapter 1

Introduction to events management

Contents

1.1 Introduction to the second edition

Many changes have transpired since we wrote the first edition of this book. The events sector and the profession have greatly developed, as have the geopolitical and economic environments surrounding them. This chapter, in addition to introducing the rest of the book, is intended to 'set the scene' for the reader in terms of the crucial role of events in human history through to the present day. The emphasis of events as an artefact of human culture, which developed into a fast-growing industry, has more recently and increasingly appeared to establish itself as an expediter of local and global strategies for many kinds of change, in national, international and digital realms. At the time of the publication of this second edition, the authors have endeavoured to incorporate key changes to the events sector by advances in technology, as well as cultural and geopolitical changes by the election of new world leaders and the realignment of democratic and economic boundaries. The book also attempts to address other contemporary questions that are raised by the continued development of the events sector, and the education provisions designed to serve it.

1.2 Aims of the second edition

By the end of the chapter the student will be able to:

- describe the main characteristics of events;
- explain the evolution and history of events;
- analyse the structure of the contemporary events industry;
- understand the relationships between the events industry and the education sector; and
- navigate this book in order to develop their knowledge of event management.

1.3 What is an event?

There are various answers to this question, depending on the viewpoint of the person defining it. There are many definitions of 'events' available from various academic writers such as Getz (2007) and Goldblatt (2008). As such definitions become more detailed, their 'real world' application becomes more problematic. Thus, this book provides a general definition as follows:

> Events are temporary and purposive gatherings of people.

It follows that 'Events Management' as a field of industrial practice should be defined as:

> The organisation and coordination of the activities required to achieve the objectives of events.

The aims of this text are to discuss and evaluate the management of these activities in the context of various and common types of events within their wider industrial and societal context. In order to do this, a clearer discussion of the features of events which make them distinct from more general business activities is required.

Events generally possess the following characteristics:

- They are temporary in nature.
- They are gatherings of people.
- They are often displays of ritual.
- They are, in some sense, unique occurrences.

Though these points may seem rather obvious, the more we observe the phenomenon of events in our society, and its influence on our business and social lives, the more we could be forgiven for finding inconsistencies between these basic descriptors and that which we witness daily in the media, our neighbourhoods and even our own families.

1.3.1 Events are temporary

Events differ from other, more common, organisational activities because they possess a finite beginning and end. Managers and students probably agree that most events have a start time, a programme and a finishing time. Though this is certainly true of managed events, it is generally not the case with 'spontaneous events' which generally take place without much specific planning.

It is necessary to plan times and programmes for the successful delivery of a planned event yet these 'spontaneous' displays of ritual, events that take place without much specific planning, can be wide-ranging in nature and expression. For example, there has been much publicity in the media about the governmental changes that have taken place due to the widespread uprising of nations in the so-called 'Arab Spring', a series of anti-government protests, which have led to significant changes in the rule of several of these countries. Similar informal events have accompanied more formal, programmed events in other parts of the world, such as those ongoing, spontaneous protest events facilitated by the Occupy Movement in Wall Street, New York, USA; the demonstrations against the election of the 45th President of the United States, Donald J. Trump; and those who celebrated (or protested against) the June 2016 referendum result which signalled the decision of the United Kingdom to leave the European Union.

There are also important differences between events and the attractions in or around which they are held. Getz (2007) focuses on the differences between events and permanent attractions such as historical venues; though many events take place for a pre-planned period at such venues. For example, permanent art galleries, such as Thyssen-Bornemisza Museum in Madrid, regularly hold events within their venues to display works by artists for a limited period only. Such events can last for several weeks, and while their attraction to tourists is clear, their limited duration still places them in the category of events.

1.3.2 Events are gatherings of people

So far, we have established that events are comprised of people, though numbers of such attendees may vary considerably. A clear definition of an event attendee is often easier to define in certain situations than in others. Somebody attending a sports or music event is unlikely to be allowed to enter without a ticket, whether paid for or not. However, as will be discussed in Chapter 10, mega-events include in their scope entire locations, destinations and even the whole world in the form of international media coverage.

Events can involve single people as the focus, as in the case of concerts by solo music celebrities, or whole groups, such as those who attended the event discussed in the following case study.

CASE STUDY 1.1

Good Food & Wine Show Gauteng, South Africa

As the largest African annual food event of its kind, The Good Food & Wine Show showcases the latest food and beverage products, innovations, lifestyle home gadgets and appliances. The events have been held at various South African cities, including Johannesburg, with more recent event extensions in Cape Town and Durban.

The prosperity of economy and image experienced by South Africa in the post-Mandela era has arguably been tarnished by what many regard as misgovernment, leading in particular to a devalued currency and falling wine sales. This festival has therefore been heralded as one of the important avenues by which these deficits might be corrected.

The core concepts of the show include themes, such as 'Eat Well, Live Well', 'Fresh', 'lifestyle' and 'baking'. The live theatre includes sessions on wine and cookery, including presentations by top chefs. The event has social media support, regularly tweeting on the @goodfoodSA Twitter timeline, as well as involvement with many leading sponsors from related industries. The recent relaunches in all three of these destinations have repositioned the events as much more than straightforward trade shows, focusing more on global sustainability of urban farming.

Study activity

1 Which are the main groups of people being gathered by this event?
2 What, do you think, are some of the possible event planning aspects that need to be considered for this event?
3 What are your ideas about potential future developments of the Food and Wine Show concept?

As can be seen from this example, events can comprise both planned staging elements and unplanned spontaneity. The scale and formality of events can vary considerably as can the levels of ritual display.

When considering such events as gatherings, we should also consider the impacts of more recent technologies on these otherwise age-old practices. Certainly web conferencing – the ability through media to share information from widespread geographic locations – has progressed in terms of effectiveness and popularity in recent years. In a sense, the participants gather without travelling.

Applications of web conferencing include meetings, training events, lectures or presentations and have the advantage of being real-time, and carry the facility to be recorded, which is a valuable service for many businesses. Downsides of web conferencing include technological failure which can fast make a promising event a complete non-event. This is particularly frustrating for organisers of larger web conferences as the technology is rarely under their direct control.

Webinars or webcasts have been born of these technologies, making one-way mass-presentations possible to international audiences, with webinars tending to be more interactive than webcasts. Workshops can also be effectively held by organisers using online tools.

Despite certain suggestions at one time about the possibility that web conferencing would end 'real' conferencing completely, it has proven to be used as a supplement to face-to-face contact rather than its replacement. One of the main limitations of web conferencing is that it cannot replace the richness of face-to-face interactions.

1.3.3 Events are often displays of ritual

Humans are the most socially evolved species on the planet. As such, we develop social interactions beyond our family structures which facilitate the need for events. According to Maslow (1943), the relationship of these social needs relate to other human needs as shown in Figure 1.1.

As this early model suggests, humans are on a journey to the achievement of self-actualisation, which relates to the ultimate fulfilment of one's potential. Initially, physiological needs, followed by safety needs should be satisfied before a person can go about satisfying their needs for love and belonging to a social group. Clearly these latter needs are partially fulfilled through family ties and social relationships, but they could also be said to form the main motivating factor behind the age-old practice of holding events.

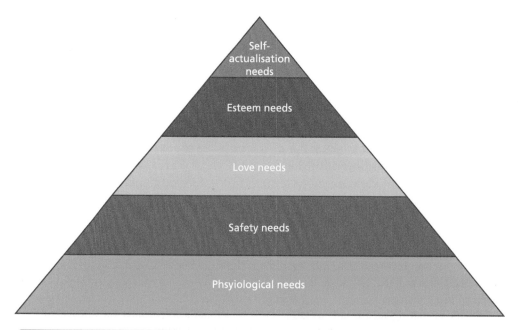

Figure 1.1 Maslow's hierarchy of needs
Source: Adapted from Maslow 1943

Events are characterised by rituals, symbols and artefacts which themselves denote meaning. For example, one has only to consider the average wedding event, which will likely be comprised of various costumes, food and drink, speeches and behaviours, which denote the meanings of the culture in question. More discussion of how these meanings can be designed is provided in Chapter 3.

1.3.4 Events are unique occurrences

Events, because they are not permanent, are held at different times, in different locations for different reasons. Even the same event held annually can differ considerably in its characteristics. These features make every event, in a sense, unique. As will be discussed in Chapter 14, this makes planning for event legacy particularly challenging, as the enduring things left over after the event are often very difficult to predict.

1.4 Events management challenges

The previous discussion raises some important challenges for anybody seeking to manage the delivery of an event. Whether the reader is an event professional or a student, they could be forgiven for concluding that a coherent understanding of the events industry and its effective 'management' is almost impossible due to its very breadth, complexity and fast-moving nature. A definition and categorisation of different events has been attempted and results in some common labels, which include mega-events, cultural events, special events, corporate events, sporting events and so on.

Although such a clean categorisation of events should enable their management requirements to be easily communicated, in practice it seems that these labels are often too broad and unclear to be useful. For example, many of the special events upon which Goldblatt (2010) bases his discussions could also be categorised by several other classifications. While clearly recognising such problems, it was decided to use many of these classifications as chapter headings. Industry professionals do still use many classifications, such as 'special events', to define certain event concepts, but terms such as 'corporate events' are widely recognised to encompass a variety of concepts, such as conferences, exhibitions or brand experience events, which are generally more useful in conveying their ideas.

However, the aims of this book focus on the systematic management of these practices involved in the delivery of events as formal projects on a variety of scales. As discussed in Chapter 2, the origination, planning and delivery of events, regardless of their classifications, tend to require similar frameworks, based upon the events management theory accumulated.

1.5 Events, human history and culture

Despite the obvious advantages of clear and definite information, particularly to those embarking on new study of this exciting and fast-evolving field, it should be worth remembering that events management is largely the modern-day practice of age-old expressions of human social interactions and activities. Before commencing an understanding of some of the mechanics of modern-day events management, a more historical view of their development throughout the ages may enable the reader to put contemporary events management into the context of its origins.

Ancient texts, such as those used to translate the Christian and Jewish Old Testaments, record the early practice of festivals. These were enshrined in law and primarily took the form of the seven feasts of Israel, where the people of the nation gathered seven times throughout the year in religious celebration and remembrance. Such records show various customs and rituals were carried out, from the eating of the Passover feast through to the offering of various sacrifices. Variations of these different feasts are still carried out today. World religions, such as Islam, later developed their own annual pilgrimages, like the one to Mecca (see p. 213 this edition), which in the present day has led to a number of significant crowd safety challenges. Indeed, it was religious observance to the gods of Greece which birthed the first ancient Olympic Games. Modern-day festivals such as Christmas and Halloween also find their roots in such observances, whether pagan or otherwise. The development of modern-day events from their origins is illustrated in the following case study.

CASE STUDY 1.2

The Nehru Trophy Boat Race, India

The Nehru Trophy Boat Race, also known as the Snake Boat Race in English, is held on the second Saturday of each August, near Alappuzha, Kerala, India. The boat race is named after Jawaharlal Nehru, the first prime minister of the new, independent India, who in 1952 was escorted by the people of Alleppey, in snake boats, and donated a silver trophy of a snake boat to be awarded to the annual winner of the race. The event has grown in recognition and international interest over the decades that it has been held and has become widely televised and, more recently, races have been disseminated via YouTube.

Image 1.1 **The Nehru Trophy Boat Race, India**
Credit: STRDEL/Stringer/Getty Images

Study activity

1 Research the Nehru Trophy Boat Race online and compare and contrast some of its traditional and more modern-day characteristics. What do you think are the main reasons for any changes or new developments?
2 Choose a similar, more familiar festival to you and establish its:

- Origins – how did it come about? What were the original reasons for it being held?
- Main rituals – what are the reasons for these?
- Modern developments – how has the event changed from its origins to its present expression? What are the reasons for these changes?

1.6 The events 'business'

In the previous case study, one of the reasons for the modernisation of the event from its traditional origins was the changing culture and other aspects of the way people live as members of a fast-developing, global economy.

Festivals are generally common forms of cultural practice and, although many have long histories, the majority have been founded in the much more recent past (Getz 2005). The International Festivals and Events Association estimates that there are over 4.5 million recurring festivals worldwide per year (IFEA 2009: 1).

The influence on the UK national economy alone of all types of events is clearly substantial.

In a 2014 report entitled 'Events are GREAT Britain', compiled on behalf of the Business Visits and Events Partnership (BVEP) about the presence of the events in UK industry, many useful conclusions were reached, including:

- The sector is worth £39.1 billion per annum to the national economy.
- Leisure visitors spend £583 per visit while visitors to UK exhibitions from overseas spend £611 per visit, worth £4.4 billion annually, and the spend by those accompanying attendees at business events is worth an additional £7.7 billion.
- Events account for 35 per cent of the UK visitor economy.
- Trade transacted at exhibitions and other business events held in the UK is conservatively estimated to be worth over £100 billion.
- There are more than 25,000 businesses in the sector, which sustain at least 530,000 full-time equivalent (FTE) jobs.
- Inbound business visits to Britain equate to 23.5 per cent of all visits and, at £4.4 billion, 24.4 per cent of the total spend.
- Business events account for 30 per cent of the UK visitor economy.

The economic influence of the industry alone is substantial and the report illustrates this in Figure 1.2 with a breakdown according to many of the different types of events discussed in our later chapters:

Total value £36.1bn			
Corporate events £30.3bn	Cultural events and festivals £2.3bn	Sports events £2.3bn	Outdoor events £1bn

Figure 1.2 The value of Britain's events industry by sector
Source: Adapted from *Events are GREAT Britain Report* 2014

1.7 Role of events managers

Such a presence and development of just one nation's events industry as part of the overall international and global picture has prompted a greater need for trained specialists to plan, organise and deliver such events. Such undertakings, often mammoth in scope, have raised new requirements of those tasked with them. As with most professionalising fields, there has been some discussion of the most suitable traits, attributes and skills needed by the modern-day events manager. Their leadership style and qualities are discussed further in Chapter 2, and the skills they need to be able to apply are touched upon in each of the relevant, subsequent chapters. These newer industry requirements logically present questions about how such skills are acquired and the role of events management education in the professionalisation of future events managers.

CASE STUDY 1.3

Is events management a profession?

Presumably most readers and practitioners in the field would immediately confirm that it was, without reservation. In fact many of us speak of the 'events management profession' all the time, yet often do not compare it to other, more traditional examples of professions in our society, such as doctors, accountants or teachers. Part of the problem in referring to the events field as 'a profession' and its managers as 'professionals', lies in the historical definition of such terms, which is probably now quite outdated.

Undergraduate education for the 21st-century events profession

This discussion about the events sector boasting a single, coherent profession has prompted contemporary discussion about the provision of undergraduate education to students who eventually intend to enter a career in events management.

Bladen and Kennell (2014) discuss whether the traditional university model of academic education is currently fit for purpose, whether the events sector can even be considered as a profession in the traditional sense and how provision can be more effectively tailored to what is an extremely important yet diverse sector of world economies.

Within this UK-centric discussion, the authors discuss both the fast development of Events Management degrees, with little unified support from the wide number of regulatory and industry bodies responsible for its oversight, as well as who benefits from the skills and competencies of the graduates produced by such programmes.

Wilensky's (1964) model of a profession concluded that it must have:

1 The emergence of a full-time occupation.
2 The establishment of a training school.
3 The founding of a professional association.
4 Political agitation directed towards the protection of the association by law.
5 The adoption of a formal code.

However, to date, there appears to be little progress made in many of the above qualifiers. There still exists great employment flexibility and insecurity present in the events industries that make up the sector. There is likewise a series of different pathways in events education and training, still with many successful events managers foregoing any formal events education whatsoever. There exists a plethora of events-related professional bodies, which tend to represent only their own particular industry. Many events employees still have no formal professional, legal or collective representation. Also, outside the areas already legislated, or general quality management or environmental initiatives, there is still no formal events code of practice, mainly because of the diverse activities of the sector.

Though useful for academic programme development (Barron and Leask 2012), criticisms of the Events Management Body of Knowledge continue, mainly due to its static nature and limited breadth of use for educators and industry specialists. Certification programmes by international professional initiatives, such as those by the Canadian Tourism Human Resource Council (CTHRC), still await wider and more universal adoption, as does its Events Management International Competency Standards project (EMICS).

As all these works progress towards the establishment of Events Management as a profession, the sector continues to require large numbers of appropriately skilled workers. One solution has been to recruit large numbers of often unpaid volunteers from colleges and universities. However, the arguments used to justify this free use of unpaid labour by events managers have largely been discredited due to the imposition of UK minimum-wage legislation. Thus, this makes the gaining of useful work experience to bolster their academic profiles more difficult for students to obtain.

Certainly, there continues to be a need for graduates to gain employment and for events industry organisations to acquire large amounts of cost-effective, skilled labour. Therefore, there needs to be continued discussion about the future shape events education, training and the related certifications take, in order that the value for money sought by students translates into the professionals needed to populate the ever-growing Events Management profession.

> ### Study activity
>
> 1 In your opinion, to what extent is events management a profession? Use evidence to support your answer.
> 2 How far does the present approach of defining the attributes of the events management profession resemble the various approaches presented in this case?
> 3 How can you suggest event professionalism can be more effectively achieved?

1.8 About this book

As previously stated, the overarching aim of this book is to provide a working knowledge of the field of events management. Following our general review of the development of the present-day industry, and some of the fundamental questions raised for both students and practitioners of the field, a review of the key debates which this book attempts to facilitate in the chapters which follow should be noted.

This book has been designed to cover the wide variety of events that make up the subject matter of most events management courses, as well as to provide practical event planning and events management skills and knowledge. There follows a brief outline of each chapter.

To support students in developing their understanding of the topics covered in each section, a number of features have been included in each chapter:

- clearly stated aims at the start of each chapter;
- international case studies;
- student activities; and
- further reading suggestions.

There are also a variety of industry-focused features available on the book's companion website.

1.8.1 Chapter 1: Introduction

This first chapter analyses the role and significance of events from historical times until the present day. It sets out how events have evolved and describes the current state of the events industry. Importantly, it contains this summary section, setting out the book's structure. When researching any aspect of events management, this chapter will provide a key starting point from which the rest of the text can be navigated.

1.8.2 Chapter 2: Event project management

This chapter analyses events as projects, with specific features that need to be planned, managed and evaluated in order for a successful event project to be delivered. As projects, events generally have fixed budgets, precise timelines and limited resources, including employees, suppliers, venues and volunteers. In this chapter, students will be introduced to the principles of project management and shown how these principles can be applied to events. This chapter discusses these techniques outside the simple application of limited, functional management theories and argues that, when applied correctly, event project management can produce better and faster results to plan and deliver events.

1.8.3 Chapter 3: Event design and production

Event design, as a core process in events management, is rarely covered outside logistical considerations in the events literature. This chapter evaluates the value of a range of social and psychological approaches to understanding the event experience and explores how these can be applied in the design of events to produce authentic and exciting attendee experiences. Working through this chapter will support event managers to design events from the initial event concept through to design development and production considerations.

1.8.4 Chapter 4: Event operations

Operational planning begins once the event concept has been decided upon, a venue has been chosen, the event has been designed and a project plan put in place. To deliver an event successfully, event managers must consider all of its elements and decide the resources, skills and equipment needed to deliver them. This chapter covers all aspects of operational planning and management, including the legal external environment – the consideration of legalities, regulations, licenses, permits and contracts involved when managing an event – and the event logistics – including the logistical planning for both customers and on-site at venues or event sites.

1.8.5 Chapter 5: Event human resources

This chapter provides an overview and analysis of core human resource management issues in the events industry, including recruiting, motivating and rewarding staff, the role of volunteers in events and the requirements of key legislation affecting the human resources function of events management. The relationship between event organisations and their staff will be considered from the perspective of the 'pulsating organisation'. Finally, the issues of professionalism in the contemporary events industry will be evaluated.

1.8.6 Chapter 6: Event finance

Financial management is vital to the success of an event and forms a core area of competence for any event manager. This chapter examines the key aspects of event finance, at a variety of scales, supporting students to develop their knowledge of important financial terms and methods. The chapter has been written to provide event managers with the ability to write, interpret and present financial documents that will be required by colleagues, internal and external stakeholders and clients.

1.8.7 Chapter 7: Event marketing and sponsorship

As the events industry has grown, so has the wealth of research and practical guidance on how to market events. This chapter sets out the key areas of marketing, such as market analysis, marketing planning, marketing techniques, control methods and evaluation. As well as these established areas of event marketing, this chapter also explores the role of sponsorship within the events industry and the advantages and challenges that this presents to event managers. Connections are made between the development of the marketing function for modern events, the scope for communication of sponsorship messages to specific audiences and the significant cost-recovery potential to event managers of developing relationships with sponsors.

1.8.8 Chapter 8: Event health, safety and risk management

Historically, issues of health and safety have been perceived as a bureaucratic burden on event managers and event organisations. In recent years, however, a number of high-profile accidents and disasters have occurred that have focused the industry on the importance of developing excellence in the management of health, safety and risk for organisations, their staff and event attendees. As well as this focus from within the industry, governments and other regulatory agencies have promoted and enforced new legislation and standards on the events industry that organisations must comply with or face hefty financial and criminal penalties. Individual event managers have a significant responsibility to deliver events that reflect this new reality and this chapter evaluates key areas of risk facing event managers and supplies important techniques for managing these.

1.8.9 Chapter 9: Sporting events

In this chapter, the specific characteristics of sporting events are analysed. They have been hugely significant in the development of the events industry and continue to feature prominently on the events landscape, from the smallest community competition to mega-events responsible for billions of dollars of turnover. The chapter considers the factors affecting attendance at sporting events, and the behaviour of these spectators, as well as how this sector has developed to meet the changing profile of sporting events audiences – who may attend in person or form part of the huge global sports media audience. Issues of crowd management and venue design are explored in detail, enabling readers to learn about these cutting-edge aspects of events management in which sporting events lead the field.

1.8.10 Chapter 10: Mega-events

Mega-events such as the Olympic Games and the World Expositions have become features of the global economic and cultural landscape. Governments compete to bring them to their cities to catalyse economic, social and cultural change. This chapter analyses the rise of the mega-event as an instrumental device for promoting development and regeneration, and also examines vital aspects of the management of these global media events, including the bidding process, resourcing, media, security and event tourism.

1.8.11 Chapter 11: Public and third sector events

In this chapter, the differences between the private, public and third sectors of event organisations are explained. The public and third sectors operate in a different context to the profit-seeking private sector, which has been the focus of the majority of events management texts. Building on the material elsewhere in this book on key aspects of events management that are applicable to events in all sectors of the economy, this chapter attempts to highlight the particular characteristics of the third sector and public sector events and the different nature and style of managing their success. Forms of event that are unique to these sectors are analysed, including consultations, fundraising events, political events and faith events, along with issues such as the political impacts of public sector events and the funding challenges facing third sector event organisations.

1.8.12 Chapter 12: Corporate events

The corporate events sector is extremely broad and diverse. This chapter introduces readers to this complexity, exploring the success factors and challenges for meetings and conferences, incentives, networking events, corporate hospitality and exhibitions and trade shows. As well as analysing the different forms of corporate events, this chapter also presents an analysis of the corporate event consumer and looks at the influences on the contemporary corporate events industry from the perspectives of both suppliers and consumers.

1.8.13 Chapter 13: Cultural events and festivals

This chapter provides an overview of the cultural events and festival sector of the events industry. Cultural events and festivals can often only be understood by reference to the relationship that they have to the expressions of individual and group identities and cultures and this chapter provides a categorisation of cultural events from this perspective, as well as an overview of arts and entertainment events. In addition to this categorisation, management approaches for cultural events are also introduced that are specific to this sector, including audience development and specialised marketing techniques.

1.8.14 Chapter 14: Event impacts, sustainability and legacy

The issue of the impact of events is central to both events management education and the sustainable management of the events industry. This chapter analyses the economic, environmental and social impacts of events and provides techniques for the management and evaluation of these impacts. The concepts of sustainability and sustainable events are introduced in this chapter and these are put into the context of the changing global climate and the global economic crisis. In this chapter, a new model of sustainable economic development is put forward that offers a novel perspective on the future growth of the events industry.

1.8.15 Chapter 15: Events and the media

The relationship between events and the media is critical, both in terms of how events are represented in the media and how event managers make use of the media to communicate with their stakeholders. Media coverage of an event can shape how that event is perceived, with positive and negative implications for how those events are managed. This chapter explores the ways in which event managers can obtain and shape media messages – understanding how the media operates and how to develop positive relationships with journalists and editors and work with new forms of social media can be vital in delivering a successful event.

Industry voice

Adam Mussett, Professional Event Freelance Specialist

 I started my career in the events industry almost 20 years ago, selling programmes at a music festival. It was the beginning of the British music festival boom and felt, to me, like a period in which both corporate and leisure sectors were beginning to realise the full industrial potential of the events. At the time, there were a handful of music festivals, bands were touring less frequently, and no major companies owned a large proportion of the UK music venues and theatres. Much of the music in the charts was indie and much of the live music sector was also independent.

Other types of events, that have subsequently increased in popularity, such as comic and film industry conventions, were much rarer and their scale of production much smaller. Hotels were beginning to look further afield than just their delivery of wedding events and were starting to tap into the rapidly growing market for conferences and trade fairs, thus not only selling their event spaces but also their rooms and other revenue centres. At that time, many of these events generally relied on potential attendees seeing a 'physical' advertisement, and this is possibly why the events industry was somewhat smaller in scale and more limited in scope than it is today. The events that were generally deemed more successful were often those that exhibited more niche appeal and were of special interest to their potential customers.

In comparison with the present day, it is immediately apparent how these features of what is now referred to as the international events sector have changed. For example, music festivals in the UK alone occur every weekend from May to October and even now, to some extent, throughout the winter months as well. International promoters are stakeholders in not only their own businesses but also in the businesses of festivals and venues. Bands tour more often, now that people have stopped buying music. While previously the album would create a large revenue that the label or management would, in turn, use to pay for a tour, now the tour is necessary to pay for the album. I would add that, as I write, I am also working for a band that has played 111 shows, across all continents, in the last year alone.

In contemporary music events, the biggest revenue for a band on tour is often the sale of merchandise. While fans sometimes bemoan the prices, little is done to explain that the promoter has often arranged a show at a venue where the band is forced to use a salesperson from the venue, with the venue charging as much as 25 per cent commission, plus sales tax, for this service. This means the venue earns more per sale than it costs the band to produce them in the first place. In certain cases, international promoters can own a controlling share of chains of venues. Merchandise revenues can also be affected by falling ticket sales due to market saturation.

However, these are not the only aspects of this part of the events sector that have suffered due to recent developments. It could be argued that music event attendees' motivations for visiting events have changed from an interest, or 'love' for what the event might offer, more to a 'rite of passage'; in other words, possibly more concerned with an attendee's stage of life and personal experiences rather than fandom, or loyalty to the band they see perform. This has meant that the grassroots, loyal fans can be put off by those they regard as crowds of marauding 'imposters' rather than those who share their values. It can be argued that comic, film and games events, alongside beer festivals and record fairs are a prime example of this.

Also, more and more of the same type of events are appearing. For example, food festivals have become increasingly popular, 'German' Christmas markets are appearing in many major cities in the UK, and rooftop cinemas seem to appear in more plentiful numbers each year. As more such events occur, the attendees become more expectant and this is something that event managers need to be more aware of when planning, budgeting and advertising them. Because the events industry has become such a large business within the UK and internationally, there have been notable increases in health, safety and fire regulation requirements. There is more training given to everyone from the ground up, so that people can be properly educated in what is needed for each given event. Having said this, the sector can still appear quite unscrupulous in methods of employment, with internships being incredibly common.

On a more upbeat note, the future of events is something that we should be increasingly excited about. There is still room for the events sector to expand, and the rise of 'boutique' and 'pop-up' events prove this point. Alongside this, the revenue from advertising and marketing has grown exponentially and so have the use and incorporation of technology. Fundamentally, it's the easiest form of advertising, but increasingly apps can be used for an infinite number of things, including purchasing drinks before you have approached the bar, to check which act is due to appear next, or to find more information about a product using QR codes. Some event spaces are already offering virtual tours and even virtual playback of the event attendees have just seen. In addition, 3D printing can be used to customise souvenirs or conference packs. Overall, technology is becoming more prevalent, and event managers should look to incorporate it into projects, to ensure that the excitement generated by an experience is as strong in the digital, as in the physical realm.

1.9 Summary

This chapter has discussed the evolution of events as part of human culture, from their historical foundations to their present-day status as part of a prominent global industry which is a major revenue earner for entire national economies. Such rapid and substantial contemporary development has nevertheless included the revival of many traditional events in a modern-day context, and the introduction of many new events, requiring the necessity for knowledgeable, qualified and professional event managers to deliver them.

All of the chapters in this book take the approach of presenting basic definitions and descriptions of the key management practices presently employed in the events industry, while linking these to the most important theoretical and management frameworks used to inform their successful practice. As event academics and practitioners, the authors have taken care to reflect present industry thinking and practice, while simultaneously attempting to challenge that which might be considered to be outdated or inconsistent. In such cases, an attempt has been made to propose new or adapted models and theories in order to stimulate debate and new practice in this fast-moving, international industry. To supplement this approach, many industry leaders and practitioners have been chosen to share their experiences in the 'Industry voice' sections.

Further reading

Bladen, C. and Kennell, J. (2014) Educating the 21st Century Event Management Graduate: Pedagogy, Practice, Professionalism and Professionalization, *International Journal of Events Management*. For a broader coverage of the points summarised above.

Getz, D. (2008) Event Tourism: Definition, Evolution, and Research, *Tourism Management* 29 (3): 403–428. This is a very useful article for gaining an overview of the study of events and also includes references to many important sources.

Maslow, A. H. (1943) A Theory of Human Motivation, *Psychological Review*, 50 (4): 370–396. Available at: http://psychclassics.yorku.ca/Maslow/motivation.htm. Accessed 29 June 2011. This article is the original source of Maslow's 'hierarchy of needs' model, a recurring feature of management literature.

References

Barron, P. and Leask, A. (2012) Events Management Education. In S. J. Page and J. Connell (eds) *The Routledge Handbook of Events*: 473–488, Oxon: Routledge.

Bowdin, G., Allen, J., O'Toole, W., Harris, R. and McDonnell, I. (2011) *Events Management* (4th edn), London: Elsevier.

Events are GREAT Britain Report (2014) Available at www.businessvisitsandeventspartnership. com/. Accessed 12 April 2016.

Getz, D. (2005) *Event Management and Event Tourism*, New York: Cognizant Communications.

Getz, D. (2007) *Event Studies*, Oxford: Butterworth-Heinemann.

Goldblatt, J. (2008) *Special Events: The Roots and Wings of Celebration*, Chichester: John Wiley & Sons.

Goldblatt, J. (2010) *Special Events: A New Generation and the Next Frontier*, Chichester: John Wiley & Sons.

Wilensky, H. (1964) The Professionalization of Everyone? *American Journal of Sociology*, 69: 142–146.

Chapter 2

Event project management: feasibility, planning, delivery and evaluation

Contents

2.1 Aims

By the end of this chapter the student will be able to:

- understand the importance of event project management to the international events industry;
- explain the organisational issues that must be taken into consideration when managing event projects;
- relate event project management to conventional event planning theories and practices; and
- explain the processes related to effective event project management throughout the event cycle.

2.2 Introduction

Following our Chapter 1 discussion of the common event types that specialists are responsible for organising, we come to more of the considerations necessary when planning, delivering and evaluating such projects. As projects, events generally have fixed budgets, precise time-lines and limited resources, including employees, suppliers, venues and volunteers. Organisers of such events are therefore responsible for the management and delivery of projects. Project management has developed processes and techniques to help plan, organise, lead and control events and can be used to make event projects more successful. This chapter discusses these techniques outside the simple application of limited, functional management theories and argues that, when applied correctly, event project management can produce better and faster results to plan and deliver events.

2.3 Events as projects

As can be seen in Figure 2.1, most events exhibit the characteristics of projects. This tendency generally increases with the size and scale of the event. Each of the characteristics of events are expanded in the following subsections.

2.3.1 Leadership

Events are often the ultimate responsibility of one lead events manager who coordinates specialist functions. The centralised and hierarchical nature of the leadership role can be dependent upon the scale of the event. A mega-event, such as the Olympic Games, has a national planning committee ultimately accountable to its international parent, while corporate events are often under the direct leadership of a single event manager. There will be more discussion of this unusual leadership role later in this chapter.

2.3.2 Budget

Events almost always have specific budgets allocated to them. As discussed in our chapter about events finance, the accurate calculation of such budgets will often include difficult predictions of fixed and projected variable costs in relation to forecasted attendee numbers. Such calculations

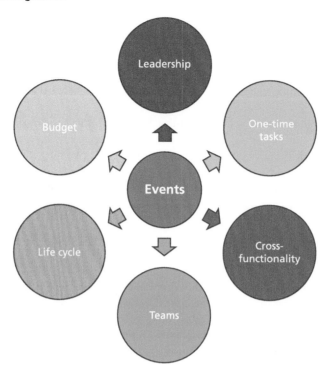

Figure 2.1 The characteristics of events as projects

cannot be considered reliable if made in isolation to other important project factors such as schedules, timelines and project lifecycle stages. For example, cuts in government funding will inevitably curtail the provision and/or scale of public sector events.

2.3.3 Life cycle

Each event has a defined beginning and end within its life cycle. There are a variety of life cycles proposed in the field of project management to aid managers in distinguishing key phases throughout a project's life. However, such cycles for use by industries such as engineering or software development tend to accommodate the tendency in such industries for phases to be completed, leading to the definite beginning of the next. Event project managers do not often have this luxury, as they are required to handle multiple tasks, contractors and other (often complex and interrelated) factors simultaneously. This is particularly the case with large exhibitions, which can often take two years to plan and execute for delivery over a single week. In practice, this means that major exhibition organisers are likely to find themselves managing both this year's and next year's events at the same time. An international organisation such as Gartner, which operates across a number of continents at any one time, often has to have team members who are geographically spread, working on a variety of different projects at any given time. This requires effective communications, which can also make project management software packages such as Microsoft Project and use of international databases imperative, so that team members can alter event details and immediate project updates can be sent to their colleagues using the company's international intranet.

2.3.4 Tasks

Events often require tasks to be performed that will not be repeated, even in the case of recurring annual events. The complexity of certain larger events requires that often the seemingly simplest of tasks or functions, such as catering, volunteer recruitment or theming, can be approached in a distinct manner in order to reinforce the uniqueness of a particular event from year to year. This obviously becomes even more complicated when an event changes location or venue, even if the concept of an annual event remains consistent. When the design and production details discussed in Chapter 3 are considered, they make the tasks involved even more complex and variable for different events. Successive Summer and Winter Olympics organising committees have experienced challenges as they try to learn from past events. Although the basic format of such mega-events remains constant, many of the problems and complexities differ due to changes in the city where the event is being held and factors such as culture, government legislation and even the basis on which initial bids by individual cities are made.

2.3.5 Cross-functionality

Event organisations are likely to be required to work cross-functionally without formal authority. This principle mainly depends on the type of event project being managed and the corresponding organisational structure required for optimal effectiveness and efficiency of execution. In other words, as most industries have clearly needed to adopt project management techniques in order to improve their performances, event managers have always, in a sense, been project managers because of an ongoing need for them to have versatile skills in a number of key business areas in order to be successful. Indeed, as this book suggests throughout, event project managers do not have the luxury of simply being good financial managers; they must also be effective marketers and human resource managers, as well as almost anything else that is required.

2.3.6 Teams

Events require working teams to be brought together only for the duration of a particular project. Most event organisations tend to vary their approach towards formality of event leadership and the corresponding organisational structure; it is not uncommon for the teams being employed on particular events to vary according to different factors. Goldblatt (2005) applies Toffler's (1990) earlier discussion of the 'pulsating organisation' to events, particularly in relation to the fluctuating numbers of volunteers required throughout the events cycle. Events such as trade exhibitions have often staggered delegate registration, giving priority to trade deals on the first day, the general public on the second day and students towards the end of the third day. Obviously, this is done for trade considerations, but it can result in some exhibitors leaving early and there being a need for fewer volunteers and other workers. These workers are required in larger numbers for the event setup and breakdown, but not during the event. Thus this organisation 'pulsation' takes place in accordance with the event cycle.

2.3.7 The event project life cycle

Events have a distinct timeline and life cycle. In Figure 2.2, Silvers demonstrates the link between an event's stages from initiation to closure and the levels of activity associated with these stages throughout an event's life, from start to finish. This classification has proven generally useful to event project managers in order to understand levels of activity required at the progressive stages of an event's conception, research, planning, delivery and evaluation, as discussed in Chapter 1.

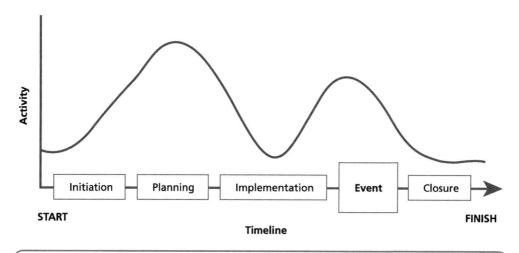

Figure 2.2 The event project life cycle
Source: Silvers 2007: 159

2.4 Project management perspectives

When considering how to apply project management to events, a project leader should consider their overall perspective. As discussed by Kolltveit *et al.* (2007), there are six major perspectives to project management, all of which can be applied directly to the management of the event project.

● The *task perspective* focuses on the delivery of the event as specified, on time and within the set budget. Certainly, it is important to clients that such projects as most corporate events or weddings should meet the criteria specified beforehand since they represent the most tangible and measureable success factors for the event. Any event project team will need to focus on the scope of the event concept and operations, as well as clear targets, measureable results for evaluation, high levels of ongoing project supervision and tangible event legacy criteria. This has clearly been the approach thus far with the types of modern mega-events described in Chapter 10. These events, such as the Olympic Games, focus on the tangible measures necessitated by the adoption of the task perspective to events.
● The *leadership perspective* to event projects depends upon theories of leadership styles, communication styles and processes, decision-making, management of team characteristics and organisation, clear allocations of team members' functions and responsibilities, interim milestone delivery dates, reviews and feedback.
● The *stakeholder perspective* to event projects is heavily used in the events industry and focuses on identification of key stakeholder groups and the management of their relations to ensure event success.
● The *transaction-cost perspective* to event projects views the production of an event as a commercial transaction and mainly focuses on governance of the project and its cost structure with particular reliance upon contracts and innovation.
● The *systems perspective* to event projects views the event as an overall holistic system, rather than made up of individual, functional components such as marketing, finance, design and so on.

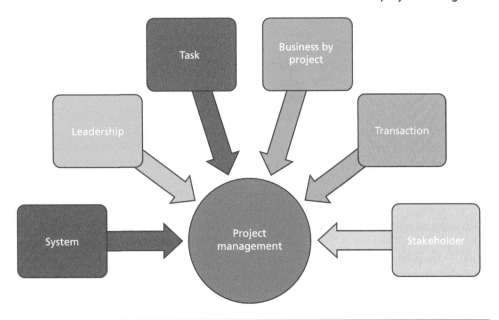

Figure 2.3 Perspectives on project management
Source: Adapted from Kolltveit *et al.* 2007: 4

- The *business-by-project perspective* to event projects views events as individual investments which yield returns or benefits in their own right. This perspective relies upon investment methods and portfolio management, among others. While this approach is probably more common with the development of technological innovations through business start-ups, most large events management companies do, to some extent, maintain proprietary interests over a series of different event product concepts at any one time.

Kolltveit *et al.* (2007) found that the writers in the general project management field centre on the 'leadership' and 'task' perspectives. Certainly, the main perspectives adopted by events management writers to date tend to be based mainly on project tasks and stakeholder perspectives. It is argued that more investigation should be made into the relevance of the other perspectives to the field, in particular those related to event leadership, due to the specific nature of the event planner's role as project manager of the complex and highly variable events.

2.4.1 The emerging importance of projects

The origins of project management can be traced back to its use during the large-scale government projects of the nineteenth century. It developed further through the building projects initiated as a result of the Second World War, moving project management on to the same methods used in events management today. The field developed its own project management body of knowledge (PMBOK) and its own professional certifications, such as the Project Management Professional (PMP) Certification.

2.4.2 The core competencies of an event project manager

By applying the information provided by the PMP certification (see LaBrosse 2007: 99–100), we can see that an effective event project manager requires a variety of diverse yet interrelated core competencies that should be applied throughout the event project stages of initiation, planning, implementation, delivery and closure.

Event managers need to be able to select suitable projects, and in the event of multiple products they must be able to prioritise between them in relation to the requirements of their organisation. Such prioritisation will likely be related to strategic factors and overall feasibility. Initiation of the project will require the event manager to be able to assemble the initial project team and stakeholders, which may include provisional agreements from key personalities associated with such an event, such as top entertainers, leading sponsors, specialised designers and producers, as well as possible donors and benefactors in the case of voluntary and fundraising events. An event manager's ability to initiate an event project is also dependent upon their skill to develop an effective project contract so that further planning may proceed.

The event project manager will need to be a competent project planner of the event's key delivery milestones, processes and reviews in order to ensure that the project is kept on track through effective ongoing performance measurement. There is also a need to highlight possible areas of conflict between different functions of the event team. Additionally, this person must be a project leader throughout the event, careful to ensure that they capitalise on the skills of others who are involved in the project, and knowing when specific tasks should be contracted out to other event specialists.

The event project manager will need to be competent to manage the event's scope, schedule, cost, procurement and resources. The risks to the satisfactory and successful delivery of the event itself (as opposed to 'Risk Management' of the health, safety and welfare of those associated with it, as covered in Chapter 8) will need to be accurately assessed and managed in the form of insurance and contingencies. As the planning and delivery of the event progresses, required changes will need to be identified and managed, aided by associated performance tracking and reporting. The appropriate media will facilitate communication throughout the event. In particular, stakeholders may need to be kept up to date with developments and teams will be involved in meetings to foster a constructive atmosphere of teamwork, consultation and feedback. Communication skills will also include the ability to negotiate with all parties associated with the event, both inside and outside the project organisation. The event project manager will eventually have to evaluate the overall accomplishment of the event's objectives and legacy, as well as document these findings.

2.5 Event project definition, organisation and framework

Following the foregoing discussion of events as projects and the various approaches an event manager can take towards them, it will be necessary to consider the most effective type of organisational structure for the event.

2.5.1 Functional and project-led organisations

Event organisations are often temporary and differ slightly depending on the project concerned. They will have a structure with predefined reporting relationships, functional 'departments' and systems to carry out the project. *Functional organisations* group their people into departments performing similar tasks, as is shown in Figure 2.4.

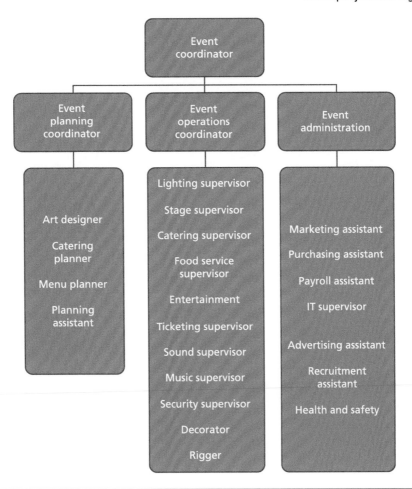

Figure 2.4 Functional event organisation

Project-led organisations group people into temporary teams for the duration of a project. The events industry clearly comprise both types of organisation. An international event venue, such as Excel in London, will have a functional infrastructure of departments responsible for such activities as financial management, operational management, human resource management and so on. Event organisations, such as Gartner, a project-led organisation, will use different people on different events as the concept and brief dictate. An example of a project-led organisational structure is shown in Figure 2.5.

Matrix organisations combine functional and project-led structures in order to perform both focuses at the same time, as illustrated in Figure 2.6.

This structure enables both a project-led and a functional approach to events and is therefore particularly suitable for this industry. However, in order for the matrix to be project-led, it is important that key authority and responsibilities for important event project elements, such as budgetary and other resource control, reside with the project manager at the event level, rather than with the functional manager of the department under which the event is being delivered. Failure to adopt this approach will tend to weaken the matrix and relegate the event project manager to the more minor role of administrator.

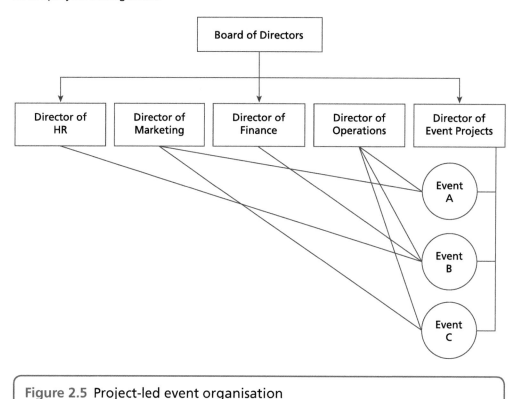

Figure 2.5 Project-led event organisation

It may be tempting to adopt the matrix structure without reservation, considering its appeal in combining the best of both functional and project-led structures. In many cases, this structure does profit the event in question, but there are a number of problems often associated with this structure. In particular, the decision-making processes of an event, especially during the delivery stage, must often be adaptable in response to crises or changes in the event's micro or macro environments. The matrix approach often slows down these processes since the project group must spend too much time in consultation across areas of responsibility before reaching a consensus. This can lead to serious delays and unnecessary project failures.

Study activity

1 List the strengths and weaknesses of each of the above event organisation structures.
2 Discuss the most suitable organisation type for each of the following:

(a) A venue specialising in corporate events.
(b) An event company involved in creating and delivering one-off corporate events for a variety of leading brand clients.
(c) The planning committee of the 2018 World Cup.

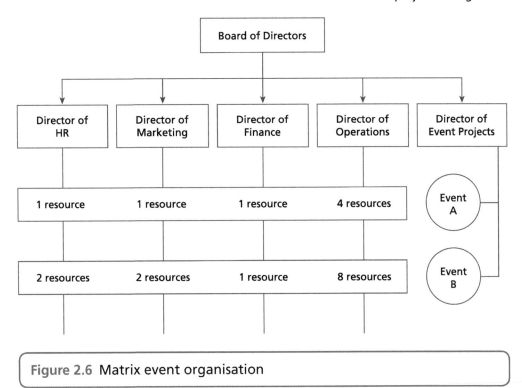

Figure 2.6 Matrix event organisation

2.5.2 Project leadership

Whether an event organisation uses a functional, project-led or matrix structure for its events, its choice will, for the most part, dictate the type of leadership which is most practical for that particular structure. The leadership of the organisation, along with its structure, will in turn heavily influence its project culture, which will have its own influences on the delivery of the event. According to Pinto (2010: 130), project leadership 'involves inspiring, motivating, influencing, and changing behaviours of others in pursuit of a common goal'. Event project leadership therefore differs from management and administration tasks and responsibilities that are mostly functional, and focuses on the actions of an individual's relationship with others involved in the event.

Kurt Lewin, one of the pioneers of analysing organisations, carried out research into leadership styles. In their 1939 paper, Lewin *et al.* identified three main, prevailing leadership styles which shaped:

- authoritarian;
- democratic; and
- laissez-faire work environments.

Authoritarian work environments are led by an autocratic leader who makes decisions on behalf of the team and divides work tasks and processes accordingly, providing critique of the team's performance while often not engaging closely with either the team or their activities. Democratic work environments have leaders who consult team members in order to arrive at a consensus regarding important decisions, offering guidance as required, as well as praise and constructive criticism throughout. Laissez-faire work environments have little tangible leadership input and the leader allows all major decisions to be made and executed by the team members, who demonstrate 'free-reign' and receive little input or feedback from their leader.

Turner *et al.* (2009) found that project success was increasingly linked to leadership competencies rather than tools and techniques, as had previously been thought. This finding

---

Study activity

1 Which of Lewin's work environments would be best for:

   (a) encouraging motivation and participation by event team members?
   (b) encouraging innovation?

2 What do you think are the advantages and disadvantages of each?
3 Which type of leadership would you prefer to be following? Why?
4 Complete Table 2.1, adding 'High' or 'Low' to each cell:

Table 2.1 Leadership styles

	Leadership style		
	Autocratic	Democratic	Laissez-faire
Time required for decision-making			
Scope for innovation			
Promotion of participation			
Team member motivation			
Ability of team members to voice disagreement			
Scope for leader to make mistakes			
Direct/formal communication			
Open team discussion			
Quality of decision-making			
Clarity of mission			

---

built on the work of Dulewicz and Higgs (2005), which isolated three main project leadership styles: goal-orientated leadership, involving leadership and engaging leadership. Ironically, goal-orientated leadership, which involves the 'management by objectives' approach to events towards clearly defined results espoused by leading authors in the field (e.g. Bowdin *et al.* 2011; Goldblatt 2005; Shone and Parry 2010), appears more useful in environments that remain mainly stable in nature. However, many event practitioners might suggest that an event project can be quite an unstable context for management, perhaps due to the intangibility of the perceived end result and the fluidity of the context in which it is being delivered. Involving leadership may therefore be more suitable for dealing with the transitory features common to events project organisation. Industry managers often find definitions, plans, resources and many other important project variables in a state of flux. The engaging leadership approach, however, appears to be impractical for anything other than the smallest or most specialised of event teams, due to the transformative nature of the leadership role and the necessary level of corresponding employee commitment. The particular attributes and competencies of such leaders are discussed later in this chapter.

2.5.3 Project organisation

Forming teams is an essential activity of any event project manager and is vital to the success of any event's production. The general considerations required in the management of event teams are mainly considered in Chapter 5 of this book. However, simply selecting team members and allocating them to functional groups is not the most efficient or effective way of staffing an event, as this does not suit the common structure of the event organisation. It may also stifle the creativity of design described in Chapter 3. Therefore, team members and their formal and informal interrelationship should ideally reflect accommodation of the cross-functional activities associated with the events industry. For example, some of the tasks of the event's security detail will often also be involved with safety and customer service provision, so the team should be constructed to enable these important and interrelated capacities.

Teams and teamwork are usually more effective than individuals in events projects because:

- They allow more to be achieved as they can accomplish a much wider range of tasks and workloads.
- Team members usually have a wider range of skills, specialisations and thought processes which can be drawn upon in the solution of event problems.
- Team often make better decisions.
- They often provide a better environment for motivation and can better support each other.
- They are more open to risk-taking as risk is spread across more people associated with an event.

On further consideration of event project teams, according to Maylor (2010: 248–249), effective project teams require:

- clear goals
- a results-driven structure
- competent team members
- unified commitment
- a collaborative climate
- standards of excellence
- external support and recognition
- effective leadership.

For further discussion of important issues related to team management in events which include team culture, roles, motivation and evaluation, please see Chapter 5 on the management of the events human resource.

2.6 Project parameters

2.6.1 Project scope

Project scope, though rarely called that, is probably the largest current area in events management literature. Most process diagrams, including the one shown in Figure 2.7, tend to relate to 'event planning'.

Figure 2.7 incorporates the main scope aspects, which according to Pinto (2010: 157) include concept development, statement of scope, work authorisation, scope reporting, control systems and project closeout.

The problem statement essentially denotes the *raison d'être* of the event, that is, the reason why it is taking place and what it intends to achieve. This can vary even when the same annual event is held in consecutive years at the same venue. It is vital to gather accurate information, from basic general observations to extensive environmental and other analyses. These activities can take months, or even years in the case of mega-events, and can form the largest part of the overall feasibility study for the event.

2.6.2 Project requirements and constraints

Constraints to the event's staging, financing and other practical options need to be considered as do contingencies and alternatives. Alternative design, themes, venues and entertainment options are often considered at this point in the event concept's development.

Figure 2.7 Event planning process
Source: Shone and Parry 2010

2.7 Stakeholder requirements and needs

Stakeholder analysis is currently an important topic in events literature, with a much wider definition of the number of parties affected by an event's activities preferred to the narrower, profit-orientated definition used by other business-related fields. In other words, the wide-encompassing influences and impacts of events in communities and nations make it necessary to consider the needs of all parties affected by them in stakeholder analysis, whether they actively participate or not. This project stage will therefore include the analysis, monitoring and evaluation of the needs and requirements of investors, employees and attendees who seek to benefit from the event's delivery, as well as those of local area residents who may even try to avoid the event and its impacts completely, yet are greatly affected by them. This is discussed in depth in Chapter 14.

2.8 The project objective statement

Event objectives form the key direction for the following stages of the project's planning, delivery and evaluation. These objectives provide specifics for concept screening and feasibility analysis and form the overall direction of activities for the project team and associated event contractors to arrive at the accomplishment of the event's outcomes. These must be specific and measureable where possible in order to be effective indicators by which the event can be conceived, kept on track, effectively delivered and evaluated. To aid this, Doran's (1981) popular SMART acronym is often used to describe effective event project objectives:

- Specific
- Measureable
- Assignable
- Realistic
- Time-related.

This acronym, though not at all scientific, is a useful guide to the formation of useful objectives. As with any business system, the project objectives will only be as effective as the consideration of the team that sets them, but making them as clear and communicable as possible will help to ensure their effective decoding by important stakeholders, contractors and others associated with the effective outcome of the event.

There is a great deal of discussion about the suitability of the application of such a 'management by objectives' approach to events management projects. Certainly, the prospect of a project team setting, achieving and evaluating the same objectives may potentially appear circular and self-fulfilling. However, the sheer scope of certain events and their potential for instability demands the clear formulation and communication of an effective project objective statement, although this may be modified as the project progresses.

Study activity

Set effective objectives for an event of your choice. Make sure they are specific and measureable. Can their achievement be effectively evaluated by a third party? Check them with someone else. What improvements can be made?

2.9 Project planning

2.9.1 Work breakdown structures

The process of an event project involves a variety of interrelated tasks and functions that must be broken down into smaller, more clearly distinguishable and easier-to-manage subsections. This work breakdown structure is essentially the basis for the Event Management Body of Knowledge (EMBOK) model and once again attempts to 'departmentalise' event activities into the previously criticised functional structure. On the other hand, it is reasonable to suggest that the successful future of the events management industry depends upon employees who can understand the working dynamics of the smaller elements of event work breakdown.

Work breakdown is important in event projects in order that a clear link can be observed between the event objectives and the tasks required to achieve them. Tasks might be practically divided into functional responsibilities, and event progress can be made more tangible for those participating in the event's delivery as well as for its stakeholders. It also enables more effective evaluation and cost allocation.

2.9.2 Project schedules

Time is crucial to the management and delivery of event projects, not least since event dates are often fixed because of venue and other resource availability as well as the need for upfront procurement payments and deposits. The flexibility of these factors also makes delays more likely than they might be in other project-related industries.

2.9.3 Resource breakdown structures

The main event project resources can be broken down into:

- *People* – including the expertise and skills of event specialists, such as designers, specialist entertainers, decorators, those associated with specialist staging activities and front-line personnel engaged in customer service delivery and other interactions.
- *Facilities* – including the venue, site and associated amenities, which can also include location and even destination attributes that contribute greatly to the success of any event.
- *Equipment* – including all plant and machinery, from transportation vehicles through to cooking equipment, lighting rigs, sound systems, scaffolds, portable dance floors, toilets and even personnel uniforms.
- *Finance* – as discussed in section 2.14 and Chapter 6.
- *Materials* – involving anything which can be used to make something else, such as timber, decorations, foodstuffs and paints.

2.10 Project optimisation

2.10.1 Critical path analysis methodology

Critical path analysis requires the analysis of all project tasks. Task dependency, that is, the relationship between the completion of one task before another can be commenced, also needs to be carefully considered. The construction of the critical path analysis of an activity network

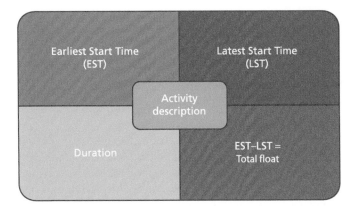

Figure 2.8 Activity notation

usually begins with breaking down the activities necessary for the planning of an event and estimating as accurately as possible the earliest and latest start times and duration of each. This can then be represented as shown in Figure 2.8.

By noting each event activity using this method, they can then be represented as an activity network, displaying the relationships and dependencies of tasks to each other. The values in the bottom left of the boxes can be calculated in order to determine how long the project will take. The critical path is the longest path through the dependent activities. Please refer to the companion website for a worked example.

Critical paths often incorporate capacity planning, also known as capacity constraint buffers (CCB); a reserve allocated to project tasks that use the same resources. For example, project managers of specialist corporate events that use an event producer as a central agent for all event concept development, design and logistical arrangements will need to protect them as a resource at each stage of the project process. This becomes even more necessary if the producer is working on a number of different event projects simultaneously. A CCB must be applied to protect the producer's time as they transition from one part of a single project to another or from one project to the next.

2.11 Project evaluation and review techniques

An event project requires ongoing evaluation and review to avoid delays and to manage ongoing changes. Such delays or changes might lead to undesirable increases in costs in other types of project, but for event projects they might be lethal to effective delivery.

2.11.1 Evaluation criteria

It is important that the event project team have methods in place to ensure the ongoing evaluation of project scope in terms of its continued adherence to the parameters set by the event objectives. These controls will concern each of the financial, marketing, design and operational areas associated with the event. They will need to be supported by relevant documentation of such aspects as expenditure and communication to ensure that the initial event plan is being adhered to and not changed without authorisation.

These concerns will also extend to the ongoing monitoring of the event macro and micro environments. For example, international events rely heavily on attendance by visitors who arrive by air. Any major changes in airline pricing, perhaps as a result of government taxation or direct market factors, may greatly affect potential ticket purchases before the event and may require some corresponding strategic changes to be made.

2.11.2 Review techniques

The event project will require continual evaluation throughout its life cycle. In particular, many event projects are heavily reliant on stakeholder involvement and their promised legacy as well as being commonly subjected to ongoing, critical media scrutiny. These factors, in addition to the usual financial requirements associated with non-event projects, such as return on investment and protection of profits, require that regular systems are in place to evaluate event achievement of its key deliverables. The basic process of event project evaluation involves four main reflective stages, as shown in Figure 2.9.

Key event areas which will require evaluation will likely include activity tasks, project milestones and budgetary indicators. Milestones, while being clear enough for all team members to readily understand, present problems if the project suffers serious delays. In such cases, the shortfalls are often revealed too late to be remedied effectively. One common way of evaluating and tracking project baselines is with the use of Gantt charts as shown in Figure 2.10.

The evaluation of any event project depends upon the clear definition and use of critical success factors. Pinto (2010) classifies these factors into the following areas:

- project mission
- top management support
- project plans and schedules
- client consultation
- personnel

- technical tasks
- client acceptance
- monitoring and feedback
- communication
- troubleshooting.

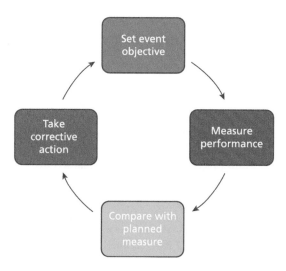

Figure 2.9 The event project evaluation cycle

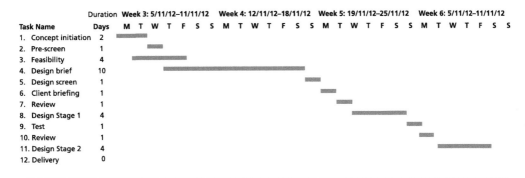

Figure 2.10 Event project tracking Gantt chart

2.12 Project crashing

Project crashing in events refers to speeding up the delivery process. This becomes necessary when costs can be saved, and when competitor offerings seem likely to steal innovation or successfully imitate other aspects of competitive advantage. Finishing event production early can significantly cut development costs, which may be distinctly advantageous, particularly if this development process has fallen far behind schedule.

The actual process of project crashing in events will involve increasing the productivity of the existing events team, increasing the resources allocated to the event, which may mean more people, plant and/or equipment, or altering the working methods. One way that crashing can be accomplished is by using technology more efficiently for such activities as project meetings, information sharing, ongoing team communication and operational concerns, such as ticketing, sales and reporting. As the project team becomes more liable for financial penalties due to delivery delays, the more likely it is that project crashing options will become attractive. Crashing can also be achieved by simply contracting out event-related tasks to third party agencies instead of handling them in-house, thus freeing up resources for reallocation elsewhere. Of course, outsourcing attracts its own set of problems and considerations.

Study activity

You have decided to crash an event project in order to save costs. Discuss some of the problems associated with contracting out your events management functions to third parties.

2.13 Project risk management

2.13.1 Definition of project risk management

Pinto (2010: 221) defines risk management as: 'the art and science of identifying, analysing, and responding to risk factors throughout the life of a project and in the best interests of its objectives'. In this section we intend to discuss risk management in the context of event projects from the perspective of loss in terms of the successful completion of an event. While we recognise that risks associated with the health, safety and welfare of event attendees and employees is an important area of management for event project leaders, we will discuss this in Chapter 8. Entrepreneurial risk management, which involves consideration of both monetary loss and gain, will be discussed in Chapter 6.

Anyone who has worked on even the simplest event project will recognise the complications caused by the unpredicted intervention of problems relating to resources, timings and changes, particularly in the context of the uncontrollable event macro environment. The ultimate success of such event projects invariably rests on the project team's ability to solve or lessen the impact of these problems. However, it cannot be argued that a successful project simply faces fewer problems than an unsuccessful one. It is more likely that the successful project manager can more accurately predict outstanding potential hazards that may come along throughout the duration of the project's schedule and has implemented satisfactory contingency measures well in advance. Thus, the art or science of successful event project risk management has to be in the manager's ability to predict the future as accurately as possible.

In order to predict such intervening variables before they cause problems, event organisers will need to ask themselves:

- How might these problems present themselves?
- What will be the symptoms or signs that such problems are occurring?
- What are the likely consequences of doing nothing?
- If something needs to be done, what should it be?

These questions are addressed as part of an internal and external analysis of the event organisation's environment, as discussed in Chapter 1.

2.13.2 Classification of project risk management

Risks need to be assessed in terms of their potential impact on the success of the project and where the source of their control lies. Wysocki (2007) classifies risk in the following four areas:

- technical
- project
- organisational
- external.

Sometimes projects fail because suitable technical resources, such as people, expertise or equipment, are unavailable. For example, in production-driven events (as discussed in Chapter 3), there is often an inevitable dependence on the creativity of the design team. Staff changes, departure from companies, disagreements and even illness or death can cause key team members to leave important projects, resulting in serious gaps. When this happens, it is not simply a case of replacing one person or role with another. For example, two events industry design directors may be considered of equal calibre, but they may have significant creative differences in the way they approach a project.

Charity events often rely on a steady stream of willing volunteers to maintain effective delivery levels. Failure to attract a suitable profile of volunteer can greatly impact on the success of event projects.

2.13.3 Use of buffers

Though work tends to fill the time available, event project managers can use time and cost buffers in order to offset the impact of several of these problems. As their name suggests, cost buffers include extra budget, which is allocated in emergencies, while time buffers are extra hours that can be allocated before the project delivery deadline to offset delays in the schedule. Again, though the application of these buffers seems fairly obvious in the context of traditional projects, the constraints of events as projects dictate unusual difficulties in a simple application of these principles. For example, the project managers for the Glastonbury Festival decided not to hold the world-class, internationally renowned music festival in 2012 due to reported resource shortages, which are claimed to have been caused by the London 2012 Olympic Games. According to one article, the key resources that were thought to be in short supply were police officers and portable toilets (Nicholl 2010).

2.14 Project cost breakdown structures

2.14.1 Total costs

Costing of event projects will likely emphasise price, cost or profit, according to which is the most relevant to the project in question. It can generally be approached from a top-down or add-on perspective, depending on whether a fixed budget is provided. Costs will generally be forecast for events using fixed and variable costs for the resource groups already listed earlier in this chapter, which will be subtracted from the forecast revenues eventually gained from ticket sales made at target prices. Clearly, there are complications to this approach, which relate to returns on investment, the cash flow considerations associated with events and other event-specific financial issues, which are covered in more depth in Chapter 6. However, it should be noted that the conventional project management methods regarding cost management tend not to be directly applicable to events as projects because events rarely present opportunities for guaranteed financial returns. Cost reductions to event projects can rarely be achieved by simple labour reductions, as is possible in other project-based industries, because of the labour-intensive nature of event projects. Also, many events are produced for the not-for-profit and public sectors.

2.14.2 Cost monitoring

For cost monitoring to be successful, the event project manager must allocate costs correctly to each of the project tasks. These should be reported at regular intervals by the individuals in charge of the relevant tasks' completion. In particular, it is essential with events that contractors are paid correctly, that ongoing expenses are carefully monitored and centrally authorised, and that costs are correctly allocated to the relevant event-department budgets.

2.15 Project implementation

Project implementation concerns the delivery of the event from its live opening to its close. This will involve the practical completion of all the processes related to the tasks with all their associated considerations covered so far in this chapter. The main articulation of this phase of an event will be incorporated into the events programme, which will include a statement beforehand of all the activities intended to be carried out, with the clear assignment of responsibilities for each. Depending on the type of event being staged, the project manager may decide to use a responsibility chart for each of the event programme elements, with an associated time schedule for their completion, as well as other relevant programme details, such as locations and other resource information. Each part of the event's delivery will require ongoing monitoring and reporting systems that should be as simple and as user-friendly as possible. These will enable each party to carry out the work successfully and to take effective remedial action if required. The major evaluative criteria the event manager is most likely to be concerned with include the completion of event delivery tasks, timings and associated cost controls. The more forthcoming and useful this review, the more likely it is that the project manager can remedy shortfalls in these important areas. Likely remedies will include the application of predetermined, contingent strategies that will often need to be applied in coordination with the most important event stakeholders. As complicated as these processes may sound, their successful implementation will depend directly on the soundness of the initial event project plan. They might well concern unforeseen circumstances stemming from the event's macro environment, such as adverse weather conditions or terrorist attacks, which may well require the overall strategic direction of the event to be significantly altered or even abandoned altogether.

2.16 Project shut-down

Event project shut-down can prove much quicker to implement than its initiation. An events-focused adaptation of Turner's earlier (1999) framework for finishing the work can be useful here and includes the following elements that can be applied to event completion:

- Produce checklists of outstanding work.
- Hold frequent meetings of event teams to ensure that closedown problems are identified and solved.
- Release event personnel from certain teams as they are no longer required, either onto other parts of the event closedown or from the project completely.
- Create a specific event closedown 'task-force' to complete outstanding work.
- Close down contractors and suppliers that are no longer required in order to avoid unnecessary cost.
- Support the event project manager with a deputy with finishing skills.

Considering this importance of stakeholder management, event objectives and planned legacies, it is also important for the evaluations of the event to be documented, including its problems, achievements and benefits. Some large event project management organisations, such as Gartner, also use this stage of an event to elicit attendee feedback through formal research processes, such as interviews and focus groups. Overall event evaluation will be a requirement for events that have involved the investment of public funds and those attracting a high degree of media coverage. Additionally, it will be useful in particular for events that will be repeated. Therefore, the project manager should ensure that the relevant information is planned for well before the event is delivered.

Disbanding event teams can be problematic if not planned well in advance. Many event personnel experience concerns about future employment, so there can be a tapering of team morale. It is therefore useful to plan for the schedule closedown as early as possible and some event organisations hold debriefing meetings and end-of-event parties, which may include recognition and rewards for performance achievement.

2.17 The required competencies of an event project leader

Following this in-depth analysis of the tasks of an event project leader, it is logical to present a brief consideration of some of the competencies needed for leading an event project effectively. Several studies (e.g. Dulewicz and Higgs 2005) suggest that an effective project leader should possess the intellectual, emotional and managerial skills outlined in Table 2.2.

Table 2.2 **Event project leader competencies**

Intellectual	Emotional	Managerial
Critical analysis and judgement	Self-awareness	Engaging communication
Vision and imagination	Emotional resilience	Managing resources
Strategic perspective	Motivation	Empowering
	Sensitivity	Developing
	Influence	Achieving
	Intuitiveness	
	Conscientiousness	

CASE STUDY 2.1

#BodastoryAlbirPlaya

Location: Southern Spain
Event type: Consumer show

One of the unique challenges associated with providing professional events management case studies is the competitive nature of this fast-growing industry and the resulting confidentiality that often surrounds its best examples of outstanding practice. However, the following is a real-world, industry case of event project management in action. It is based on the activities of Bodastory, part of a young, fast-growing events management company based in southern Spain.

Project background

Bodastory is one of a group of companies run by a small management company. They dedicate themselves to bringing together their two sets of clients who are members of the general buying public, looking for particular goods and services, and their other clients, who supply those goods and services. This is done through a webpage and events such as consumer shows. Although a recent company, established in 2009, Bodastory has built an extremely successful reputation for organising and managing high-profile events with a unique emphasis on delivering those events as emotional experiences. This track record has been achieved by well-designed events, and by Bodastory's high-impact social media presence due to their expertise in community management and the considerable traffic generated through their social media platforms. This has also contributed significantly to the elevated attendee numbers at their events.

The intention at the heart of the event series concept was to enhance the Bodastory brand image, to create opportunities for further events – the evaluation of the event project being crucial to planning the next event; its type, size and design. They also wanted to cultivate new business, both for Bodastory and for the supplier clients by bringing those suppliers and the customers together in the same venue, all within the limits of the company's available funds and resources. This could only be achieved through strategic planning and execution.

Project management outline

The following outline for the event was agreed:

- Management team meetings and feasibility testing (could they deliver – financial considerations, staffing, costs and so on).
- Deciding on venue and decision to pitch.
- Pitching project:

  - creative ideas and concept development
  - proposal document
  - pitch content
  - pitch processes and practice
  - pitch.

- Decision.
- Procurement and feasibility testing, including negotiation of venue client brief.

Project management of project

The Project Leader, as the key contact, liaised throughout the project with the company's central marketing team, headed by the Marketing and Social Media Manager and the venue's Event Manager. They had regular meetings as well as daily phone calls and emails. Each event was hosted by the Project Leader and the Marketing and Social Media Manager, and attended by staff from the local area; a small, highly trained and specialised team as well as extra hand-picked staff brought in for the actual days on site. Special weekend event guests were selected by Bodastory from their most important local business customers and professional contacts, local politicians, three of the top most influential bloggers in Spain and members of the press, all of whom could potentially introduce future new business to their company.

- Planning:

  - duration – it was decided that the event would run for two days over a weekend
  - client and stakeholder contact
  - finance
  - design
  - selection of key elements: speakers and bloggers
  - marketing
  - social media
  - risk and health and safety
  - suppliers
  - human resource management – choosing and training staff
  - critical path development.

- Implementation.
- Evaluation.

Project management approach

The project was approached holistically. A project plan was formed, which outlined the date and specific details running up to the event, and focused on specific aspects, such as the venue's obligations, design, guests, budget, suppliers and client (both invited guest and attendee) profile and information, and social media strategy.

Series project management

The project had a management plan. The main project management areas for the entire project could be listed as:

- Client contact and administration.
- Staff:

  - Roles and responsibilities of existing staff
  - Deployment of internal marketing and design staff to support project
  - Recruitment and training of staff to work at the event.

- Finance:

  - maintenance of overall budget to ensure no overspend
  - payment term negotiations for suppliers/vendors
  - analysis of resources.

- Suppliers:

  - supplier selection – audiovisual (AV) contracts, speaker contracts.

- Marketing and design of entire project:

  - This was fundamental to the success of the event. It allowed suppliers to present their products in a manner that was approachable, friendly and fun in order to ensure an important return on their investment.

- Evaluation and feedback to client(s).
- Logistical concerns: health and safety; special needs; Wi-Fi; security; parking.

The process began with Bodastory deciding on a venue; the Albir Playa Hotel, and then approaching the hotel's Events Manager. A meeting was arranged with the Director of the hotel, the hotel's Events Manager and the Project Leader and Marketing and Social Media Manager from Bodastory, where the project was pitched and accepted. Bodastory and the hotel team worked together to decide on an event date and the obligations of both parties (catering by the hotel, for example). Bodastory decided upon the inspirational speakers for the round table and organised suppliers' stands, the fashion show catwalk, a flash mob and an official wedding ceremony, which was to take place at the event. At that stage, the project was broken down into individual components, with plans devised for the venue, other suppliers, guests, guests as clients, video reviews, social media drive and budget. These plans were issued as Gantt charts for a breakdown of the project structure so that both Bodastory and the venue knew what had to be done, by whom and by when. Bodastory also used critical paths to ensure that all elements of each component were delivered effectively and on time. These critical paths enabled Bodastory to implement all the processes required in the planning of the event.

Client plan (venue)

- Communication lines set up – weekly meetings, daily email exchange.
- Liaison on key decisions.
- Budget discussions.
- Client staff attendance.
- Client staff briefing.
- Client staff joining instructions issued.
- Post-event evaluation.
- Post-event feedback and budget collation.

Guest and attendee plan

- Data gathered from clients of the webpage and the social media marketing campaign.
- Guest list generation – social media campaign; specific website clients invited through Facebook.
- Invite designed.
- Invites sent out on Facebook.
- Invites chased.
- Invite responses collated.
- More invites sent if necessary.
- Final invite responses collated.
- Final guest list created.
- Seating plan drawn up for each individual activity over the event duration, e.g. round table, catwalk and so on.
- Guests joining and registration instructions issued.
- Dietary requirements information gathered.
- Venue informed of numbers, details, dietary requirements and special needs requirements.
- Guests reminded of event individually through Facebook and general public attendees over all social media platforms.
- Special needs requirements collated and communicated to relevant responsible parties.

Venue plan – logistical concerns

- Venue visits.
- Layout of main salon, reception, round table restaurant area, poolside area for the opening ceremony, catwalk and cocktail area.
- Catering – menu tasting, menu selection.

- Beverages.
- Budgets and projected costs.
- Staffing.
- Bedroom booking.
- Health, safety and risk assessments.
- Guest and attendee numbers confirmed (with constant communication of attendee numbers at all times in case of fluctuation).
- Seating plans supplied.
- Theming and design elements confirmed.
- Wi-Fi.

Supplier plans (excluding venue)

- Initial briefs sent to suppliers – AV; video reviews; speakers; entertainment.
- The unique entertainment elements of the event.
- Prices negotiated.
- Suppliers secured.
- Briefs issued.
- Individual requirements met for suppliers as vendors.
- Approval of stage sets/lighting/sound/entertainment content and so on.
- Liaison as required.

Budget plan

It is usually an industry standard for the organisers of a consumer show to charge a small entry fee but #BodastoryAlbirPlaya was free to attend.

- Initial budget development.
- Budget control and monitoring.
- Budget evaluation.

Implementation

Once all of these planning stages were completed, Bodastory could implement the event. They used an event timeline, production schedules and briefing document (including contacts, seating plans and site maps) that enabled all staff (the venue's Event Manager, the Bodastory team and suppliers) to fully understand the event. Time lines started from the evening before the event and listed, by role and by time, each action that needed to happen during the setup, delivery and breakdown of the event. Production schedules provided clear guidance on when every element of the event took place.

Evaluation

Attendees' details had been noted at reception so they could be registered as new clients on the webpage and evaluation of the event had two approaches – the guests were asked on Facebook and on the webpage to give feedback, and the supplier clients were asked to do so via email. This was collated into one large document, providing a comprehensive evaluation of the event as well as an appraisal of its profit and loss and budget. The document included the benefits offered to each client, both the venue and suppliers, and their businesses (suppliers had seen a tremendous return on investment, for example). It also challenged experienced and critical recommendations for future events in the series and the evaluation of whether the event had met its objectives was presented.

(Stephens 2014)

Industry voice

Mariano Martín, Founder and CEO of The Word Of Mouth TV, Bodastory

Events as projects

Events are projects. Our little company has been organising events for quite some time, both for ourselves and for others, with remarkable success because we organise events as such, as projects.

Spain is very different to other countries, or maybe the same; it has a deep sense of community, and family, cultural and community traditions. It is old-fashioned, change is steeped in fear of losing these traditions, and it has been hit heavily by the economic recession, having the worst unemployment rate in Europe in real terms; the statistics confused by prolific under-the-table trading. Because of all these factors, change to events and how they are perceived needed new vision. So we, as a young company, surrounded by fresh ideas and with the clear support of the local business school, itself innovative and with a coherent voice, pushed for that change, by understanding that events are projects and by implementing change in them and their organisation.

My team has versatile skills in a number of key business areas, drawn from a vast vat of experience. We work with event managers in venues who are ill-prepared, so they could become obstacles without our careful training and monitoring. We are vigilant to ensure we capitalise on the skills of all others involved in our projects, and we understand when it is necessary to contract out areas to other specialists.

The key to it all is to have clear event project objectives concerning the financial, marketing, design and operational areas and initiation to closure, and to bear in mind the following:

- Time as a resource is critical to the management and delivery of event projects, planning, implementation and event delivery and closure.
- Monitoring of ongoing costs is essential.
- We have to be able to predict the future and all potential problems and setbacks accurately, and have contingency plans in place well beforehand.
- The event project requires continual evaluation throughout its life cycle from initiation to closure.
- To create opportunities for further business, the evaluation of the whole event project is crucial.

2.18 Summary

This chapter has attempted to demonstrate that events are projects, yet they are managed quite differently from those in other industries. The importance of proper applications of project management to the international events industry should now be apparent. Proper application depends on an initial understanding of the difference between the organisational structures and processes of event organisation, when compared to other types of business. While it is clearly possible to relate project management to many of the conventional event planning theories and practices discussed elsewhere, the particular processes related to effective event project management throughout the event cycle should be noted.

Further reading

Doran, G. T. (1981) There's a SMART way to write management goals and objectives, *Management Review*, November: 35–36. This is the often-quoted, foundational paper for the understanding of SMART objectives, which is definitely required reading for any student of events management.

Kolltveit, B. J., Karlsen, J. T. and Gronhaug, K. (2007) Perspectives on Project Management, *International Journal of Project Management*, 25: 3–9. This paper provides a fuller discussion of our basic summary of project management perspectives, which provides useful models for understanding how to apply project management to events.

Pinto, J. K. (2010) *Project Management*, New Jersey: Pearson. This book is a thorough overview of project management and includes many models and supporting examples from a variety of industries.

Silvers, J. R. (2007) *Risk Management for Meetings and Events*, London: Elsevier. This book is particularly useful for those wanting to understand more about project management and the risks associated with projects in particular.

References

Bowdin, G., Allen, J., O'Toole, W., Harris, R. and McDonnell, I. (2011) *Events Management* (4th edn), Oxford: Butterworth-Heinemann.

Dulewicz, V. and Higgs, M. (2005) Assessing leadership styles and organisational context, *Journal of Managerial Psychology*, 20 (1): 105–123.

Frame, J. D. (1995) *Managing Projects in Organizations* (2nd edn), San Francisco, CA: Jossey-Bass.

Goldblatt, J. (2005) *Special Events: Event Leadership for a New World* (4th edn), Chichester: John Wiley & Sons.

LaBrosse, M. (2007) The Evolution of Project Management, *Employment Relations Today*, Spring: 97–104.

Lewin, K., Lippitt, R. and White, R. K. (1939) Patterns of Aggressive Behavior in Experimentally Created Social Climates. *Journal of Social Psychology*, 10: 271–301.

Maylor, H. (2010) *Project Management* (4th edn), Harlow: Pearson.

Nicholl, K. (2010) Glastonbury loses Battle of Portaloo: 2012 festival off because Olympics needs all the police and portable toilets. *Daily Mail*, 16 October. Retrieved 12 November 2010 from: www.dailymail.co.uk/news/article-1321160/Glastonbury-2012-cancelled-London-Olympics-need-police-Portaloos.html.

Project Management Certification website, www.pmcertification.net/.

Schwalbe, K. (2009) *An Introduction to Project Management* (2nd edn), Boston: Cengage.

Shone, A. and Parry, B. (2010) *Successful Event Management* (3rd edn), Hampshire: Cengage Learning.

Stephens, K. (2014) #BodastoryAlbirplaya | Bodastory Blog. Bodastory.es. Available at: www.bodastory.es/blog/category/bodastoryalbirplaya/. Accessed 10 February 2016.

Toffler, A. (1990) *Powershift: Knowledge, Wealth, and Power at the Edge of the 21st Century*, New York: Bantam Books.

Turner J. R. (1999) *The Handbook of Project-based Management* (2nd edn), Berkshire: McGraw-Hill.

Turner, R. T., Müller, R. and Dulewicz, V. (2009) Comparing the Leadership Styles of Functional and Project Managers, *International Journal of Managing Projects in Business*, 2 (2): 198–216.

Wysocki, R. K. (2007) *Effective Project Management* (4th edn), Indianapolis: John Wiley & Sons.

Chapter 3

Event design and production

Contents

3.1 Aims

By the end of this chapter, the student will be able to:

- explain the relationship between the event production steps of concept, design and staging;
- develop an understanding of events design as the production of experiences rather than the management of staging elements; and
- describe the common elements of the event attendee experience.

3.2 Introduction

Event design and production are among the greatest challenges facing the events specialist. As clients continue to demand ever more memorable and remarkable events for their participants, it is left to the event designer to fulfil the brief and the event producer to deliver desired outcomes. However, event design and production are difficult processes, which are also embodied in the wider activities associated with planning events.

Event design and production are distinct sets of activities from each other and are different skills from what are widely regarded as the functions of management. They therefore do not rely on the more specific management processes discussed in Chapter 2; instead they are generally creative and artistic, as well as being strongly grounded in traditional design principles.

'Event Design' simply refers to the mental creation of an event before it takes place, first in the mind of the designer and then as it is communicated to those responsible for its production. 'Event Production' therefore refers to the subsequent action of manufacturing or engineering an event's delivery, based on its initial design.

However, when approaching this topic with a view to successful industry practice, it is worth noting that the literature about event design and production is sparse, and also there are wide differences among industry practitioners about how to approach both areas. This chapter attempts to unravel some of this controversy and confusion about this important topic. Literature about processes and procedures in the industry has led to what many view as a 'managementisation' of what should be the production of authentic event attendee experiences. This emphasis has also led to confusion between both event design *and* production. Practitioners and academics have generally focused on staging and logistics when discussing both of these elements. What is really required from *design* is the clear establishment of an initial event concept, with corresponding design development following. Event *production* then involves putting this design into practice, using practical staging elements.

3.3 Recent developments

Recent developments in event design and production have been influenced by this need to produce authentic event attendee experiences. There is a demand to design an event to run as closely as possible to its theme. One of the ways this is evolving is a move away from the traditional event venues of conference halls or large hotels, and selecting instead unique venues to capture the event theme, such as art galleries or venues with a history relevant to the theme. An example of this was the opening night event of New York Fashion Week in September 2014, where the event was held at the Irving Plaza because of its history as a rock venue. Another example was the 'What You Will, Celebrating 400 Years of Shakespeare' event in the case study later in this chapter, which was held in the same room, and at the same venue as the very first performance of Shakespeare's *Twelfth Night* – the Middle Temple Hall in London. This created an authentic experience both for the live audience and the online one on YouTube. The décor incorporated the original wood panelling, and the 30ft table on which the catering was served had been built inside the room more than 400 years before, from a 600-year-old tree, making the wood in the present-day table 1,000 years old. It was the same table on which food had been served to Shakespeare, his players and guests on that night in 1602. The music was of the day, using instruments from the 1600s, and lit candles in the original candlesticks were placed at either end of a replica Shakespearean stage.

Advanced technology, using an iPad to order food preferences, or to vote in mini-questionnaires, for example, can be appropriate since they enable attendees to make prompt decisions about their own experiences, giving them choices, and providing them with instant gratification as their input becomes reality.

AV effects and lighting can create the atmosphere and visual effects necessary to complement event themes.

Live entertainers can be streamed in as holograms, both to create a unique space for an attendee's authentic experience and to heighten that experience by providing sensory stimulation. It is far less expensive to use holograms than to pay for live acts to travel, and therefore more entertainers can be employed at an event, which further adds to the attendees' experience.

3.4. Events as designed experiences

3.4.1 Events as part of the growing experience economy

In Chapter 1, the diverse scope of events was discussed, and it was established that it is often difficult to categorise, or even define, what they are. However, one common thread shared by all events is that they are experiences for those who attend them. Certainly, masses of attendees flock to the annual Glastonbury Music Festival, not because they cannot see its extensive, televised coverage, but because attending offers a particular experience that cannot be gained elsewhere. In fact, many music performers have overcome the impact to their earnings from revenues lost through illegal music downloading by switching their emphasis from generating profits through music sales to performing at live events. This change has led many previously retired acts to come back and play at large music event venues, such as the O2 in London.

In general, events, whether formally managed or not, can be considered as an industry that forms part of what Pine and Gilmore (1999) described as an emerging 'experience economy'. In a social, cultural and technical transition, our society, which used to be very much based on the consumption of products, now consumes a much higher proportion of services. The third phase of this consumption evolution has resulted not only in customers demanding services but also in having those services delivered as part of an overall, packaged experience.

Thus, the focus for event companies has changed over time. Industry successes, which are changing the face of the modern events industry, such as Top Gear Live, have moved from the traditional approach of car shows, which were largely presentations of manufacturers' vehicles. Potential customers and enthusiasts could try these cars and obtain information about them since they were consistent, durable products. These products, in turn, were being exhibited by company employees who, as service providers, customised their service offering, depending on the requirements and expectations of their customers. However, Top Gear Live turned this product and service relationship into an experience through the designed and produced event. This redefined the car event and produced a prosperous franchise for the organisers, who now hold five such events worldwide.

There has also been recent growth in the popularity of music and cultural festivals, increased media coverage of sporting and mega-events and an increasing reliance on the strategic value of faith, voluntary and corporate events to promote brand relationships. Clearly, the modern, international events industry represents a crucial facet of this new social architecture. These indications seem to support Jensen's (1999) observations that, as consumers of such experiences, we seem to be living in an ever developing 'dream society', where consumer perceptions of value, recognition of rarity and willingness to justify premium expenditure focus on the ability of successful business organisations to produce unique customer experiences. With such profound social and industrial changes, one could argue that the traditional management practices of the twentieth century might require reconsideration.

3.4.2 The event production process

Event planning is often presented as a rather simple process, comprising stages that build on each other towards the achievement of preset objectives. Watt (1998), Shone and Parry (2010), and Bowdin *et al.* (2011) all suggest this approach. However, event design is more of a creative set of activities that can often appear chaotic in its development due to its need to be revised. These activities are embodied in the 'spirit' of the event planning process. However, because *doing* event design and *learning* event design often involve very different outcomes, the specific explanation of what event design involves has proved more difficult to express. Anybody who has worked closely with expert event designers will often be impressed by how different their thinking processes and their verbalisation are, compared with those involved in more structured businesses, such as accountancy or law. It often seems that the 'out-of-the-box thinking' associated with design is difficult to put into ordinary speech.

Edward De Bono (1976) highlighted that thinking encompassed not only the logical and analytical 'types' of thinking we seem to spend so much of our studies and work lives practicing and perfecting, but also the importance of 'lateral' thinking, particularly in creative or artistic work, and that these three 'types' of thinking interact, as shown in Figure 3.1.

Lateral thinking involves the movement value of ideas. It is often concerned with taking an initial idea as a starting point and moving to the creation of new ideas. De Bono (2006) proposed four types of thinking tool to facilitate this process:

- *idea-generating tools* that are designed to break current thinking patterns—routine patterns, the status quo;
- *focus tools* that are designed to broaden where to search for new ideas;
- *harvest tools* that are designed to ensure more value is received from idea-generating output;
- *treatment tools* that are designed to consider real-world constraints, resources and support.

The realisation that artistic endeavour requires creative thinking processes is not new, particularly to those associated with the arts and the creative industries. However, the nature of the outcomes associated with events often requires much more final measurement of tangible success. Much of traditional business school education, particularly in the western world, is concerned with the development of critical reasoning skills, relating to the evaluation of true statements and the questioning of errors – skills that mainly require analytical and logical thinking processes. While critical reasoning is obviously an important skill for events management specialists to develop and use in their work, it is much less useful for the event designer, whose 'craft' concerns the accomplishment of business outcomes through creative problem-solving.

3.4.3 The need for event designers to develop reflective practice

If the path to effective experience design in events cannot be satisfactorily pursued through the channels of traditional analytical, logical and therefore critical thought processes provided by mainstream business management practice and education, then the methods employed should perhaps attempt to incorporate more creative processes, possibly providing more opportunity to utilise right-brain functions. Certainly, the tasks associated with the more straightforward and organisational activities commonly associated with event planning may need to be rethought because of the creative requirements of reflective design.

Donald Schön (1987) proposed that in order to develop 'education for artistry' there would be a necessity for the formation of a 'reflective practicum', which represents a departure from the delivery and use of school knowledge and a move towards the use of reflection in action. For event designers to develop creative design practice which applies the tools of experience design literally 'outside the box' of conventional management activities, there is a need to articulate the difference between the two spheres of design knowledge, as compared in Table 3.1.

3.4.4 Content-based versus production-driven events

Berridge (2007) distinguished traditional management processes from the importance of recognising a particular design 'component' required throughout the event cycle to ensure the success of production-driven, creative events. This view has more recently gained popularity among events academics and practitioners alike.

Building upon the model of creative and reflective practice for event design, it is logical also to question the dominance of the linear event planning process models in which design seems to figure only as an implied part. For more detailed discussion on this topic, Berridge (2007) highlights at some length the fundamental distinction between management and design of event experiences.

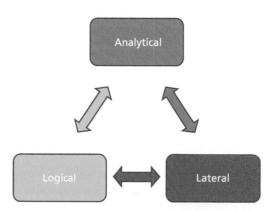

Figure 3.1 Three types of thinking
Source: Adapted from De Bono 1976

Table 3.1 Comparison of 'school knowledge' versus 'reflection in action' as applied to event design

Event design according to 'school knowledge'	Event design according to 'reflection in action'
Designer relies upon critical reasoning – that is, the designer completes a preset schedule of logical steps.	Designer 'knows' in action – that is, various approaches are creatively synthesised using familiar pre-existing models from familiar past representations (e.g. culture) and other design settings in new combinations according to the design concept until an intuitive goal is reached.
The design process can be 'managed' or controlled according to predictability and bureaucracy. This allows the project to be constantly evaluated according to goals, timelines and tangible, measureable standards.	The design process becomes difficult for external parties and stakeholders to evaluate clearly. Measures of 'quality' are mainly perceived and realised from the reflective point of view of the designer.
The designer uses formal, commonly agreed categories of knowledge to inform the design process. This usually relies on a common body of knowledge and clearly 'right answers' which can be clearly articulated.	There is more of a view that design is somewhat about knowing more than we can say. Sensory design in particular often cannot be satisfactorily verbalised and also is not simply an intellectual activity.
The designer may view the design environment and its experience as separate from everyday life.	A designer may help the event attendee to coordinate everyday knowledge in action with other forms of privileged or received knowledge.
The designer's theory and experience are considered valuable, with higher levels of theory being brought to design having higher status. Design knowledge is also 'molecular' and not interconnected and there is a view of a more 'set' way and rigid answer to the set design task. Often there are single or set methods towards the required outcome.	The reflective designer uses on-the-spot experimentation, thinking about what they are doing as they are doing it. The designer allows himself/herself to be surprised and puzzled, responding to the puzzle as it progresses and unfolds, resetting the problem as appropriate. Separate methods are used, depending on the nature of the problem, including the invention of new ways to achieve outcomes in different projects. Overall, the practice is less of a method, but more of an art.
'Junk' categories are created for people who do not receive the design and event concept as expected.	The designer attempts to meet the attendee at their level of understanding.

Of course, linear models, such as those proposed by Shone and Parry (2010), should not be completely discarded, particularly in favour of a seemingly random replacement. It is simply hoped that there might be a proposition made that may assist the theoretical operationalisation of the design 'function' or component of the overall event planning process. Thus, the creative component of event design is carried out on the basis of a rationale for each event, which is based on traditional planning tools. The place of design in events is illustrated in Figure 3.2.

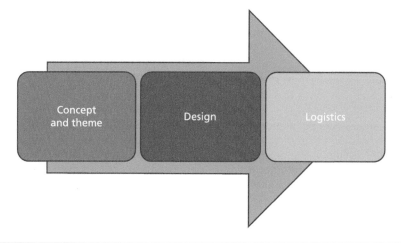

Figure 3.2 The three-stage event design model

CASE STUDY 3.1

The opening ceremony of the London Olympic Games 2012

On 27 July in the Olympic Stadium in London the opening ceremony of the 2012 Summer Olympic Games took place. The Games were formally opened by Queen Elizabeth II and the opening ceremony spectacle was directed by the British film director Danny Boyle, and performed to music entitled 'Isles of Wonder'.

The important elements of the event's design are summarised as follows:

- There was a budget of £27 million for the opening event – higher than the cost of many motion pictures.
- The title, 'Isles of Wonder', was inspired by Shakespeare's play *The Tempest* and designed to reflect aspects of British history and culture.
- There were three, principal sections: Britain's Industrial Revolution, the National Health Service and its literary heritage.
- It involved a cast of professional performers and 7,500 volunteers.

Image 3.1 **2012 Summer Olympics**
Credit: Paul Drinkwater/NBC/Getty Images

- The programme relied heavily on children and young people, building around themes that would relate to youth. Twenty-five schools from East London boroughs recruited child volunteers for the performance plus 170 sixth formers, speaking more than 50 languages.
- The cast was cued and coordinated by verbal directions received through earphones, which also carried a continuous electronic metronomic four-beat to keep performers moving in time with the music.
- The Red Arrows performed a flypast over the stadium, and there was a concert in Hyde Park featuring artists selected to represent the four nations of the UK.
- Various film clips were used throughout, including shots of London, and a journey along the Thames, taking in famous landmarks and characters from British popular and literary culture. One sequence starred James Bond and Queen Elizabeth herself.
- The first segment, 'Pandemonium', encapsulated British economic and social development from rural economy through from the Industrial Revolution to the 1960s.
- Volunteers represented groups that had changed the face of Britain: the women's suffrage movement, the Jarrow Crusade, the first Caribbean immigrants arriving in 1948 on board the *Empire Windrush*, a 1970s DJ float, the Nostalgia Steel Band and the Beatles.

- Clever stimulation of the senses using sound, included workers casting an iron ring. As the noise level and tension built, driven by the relentless rhythm of the music and drumming, participants mimed repetitive mechanical movements associated with industrial processes. This resulted in four glowing orange rings, which were carried high and became the five rings of the Olympic symbol that ignited and rained fire in silver and gold.
- The second section included a salute to the NHS, and a celebration of British children's literature.
- The third section celebrated British popular music and culture, and paid homage to each decade since the 1960s.
- Tim Berners-Lee, inventor of the World Wide Web, tweeted: 'This is for everyone', which was instantly spelled out in LED lights around the stadium.
- Next came a filmed sequence showing extracts from the UK torch relay, followed by David Beckham driving an illuminated motor boat with footballer Jade Bailey holding the Olympic torch down the River Thames and under Tower Bridge. There was then a tribute to the victims of the 7 July 2005 London bombings.
- In the Parade of Nations each team of athletes was led by a flag-bearer, a youngster wearing a dress made from fabric printed with photos of Olympic volunteers, and carrying a sign with the country's name.
- The Olympic Flag was carried by eight people chosen from around the world as symbols of the Olympic values.

(Olympic.org 2016)

Study activity

Watch the video clip at www.youtube.com/watch?v=4As0e4de-rl and answer the following questions:

1 Choose another country to hold an Olympics opening ceremony. Write notes about the symbols you would use and the meanings they would convey.
2 Analyse the case and discuss to what extent the designer has successfully promoted a sense of inclusion, for all members of British society.

3.5 Concept and theme

3.5.1 Event concept

The concept of an event and its theme, although different steps in the design process, are cohesive aspects, with the theme essentially becoming the main 'vehicle' through which the outcomes of the event are to be achieved. Goldblatt (2005) provided a useful framework, named the '5Ws', which has become the bedrock of most events, whether content-based or production-driven in nature. The 5Ws are explained by Goldblatt as the essential questions that should be asked and answered as the basis for any event before further decisions should be made. He phrases these questions in Figure 3.3.

While these questions have their own context in the overall planning of the event and form the basis of the widely accepted event planning frameworks, such as the one proposed by Shone and Parry (2010), they pose particular problems for the event designer in terms of the overall event outcomes to be accomplished by its design.

The focus on event attendees' experiences, as opposed to the simple management of an events process, is a major departure from the more traditional practice of gathering together various logistical elements, such as catering, entertainment, sound, light and service, in the hope that somehow, with the right timings and programme, all those who attend will experience something special. Instead, the focus is on the psychology of event attendees and what will be achieved in their own experience. While in the planning context, discussed in Chapters 1 and 2, these five questions and their answers lead the quest for the establishment of event feasibility and they present the event designer with more complex, creative problems to solve. In design terms, the reason why the event should be held becomes a question about what is to be achieved in the experience of its attendees. The event stakeholders often become agents in the creative process of design and may require accommodation by the event designer. This could also prove troublesome, making the design process more complex because of having to consider the additional opinions of the interested, yet not necessarily expert, parties. The venue and the date and time of the event, though often dictated to the designer, become crucial features of design, which either greatly complement or sometimes greatly hinder the cohesion with the theme and other important aspects of the event's delivery. The event product, or 'the event

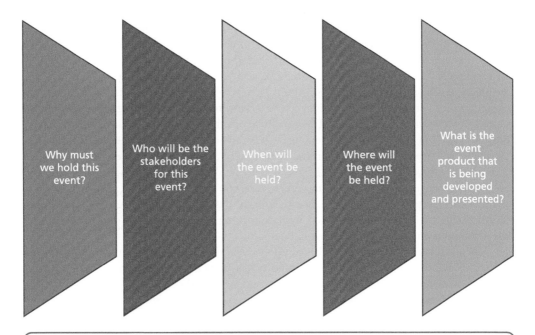

Figure 3.3 The '5Ws' of the event concept
Source: Adapted from Goldblatt 2005: 44

take-home', relates to the psychological, physical or even spiritual experience attendees should remember, perhaps reflecting on or acting upon them afterwards.

With respect to the event product, the design outcomes can be divided into cognitive, affective, decisional and psychomotor domains. Cognitive outcomes relate to the use of attendees' minds and may involve learning, which could include the delivery and assimilation of new knowledge. For example, an exhibition might seek to inform the public about the life and achievements of a particular historical figure. This would involve the conveyance of various types of information suitable for absorption by attendees, which could be retained in their memories.

Affective outcomes involve appealing to the emotions of attendees and can include their registration of new awareness, or surprise, excitement or even fear. Certainly, new awareness and appreciation of social issues, such as environmental sustainability, can be successfully achieved in event attendees by using suitable emotional stimuli, such as personal appeals or visual materials.

Decisional outcomes involve attendees making choices, such as those concerned with new purchases, voting or supporting causes.

Psychomotor outcomes involve physical activities, such as running marathons, playing sports or making political protests.

Once the answers demanded by the 5Ws have been ascertained, the relevant particulars from the outcome domains can then be decided and articulated, and the designer can set specific design objectives. When these have been decided, this concept can be linked to an appropriate theme.

3.5.2 Theme

Defining this important term from the existing literature has proved problematic. Authors such as Goldblatt (2005) and Monroe (2005) tend to apply the term in relation to a more traditional concept of the 'themed event,' perhaps denoting a national flavour to food, entertainment, décor and other staging aspects. Getz (2007: 223) has provided the clearest definition so far stating: 'A "theme" is a unifying idea or concept which gives meaning to the event, or is the object of celebration or commemoration.' Therefore, the theme, often established with the participation of stakeholders, is assigned with a view to being a dictating influence over all aspects of subsequent event design. This is contrary to the more traditional view presented by Bowdin *et al.* (2011), which places theming at the centre of logistics, without the key mediation of the distinct role of design in the production of event attendee experiences.

A more helpful analogy might be the use of genre in film and theatre production, which has been used to convey ideas and meanings more efficiently between directors, writers, costumers and all other parties responsible for every aspect of design. Part of the necessity for the use of genre was the difficulty associated with conveying ideas verbally. Words often convey linear thoughts and prove problematic in communicating creative ideas. As a result, directors developed forms of communication based upon visual media, such as storyboards. They also learned to talk to others responsible for important aspects of the creative process in terms of 'horror', 'romance', 'action' and other genre-based terms and concepts. This filtered into the marketing communication messages of studio advertising so that potential viewers of movie products might obtain clear ideas beforehand about particular offerings. Architectural firms have followed the same practice when communicating complicated building-design concepts to clients and other stakeholders through such devices as concept boards and scale models.

Similarly, in the case of event design, often the parties involved are unable to convey design ideas and instructions clearly without 'leakage' of meaning, potential loss of detail, as well as serious risk of potentially expensive design errors and client misunderstandings. Therefore, in addition to the theme being a central idea by which all the other elements of design can be determined, it also serves as an effective communication medium.

However, theming has thus far been approached at a level of complexity little more sophisticated than that offered by the existing tourism and hospitality management literature. For example, Getz (2007) briefly combines the topic with programme design. Malouf (1999) provides theming advice ranging from table plans to options for napkin folds. Goldblatt (2005) writes a section about themed events, which offers suggestions about suitable design elements for events ranging from 'Hooray for Hollywood' through to 'Dickens of a Christmas'. Monroe provides a more extensive glossary of event themes including 'MASH', 'Dinosaur Dance' and 'Roman Empire'. Only Berridge (2007) has attempted to incorporate the components of theme into a clearer conceptual framework, which appears wholly inseparable from the design process itself and its planned outcomes.

Just as the big studio system of the twentieth century was often accused of effectively 'recycling' standardised and mass-produced art forms for general public consumption, the events industry may have also developed its own standardised forms. This has led to concern about inauthentic, artificially produced events.

As an important part of this ongoing debate, Brown and James (2004) notably discuss the potential risk of what they term 'ritual sacrifice' in the events industry. They argue that in its haste to become recognised as a mature field and profession, the industry is unconsciously deviating from its roots; the age-old foundations of events which were discussed in Chapter 1. These events were 'grassroots', cultural experiences that developed over centuries as authentic expressions of social community gatherings. However, Brown and James argue that these natural and often spontaneous expressions of social existence have been replaced by inauthentic, artificial, 'packaged' consumer experiences for generating profit.

CASE STUDY 3.2

What You Will, Celebrating 400 Years of Shakespeare in the English Language

Location: Middle Temple Hall, London, United Kingdom
Event type: Organised by the British Council and part of the British Council *Shakespeare Lives, Live* series of events

The What You Will, Celebrating 400 Years of Shakespeare in the English Language event was organised by the British Council as part of their 'Shakespeare Lives, Live' series of events, and held to celebrate the very first performance of Shakespeare's *Twelfth Night*, exactly 414 years to the day of the event, Candlemas, 2 February 1602.

2016 is the 400th anniversary of Shakespeare's death, so is marked by events across the world. This event responded to one of the prompts by the #Shakespeare400 activities to celebrate 400 years of Shakespeare in the English

Language, and its aim was specifically to demonstrate the continuity and contribution of that language to modern everyday English.

This aim was met by the reflection of the theme in the event design, thus giving authenticity to the attendees' experience.

Attention to detail was paramount. The event was held in the same room, and at the same venue as that first performance of *Twelfth Night*; the Middle Temple Hall in London. This created an authentic experience both for the attendees and for the online audience on YouTube. The room's décor was the original wood panelling from when Shakespeare stood there, and the furniture used was mostly original too. For instance, the 30ft long table displayed a scroll of the 1,167 words that are first credited to Shakespeare, and are still in use today, had been built inside the room, more than 400 years before from a 600-year-old tree. The wood in this table is over a thousand years old and it was from this same table that Shakespeare, his players and guests ate on that night in 1602. The music was of the day, using instruments dating from the 1600s. Candles were lit and set in the original candlesticks, which were then placed at either end of a replica Shakespearean stage.

The evening comprised an **ensemble** of musicians and players, and various speakers, and experts, for a celebration of literature, language and theatre. It began with an adaptation of *Twelfth Night*, which continued, interspersed with mini-lectures, performances and forums throughout the evening. All those words from the scroll, first credited to Shakespeare and still in use today, were spoken during the evening's proceedings.

By representing the language of Shakespeare over the last 400 years, the performers and speakers demonstrated that the language is still alive and well in the present day, in the mouths, ears, eyes and hearts of people around the world.

The authenticity of this theme was enforced by the event design. It was credible to the audience, both attendees as well as teachers online from all around the world, that the words were still part of a living language today because they were spoken in the same surroundings as when they were first uttered.

The proceedings then moved on to a question-and-answer session, for the seated audience, the online audience using the Twitter hashtag #ShakespeareLives, and a discussion on YouTube. The live audience was offered refreshments and tours of the venue with its various artefacts.

This presented a perfect example of correctly using event design to authenticate an experience while fully embracing recent developments and technical advancements in the events industry.

(London, U. 2016)

As is discussed more fully in Chapter 13, some produced events do still provide an escape for attendees from their usual routines. Chapter 12 highlights the essential part that event production plays in disengaging attendees from their normal thought processes, thereby enabling them to enter into a new set of relationships and experiences that are often related to unfamiliar branding concepts.

Pine and Gilmore (1999: 36) counter Brown and James's criticism by stating: 'There's no such thing as an artificial experience. Every experience created within the individual is real, whether the stimuli be natural or simulated.' Thus, while some in the marketing community continue to discuss more effective ways to deliver standardised products in customised service environments, the events industry's focus on the production of attendee experiences requires more consideration of an artificially produced 'experiencescape' in which the event attendee can engage in his or her personalised experiences at three operational levels of design, as shown in Figure 3.4.

Figure 3.4 demonstrates that the event attendee is often consuming standardised, tangible products, such as a branded soft drink, which is delivered through the medium of customised service provided by event employees, such as waiting or sales counter staff, within a personalised experiencescape that incorporates ambience, fragrances, light, space and other design aspects. It should be remembered that such attendees will always form their own personalised experience, which will often be as a result of stimuli artificially produced by the activities of the event organisation. These experiences will be positive or negative with respect to the achievement of the intended event outcomes. It is therefore the responsibility of the event designer to ensure that the experience which is personalised by each attendee mirrors these event objectives as closely as possible.

3.5.3 Inadequacy of the service design research

Since the popularity of service management literature began in the 1980s, several useful models for the design, delivery, measurement and recovery of customer service have been proposed. Foremost among these has been Zeithaml *et al.*'s (2006) model of service gaps and their associated measurement using the SERVQUAL questionnaire tool. Obviously, the events industry remains in many respects a service industry, and while the measurement of gaps in customer satisfaction related to service delivery remains relevant, from an event designer's viewpoint its use as an instrument of customer experience measurement appears limited. Such scientific methods are as inadequate in their capacity to evaluate the successful design and delivery of event experiences as they are in their measurement of people's opinions about art exhibits, or their views about theatrical productions. Major event organisations, such as Gartner, have attempted to address these issues by using flexible, one-to-one interviews with

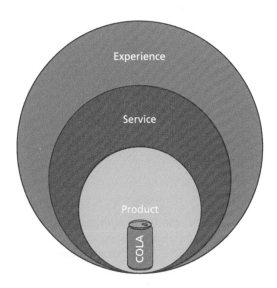

Figure 3.4 Three levels of the 'experiencescape'

key event attendees after major productions. Event evaluation is discussed in greater detail in Chapter 14, but it seems that much more research is required into new ways to investigate the creative impacts of 'wow' factors on event attendees' perceptions of events and memory formation, in particular.

Study activity

Write a basic research plan of how you would investigate attendees' perceptions of:

- A major community firework display.
- The performance of a headlining act at an international music festival.
- The awards ceremony at a Formula 1 racing championship.

What challenges do you predict in your ability to measure these perceptions?

3.5.4 Experience blueprinting

It is therefore proposed that designers of the event experience clearly articulate, at least for their own reference, a 'blueprint' of intended attendee experiences throughout the event. This approach is an adaptation of Zeithaml *et al.*'s (2006) initial application of blueprinting to service design, which attempts to articulate service delivery actions, such as employee scripts, interactions and their associated performance standards. It is suggested here that the experience blueprint for an event includes similar details, though it should be supplemented by clear reference to the 'activities' of the various sensory stimuli involved in the design, such as programme, staging and timing elements, as well as their intended outcomes, such as attendees' memory formations, emotional flow, engagement and so on.

Such blueprinting of planned experiences should be carried out for the whole of the event cycle, which cannot be limited simply to the timelines required for operational delivery, but need to be centred on the experiences the attendee has at each stage. Just as marketers often find it essential to view a simple purchase as a multi-staged cognitive and emotional process, so event designers need to predict and design for the multi-phased nature of experience before, at and after events. Clawson's (1963) multi-phased nature of experience model helps to isolate some relevant, key stages of the attendee's experience, as shown in Figure 3.5.

It is also practical to suggest that some of the marketing and sponsorship issues discussed in later chapters should be carefully considered here to ensure cohesion of the event's design in relation to its overall branding and competitive positioning, as well as the service delivery aspects common to ticket sales and pre-event advertising and social media. These will also be important aspects of Clawson's 'anticipation' stage of attendee experience.

3.5.5 Attendee absorption and immersion

Any proposed blueprint, though subject to change as the event delivery progresses, should clearly provide an understanding of the levels of immersion and/or absorption, as well as the participation requirements and activities of attendees. Once again, such considerations should mirror the event concept requirements and will be informed by, and in turn inform,

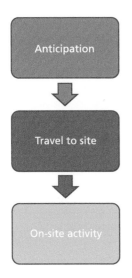

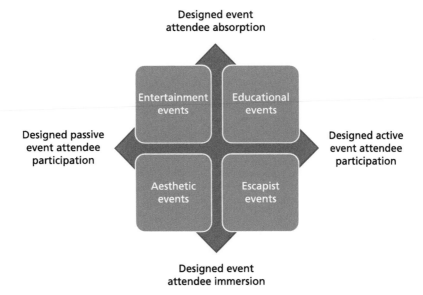

Figure 3.6 The event experience realm
Source: Adapted from Pine and Gilmore 1999: 30

its chosen theme, thus influencing the event's design. Pine and Gilmore's (1999) 'experience realm' model helps us to understand these basic combinations of immersion and absorption, with participation levels at various stages of the event experience, as shown in Figure 3.6.

'Participation' can be active or passive, depending on whether event attendees directly influence the experience being produced. Classical music concert events generally involve little audience participation until the final applause, whereas the annual London Marathon depends upon the active participation throughout of its attendees, that is, the runners. 'Absorption' involves 'occupying a person's attention by bringing the experience into the mind', and 'immersion' is 'becoming physically (or virtually) a part of the experience itself' (Pine and Gilmore 1999: 31). The combination of these elements produces the four 'experience realms' of entertainment, educational, aesthetic and escapist events.

This model is not intended to depict a static rationale for an event, but refers to different levels of participation combined with absorption or immersion at different points of the event, depending on the prescribed outcomes of each stage. The level of participation by attendees at events needs to be carefully designed beforehand to ensure their appropriate level of engagement. Additionally, failure to implement the correct level of immersion can lead to serious shortfalls in attendee engagement and a lack of satisfaction. It might also be worth noting that attendees sometimes attempt 'unauthorised' immersion of themselves in experiences, which are mainly intended for absorption, such as football matches, the outcomes of which have suffered as a result of pitch invasions. In such cases, designers with planners, and even contract agents such as law enforcement officers, should ensure that steps are taken to minimise such disruptions.

3.6 Understanding event experiences

This view of the event designer's role therefore moves away from the traditional approach of simply planning events by using logistics. It focuses more on clearly defining the required experiences that attendees should have in relation to the planned outcomes and objectives set for the event, as well as the levels of required participation and immersion or absorption at its different stages.

3.6.1 The role of sensory experience

The basis of event attendee experience formation is sensory stimulation. Authors such as Goldblatt (2005), Monroe (2005) and Getz (2007) acknowledge the necessity of appealing to attendees' senses of sight, hearing, taste, touch, speech and emotions within the experience environment of the event. However, they tend to revert to lists of sensory categories and associated logistical options, without much explanation of their use or how they stimulate attendees to form experiences. The EMBOK model (EMBOK 2010) and the corresponding website of leading events industry authority Silvers (juliasilvers.com 2010) generally attempt to list design on behalf of the events industry as comprising:

- content design
- theme design
- program design
- environment design
- production design
- entertainment design
- catering design.

Silvers also attempts to develop each of these categories, with a selection of logistical options under the heading of 'Management'. Not referring to EMBOK specifically, but more to the historical tendency of such lists, Berridge (2007: 34) observes:

> Oddly these are not always aligned with detailed examples of their use. Or any further explorations of the types of experiences that might be subsequently created. This is a common characteristic of academic study of events in general, to produce checklists of

what could be included without necessarily any accompanying explanation of how they should be used or what they will produce.

3.6.2 Basic event attendee psychology

Bearing in mind that sensory stimulation provokes a psychological formation of experience in event attendees, general reference to some basic theories of psychology is appropriate here. Though it is not within the scope of this text to explain or critique these approaches, their importance and application to the design of event attendee experiences is crucial to the understanding of event design by the event designer.

3.6.2.1 Behaviourism

Behaviourism, one of the earliest schools of popular psychology, proposes that individuals learn through conditioning as a result of stimuli in their environment, as shown in Figure 3.7.

This school of learning is based on the two main theories: classical conditioning and operant conditioning. Classical conditioning was developed through experimentation on dogs by Ivan Pavlov (1927) and involved associative learning. Briefly, Pavlov demonstrated that individuals' naturally occurring stimuli – such as smelling food, which leads to the response of increased hunger – could be modified through conditioning to become a conditioned response associated with a modified stimulus. For example, when attendees arrive at a dinner event it would be usual for them to expect to eat at some later point. Seeing or smelling attractive food can stimulate hunger and appetite, but the event designer can use various sensory cues in the environment that are not directly related to food in order to condition the attendees to anticipate certain levels of luxury or extravagance in the pleasurable experiences awaiting them. Canapés, fine champagne and the dress code, as well as formality and attentiveness of the food service staff, can all cause a conditioned response, as can table linen, cutlery choice and accompanying music.

B. F. Skinner's (1957) theory of operant conditioning as a development of Pavlov's classical theory demonstrated that individuals can learn as a result of punishment and reward from external stimuli, as is shown in Table 3.2.

This approach focuses on a person's response to stimuli and can be used with the correct corresponding reinforcement to modify behaviour. For example, attendees at an event often need to pass through processes which they do not consider satisfying or central to their overall event experience. These processes can include long queuing periods, or compliance

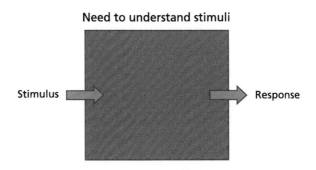

Figure 3.7 The stimulus–response mechanism

Table 3.2	Basic summary of stimulus–response via operant conditioning

	Outcome of conditioning	
	Increase behaviour	*Decrease behaviour*
Positive stimulus	Positive reinforcement (add stimulus)	Response cost (remove stimulus)
Negative stimulus	Negative reinforcement (remove stimulus)	Punishment (add stimulus)

with security or other necessary crowd management procedures. Correct design can stimulate an appropriate response to verbal, visual or other cues which can instruct attendees in their required behaviours. Formally dressed security personnel can reinforce the need for adequate compliance with bag checks at events where there are valuable artefacts, camera use at art exhibitions or even physical examinations for weapons at football matches. Queuing configuration design can play a large part in the ambience of an event, reinforcing attendees' satisfaction levels and first impressions.

3.6.2.2 Psychoanalysis

The work of Freud, Jung and other popular psychoanalysts can also provide useful understanding to the event designer, who will often access previous experiences and associations from an event attendee's background and particularly their childhood. Many design strategies used in order to stimulate event attendee immersion encourage the use of basic and familiar instincts, often delivered in unfamiliar contexts. For example, businesses often use paintball competitions for team-building events, which could be little more than the re-enactment of school playtime. Dressing up in costume is common in events as diverse as carnivals, graduation ceremonies and Halloween. The gamut of childhood emotions, including fear, euphoria and competitiveness, can be variously called upon in event contexts by the appropriate design of sensory stimulation. As human beings, many of these instincts are experienced at an almost primal level and they can be enhanced by the tastes and textures of foods, food service, familiar music, colours and even smells. These can be used to stimulate attendees' memories, which in turn stimulate the required sensory outcomes. The deeper meaning of cultural symbols, rituals and contexts are discussed later in this chapter.

3.6.2.3 Cognitivism

Cognitivist psychologists such as Rogers or Schön extended the humanist agenda which resulted from the practical applications of the theories of the two foregoing psychological schools to propose that humans are sentient beings capable of forming their individual meanings from the world around them. The relevance of reflective processes to the design of event experiences has already been discussed in some detail with respect to the role of designer, but similar application could be made to the process by which event attendees make meaning of their experiences for themselves. Certainly, this approach will rely in part on those that have previously been mentioned, but attendees' past experiences will influence how they process a particular event's stimuli.

3.6.3 Sensory perception

An event designer should recognise the application of these schools in association with the role of perception. Perception refers to the interpretation of the information we receive through our five senses. Attendees at events constantly receive stimulation through visual, auditory, olfactory, tactile and gustatory cues in various amounts and combinations, depending on the particular event in question. It is the perception of our environment that distinguishes us from other mammals. Gestalt psychology, which is concerned with 'the whole', suggests we organise stimuli into groups according to four main types: similarity, proximity, continuity and closure. This means that event attendees group items based upon how similar they are, how close they are to each other, according to continuous patterns, and they form their own interpretations of familiar objects in order to create their own experiences. Perceptual constancy allows event attendees to maintain their view of an object even though it changes in terms of size, shape and brightness.

Visual perception allows us to interpret size, texture, overlap, shading, height, clarity and depth. Visual perception is therefore an important consideration when designing events.

For example, attendees associate groups of dishes on a wedding buffet table in terms of food groups such as fish dishes, salads or vegetarian options, or visual indication of likely flavours, such as cultural specialities or desserts. They will expect to see a progression of courses at a typical wedding in the west; from hors d'oeuvres, to fish courses, main courses and desserts. Colours will provide indications of the variety of ingredients, possible freshness and potentially important differences between flavours of diverse items, such as cheeses. Cleanliness of the surroundings will be visually perceived. Grandeur of the setting can be communicated by the visual perception of the silver plate on the guest cutlery and the texture and brightness of the table linen. Though psychologists and philosophers understand more about visual perception than they do about any other type of perception, it is still crucial for the event designer to consider carefully its interaction with the other senses.

Auditory perception is the ability to identify, interpret and attach meaning to sound. Sounds are what we hear (McLachlan 1989), and are internal sensations which we experience directly as a result of public occurrences in the outside world of the event. For example, loud music at a music event can provide feelings of euphoria in one attendee and a physical headache in another. In 2009, a student suffered sudden arrhythmic death syndrome (SADS) after attending a club event and heart specialists thought the cause could have been linked to the loud bass music. Though much discussion surrounds the nature of sounds in relation to the objects that produce them and the act of hearing, it is sufficient for our purposes here to state that objects produce distinct sounds and event attendees use the distinction between these sounds to make sense of their environment and the occurrences within them. With this in mind, the effects of music on human experience have been recognised since time immemorial. The effectiveness of themes can be reinforced or compromised by the suitability of the accompanying music and sound system logistics. Obviously, some events, such as music festivals, revolve completely around music. This has more recently led to discussions regarding the suitability of some popular music artistes' participation in such long-standing events as the Glastonbury Festival in the UK. Music was a key design feature of the opening ceremony of the 2012 London Olympic Games, as the range of music was almost exclusively British, including classical works by British composers, performances by UK choirs and UK music from the 1960s onwards. Musical motifs were used to bind the event together; a whistling theme for the ceremony and a bells theme for the entire opening day of the Olympics.

The other main senses involved in event design, though less well-documented, nevertheless remain crucial to the success of the event. *Olfactory design* involves appealing to the event attendees' sense of smell and has probably been the fastest developing area of experience design, thanks in part to its use by fast-food, retail, hospitality and leisure companies. *Gustatory design* relates to the sense of taste. While it is naturally closely allied with the olfactory sense, it has been used at events in catering for millennia. *Tactile design* involves the stimulation of the attendees' sense of touch to achieve outcomes in the psychomotor realm.

3.6.4 Memory

As attendees return home, the main residual effects of the event's concept and outcomes remain in their memories. Sometimes, whole societies can share a powerful collective memory of a particular event. It is therefore crucial that the most important moments in an event are signposted for its attendees and distinguished from the often huge quantity of other, peripheral information and stimuli being provided. Attendees can form and retain lasting memories of the event. It is vital in this process that various subsections of the experience are carefully designed and programmed. The psychological aspects of such subsections include a sense of time, excitement and mood, ambience and emotional flow. These are discussed at length by Graham Berridge (2007) and are often carefully combined to produce 'wow' factors, which can be defined as sensory crescendos where attendee consciousness reaches its peak. Such wow factors are designed moments when the *raison d'être* of the event is signified to all participants. For example, the captain of the World Cup's winning team raises the trophy in triumph as the high point and culmination of the whole tournament. Similarly, the torch-lighting ceremony of the Olympic Games often attracts the largest international media viewership. Film and other entertainment award ceremony presentations will schedule a specific moment to recognise a famous director for their lifetime achievement and contribution to the art form. Sometimes, though, wow factors are unplanned, such as the famous moment during the 1985 Live Aid event when Bono, lead singer of rock band U2, rescued a spectator from being crushed against security railings, creating an iconic, collective, cultural memory of a key event high point.

> **Study activity**
>
> Choose an event you attended. Try to recall its main memorable incidents and especially its wow factors. How were these delivered?

3.7 Event staging and logistics

Having decided the event concept and the specific design characteristics, it becomes more straightforward for the event designer to draw together a cohesive system of logistics in order to deliver the experience to event participants. Hopefully, the foregoing discussion has further clarified the importance of keeping to this order of design elements. Only when the event's outcomes are clear, can it be determined on a sensory level which design elements will deliver them and which are the tools necessary for achieving this. Finally, the specific staging elements – such as timings, programming, service, audience participants, queuing arrangements, entertainment, sets and decorations, plants and flowers, seating design, table settings, catering and food service, lighting and rigging, colours and themes, sound and use of technology – can be definitively set, planned and delivered.

3.8 Summary

This chapter attempts to provide a clear, introductory overview to a topic which is crucial to the success of designed and production-driven events, yet about which remains much misunderstanding and confusion. The relationship between the event production steps of concept, design and staging has been highlighted, with a focus on events as the production of experiences rather than the simplistic, yet common, management of staging elements. This has been discussed from the perspective of the event attendee's experience, with a focus on the psychological outcomes of design and production.

Industry voice

Joanna Griffith

 I joined the British Council as an events officer, just after they had started planning the launch of a series of seminars to commemorate the 400th anniversary of world-famous playwright William Shakespeare's death.

When I was being interviewed, the initial plan was that the event, based on Shakespeare's play Twelfth Night, was to take place on the twelfth day after Christmas. However, by the time I commenced employment, the event had been rescheduled for performance on its original date, 2 February, at its original venue, Middle Temple, in London.

As a fairly recent graduate of Events Management, I was so excited to join the British Council team and the launch of the 'Shakespeare Lives Seminar Series' on such a significant date and venue.

We found out that Middle Temple has the bell of the Golden Hind and we used that to signal the start of the event. In addition, the walls of Middle Temple are lined with the coats of arms of teachers who have given lectures to law students. In fact, Shakespeare's cousin, Thomas Greene, once gave a lecture at Middle Temple. His coat of arms you can find adorning one of the walls. Attendees got a feel for the greatness of these hangings as they walked passed them to their respective waiting areas.

We wanted to create a spectacular entrance, the great reveal. The doors to the main hall were shut as attendees entered the venue, and were opened on the sound of the Bell of the Golden Hind. Little details were mentioned in the opening and closing speeches, such as the fact that there was a 400-year-old chest in one of the hallways, and the table which lay to the side of the audience was built in that room. The performers laid out a scroll of more than 1,000 words which were first recorded by Shakespeare and that we still use in the English language. Our actors recited these words in a record 8 minutes and 11 seconds.

We were able to incorporate elements into the event, such as the lighting, refreshments and setup of the venue. The performance was partly by candlelight, decreasing the use of LEDs and creating atmospheric lighting similar to what would have been used in the 1600s. The canapés served after the performance were also Shakespearean-themed. These elements, these components, were brought together to create a memorable event because there is so much history to Middle Temple itself that it would have been a wasted opportunity not to include these as part of the event.

The performance itself was a modern take, though Shakespeare's language was used in the scenes, and the travelling actors, if you will, wore modern clothing. The performance focused on the language of Shakespeare and how it relates to the Modern English and was presented by the renowned linguist David Crystal, while the travelling actors were from the performance group Passion in Practice.

These concepts, combined, made for an inspiring and engaging seminar, which was fundamentally a lecture, given through entertainment. The attendees managed to have a sense of Shakespeare, Shakespearean times and still were able to take away the key messages of the event focused around Shakespeare's language. It opened up their minds and suggested ways that they could use the content in their own professions as English Language teachers and inspire their generation of future English speakers.

This event was very different to those that I have worked on before and was my first corporate-styled event where I have assisted from planning stages, through to production and post-production. I have now seen how event designs allow for a more engaging event in both art-based event settings and a more corporate setting. Business-based events should look more towards these community and public events, absorb the reactions and the engagements from those audiences and recreate and modernise the corporate sector.

Further reading

Berridge, G. (2007) *Event Design for Experience*, Oxford: Butterworth-Heinemann. This well-written book provides a thorough, literature-based review of some of the concepts discussed in this chapter from the multidisciplinary development of experience design.

Brown, S. and James, J. (2004) Event Design and Management: A Ritual sacrifice? In Ian Yeoman, Martin Robertson *et al.* (eds) *Festival and Events Management*. Oxford: Butterworth-Heinemann. This seminal chapter provides an interesting and critical discussion of some of the issues associated in event design and production regarding cultural authenticity and the wider implications of escapist events.

Jensen, R. (1999) *The Dream Society: How the Coming Shift from Information to Imagination Will Transform Your Business*, New York: McGraw-Hill. Though not directly related to the events industry, Jensen's thoughtful and well-written book discusses the movement in society away from tangible products and services to the demand by consumers for the designed experience and the importance of story-telling other methods applied by the modern-day marketers of such offerings.

Pine, B. J. and Gilmore, J. H. (1999) The Experience Economy, Massachusetts: *Harvard Business Review*. A foundational text for anybody interested in the models of experience design, which also uses many examples from a variety of consumer industries.

References

Bowdin, G., Allen, J., O'Toole, W., Harris, R. and McDonnell, I. (2011) *Events Management* (3rd edn), Oxford: Butterworth-Heinemann.

Burr, A., (2006) The 'Freedom of the Slaves to Walk the Streets'; Celebration, Spontaneity and Revelry Versus Logistics at the Notting Hill Carnival, in Picard and Robinson (eds) *Festivals, Tourism and Social Change: Remaking Worlds*, Clevedon: Channel View Publications,

Clawson, M. (1963) *Land and Water for Recreation: Opportunities, Problems and Policies.* Chicago, IL: Rand McNally.

De Bono, E. (1967) *New Think: The Use of Lateral Thinking.* London: Avon Books.

De Bono, E. (1976) *Teaching Thinking.* London: Penguin Books.

De Bono, E. (2006) *Thinking Systems Lateral Thinking: The Power of Provocation manual,* Clive: De Bono Thinking Systems.

Getz, D. (2007) *Events Studies,* Oxford: Butterworth-Heinemann.

Goldblatt, J. (2005) *Special Events: Event Leadership for a New World* (4th edn), Chichester: John Wiley & Sons.

Maclachlan, D. L. C. (1989) *Philosophy of Perception,* Englewood Cliffs, NJ: Prentice Hall.

Malouf, L. (1999) *Behind the Scenes at Special Events: Flowers, Props and Design,* New York: John Wiley & Sons.

Monroe, J. C. (2005) *Art of the Event: Complete Guide to Designing and Decorating Special Events,* New York: John Wiley & Sons.

Pavlov, I. P. (1927) *Conditioned Reflexes: An Investigation of the Physiological Activity of the Cerebral Cortex,* translated and edited by G. V. Anrep, London: Oxford University Press.

Schön, D. (1987) Educating the Reflective Practitioner, presentation to the meeting of the American Educational Research Association, Washington, DC.

Shone, A. and Parry, B. (2010) *Successful Event Management* (3rd edn), Hampshire: Cengage Learning.

Skinner, B. F. (1957) *Verbal Learning,* New York: Appleton-Century-Crofts.

Skinner, B. F. (1974) *About Behaviorism,* New York: Knopf.

Watt, D. C. (1998) *Event Management in Leisure and Tourism,* Harlow: Longman.

Zeithaml, V., Bitner, M. and Gremler, D. (2006), *Services Marketing,* Berkshire: McGraw-Hill.

Websites

www.juliasilvers.com.

www.embok.org.

news.bbc.co.uk/1/hi/england/london/8699866.stm.

London, U. (2016) What You Will: Celebrating 400 Years of Shakespeare in the English Language. Eventbrite. Available at: www.eventbrite.co.uk/e/what-you-will-celebrating-400-years-of-shakespeare-in-the-english-language-tickets-8478155391. Accessed 13 April 2016.

Olympic.org (2016) London 2012 – The Opening Ceremony. Available at: www.olympic.org/news/london-2012-the-opening-ceremony/204829 Accessed 22 February 2016.

Thomas, K. (2008) I.O.C. Issues Glowing Review of Beijing Games, *New York Times*. Available at: www.nytimes.com/2008/11/27/sports/olympics/27olympics.html?_r=0. Accessed 11 March 2016.

Chapter 4

Event operations

Contents

4.1 Aims

By the end of this chapter, students will be able to:

- explain the key elements of event operations;
- evaluate the need for event operations within the wider framework of event planning;
- discuss the external legal framework and frameworks that events operate within;
- recognise the importance of contracts and understand the basic contractual requirements for events; and
- analyse individual event requirements from a logistical perspective.

4.2 Introduction

Operational planning takes place after the strategic plans have been put in place – the event manager has developed a concept, tested it for feasibility (using situational analysis and market segmentation), chosen a venue, considered the event design and drawn up a strategic project plan. The next stage is to develop and implement the operational plan.

Operational planning consists of a set of plans for each key aspect of managing an event. It is the detailing of the skills and resources needed to deliver an event (Bowdin *et al.* 2010) and must therefore consider all areas central to event delivery. The event manager must consider all elements of the event and decide what resources, skills and equipment will be needed to deliver them – this, in a nutshell, is event operations. As every event is different and individually complex, there is no set formula for which operations will need to be planned. However, we can generalise, to some extent. Typical areas for planning include decisions around a

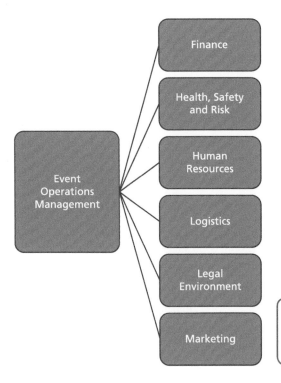

Figure 4.1 The key areas of managing event operations

staffing strategy; plans that cover the organisational approach to marketing and sponsorship; operational planning to evaluate health, safety and risk factors; and financial control systems. All of these issues are key event operations requirements and are therefore explored in detail in the chapters that follow this one. Figure 4.1 shows the key areas of operational management.

In addition to these key operational areas, the planning process of an event must consider a wider range of operations. This chapter will focus on the legal external environment – the consideration of legalities, regulations, licences, permits and contracts involved when managing an event – and event logistics – including the logistical planning for both customers and on-site at venues/event sites.

Study activity

Draw a model that demonstrates the event planning process as described in the book so far. It should include the order of the processes. Indicate how one element feeds into another. Include the following areas:

- The planning process:

  o event concept development including 5Ws and SMART event objective setting
  o event design
  o event feasibility testing including SWOT/PEST analysis
  o event project planning.

- The operations process:

  o financial planning
  o health, safety and risk
  o human resource management
  o logistical operations
  o the legal environment
  o marketing.

4.3 The legal environment

The consideration of and adherence to legalities is seen as the key to secure operations (Shone and Parry 2010). It is therefore essential that event managers keep abreast of the legal framework and relevant events legislation. Goldblatt (2008: 379) suggests four primary reasons for complying with laws and regulations: 'to protect your legal interests, to abide by ethical practices, to ensure the safety and security of your event stakeholders, and to protect your financial investment'. It is also important to comply in order to avoid adverse legal consequences, such as being sued for negligence or losing permits and licences that allow you to operate in the industry.

Legislation changes continually and there are many issues that cannot be fully explored here, so it is essential that event managers keep up to date with the ever-changing legal landscapes. Laws also vary from country to country. However, there are some common legal themes that event managers need to consider. (More information on legal requirements for events can be found in Chapter 8; particular attention should be paid to the various Health and Safety at Work Acts, which underpin much events legislation.)

> ## Study activity
>
> Using the internet, look up the key legislative requirements for events management in your country. Tip: This chapter gives you the broad headings and indicative laws, regulations and licences that will help you to frame your search.

4.3.1

'Who owns the event?' is one of the key questions in the legal external environment. As Bowdin *et al.* (2010) point out, establishing who owns the event is a crucial point – whoever owns the event has legal responsibility and is therefore liable; and liability opens up the event owner to potential claims of negligence and costly litigations. The legal owner of the event could be the event manager, the organising body, the event organisation, the event committee or even the client. The question of ownership is vital to establishing outcomes in legal situations, as potentially negligent activities can lead to expensive and drawn-out litigation processes, and can ultimately have disastrous impacts on the event owner. It is therefore important that the answer is established from the outset – ownership of the event should be implicit throughout all pitching, proposals and contractual negotiations. Issues surrounding intellectual property (who owns the idea or concept) should also be established at the start of any event.

Once the ownership of the event is established – and the responsibility (liability) in the eyes of the law is therefore apparent – the event owner is endowed with a duty of care. This is a fundamental legal principle that, when applied to events, means 'taking all reasonable care to avoid acts or omissions that could injure employees, contractors, users, participants and visitors' (Bowdin *et al.* 2010: 339).

> ## Study activity
>
> In 50 words or less, explain why the principles of duty of care and event ownership are integral to the events industry.

4.3.2 Equality Acts

Event managers need to ensure that their event is accessible to all members of society. In the UK, legislation exists in order to ensure that events are accessible. This is covered by the Equality Act of 2010, and it legislates against discrimination across a number of protected characteristics. Of the eight protected characteristics (age, disability, gender reassignment, marriage and civil partnerships, race, religion or belief, sex and sexual orientation), disability is one of the key concerns for event managers. It is unlawful for a service provider to discriminate against a disabled person by refusing to supply any service that it provides for other members of the public (Bowdin *et al.* 2010). In real terms, this means that event managers must consider issues relating to access to venues, ensuring that disabled guests have access to all services offered, and fair treatment of disabled employees. Other countries have similar laws and legislations, and it is advisable that event managers keep abreast of these and seek advice on how to adhere to them. In the USA, laws such as the Civil Rights Act of 1964, the Equal Pay Act of 1963 and Title 1 of the Americans with Disabilities Act of 1990 need to be considered. Websites such as www.gov/uk, www.eeoc.gov (US Equal Employment Opportunity Commission), www.humanrights.gov.uk (Australian Human Rights Commission) and www.india.gov.in (Indian Fundamental Rights) are invaluable tools for the event manager seeking further information.

4.3.3 Sustainable events

The BS8901 standard was developed in the UK in November 2007 specifically for the events industry, in order for all aspects of events to be measured in terms of their sustainability. The standard sets out a system that helps organisations to consider the economic, environmental and social impacts of organising their events and ensures that every choice made, from the transportation of goods through to the contents of the delegate pack, are designed to be as ecologically and socially responsible as possible.

However, BS8901 is a standard, not a legal requirement, which is an important distinction. A standard sets out a framework of good practice; if an event organisation is granted the standard, it will be certified as meeting the BSI standard. But the law does not insist that it must comply with the standard.

On an international level, the International Standards Organisation created a new standard in 2012. This standard, ISO 20121, seeks to ensure that the international events industry will address social, economic and environmental impacts. In order to achieve ISO 20121, and receive the associated certification, organisations must demonstrate that they have considered their management systems from an event sustainability perspective. This includes not just environmental issues, but also financial and social aspects of sustainability. The benefits of achieving this standard include allowing events management organisations to evidence that they have their own sustainable policies, and therefore increasing chances of winning contracts. Approximately thirty countries are involved as participants or observers (Quainton 2010). The aim is to have one internationally recognised framework for the implementation of sustainability in events (see Chapter 14).

CASE STUDY 4.1

Goodwood Event Operations team – Sustainable events management, taken seriously

Location: UK

Multi-venue site: Major international events such as Festival of Speed with 180,000 visitors, Glorious Goodwood and Goodwood Revival, as well as numerous horseracing events throughout the year, weddings and many more events.

Goodwood House and Estate run a variety of events throughout the year. These events vary from horseracing to motorsport. The event operations team recognise that events have a huge impact on resources and they have therefore adopted sustainability as a guiding principle, in order to protect the estate for future generations. As such, they have applied for, and gained, certification in ISO 20121. Goodwood had several objectives that related to an increase in a sustainable focus for their event output; these included retaining their reputation for excellence and a wish to be recognised as a pioneer for sustainable events management; to demonstrate to suppliers that Goodwood events are managed in a responsible way, and to embed a sustainable conscience throughout the organisation.

The process of becoming a sustainable event organisation began in 2011 when Goodwood worked towards the requirements of BS9801. They achieved this via self-certification within six months and, in May 2012 they became one of the first organisations worldwide to gain certification to ISO 20121. For the team, the standard provides a structured framework to formalise procedures and increase awareness of sustainability within the business. The International Standard has a focus on management, which has resulted in Goodwood using a new management system, with redeveloped stakeholder engagement and a focus on waste, utilities and procurement. The team have improved recycling opportunities, trialled a tri-ticketing system with rail and buses and implemented schemes to reduce paper consumption.

Goodwood worked with BSI in order to achieve the ISO 20121. They audited the business and identified gaps that can be developed and improved upon. As a result of their sustainable events management system, they have seen a 40 per cent increase in public transport to events, 50 per cent reduction in paper consumption for printing, identification of business trends which have provided opportunities for the future and have significantly improved their waste management and recycling at events.

(www.bsigroup.com/en-GB/iso-20121-sustainable-events-management/case-studies/)

4.4 Insurance

Events are susceptible to any number of issues that are often outside the event organisation's control. Disasters, such as an outbreak of a contagious disease (for example, bird and swine flu in Asia and South America, respectively, and foot and mouth in the UK) or extreme weather conditions (such as flooding or blizzards), can have severe effects on an event's performance. The industry has witnessed a shift towards a larger number of claims made from attendees who have injured themselves at an event or who make claims when they perceive the event to be unsatisfactory – perhaps due to the cancellation of the main act or a change of venue. Event insurance is therefore now essential, and it has become one of the key issues for the industry.

Event insurance will typically cover such items as cancellation of the event, venue bankruptcy, non-appearance of celebrities, failure to vacate the venue, damage to property or premises, legal liabilities, damage to equipment and public liabilities (Shone and Parry 2010).

The importance of event insurance was illustrated when Unique Events was forced to cancel the New Year's Eve 2006 celebrations in Edinburgh, Scotland, due to severe weather.

Fortunately, the company had sufficient cancellation insurance to cover ticket refunds and any financial loss (Francisco 2008); the picture would have been very different if the organisers had not taken out this policy. Cancellation is usually the very last option for event organisers, though – often, they will approach their insurance company to fund preventative action. Insurance companies will often cover smaller amounts that enable the show to go on: for instance, they might make funds available for extra transport to ensure that guests can beat transport strikes, or to a change of venue at the last minute. Both organisers and insurers will obviously explore such options in preference to cancellation of the whole event.

Insurance that covers theft, fire, weather and workers' compensation is also important, as is public liability (sometimes known as personal accident) insurance and property damage insurance. Any special insurance for particular elements of the event should also be acquired (for example, marquees often require special insurance and events that take place outside can sometimes ask for weather insurance), and consideration should be given to event equipment and property cover to ensure that any hired equipment is covered. Many insurance policies exclude terrorist attacks and 'acts of God' (typically defined as acts that are outside human control, such as natural disasters).

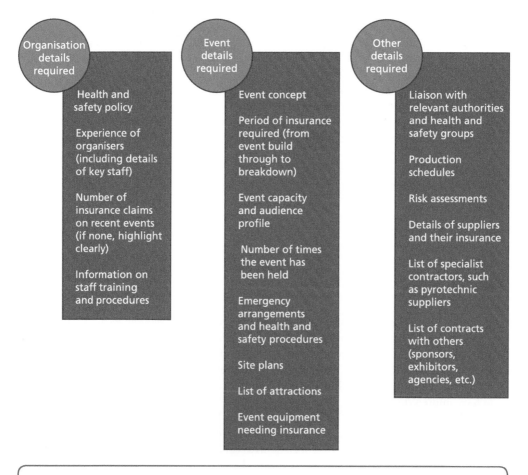

Figure 4.2 Details insurance companies require
Source: Adapted from EventScotland 2006

Event managers should also always check that suppliers – such as the artists, venue, audiovisual suppliers, entertainment agencies, staffing agencies and so on – have their own insurance and liability cover and are in compliance with industry and legal regulations.

Insurance policies and the clauses within them are often very specific and should be read carefully. It is also important to give the insurers the right information. Equipment used on-site will need to be detailed carefully: for example, expensive musical instruments are often not covered by standard insurance policies. Figure 4.2 provides a sample checklist of information that the insurance company or brokers will require.

Event insurance should therefore be in place for the entire planning process and, in order to gain the correct cover, insurance requirements should be investigated in good time, preferably with an insurance broker or with specialist event insurance companies (Shone and Parry 2010). It is advisable to aim to confirm event insurance two to three months before and certainly no less than one month before the event date (EventScotland 2006).

4.5 Regulations, licences and permits

No matter which country an event is organised in, there are myriad regulations with which the event manager must comply. These regulations change from country to country, and indeed from region to region (regulations are often governed by local authorities or regional councils). Generally, the larger the event, the more regulations, licences and permits that will be required. It is important to note that the event organiser is legally required to obtain the right permits and licences, and failure to do so may well result in fines and penalties. It should also be noted that authorities have the right to cancel events if the right permits are not obtained.

Image 4.1 **Races cancelled at Rio Olympics 2016**
Credit: Damien Meyer/afp/Getty Images

An example of this can be seen with the Lapland West Midlands event (nicknamed 'Blunderland' by the industry press in the UK), which was cancelled just a few days before it was due to open in 2008. In part, this was due to the organisers' failure to apply for an entertainment licence from South Staffordshire District Council (Francisco and Quainton 2008) who claimed to have only been informed of the event a week before it was due to open.

It is perhaps easier for event managers to consider the event components that need licences and permits, rather than to try to keep abreast of the ever-changing regulations. Therefore, below, we suggest some of the event elements that may need permits or licences. As each event varies significantly, the list is dictated by the event design and the event product. However, once established, this list can act as a standard plan that merely needs revising and evaluating every time the event is repeated. Again, it should be stressed that many of these licences are legal requirements, so event managers should check carefully.

Event managers should consider the following issues and the regulations, permits and licences that might apply to each one:

- alcohol consumption
- food handling
- staffing
- noise
- building regulations/standards
- fire precautions
- health and safety at work
- first-aid regulations
- lifting equipment and manual handling operations
- occupancy levels
- music and performance rights and licences
- intellectual property
- electricity at work
- environmental protection
- signs and signal regulations
- waste disposal
- street trader or temporary market trader licences
- street closures
- public entertainment licences
- Criminal Record Bureau checks (required for events involving minors; similar police checks are required internationally).

As Bowdin et al. (2010) suggest, the principal rule is that event managers should carry out careful research in order to ensure they understand and comply with all regulations that relate to their event. It should also be noted that the time taken to identify and comply with regulations can vary enormously – the process should be started at the earliest point in order to deal with such issues as delays in the granting of licences.

A list of resources that will help to identify relevant health and safety legislation is given in Chapter 8.

Study activity

You are organising an outdoor music festival for 1,500 attendees in your town or city. The venue is a local park, which has a capacity of 1,600. Write a list of the key event components that might have regulatory considerations and those which might require a permit or licence. Then, using the internet as your primary resource, research the regulations and obtain information about which permits or licences will be needed.

4.6 Events contracts

'The contract is the documentation of the relationship between the event and the various stakeholders' (Bowdin *et al.* 2010: 330); it is an agreement that sets out the responsibilities between two or more parties and it is legally binding. Typically, contracts are written; oral contracts are becoming less common in the industry, as all stakeholders understand the need to have formal contractual obligations in order to guard against future problems.

4.6.1 Contract law

Contract preparation and execution are vital parts of the events management role, so it is important that event managers understand the key terms used within them. Goldblatt (2008: 311–314) defines the key terms of an events contract as:

- *Parties* – names of parties must be clearly defined.
- *Offer* – 'the offer is the service or product tendered by one party to another', including consulting services, products, entertainment, sponsorship deals and so on.
- *Consideration* – the consideration clause defines what one party will provide the other upon acceptance of an offer. This is usually money or rights.
- *Acceptance* – 'when both parties accept an offer, they execute (sign) the agreement confirming that they understand and agree to comply with the terms and conditions of the agreement'.

Matthews (2008) offers a comprehensive breakdown of the requirements of contract provision. He suggests that a contract is made up of two main parts: terms and conditions, and the clauses. *Terms and conditions* are considered essential to the contract and include contact information (including legal names, full addresses and so on); event details (including venue, specifics of product/services, additional requirements, details of general liability and additional insurance, and compliance with regulations and standards); financial information (including details of cancellation and compensation, plus taxes and deposits); rider information.

Clauses comprise the fixed part of the contract. They define and expand upon the terms and conditions, and might include:

- *Cancellation* – usually this is expressed as a percentage of the total value of the contract, which is payable upon cancellation by either party. Cancellation policies usually operate on a sliding scale, with 100 per cent of the contract value within fourteen days of the event date.
- *Force majeure* (act of God) – this clause removes liability from the contracted party should they be prevented from delivering their obligations due to an act of God. Acts of God are defined as unavoidable circumstances that are outside the party's control – in event contracts, they tend to relate to the weather, natural disasters, transportation issues and terrorism.
- *Billing* – including payment terms and schedules.
- *Insurance* – including details of insurance held by the contracted parties.
- *Indemnification* – protection of the contract signatory against losses incurred by an event. Liability clauses are also included and are important for events, as many suppliers will not expose themselves to liability and will attempt to remove this clause. Event managers are advised to seek legal advice on this clause, as it relates closely to insurance and can invalidate policies and contracts.

(List adapted from Goldblatt 2008)

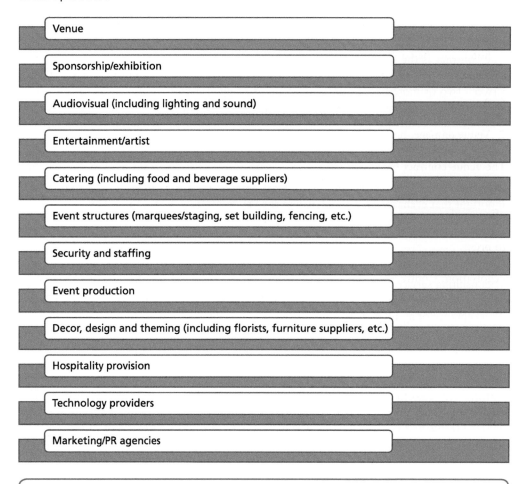

Venue

Sponsorship/exhibition

Audiovisual (including lighting and sound)

Entertainment/artist

Catering (including food and beverage suppliers)

Event structures (marquees/staging, set building, fencing, etc.)

Security and staffing

Event production

Decor, design and theming (including florists, furniture suppliers, etc.)

Hospitality provision

Technology providers

Marketing/PR agencies

Figure 4.3 Event contracts may be required for a number of suppliers and providers

While these lists and generalisations are useful as a background to event contracts, some contracts are vital to the successful delivery of an event and require special consideration. These are listed in Figure 4.3 and explored in more detail in the following sections.

4.6.2 Venue contracts

The venue contract is one of the most complex contracts. It contains many specific clauses and, when dealing with these agreements, a number of issues must be taken into consideration. Again, these are usually legally binding. They can be summarised as:

1 Cancellation clauses, including details of refunds available and costs payable in the event of a cancellation by either party.
2 Payment terms, including deposit details and payment schedules.
3 Full details of costs and estimated event spend at the venue (including projected food and beverage costs, room hire charges, furniture and linen hire, tips and service charges, taxes, set-up charges and so on).

4 Attrition clause, which sets out the food and beverage minimum spend. If your customers do not attend, the event organiser will be required to pay this fixed fee. If the venue is a hotel, and the contract includes room bookings, there will be an attrition clause regarding the minimum number of rooms that must be paid for, even if they are not occupied.
5 Provision of personnel and security, including overtime rates and numbers of staff required.
6 Access times and overrunning clauses, including date of event, start and end times and service times for food and beverages.
7 Venue damage, including indemnification, insurance, liability issues, licences and permits.

The venue contract should be viewed as an opportunity for the event organiser to negotiate rates and charges. Particular attention should be paid to the payment terms. Getting this right will ease cash flow and ensure financial stability throughout the event process. The venue is often the largest expense on an events budget, so ensuring that the payment schedule allows the event manager to generate some revenue before meeting the majority of the costs will help to prevent cash flow issues.

Similarly, cancellation terms and penalties need close attention and are often open to negotiation. Contracts with venues also usually set out the minimum numbers required for the event – this figure represents the least number of guests the event organiser must pay for, no matter how many guests actually attend. It should *always* be negotiated, as it is usually possible to cut it by 10–20 per cent. Event managers should also look closely at food and beverage prices, which are often highly negotiable and may contain hidden costs, such as the supply of linen, chairs and tables, which can be easily removed.

Figure 4.4 shows a sample venue contract.

Organisers should note too, that many venues will issue operational and safety guidelines, detailed in their terms and conditions and hiring policy. These must be in place during the organisation and running of an event in their space; failure to comply with these guidelines can result in the cancellation of your event. An example of this can be seen in the case study below.

CASE STUDY 4.2

Oktoberfest

Location: London, UK
Venue: Tobacco Docks, London

In 2015, Oktoberfest London, opened for one night only and was cancelled the next day, before the majority of the weekend activities could take place. Oktoberfest London was set to be a version of the German beer festival, in the UK. It was expected that around 24,000 people would attend – tickets ranged from £10 to £1,000 for tickets for groups, inclusive of food and drinks. It was due to run from Thursday to Sunday inclusively, with a number of 'sessions' running each day.

The venue pulled the event after one day because of issues with staffing and other managerial and operational aspects on the opening night and due to concerns with their compliance with the 2003 Licensing Act. The venue released a statement that said: 'We were not convinced the operational changes we required the organiser to make would be able to be put in place by Oktoberfest UK in time for this weekend's events to run safely and efficiently, and at that point agreed with them that these events should be cancelled' (Tobaccodocklondon.com/news). In addition, the venue's statement said: 'The decision [to cancel the event] was not based on guest numbers nor the nature of the event – both of these were well understood in advance – but on the management and operational systems and insufficient serving staff both in terms of numbers and experience that had been put in place by Oktoberfest UK.'

The company organising Oktoberfest UK went into administration, and are currently not trading. Ticket holders for the cancelled session needed to apply to the administrators for a ticket refund. Other event organisers have been more successful in bringing Oktoberfest to the UK – see Image 4.2.

Image 4.2 Oktoberfest in Munich, which event organisers tried to replicate in the UK – to varying degrees of success
Credit: photo75/Getty Images
Sources: www.oktoberfest.london; www.standard.co.uk

Unless otherwise agreed in writing by the University, these conditions apply and are additional to any specific agreement concluded for the hiring of University Premises and/or Facilities.

1. Definitions

"Hirer" means the company, entity, institution or person hiring the Premises and/or Facilities from the University. "Premises" means all premises which are being hired by the Hirer (including car parks and grounds).

"University" means University of Greenwich.

"Facilities" means all services, equipment and apparatus belonging to or provided by or on behalf of the University to the Hirer.

2. Booking, Deposit and Confirmation

2.1 The submission of a Hiring Agreement does not constitute a hiring. The University reserves the right to decline an application at its sole discretion.

2.2 This Agreement shall not be effective until the potential hirer has submitted a signed Hiring Agreement and paid a non-refundable deposit for the Hire of Premises and/or Facilities to the University and the University has accepted such Hiring Agreement.

2.3 The Hiring Agreement sets out the amount of non-refundable deposit(s) and the date(s) by which such deposit(s) shall be paid by the Hirer. The Hirer acknowledges that if the University does not receive the non-refundable deposit (s) by or before the relevant date(s), the Premises may be hired to a third party or become non-available. The non-refundable deposit(s) will be based on minimum number of guests or attendees.

The Hirer agrees that the initial pre-paid deposit(s) are non-refundable and non-transferable in the event of the booking being cancelled for whatever reason.

2.4 All catering will be undertaken by the University unless agreed prior in writing by the parties. Final confirmation of the number of guests or attendees for catering purposes must be received by the University one week before the start of the period of hire.

3. Charges, Deposits and Payment

3.1 The charges for the Facilities and the Premises will be communicated to the Hirer prior to or at the time of booking and will be set out in the University Hiring Agreement.

3.2 The Hirer agrees that these charges may be increased by the University between the time of booking and the period of hire in the event of any increase in the costs to the University of providing the Facilities and/or Premises for reasons beyond the University's control.

3.3 The University shall issue (after the period of hire) a final invoice for the charges for the hire of the Premises and/or Facilities plus any applicable VAT, less any deposit(s) already pre-paid by the Hirer. The Hirer shall pay the outstanding amount within 30 days from the date of the invoice.

4. Cancellation and Charges

4.1 All cancellations must be submitted in writing to the University. Failure to confirm cancellation in writing may result in the Hirer being liable to pay the full amount of the estimated charges for the hire.

4.2 Unless minimum numbers are guaranteed by the hirer and stated on the hiring agreement the following shall apply; if the hire is cancelled or the number of guests or attendees is reduced:

a) 365 days or more before the date of hire, there is no charge other than the initial non-refundable deposit (if applicable)
b) between 364 and 180 days before the date of hire, there will be a 20% charge of the estimated total amount.
c) between 179 and 90 days before the date of hire, there will be a 40% charge on the estimated total amount.
d) between 89 and 15 days before the date of hire, there will be a 60% charge on the estimated total amount.
e) 14 days or less before the date of hire, there will be a 100% charge on the estimated total amount.

Notwithstanding the above, the University may, at its sole discretion and in any case after the period of hire, refund part of the initial pre-paid deposit(s) if the same Premises are hired to a third party.

4.3 In addition to the amounts set out in clause 4.2 above, the Hirer shall reimburse the University in full for any expenses already incurred or committed by the University (with the Hirers consent) for or on behalf of the Hirer including but not limited to musicians, florists, equipment hire, catering and accommodation.

4.4 Neither the University nor any body responsible for the management of the University shall be held liable or required to pay compensation to the Hirer or any third party for any loss or damage sustained as a result of or in any way arising out of the cancellation of the hiring.

4.5 The hire charges relate to the times of the booking. The Hirer will be responsible for ensuring that the Premises are vacated by the finishing time agreed at the time of the hiring. In addition to the rights and remedies that the University may have against the Hirer, if an event continues beyond thes times the Hirer will incur additional hire charges.

4.6 In any case, the University reserves the right to enter the Premises and
terminate any event which extends beyond the contracted times of hire without any liability to the Hirer.

5. Liability

5.1 Where the Hirer is an unincorporated association, the person or any member, servant or agent thereof signing the Hiring Agreement or such other document requesting the use of the Premises and/or Facilities undertakes personal liability for all charges in respect of the hiring and for the compliance with the terms of the Agreement. The liability of the unincorporated association and such person or any member, servant or agent thereof shall be joint and several.

5.2 The Hirer shall indemnify and keep indemnified the University against all actions, claims, demands, costs and expenses of any nature which may be brought against or suffered by the University as a result of or in connection with the use of the University Premises and/or Facilities by the Hirer, its guests or any other attendees. For the avoidance of doubt, the Hirer shall be responsible for any damage, other than fair wear and tear, to University property (or that belonging to any individual or organisation).

Figure 4.4 A sample venue contract

Note: This is an example of part of the terms and conditions section of a booking contract.

5.3 The University accepts no liability for any interruption or curtailment of the hiring as a result of the actions of any third party (including any guests or attendees of the event organised by the Hirer), howsoever caused.

5.4 In no circumstances will the University be liable or accept any responsibility for loss of or damage to any personal property, car or other vehicle (or the contents thereof) which may be brought or left within the premises.
All persons using the University's Premises or Facilities must take their own precautions to protect their property.

5.5 The University reserves the right to let other parts of its Premises and/or Facilities to other persons or organisations simultaneously with the hiring and accepts no liability for the actions, omissions or conduct of such other persons or organisations.

5.6 The University's maximum aggregate liability in contract, tort or otherwise (including any liability for any neglect, act or omission) howsoever arising out of or in connection with this Agreement in respect of any one or more incidents or occurrences shall be limited to a sum equal to the charges paid by the Hirer to the University under this Agreement.

5.7 The University shall not be liable for any indirect, special, incidental, or consequential loss or damage nor for any loss of business or profit.

5.8 The limitations set out in clause 5 shall apply to the extent permitted by law. Nothing in this Agreement shall exclude or restrict either party's liability for death or personal injury resulting from the negligence of that party or to any extent not permitted by law.

5.9 The University will require the Hirer to take out such insurance policies as the University may reasonably deem appropriate in respect of the hire.

6. Health and Safety and Conduct

6.1 The Hirer shall comply and must ensure that all guests and attendees and any person entering the Premises comply with any applicable health and safety laws and regulations (including the Health & Safety at Work Act 1974) and any of the University's health and safety guidance, policies, procedures or rules.

6.2 The University reserves the right to cancel the hire, upon notice to the Hirer (and without any liability thereof), if the University reasonably believes that any condition contained in this Agreement is or may be breached or that the safety of persons or property is or may be endangered as a direct or indirect result of the hiring.

6.3 The Hirer shall be solely responsible for keeping and maintaining proper order, for observing fire, safety and security regulations at all times and for providing efficient supervision on the occasion of the hire (including controlling and regulating the ingress and egress of all persons attending the event).

6.4 The Hirer must ensure that any University Premises are maintained in a clean and tidy state at all times during the hire. If any parts of the Premises are in disorder at commencement of the hire, this should be reported to a member of University staff immediately.

6.5 In the event of any damage, the University may make good the damage and the Hirer, by acceptance of the hiring, will thereby be deemed to have undertaken to pay the cost of such reparation.

6.6 The Hirer shall not install and use on the University's premises any electrical appliance, amplification equipment or lighting fittings without the priorwritten permission of the University. The Hirer is wholly responsible for the safety of such installation at all times whilst it remains on the University's Premises and for any injury caused to any person or property arising in connection with such installation and usage. Consent by the University to such installation and usage does not imply the safety or suitability for use of the said installation or acceptance by the University of liability for damage or injury arising in connection with the said appliance.

6.7 The Hirer must ensure that no child under the age of 14 years is admitted on the University's premises unless during the whole time such child is accompanied by an adult person, (minimum requirement of one adult per 10 children).

6.8 All persons under the age of 18 years (and over 14 years) must be under the control of at least one adult who should be clearly identifiable as such and who will be held responsible for any actions or liabilities incurred by such persons, (minimum requirement of one adult per 15 children).

6.9 University property shall not be moved except with prior written permission of an authorised officer of the University.

6.10 Smoking is not permitted in any part of the University except areas which are clearly designated.

6.11 No pets or other animals, except guide dogs, are permitted on University premises without prior written permission of the University.

6.12 The authorised representatives of the University shall have free access to the Premises at all times.

6.13 No part of the Premises may be sublet, or reassigned by the Hirer to any third party.

7. Overnight Accommodation

Where the hire includes use of the University premises as overnight accommodation the Hirer shall:
- (a) provide the University with a full list of persons who will be resident on the hired premises overnight not less than 7 days before the commencement of hire;
- (b) ensure the hired overnight accommodation is used only by persons specified on said nominal list unless agreed prior in writing by the University;
- (c) receive keys on the day of arrival no earlier than 16.00 and
- (d) vacate the room and return the key(s) by 09.00 on the day of departure.

8. Licensing Considerations

8.1 The Hirer must ensure that the maximum number of persons permitted to be present in any indoor facility under the licensing arrangements shall not be exceeded at any time.

8.2 No alcoholic liquor, food or other refreshments, other than those supplied by the University, shall be sold or consumed by the Hirer (or any of the guests or attendees) on the University premises without the prior written consent of the University. Alcoholic liquor shall only be consumed on the premises upon prior written approval of the University and subject to the obtaining of any specific licence that may be necessary.

Figure 4.4 A sample venue contract (contd.)

4.6.3 Entertainment contracts

Entertainment contracts are agreements drawn up between the event organiser and those people supplying the entertainment. Typical entertainment options include after-dinner speakers, celebrities, bands, DJs, singers, cabaret acts, masters of ceremonies, comedians, magicians and musicians. Special considerations for this type of contract will include non-attendance, exclusivity (the prevention of headline acts performing at similar events around the same time), cancellation terms for either party and insurance clauses.

Particular attention should be paid to the non-attendance – or 'no-show' – clause in the contract, as artists pulling out of an event at the last minute – or simply not showing up – can be a major problem for event organisers. Having a clause that clearly states the implications of a last-minute cancellation will go some way to protecting the event organiser and will at least result in financial remuneration, if not artist replacement.

Another key element of the entertainment contract is the rider. This is usually attached to the contract (hence the name: it 'rides' the contract) and specifies particular demands that the event organiser needs to meet. These can include audiovisual and technological requirements and hospitality demands (specific food, drink, room layouts and so on). Silvers (2004) suggests that riders can run to a hundred pages or more and often contain sensitive material, such as how an entertainer achieves a specific effect. Rider requests should be carefully examined as they are often used by entertainment suppliers to increase their fees, making them extremely costly for event organisers. Event organisers should therefore enlist the help of talent buyers or agents – and should acquire legal advice from solicitors – before negotiating entertainment contracts.

4.6.4 Sponsor and exhibitor contracts

Contracts with sponsors and exhibitors are unique as they refer to a one-off relationship and the obligations that stem from that relationship. Sponsors and exhibitors are usually brought on board by a specialist sales representative and they will often draw up contracts directly. However, it is essential that the event manager directly responsible for event delivery reads these contracts carefully prior to signing to ensure that all the specifics are deliverable. Special considerations for sponsor and exhibitor contract agreements include:

- exclusivity (no other sponsors/exhibitors from the same sector can be involved)
- hospitality rights, including complimentary tickets
- branding on marketing collateral and on-site brand presence
- cancellation terms, including if the event is cancelled and if the sponsor/exhibitor wishes to terminate the relationship
- payment terms – payment is preferable upon signing the contract
- length of contract – contracts can often cover a relationship lasting for a number of years (sponsorship of a repeat event over a three-year period, for example). These contracts need to be carefully considered in order to ensure that the event will be able to deliver all obligations each year.

4.6.5 Other supplier contracts

Events involve dealing with a large number of suppliers, and each of these relationships should be legally supported through the provision of a contract. Suppliers include audiovisual, security, catering, staging, florists, marquee and furniture, staffing agencies, technology providers and marketing and PR agencies.

These contracts need to be carefully worded to ensure that there is protection for either party if the event is cancelled, and also to ensure there are provision and protection in the case of non-supply by a supplier.

4.6.6 Supplier selection

Suppliers for events are often selected via a tendering process, which involves a request for proposals (RFP) to a number of competing organisations. This typically includes a description of the event concept, details of the event plan as it currently stands and an outline of any particular business problems. It will also include a full outline of the requirements of the supplier. These RFPs are sent to a variety of organisations offering the services required, with a deadline for submissions. The potential suppliers will review the request and decide whether they wish to bid for the contract. If they decide to go ahead, they submit a proposal, which will include specific suggestions on how to meet the needs and wants of the event organiser and, depending on the type of work, may also include creative solutions to business problems outlined in the proposal. A small selection of these organisations will then be invited to pitch their proposal at a meeting, and from this the event manager will pick their preferred supplier.

Once the preferred supplier has been identified, it is often necessary to go through procurement. This is the process of making a buying decision (that is, selecting a supplier) that promotes fair and open competition and also protects the events organisation from fraud. It commonly involves all the processes from preparation of contracts through to the invoicing and receipt of payment, and often concentrates on researching the supplier, value analysis, detailed contract specifications and the agreement of financial processes.

The selection of suppliers via a tendering process is outlined in Figure 4.5.

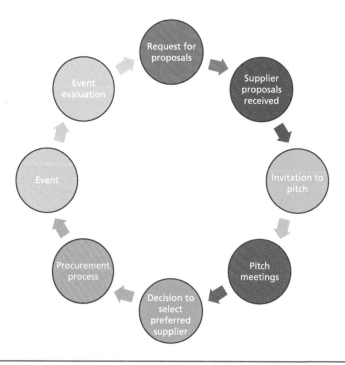

Figure 4.5 Supplier tendering process

4.7 Event logistics

The term 'logistics' is used to describe the movement of products and resources. Events management draws heavily on management logistics theory in order to understand how to manage the flow of goods, resources and information effectively. However, much of this theory relates to supplying the product to the customer – event logistics, of necessity, must consider a logistical approach that brings the customer to the product (the product cannot go to the customer; the customer must come to the product).

At first glance, event logistics can seem incredibly daunting – there is so much to plan and organise that it can feel like an impossible task. To simplify the process, it is sensible to reduce the number of logistical considerations. It is useful to consider two broad areas of event logistics – the customer and the venue/site (see Figure 4.6). (In the past, event academics

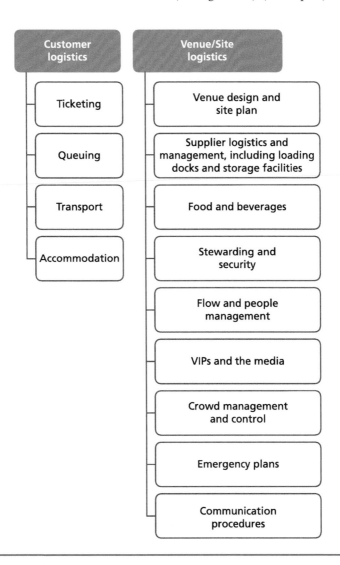

Figure 4.6 Event logistics

have talked of a third area – the product – but this is usually defined as the entire event, and is therefore confusing.)

Events can be seen as a large jigsaw puzzle, with all the elements needing to be slotted together to complete the picture – it is the role of logistics to ensure that these elements all fit and are brought together at the right moment.

4.7.1 Venue/site logistics

Event venues or sites can vary enormously. Corporate events taking place in a five-star hotel have very different on-site logistical requirements from those of a festival taking place in a desert in the middle of Arizona. The event logistics manager must therefore think carefully about their specific venue and the logistical requirements of their choice. Some of the key considerations are shown in Figure 4.7, and each will be discussed in more detail throughout this section. It is important to stress the individual nature of every event and the fact that these individual aspects will result in very different logistical requirements.

4.7.1.1 Venue design

Much of the information in this section is adapted from *The Event Safety Guide* (HSE 1999).

GENERAL PRINCIPLE OF VENUE/SITE DESIGN
The guiding principle for the design of venues or sites is to provide an arena where the audience can enjoy the entertainment in a safe and comfortable atmosphere. The venue has to be suitable for the event's needs as well as for the needs and wants of the audience.

The choice of a venue is one of the hardest and most important aspects of an event – it is often easy to get enthusiastic about a fantastic venue and forget that the audience's enjoyment

Venue/ site design

Supplier logistics and management

Food and beverages

Stewarding and security

Flow and people management

VIPs

Crowd management and crowd control

Communication

Health and safety and emergency procedures

Figure 4.7 The key areas of venue logistics

is key. Questions such as those in the list below should be paramount in any venue or site decisions:

- Will the audience like the venue?
- Do they have a clear sight of the stage?
- Can they find the location easily?
- Are the transport links adequate?
- What about the catering and general service?
- How large is the site, and how easy is it to navigate?
- What facilities are available?

SITE SUITABILITY ASSESSMENT

Once a potential site or venue has been identified, it is essential to visit it to assess suitability well before the event. In order to assess the suitability effectively, the event manager must have a proposed capacity in mind, have some ideas of the concept and theme, and have an idea of the programme – what you want to happen and when. This provisional plan will need to be flexible to work with the venue, but the more detail you have, the easier the site assessment will be.

Three crucial areas should be considered on the first visit to a new venue or site:

1 Available space for audiences and temporary structures – stages, marquees and so on.
2 Backstage facilities – how much room will the crew have? Do you want back or front projection? Is there room for performers? Crew equipment? Crew areas?
3 Parking/camping, rendezvous points and transport.

This visit allows the event manager to determine what facilities are available. Event managers should check such facilities as rooms and layouts, location and access, ground conditions, traffic routes, first-aid provision, toilets, waste-disposal areas, power, water, gas and electrical supplies, fire exits, stages, barriers, exits and entrance areas, hospitality areas, sight lines and so on.

Once the visit is completed, it is usual to produce a pre-design appraisal of the site. The final design will depend on the nature of the entertainment, location, size and duration of the event. It will also need to take account of the geographical, topographical and environmental infrastructure. This appraisal of the site visit will typically cover:

- proposed occupant capacity
- artist profile
- audience profile
- duration and timing of event
- venue evaluation
- alcohol availability
- audience: seated or standing?
- audience movement between facilities/entertainment
- single stage/multiple-arena complex, etc. (HSE 1999)

4.7.1.2 Site plans

Once the event design is in place, the event manager can begin to put together the site plan. Such plans are the primary means of ensuring communication is flowing and that the various

Figure 4.8 Contents of a site plan

managers (stage manager, lighting manager, production manager and so on) working on an event understand the key elements. Their main purpose is to indicate the proposed areas to be used by the event and the locations of various activities within the event site or venue. These plans are also key tools for communicating logistical requirements – they should, if produced correctly, alleviate the need for explanation and highlight key areas of concern.

Figure 4.8 provides a list of what should be included in a site plan. It should be noted that these plans need to be far more detailed than the venue or site maps that are given to the customer. The final site plan will often not be ready until the day of the event set-up, when all ticketing and entertainment have been finalised.

Figure 4.9 shows a site plan for the University of Greenwich. The Greenwich campus is a World Heritage Site, with a stunning location on the banks of the Thames in London and classical buildings designed by Sir Christopher Wren. It is an ideal venue for academic conferences, celebratory meals, public lectures and fundraising events, and it has a wide range of rooms and

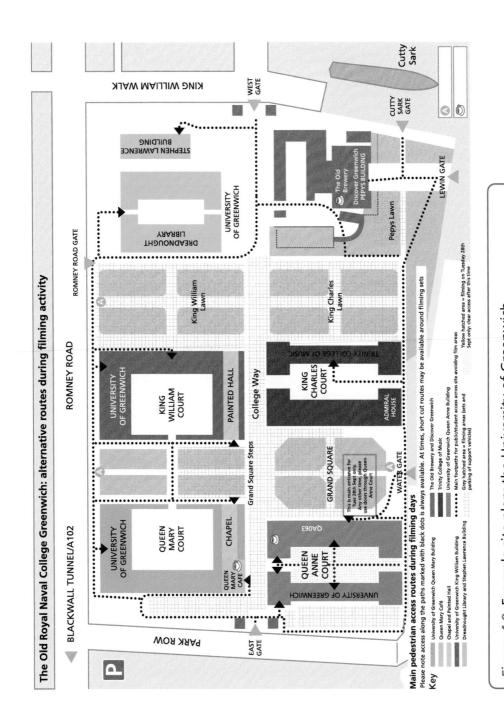

Figure 4.9 Example site plan: the University of Greenwich

facilities, making it important that event organisers, suppliers and attendees can all navigate the site easily. The site plan details the layout of the venue and allows event organisers to get a visual feel for the layout; it also directs suppliers to the right part of the campus and helps attendees arrive in the right place.

4.7.1.3 Supplier logistics and management

The main thrust of logistics is the flow of equipment, product and people around the venue and to the places where they need to be, when they need to be there.

Therefore, one of the key areas to consider is the coordination of all the event suppliers – how and when they will reach the site, and how they will move around the venue, must be planned carefully. It is the logistics manager's responsibility to do this. Ensuring that your suppliers know how to find the site and where and when they need to be available is essential, so each supplier will require a detailed briefing. This can be a very complex process. For example, a conference for a hundred delegates may require the coordination of a caterer; an audiovisual organisation; lighting and stage set production companies; room dressers to create a specific theme; furniture-hire companies; drinks suppliers; entertainment; and a cleaning company. Each of these organisations will have their own set of requirements and their own timelines for set-up. They will also require specific access (often through loading docks) and a large amount of storage space for equipment.

4.7.1.4 Food and beverages

The provision of food and beverages should be an important part of the logistics plan, with ample time built in to ensure that the catering is provided properly. Caterers at an event have very specific logistical requirements that will vary depending on the size of the event and the type of venue used. A large trade show may involve twenty different catering suppliers – each caterer must be on-site, set up and equipped with the necessary facilities in good time before the show opens. They will usually need access to running water and waste disposal, refrigeration and gas supply/electrical power points, and will have lots of equipment and a large amount of perishable goods. Moreover, they will have strict times for how long they need to set up, and how long they need to be on-site before the event opens. All of these issues must be taken into account when drawing up the logistics plan.

4.7.1.5 Stewarding and security

One of the key security issues for the logistics manager is ensuring that the right people have access to specific areas during set-up, at the event itself and during the shutdown process. This can be managed by giving suppliers or VIP guests laminated badges (for example, a creative event producer who works closely with the event manager, the audiovisual team and the entertainment will probably need an 'Access All Areas' badge). Colour-coded wristbands can also be used, acting in the same way as badges to control the movement of staff and suppliers. It is the responsibility of the logistics manager to issue these control methods (badges or wristbands), to ensure that every supplier and staff member has the correct access level.

4.7.1.6 Flow and people management

Events of any scale feature a large amount of movement in the venue or on-site. Suppliers will move around with their equipment, sponsors and exhibitors will move around with their resources, and customers will move around once the event starts. This movement of people around the event venue or site is known as the 'flow', and the people who move around are often referred to as 'event traffic'.

The flow of event traffic grows more complex as the event grows in size. A small networking dinner for 50 can be fairly straightforward, with only the caterers and the venue staff to consider during set-up, and with the flow from the kitchens to the dining room being uncomplicated (in the right venue). However, a festival with a vast number of venues within a single site will have hundreds of suppliers (including caterers, AV suppliers, lighting engineers, staging set producers, entertainment, VIP guests, security personnel, gate, fence and crush barrier builders, water and electrical engineers, first-aid operatives, toilet suppliers, vendors, media, waste removal and equipment transporters). All of these suppliers need to be controlled and need to be able to flow around the site without inhibiting other suppliers during the set-up and shutdown processes.

Once the event has started, the need to move people around the site does not lessen – in fact, the flow of event traffic becomes even harder to manage as suppliers often still need to move equipment around but will now also have to contend with customers. An experienced logistics manager will consider where the customers will be at all times, and will ensure that the rest of the event traffic flows around them. Therefore, they may suggest that suppliers cannot move equipment during peak times – such as arrival, coffee breaks or lunch sessions – or they may ensure that the supplier traffic is flowing in a different direction to the customer flow.

The Burning Man Festival – held in the Nevada Desert each August – has encountered problems with event traffic moving around the same site as event customers. In 2003, a woman was killed when she fell under the wheels of an 'art car'. In the same year, a truck carrying 30,000 pounds of ice rolled over and injured someone (*New York Times* 2003). These examples highlight the importance of considering the entire flow of event traffic prior to the event as part of the overall event plan.

4.7.1.7 VIPs

Another element that can cause problems for the logistics manager relates to dealing with VIPs and the media. It is important that the flow of VIPs around the venue or site is managed effectively and professionally. Event VIPs might be special guests for any number of reasons: they could be supporting the event financially, performers or celebrities who will add value to the brand. Ensuring that these guests are able to reach the VIP areas and the entertainment arena easily is essential, as is moving them around the site efficiently. Getting a performer from one stage to the next in plenty of time and then back to the VIP area without them experiencing congestion or being exposed to too many customers will help to ensure they take a favourable view of the event.

4.7.1.8 Crowd management and crowd control

Management of the customer base should be a priority for anyone concerned with operational planning of events – from a logistics point of view, the customer base is a crowd. Priority should be given to planning proper operating procedures since the impacts of not managing a crowd correctly can be incredibly damaging and sometimes even tragic. For example, the fire at the Colectiv club in Bucharest in October 2015, in which 41 people died – at the time of going to press, investigations are ongoing but allegations are that the venue was overcrowded and lacked the required number of emergency exits. At the German Love Parade in 2010, police attempted to stop people from reaching the parade area, which led to a stampede and the death of 19 people (BBC 2010). Unfortunately, there are a number of similar examples, all of which highlight the importance of a thorough understanding of the issues relating to crowd management and control, and of the need for a robust strategy at every event, no matter how small or large it is.

It is important to distinguish between the techniques of crowd *management* and crowd *control*. The former is concerned with moving the crowd effectively, whereas the latter is a reactive process relating to the steps that are taken once a crowd (or part of a crowd) has started to behave unexpectedly, often in a disorderly or dangerous manner (Abbott and Geddie 2001).

It is essential that event managers have a basic understanding of a crowd's basic sociological behaviour. Much has been written on this (see, for example, numerous journal articles in the *Journal of Events Management*, Berlonghi (1995), Fruin (2002), Abbott and Abbott (2000), the HSE (2000) guide *Managing Crowds Safely*, as well as online resources, such as those provided by the International Centre for Crowd Management and Security Studies (www.iccmss.co.uk) and consultants (www.crowddynamics.com)).

The main aim for logistics managers is that they have practical measures in place for an effective crowd management plan. The basics for this plan should include the control of the entry, exit and movement of people around the site. In addition, Abbott and Abbott (2000) suggest that communication, signage, ushering and security, alcohol distribution and on-site legal counselling should all be considered. Managers must also be able to identify crowd issues, and have carefully thought-through crowd control procedures in case the crowd loses control. For an in-depth analysis of crowd control plans and advice on how to formulate them, it is recommended that students read Abbott and Abbott (2000).

Crowd management is covered in more detail in Chapter 8.

4.7.1.9 Communication

Communication between staff is a key logistical concern. From an operational point of view, all staff members and suppliers need to be able to communicate quickly and effectively; finding the right solution to facilitate this is therefore essential. For small events, this can be as straight-forward as mobile phone usage. However, for larger events, this can be impractical, expensive and difficult to manage – particularly as the event manager may want to communicate the same message to more than one other person at a time. In such circumstances, the use of hand-held, two-way radio transmitters is useful. For complex events, several radio channels may well be in operation, with security operating on one, suppliers and contractors on another, and event staff on a third. The employment of runners who can physically take messages from one area to another is another common, and useful, communication technique.

It is recommended that a communications plan is devised prior to the event. Typically, this will include full contact details of all staff members and suppliers, and pager, radio call IDs, phone extension and mobile phone numbers, as well as where each person will be stationed during the set-up, event time and shutdown. Communication planning should also take into account emergency situations, should be part of the overall project management plan and should be included in the risk assessment (Bowdin *et al.* 2010).

4.7.1.10 Health and safety and emergency procedures

Event operations and the logistical planning for an event must include emergency procedures, which can range from evacuation procedures and the amount of first aid on-site through to major incident or disaster planning. Each event will need its own specific procedures, but the basic requirements are outlined in Figure 4.10.

It should be noted that much of the health and safety and emergency procedural planning will take place during the production of the risk assessment documents. It is imperative that these issues are taken seriously, as events can be shut down very quickly if the relevant authorities perceive health and safety or emergency procedures are inadequate. More detail on risk assessment is provided in Chapter 8.

4.7.2 Customer logistics

An event's customers are usually perceived as those who are paying for it, although, of course, many events (particularly culturally focused and local community events) are free. The customer is therefore better defined as someone who is attending an event.

Each event will need a different logistics plan that caters to the needs of its specific customer base. For instance, the transportation, ticketing and accommodation plans for the Burning Man Festival, which attracts customers from around the globe, will need to be vastly different from those for a community festival, such as a Holi Festival in India, whose customers all come from within a five-mile radius. The key areas for consideration in customer logistics are shown in Figure 4.11, and are discussed in detail in the following sections.

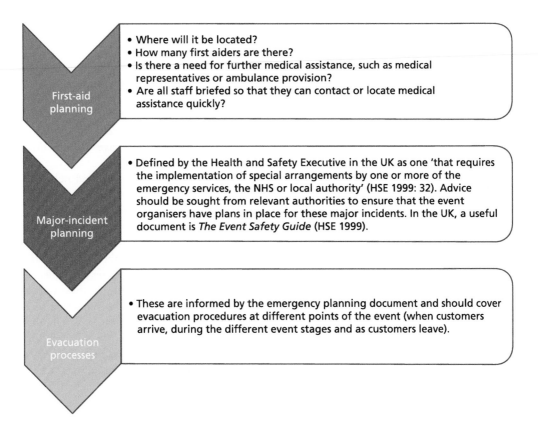

First-aid planning
- Where will it be located?
- How many first aiders are there?
- Is there a need for further medical assistance, such as medical representatives or ambulance provision?
- Are all staff briefed so that they can contact or locate medical assistance quickly?

Major-incident planning
- Defined by the Health and Safety Executive in the UK as one 'that requires the implementation of special arrangements by one or more of the emergency services, the NHS or local authority' (HSE 1999: 32). Advice should be sought from relevant authorities to ensure that the event organisers have plans in place for these major incidents. In the UK, a useful document is *The Event Safety Guide* (HSE 1999).

Evacuation processes
- These are informed by the emergency planning document and should cover evacuation procedures at different points of the event (when customers arrive, during the different event stages and as customers leave).

Figure 4.10 Key features of health, safety and emergency planning

Figure 4.11 The key areas of customer logistics

4.7.2.1 Ticketing

The distribution, collection and security requirements relating to ticketing should be a key concern for the event manager. From a customer's perspective, the process of purchasing, receiving and using tickets is often the first impression they will have of the event, and it marks the start of a relationship between the customer and the organiser. It is therefore vital that this impression is a good one.

From a logistical perspective, while not all events have an entrance fee, ticketing should always be a consideration, as it enables the organiser to control customer numbers and monitor the flow of guests throughout the event.

A key issue to consider is how much of the ticket sale allocation will be pre-event. Ticketing is usually an essential part of the cash flow – event finance tends to be unbalanced, with the majority of costs happening before the event takes place (see Chapter 6 for an in-depth look at event finance). Revenue generated by advance ticket sales therefore often covers expenses that need settling before the event date (Cherubini *et al.* 2007).

As well as helping the cash flow, selling tickets prior to the event allows the organisers to know exactly how many customers will be attending, which enables them to plan operationally in terms of food, beverages, staffing and so on.

Increasingly, events tickets are issued electronically, with barcodes or Quick Response (QR) codes that can be scanned by security staff equipped with hand-held scanners. This method increases the speed of entry and reduces the risk of fraudulent tickets. It also saves the organiser printing and mailing costs.

Another ticketing technique that often utilises QR coding technology is to send tickets to mobile phones – known as mobile ticketing. This process allows customers to order, pay for, obtain and validate tickets via their mobile phones. The most common method of mobile ticketing involves customers receiving their tickets in an SMS after texting a code to the organisers. The price of the ticket can either be added to their next mobile phone bill or debited from a previously set-up account. These mobile tickets are then visually inspected or scanned at the entrance to the event, thereby reducing production and distribution costs and increasing customer convenience.

With the increasing use of phones that support applications, it is expected that these tickets will become the main form of ticketing at future events. However, it should be noted that such tickets create a revenue issue for event organisers because mobile phone operators often insist on a large percentage of the overall ticket price.

One logistical consideration related to tickets is the resale of tickets over and above face value. There is an increased concern among the industry that secondary ticketing sites (where tickets are resold) are unfair for consumers and are creating unfair ticketing prices. In 2015, 80 leading figures from the events industry wrote to the government to ask them to introduce controls for these websites. The government voted on the relevant clause in the Consumer Rights Bill and rejected the opportunity to make secondary ticketing sites more transparent. However, sites such as Get Me In, Seatwave, Viagogo and StubHub have agreed to provide further details of the original tickets on their website (eventmagazine.co.uk).

4.7.2.2 Transport

It is a common misconception among event managers that the way in which customers travel to the event is outside their control and therefore not their concern. In fact, the way that customers are transported to an event is an important part of the overall logistics planning process. Bowdin *et al.* (2010) describe transport to the site as the customers' first physical commitment to an event.

From a logistical point of view, it is essential to establish *when* customers will arrive at an event. Event managers use two words to describe the arrival of customers: *dump* refers to customers all arriving at around the same time (for a music gig or a conference, for example); and *trickle* refers to customers arriving at different periods throughout the event (as they do at an exhibition or trade show). It is essential that those responsible for the logistics plan understand when their customers will arrive so that plans to accommodate them can be drafted.

How customers will reach an event is a key question and one that is usually considered fully during the planning stages. Below are some of the questions that should be asked of the venue, from a logistics point of view:

- Does the venue have good transport links?
- How reliable are the transport links?
- Are there likely to be problems with the transport – strikes, engineering works and so on?
- Is the venue near to major transport hubs, such as train stations and airports?
- Will travel to the venue represent an additional cost for the customer?
- If so, will this additional cost make the overall event proposal less attractive to the target market?

When considering major and mega-events (such as the Commonwealth Games or Glastonbury), transportation logistics become particularly important. As Bowdin *et al.* (2010) point out, permission must be gained from local councils, highways agencies or police, and road closures often need to be arranged as part of the logistics planning. Ensuring that roads are clear, that there is sufficient signage to direct traffic, that one-way systems are in place and so on will enable suppliers and customers to arrive and depart quickly and with minimum disruption to the local area. It is especially important to consider the transportation logistics for events that take place in usually quiet, tranquil areas, as disrupting the local community can cause repercussions for the event organisers, including pressure not to return in the future.

4.7.2.3 Queuing

Once the ticketing method has been decided, and the guests have arrived on-site, the logistics manager must consider how the guests will present their tickets for inspection in order to gain entry to the event. This will involve some form of queuing – and as this is often the customer's first physical impression of an event, it is one of the key aspects for the logistics manager to consider.

There are many techniques for managing queues, as well as a vast array of literature covering all aspects of queuing, from waiting times to physical management, much of which is too detailed to discuss here. (See, for example, Oakes and North (2008), Shelby *et al.* (1989), Jenner (2010) and the excellent work carried out by the International Centre for Crowd Management and Security Studies (www.icmss.co.uk).)

This section will touch on the three major techniques for queue management. It should be noted that we are concentrating on entrance and ticketing queues but there are similar issues and techniques for queuing once inside the event. Gaining access to toilets, catering, showers, activity booths, exhibition stands and so on usually involves queuing and therefore demands some attention to ensure that it is managed effectively.

PHYSICAL QUEUING

The most common form of queue management is the physical queue. The logistics manager must ensure that queues are designed to make the wait as pleasant as possible. Queues should be kept simple for customers, with waiting times kept to a minimum and protection from the weather in place (rain and hot sun are two important issues here). The right number of personnel should be on hand to deal with the queues and the waiting times should be signalled as often as possible to manage customer expectations.

There are several strategies that help to achieve a pleasant queue environment, including:

- *Queue capacity*: expanding the queue capacity allows more customers to join. This can be done by increasing the lane size or the length of the queue, or (more usually) by designing a line that zigzags. This shape allows for a larger number of customers to queue in a smaller area and also ensures that customers cannot perceive the true length of a particularly long queue.
- *Queue entertainment*: TV screens, music or entertainers can be used to distract customers from the length of their wait.
- *Signage*: it is advisable to indicate the length of the queue.
- *Secondary queues*: VIP queues or fast-track queues for guests who have paid a premium are becoming ever more popular at events.

Once inside, customers will be faced with queues for the toilets, food, beverages and merchandise, all of which need to be given the same level of consideration as the entrance/ticket queue, as they often have the largest impact on a customer's event experience.

VIRTUAL QUEUING

All queuing systems have problems – the main one being that the customer must arrive ahead of time and wait in line. A recent development in managing queues has sought to alleviate this through the use of virtual queues. This technique allows the customer to enter a virtual queue via their mobile phone or the internet, and await an alert that tells them when they are nearing the front of the line. They can then make their way to the event, greatly reducing their physical queuing time at the entrance. This technique seems to increase the patience of customers and ensures that there are fewer no-shows.

EXIT STRATEGIES

Techniques that ensure the safe exit (egress) of customers from an event also include elements of queuing theory. For example, staggered leaving, as operated at most football grounds (one set of fans waits in the ground until the other set of fans has left the venue and the surrounding area), ensures the safety of the customers. Stadium music gigs often empty VIP rooms first, while those standing are usually the last to leave the arena. And festivals must consider exit strategies if they are to avoid chaos – thousands of vehicles all leaving a remote area at the same time can result in long queues and extremely frustrated customers. Fruin (1984) discusses time-based control techniques, such as metering (a strategy used to control the rate of arrivals and degree of crowding at a known pedestrian bottleneck) and processing rates (the capacity and the time taken to move through or towards certain areas at the event). These strategies, when implemented properly, will help to prevent critical crowd accumulation.

4.7.2.4 Accommodation

Many events must consider customer accommodation. These are usually events that span several days or continue late into the evening, making travel home difficult or unnecessary. Examples include corporate team-building weekends and cricket Test matches. When dealing with accommodation, it is essential that the logistics manager considers the time taken to travel to the site and the efficiency of transportation links, as well as whether the available accommodation matches the needs and expectations of the customers.

4.7.3 Logistics planning folder

It is advisable to create a logistics planning folder (sometimes known as an event manual) that can be consulted when on-site. These are frequently now contained on netbooks or tablet computers, so that they can be updated easily and so that the information is available to a large number of users simultaneously. The contents of a planning folder are shown in Figure 4.12, with details of each section given below:

- Contact list, including full contact details of all contractors and suppliers, entertainment details and sponsors' and exhibitors' details. These should be up to date and include mobile phone numbers.
- Venue or site plan – there should be several spare copies.
- Project management plan – this could be presented as a critical path, a timeline or a Gantt chart. It is essentially a checklist of everything that has been done and everything that needs doing.
- Production schedule – this is a detailed schedule of all activities during the day(s) of the event.
- Contracts signed with audiovisual suppliers, entertainment suppliers, sponsors and venues will help to resolve any on-site disagreements quickly.

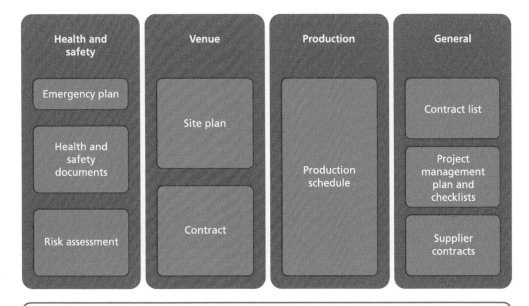

Figure 4.12 Contents of a planning folder

4.7.4 Event shutdown

The event manager's job does not end as soon as the customers have left. Rather, it continues right through the process of breaking down all the equipment and removing all signs of the event from the site or venue. This process is known variously as the event shutdown, the site phase-out or the event breakdown, and it is as important a part of the logistical planning as the set-up and staging of an event.

Smaller events may require hardly any shutdown. It may just be a case of ensuring that the venue is clear of debris and customers have not left behind any personal items. Conversely, events on a larger scale require a complex and thoughtfully put-together shutdown schedule

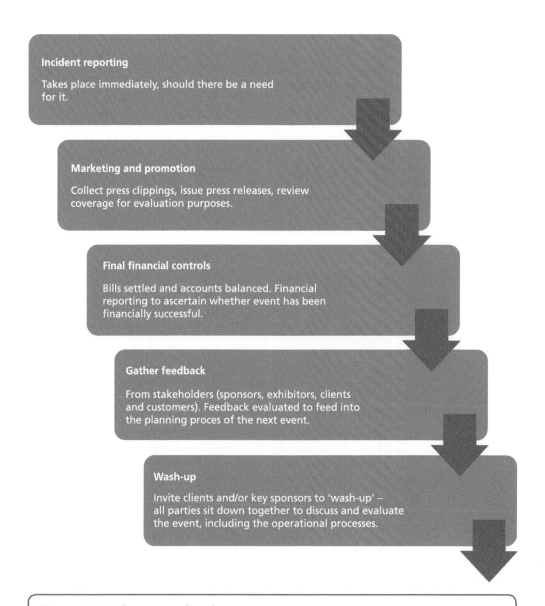

Incident reporting

Takes place immediately, should there be a need for it.

Marketing and promotion

Collect press clippings, issue press releases, review coverage for evaluation purposes.

Final financial controls

Bills settled and accounts balanced. Financial reporting to ascertain whether event has been financially successful.

Gather feedback

From stakeholders (sponsors, exhibitors, clients and customers). Feedback evaluated to feed into the planning proces of the next event.

Wash-up

Invite clients and/or key sponsors to 'wash-up' – all parties sit down together to discuss and evaluate the event, including the operational processes.

Figure 4.13 The event shutdown process

that coordinates all suppliers and works to strict timelines. The shutdown for large events will include the breaking down and removal of all equipment; the final dealings with the entertainment, including payment; cleaning and removal of staging areas; and any outstanding financial transactions. Finally, all sponsors, exhibitors, staff and contractors must be thanked and be left with positive thoughts of this event and encouragement about the next event.

Once all of this has been completed and the site is clear, the event manager's shutdown will continue for several weeks back in the office. Figure 4.13 shows the processes involved in the total shutdown of an event. The key point is that operational processes should be assessed and evaluated against original plans to examine their effectiveness. Lessons will always be learned from this process and it is essential that it takes place within a few weeks of the event, while memories are still clear.

Review Questions

1. Who owns an event? Explain event ownership and the duty of care.
2. What are the three crucial areas event managers should consider when they visit a site for a suitability assessment?
3. What is the ISO20121? What are the benefits of engaging with this process?

Industry voice

Natalie Choi, Conference and Event Manager, The Royal College of Emergency Medicine, UK

Funnily enough, I just 'fell' into events. I was always interested in the arts and dance, and therefore initially signed up to an Arts and Heritage degree. It was by chance – arriving early at a university open day – that I heard what an events course had to offer and ended up changing to an Events Management degree.

During my undergraduate studies, I volunteered whenever and wherever I could, and was lucky enough to get the opportunity to work on conferences in France and Holland, which reconfirmed that I had made the right career choice. I would strongly recommend work experience, to see if this is something that interests and inspires you. Many companies offer voluntary places on-site and, even if it is just a day of your time, it is worth having on your CV.

I graduated in 2009, in the middle of a recession, in which people were losing their jobs, and graduate roles were rarely available. I always wanted to do a master's degree, so after numerous knockbacks, and a lack of replies from job applications, I signed up to a Master of Science in Events Management.

Both the undergraduate and master's degrees had business at their core, but the master's degree progressed each area of study, advancing each subject, and thereby developed my knowledge of each topic. For example, lecture modules about 'working in organisations', developed later into modules about '*managing* organisations' and 'business finance' progressed onto 'finance *strategy*'.

Working at the same time as studying meant that I learned as much outside education, as I did on the course. It really opened my eyes as to how different people work and interact, as well as also developing my interpersonal skills. Things like group tasks, public engagement and time management are all challenging, but they taught me just as much as my studies did.

I gained my first events assistant role via an advertisement in a university alumni group. I would recommend joining such groups, networking and keeping your LinkedIn up to date. You never know where opportunities will arise! During my first role, I aspired to one day have a manager's position and lead my own team, but at the time, I did not realise just how far I would have to go to get to that level. I completely underestimated the sheer amount you learn from every event you organise, each new person you work with, and your own achievements and mistakes. Even now, when managing an event, I think of ways to run it better, next time.

After working in corporate events, I found myself working in a not-for-profit, membership organisation. There are pros and cons of working in not-for-profits, versus corporate companies, and I would suggest researching different types of organisations and seeing which one most fits your way of working. Although, career paths are never fixed, so you could end up working for both during your career.

Some of my event operations roles have been logistics-based, including booking suitable venues, project management of an event, organising AV and catering, whereas some roles have been 'all-rounders', including producing programmes, marketing, organising exhibition floor plans and selling sponsorship, for example. Again, I would suggest you consider different types of event roles, such as logistics, production, sponsorship, marketing, venue and catering.

As I have worked my way up the career ladder in various roles, I have found that some aspects of the job that I once enjoyed most have altered. For example, I do not deal directly with delegates any more, however I still enjoy managing team members who do. There is, and always will be, the need for relationship management, just in a different way, such as supplier liaison.

In all the places that I have worked, conferences involve the largest audience and group of stakeholders that a company has to deal with, so effective and efficient customer service on-site is key.

Events bring a great deal of satisfaction, but undoubtedly involve hard work and long hours. We always need to make sure our staff are cared for too – wellbeing is important in all aspects of life, as is a pair of comfortable, on-site shoes!

With enough funding, common sense and vision, you can pretty much organise any kind of event, however big, small, ambitious, or low-key. Also, with a cool head and good organisation, you can deal with any crisis that might surprise you, but it will not faze you.

4.8 Summary

This chapter has highlighted the importance of events operations. Throughout the chapter, it has been made clear that every event is different and individually complex, so there is no set formula for operations. The legislation relating to health, safety and risk changes regularly and it is important that event managers keep abreast of the current legalities and regulations.

The chapter has also focused on two key operational aspects of events: the consideration of legalities, regulations, licences, permits and contracts involved when managing an event; and event logistics, including logistical planning for customers and on-site at venues.

The planning of event operations to decide which resources, skills and equipment will be required is an essential part of the events management process and needs to be considered fully within the context of both the event planning process and health, safety and risk analysis.

Further reading

Allen, J., Harris, R., Jago, L. K. and Veal, A. J. (eds) (2000) *Events beyond 2000: Setting the Agenda: Proceedings of the Conference on Evaluation, Research and Education, Sydney July 2000*, Sydney: Australian Centre for Event Management, University of Technology. Includes useful papers on event operations, including the Abbott and Abbott paper on crowd management and control. These proceedings also cover many fundamental issues for events management studies and are thoroughly recommended.

Bentley, R. (2008) Corporate Manslaughter Law: No Place to Hide, *Personnel Today*, 17 March. Available at: www.personneltoday.com/articles/2008/03/17/44774/corporate-manslaughter-law-no-place-to-hide.html. Accessed 28 December 2010. An interesting article that offers a useful checklist for event managers operating within the regulations of the Corporate Manslaughter and Corporate Homicide Act 2007.

BSI ISO20121 Sustainability in Event Management Available at: www.bsigroup.com/en-GB/iso-20121-sustainable-events-management/. Full details on the ISO20121 standard can be found here.

Earl, C., Parker, E. and Capra, M. (2005) The Management of Crowds and Other Risks at Outdoor Music Festivals: A review of the literature *Environmental Health*, 5 (1). This article provides a significant review of the literature available on the impact of crowd behaviour on safety and success of Outdoor Music Festivals.

Jones, M. (2014) *Sustainable Event Management: A practical guide* (2nd edn), Routledge. This is a practical, step-by-step guide to identifying, evaluation and managing event sustainability issues and impacts.

Tum, J., Norton, P. and Wright, J. N. (2006) *Management of Event Operations*, Oxford: Elsevier. An incredibly detailed view of the management of event operations, useful for those who need to look in depth at a specific operational aspect. The book is particularly strong on operational techniques, such as forecasting and gap analysis. Tum *et al.* also provide a useful overview of the supply chain management of event operations. It should be noted, however, that the event operations management model proposed in this book is very complex and may well include too much under one 'umbrella' term.

References

Abbott, J. L. and Abbott, S. M. (2000) The Importance of Proper Crowd Management and Crowd Control in the Special Events Industry, in J. Allen, R. Harris, L. K. Jago and A. J. Veal (eds) *Events beyond 2000: Setting the Agenda, Proceedings of the Conference on Evaluation, Research and Education, Sydney, July 2000*, Sydney: Australian Centre for Event Management, University of Technology.

Abbott, J. L. and Geddie, M. W. (2001) Event and Venue Management: Minimizing Liability through Effective Crowd Management Techniques, in *Event Management*, 6: 259–270.

Actionsustainability (2011) BS8901: Make Your Event Sustainable. Available at: www.actionsustainability.com/news/198/BS-8901-Make-your-event-sustainable. Accessed 24 February 2011.

Allen, J., O'Toole, W., Harris, R. and McDonnell, I. (2010) *Festival and Special Event Management* (5th edn), Queensland: John Wiley & Sons Australia.

BBC (2010) Stampede at German Love Parade Festival Kills 19. Available at: www.bbc.co.uk/news/world-europe-10751899. Accessed 30 December 2010.

Berlonghi, A. (1995) Understanding and Planning for Different Spectator Crowds, *Safety Science*, 18: 239–247.

Bowdin, G., Allen, J., O'Toole, W., Harris, R. and McDonnell, I. (2010) *Events Management* (3rd edn), Oxford: Butterworth-Heinemann.

BSI (2010) – This standard has very recently been withdrawn and replaced with the BSI 12012:2012. Available at: www.bsigroup.co.uk/en-GB/iso-20121-sustainable-events-management/. Accessed 16 December 2010.

Cherubini, S., Iasevoli, G. and Lauretta, G. (2007) Events Ticketing Management: The Case of the Olympic Winter Games Torino 2006 and the FIFA World Cup Germany 2006, presentation at Marketing, Trends in Europe Conference, Paris, 26–27 January.

Corbin Ball Associates (2011) QR Codes for Meetings. Available at: https://corbinball.wordpress.com/about/new-postings/. Accessed 22 June 2017.

EventScotland (2006) *Events Management: A Practical Guide*, Edinburgh: EventScotland.

Francisco, L. (2008) Always Prepare for the Worst, *Event Magazine*, January.

Francisco, L. and Quainton, D. (2008) Second Lapland-Style Attraction Closes as Alton Towers Offers Free Alternative, *Event Magazine*, December. Available at: www.eventmagazine.co.uk/second-lapland-style-attraction-closes-alton-towers-offers-free-alternative/article/867875. Accessed 22 June 2017.

Fruin, J. (1984) Crowd Dynamics and Auditorium Management, *Auditorium News*. Available at: www.crowdmodelling.com/Fruin2.html. Accessed 4 November 2011.

Fruin, J. (2002) The Causes and Preventions of Crowd Disasters. Available at: www.crowdsafe.com/FruinCauses.pdf. Accessed 24 February 2011.

Getz, D. (2007) *Event Studies*, Oxford: Butterworth-Heinemann.

Goldblatt, J. (2008) *Special Events: The Roots and Wings of Celebration*, Chichester: John Wiley & Sons.

Health and Safety Executive (HSE) (1999) *The Event Safety Guide*, Norwich: HSE Books.

Health and Safety Executive (HSE) (2000) *Managing Crowds Safely*, Norwich: HSE Books.

Jenner, T. (2010) Whose Queue is it Anyway: A Study of Responsibilities for Post-event Queuing, *Journal of Crowd Safety and Security Management*, 2 (1): 15–23.

Matthews, D. (2008) *Special Event Production: The Process*, Oxford: Butterworth-Heinemann.

New York Times (2003) Woman Killed at Festival. Available at: www.nytimes.com/2003/09/01/us/woman-killed-at-festival.html?ref=burningmanfestival. Accessed 9 June 2011.

Oakes, S. and North, A. C. (2008) Using Music to Influence Cognitive and Affective Responses in Queues of Low and High Crowd Density, *Journal of Marketing Management*, 24 (5–6): 589–602.

Quainton, D. (2010) ISO to Create Global Event Standard, *Event Magazine*, January. Available at: www.eventmagazine.co.uk/news/975911/ISO-create-global-eventsustainability-standard. Accessed 28 December 2010.

Shelby, B., Vaske, J. J. and Heberlien, T. A. (1989) Comparative Analysis of Crowding in Multiple Locations: Results from Fifteen Years of Research, *Leisure Science*, 11: 269–291.

Shone, A. and Parry, B. (2010) *Successful Event Management* (3rd edn), Hampshire: Cengage Learning.

Silvers, J. (2004) *Professional Event Coordination*, New Jersey: John Wiley & Sons.

Tum, J., Norton, P. and Wright, J. N. (2006) *Management of Event Operations*, Oxford: Butterworth-Heinemann.

Other useful resources

Goodwood Events: www.goodwood.com/events-calendar/; www.bsigroup.com/en-GB/iso-20121-sustainable-events-management/case-studies/.

ISO2012 information: www.iso20121.org/.

Oktoberfest UK: www.oktoberfest.london.

Secret Cinema online experience: www.eventmagazine.co.uk/secret-cinema-creates-online-experience-ahead-first-nights-opening/agencies/article/1383803.

Chapter 5

Event human resource management

Contents

5.1 Aims

By the end of this chapter, students will be able to:

● explain the human resource challenges of managing events;
● model the process of event recruitment and selection with respect to events organisations;
● appreciate the complexities of leading event employees and volunteers; and
● establish suitable methods of event employee learning and development.

5.2 Introduction

Though human resource management (HRM) has been studied and practised for decades, effective staffing, training, management and motivation of event employees and volunteers differ from what is often observed in traditional, static business organisations. This is mainly because of the challenges posed by an event's vastness and the disjointed and 'pulsating' nature of the temporary, events organisation. Therefore, modern events managers need to be more proactive and flexible than managers from other professions, which deal with more permanent, ongoing, day-to-day businesses. It is argued that traditional business models, research and industry practice are not sufficient with respect to the particular uniqueness of managing the event's human resource. These variations also extend to the leadership style in the new vibrant events organisation, with a view to recognising, developing and designing the role of staff and their interactions with event attendees.

5.3 The event human resource challenge

The event human resource behaves differently from that in other organisations, requiring different planning and management activities. This runs counter to traditional views of more monolithic, hierarchical organisations, whose staffing priorities are generally filled to accommodate their own missions, goals and cultures. Instead, event organisations are required to vary staffing in accordance with each event's size, use of volunteers and permanent staff, task scheduling, roles and expertise, in addition to the particular client's and/or venue's needs.

Building on Chapter 2, the main human resource particularities of events organisations arise because, unlike static organisations such as retailers or cinemas, event organisations tend to be project-led, rather than simply designed with a view to their ongoing function. This is because project-led event organisations respond to the requirements of each individual event they undertake, making traditional functional structures, and their associated processes, less helpful when assessing how to staff events and manage event workers effectively.

Events tend to be delivered by 'pulsating organisations' (Toffler 1990), which cause their processes and practices to be constantly revised, in line with the fluctuating event environment. Different operational demands, even on different days of the same event, mean skills and numbers of workers required vary. Along with cost-control considerations, these varying personnel requirements create an ongoing need to alter demand for labour, requiring a mix between sufficient numbers of permanent employees and flexible workers, which usually include those on zero hours contracts, and volunteers.

Case – flexible staffing – zero hours

1 What are zero hours contracts? How do they work?
2 What are the benefits and drawbacks of using such contacts in the events industry?
3 Discuss some of the ethical as well as business conditions under which zero hours contracts can be managed in order to maintain efficient costs, customer satisfaction and employee loyalty.

Terminology, as it applies to event staffing, has altered significantly in recent years, in line with its increasing complexity. Twenty years ago, a practitioner or student would have referred to the staffing of an event as a function of 'personnel management', rather than using the current term 'human resource management'. This change mainly resulted from the increased complexity facing HR professionals, due to ongoing economic and cultural changes. At the same time, the expectations of how employees perform in organisations has also developed, in line with expectations of what people hope to derive from work itself.

Study activity – work–life balance

1 What do employees expect from work beyond customary contractual pay and conditions?
2 Generate some ideas about ways in which workers could have their work satisfaction and productivity improved.
3 What are some of the main initiatives that could be implemented to promote work–life balance within events organisations? Research and discuss, using examples from work organisations.

5.3.1 Event personnel

While previously the events workforce was primarily treated as a resource, to be recruited in large enough numbers from local communities (Goldblatt 2010), societal and industry changes regarding the role and treatment of temporary staff have increased the complexities and considerations associated with modern event leadership. Also, the increased academic and industry focus on holistic event design and service management has made it necessary for HR managers to evolve their function as well. Therefore, rather than simply generating staff in significant enough numbers to provide presence and atmosphere, or carrying out basic, practical tasks, HR managers must recognise that events are comprised of people; the co-producers of event customer experiences.

Thus, Van Der Wagen (2007: 5) refers to events as 'a new context for human resource management'. She argues that people are not just an essential resource for an event, but also a key success factor. Building on this important point, events as gatherings of people are conceived, designed and delivered by people, for people. They decide the all-important 'raison d'être' of the event (Brown and James 2004) which is crucial to an event's authenticity. As discussed in Chapter 2, if an event's designer needs to decide whether attendees should be immersed or absorbed in a particular experience, event staff will be essential to achieving this. Such an important role will often be key to an event's successful staging and the ultimate expression of its planned legacy.

This new strategic role of HRM for events demands greater concern for the philosophy of events and event organisations, not just attention to processes and staffing. This new view is important to event managers, considering the strategic nature of most events and the way they are managed by ad hoc organisational structures, which are often formed, revised and disbanded according to fluctuating needs.

As industry focus continues on the all-important, memorable wow factors of design-driven events (see Chapter 3), so the essential element of interaction between staff and customers also comes to the forefront of successful, quality experience-facilitation. This continues industry departure from the basic '4Ps' marketing mix of product, price, place and promotion, earlier found to be inadequate for service industry use (Booms and Bitner 1981; Bitner 1993).

Currently, successful events incorporate the additional components of people, process and physical evidence into their design and staging plans to emphasise the essential and complementary role that human resource plays in the design and production of event attendee experience within event experiencescapes. Also, the extent to which other, related event elements play their part, such as communication and the flow of activities, should not be underestimated, and are actioned by the event workforce. Even the staging elements, which comprise the remainder of the holistic experiencescape discussed in Chapter 3, are also delivered by people.

5.3.2 Understanding event professionalism

As events have continued to be mass-produced in increasing, record numbers, the industry need for workers with appropriate skills and attributes has also increased. However, though the numbers of skilled professionals required are not debated, there are conflicting opinions concerning the specific skills and attributes required.

5.3.3 Establishing the desirable attributes of event personnel

With the increasing demand for suitably skilled events personnel have come various attempts by the industry and academic institutions to define and categorise the desirable attributes of such workers in terms of competencies. As the learned capacity to do certain activities, the required competencies of event staff will vary in part according to the requirements of the particular event in question. Thus, the professionalisation of the event manager continues, as is illustrated in the following case study.

CASE STUDY 5.1

Do events management degrees adequately equip graduates for the events profession?

In an attempt to serve the recruitment needs of the growing, international events sector, there has been much recent discussion about whether degrees in events management are the most effective route towards the professionalisation of graduates within the field. As is customary with nascent, applied education programmes, there has been a tendency with some to suggest that the practical nature of the profession, if it indeed can yet be called one, can only be learned by practical, hands-on work experience.

However, as Bladen and Kennell (2014) explained, there is discussion still about whether events management can in fact even be considered a profession, due, among other factors, to its lack of a coherent professional body and professional qualifications. The authors also suggest that the way forward to equip events graduates for their careers as effective managers is to educate them in the practice of reflective thinking.

Though this appears to be the continuation of an age-old debate between those who champion practical, on-the-job training, versus those in favour of the longer-term, career emphasis provided by professional degree education, it seems that both are required for new employees wishing to pursue a career in events – from the point of first-job entry level into operations as well as far beyond this to a long-term career path and events leadership.

(Adapted from: Bladen and Kennell 2014)

5.4 Finding the right people

The task of HR planning for an event involves predicting gaps between the activities planned to take place throughout the event cycle (see Chapter 1) and the suitably competent people and teams required to complete them successfully. 'Recruitment' relates to attracting sufficient numbers of competent candidates for a position, whereas 'selection' refers to the processes used to appoint such a person. This process can be illustrated as follows:

- State specific event need.
- Use appropriate recruitment and selection methods.
- Match suitable applicant to job.
- Review recruitment and selection processes and modify as required.

Needless to say, the flexibility of the specific event, the chosen task in question and that of the individual applicant will greatly influence the level and ease of 'fit' between the person and the job. However, the consequences of errors made during this process can impact more heavily on the event organisation than they would in other more day-to-day, functional organisations because of the time-sensitive nature of the event cycle and the 'once-for-all' nature of the offering. Events cannot simply be repeated or refunds offered if shortfalls occur in the event delivery process due to the wrong people having been hired.

Another basic consideration is the building of a large supply of labour with ongoing availability for future events. Such a strategy can greatly reduce costs in the form of recruitment advertising, interviewing and other hiring expenses. Also, the costs of inducting and training new employees can be sensibly conserved if workers remain with a particular events organisation across multiple or repeat events.

Loyal event recruits can also promote improved quality of work task delivery, such as improved safety and customer service, as well as better teamwork due to familiarity with the culture of the organisation, expected standards of performance and event market segments.

5.4.1 Recruiting

For every event, there is the necessity to attract, screen and select adequately qualified workers either through a formal or informal process, which involves:

- determining the vacancies
- sourcing strategy
- preparing and publishing information
- processing and measuring applications
- notifying applicants. (Tyson and York 2000: 106–107)

Invariably, due to the sheer scale of many events, it is common practice for event organisations to use recruitment intermediaries to assist with what can often be a resource-intensive and specialised activity.

Whether the event organisers use recruitment agencies, or manage this process in-house, it is important that effective procedures and processes are formulated, possibly for each individual event if required, in order to ensure that the most suitable candidates are matched with the planned jobs. Ineffective recruitment may lead to significant shortfalls in performance, and in the events industry where, as the cliché states, 'you are only as good as your last event', failure is much more difficult to rectify than in many other industries.

Recruitment and selection methods should attract sufficient numbers of suitable applicants and should provide scope for fairness in relation to their chances of being selected. According to Pilbeam and Corbridge (2010: 137), recruitment and selection involves:

1 Attraction of suitable candidates.
2 Reduction of unsuitable candidates.
3 Selection of suitable candidates.
4 Transition of a successful candidate to an effective employee.

The typical constraints to these activities experienced by most organisations, such as a shortage of qualified candidates and issues relating to the organisation's macro environment, are even greater for event organisers. They also have to consider the temporal nature, geographical movement, complexity of stakeholder relationships and fluctuations in environmental factors, including media coverage, that are associated with the events industry.

5.4.2 Designing event jobs

Prior to beginning the process of recruitment, the event planner should complete an in-depth job analysis to assess the positions which need to be filled. This will include the collection of information about the tasks to complete before, during and following event delivery. Obviously, the more rigid and less changeable the event concept and plan are, the simpler this task will be. Any changes will require subsequent revision, perhaps adding cost buffers to timelines and budgets.

The end result of the job analysis will be a list of job descriptions, which group the various tasks coherently, and job specifications, which clarify the specific competencies of the candidates who will be recruited for these jobs.

5.4.3 Clarifying job designs and descriptions

A job description should include the following key information:

- Job/role title.
- The event-related tasks and activities that the job should achieve. These will be linked to the objectives of the role. Performance indicators can also be stipulated here.
- Levels of responsibility and any departmental affiliations within the event organisation, as well as the name of the person to whom the successful applicant would report.
- Pay scale.

5.4.4 Establishing applicant suitability

Once the parameters of the job are established, then what is required of the applicants becomes the focus, including:

- Formal qualifications, event-related certifications (such as first aid), criminal record checks, health and safety certifications and so on, as required by the event and its predicted target markets.

- Competencies, including skills, knowledge and prior experience.
- Any physical characteristics required for the role, such as heavy-lifting capabilities.

Each of these may be expressed in terms of 'essential' (minimum) and 'desirable' requirements to avoid misunderstandings during the selection phase, and to ensure that the event hires the best individuals for the various posts.

Many events are vast undertakings, requiring a diverse scope of abilities to achieve them. As Boxhall and Purcell (2008: 176) observe: 'Thus, as we move up from low-complexity work (such as routine clerical work) to jobs where greater ambiguity is involved in decision-making, differences in skills and judgement become more pronounced and are more consequential for the organisation.'

This means that, as event tasks become more complex, there is a need to find people with a wide range of skills. An event producer, for example, may possess the highest levels of innovation and creativity, yet these talents matter little if he or she is unable to communicate effectively. Obviously, the ideal candidate will be both creative *and* an effective communicator.

However, it is important not to set required competencies, skills, attributes and qualifications too high. Physical or skill requirements should not discriminate against applicants with disabilities, unless these qualities are essential for the job. Many event organisations provide on-the-job training or certifications, and carry out criminal record checks according to legislative requirements, but these can be costly and prove impractical within tight timelines so that it is often impossible to hire applicants who do not already have them.

Study activity

1 For events local to you, what are the legal requirements regulating employees? Consider the certifications you would be expected to possess in order to work in your country.
2 What are your country's main disability discrimination laws? Provide examples of steps an event manager might be able to take in order to make event jobs more accessible to the physically and mentally challenged applicants.

5.4.5 Communicating event vacancies through traditional and online media

Potential event employees are attracted by various methods, including basic advertising, word-of-mouth referral and formal recruitment sources, which include job centres, industry fairs, schools, colleges and universities. While job adverts and messages remain relatively consistent, the use of such social networks as Facebook, Twitter and LinkedIn has changed many of the ways in which recruitment takes place, presenting new challenges for both employers and applicants.

Applicants no longer maintain a passive role in the application process, but rather engage in two-way, adaptable messages, often in 'real-time'. For example, many Facebook groups have been formed specifically to publicise both paid and voluntary employment vacancies in the domestic and international events industry. Though often free, or supported by advertising, such online vehicles sometimes apply a commission for referral, which can lead to events organisations paying a variety of charges. These can range from an almost negligible 'click-through' fee to substantially larger commissions for the placement of high-level events executives. It should be noted that the legal framework governing such media is changing fast in order to bring it more in line with the laws governing offline practices, and this should be monitored closely to avoid litigation.

Study activity

Discuss, using examples from your own research, what the potential opportunities and possible pitfalls might be to the use of social media by event professionals. You might include in your discussions areas such as:

- Relationship-building between organisation and applicant.
- Legal considerations regarding contracts, descriptions.
- Management of recruitment messages and corporate image.
- Communication styles.
- Exclusion of certain social groups.

5.4.6 Screening

Following the receipt of applications via the sources discussed in the previous section, a process of screening should be applied to eliminate unsuitable applicants and reduce the numbers of less suitable candidates in favour of those who more closely match or even exceed the particulars of the planned job specification. It should be remembered that this part of the selection process involves subjectivity on the part of those responsible for selection.

There must be mutual trust and respect between employer and applicant, as a psychological contract is formed between both parties which is based on their expectations of one another as well as assumptions and inferences derived from their mutual interactions, in addition to any formal communication or legal contracts. Certainly, many premature breakdowns in the formal, contractual relationships between employers and employees can be traced back to this less formal, yet often more important, psychological understanding.

Study activity

What are your likely expectations of your employer? Which of these can be classified as comprising the 'psychological contract' between both parties? List these and discuss ways in which you think events organisations can improve their management of employee expectations from the very start of the employment relationship.

5.4.7 Selecting

Prior to any events organisation's recruitment of new employees, there is a challenging process whereby the events recruiter attempts to use selection processes to predict on-the-job performance. To this end, the events manager may employ a number of measurement tools to assess a candidate's suitability. However, this can be problematic as there is no real capacity for a trial period of employment in the events industry, as events are time-constrained and also vary considerably from each other.

Torrington *et al.* (2009: 171) highlight that selection methods can be determined on the basis of a combination of the following factors:

- selection criteria for the post to be filled
- acceptability of and appropriateness of the methods
- abilities of the staff involved in selection
- administrative ease
- time factors
- accuracy
- cost.

Because of the people-centred nature of events work, those involved in the selection process are likely to favour face-to-face contact with applicants – ideally in a one-to-one interview – in order to gain an accurate impression of their interpersonal skills. Such meetings allow the interviewer to make an assessment of the candidate's suitability and to present a realistic job preview. However, time, cost and other resource constraints usually make wholesale use of such methods unfeasible, particularly for larger events, and this has increased the popularity of the use of real-time, virtual face-to-face media such as Skype. Methods that are widely used in event selection processes include:

- application forms
- interviews – face-to-face, group, or via telephone/webcam
- aptitude tests
- group interviews and problem-solving exercises, business games, competitions and so on
- work sampling, including written work, business plans, portfolios and presentations
- references.

Several of these will usually be used in combination, depending on the type of event in question. References are especially important, with many event specialists relying on the recommendations of credible referees, such as university teaching staff and the applicant's previous employers.

5.5 The challenges in practice to the events industry

Certainly, the process discussed thus far is widely accepted and practised and it finds application in the international events industry. However, many events managers will no doubt take issue with many of the time, detail and documentation requirements implied here. This will mainly be due to the usual time and resource limitations commonly associated with events. It will also reflect the transitory and temporal nature of events, discussed earlier in this chapter. Indeed, there would appear to be little benefit in mapping out job descriptions and the qualities and qualifications of the people required to perform them if one event differs widely from the next. Most event roles maintain a large degree of consistency across different events but the processes already described are indicative of useful concepts rather than the specifics, because of the rapid changes in events organisations and the specified outcomes of their event concepts.

5.6 Formulating and conducting event induction and acculturation

5.6.1 Induction

While traditional new-employee induction to most workplace organisations is intended to promote effective adjustment and integration of the new employee into the new workplace, in the events industry it involves much more. Though it was formerly assumed that induction was a first-day familiarisation tour, in the events industry it begins at interview and continues to the end of the worker's involvement with the event, or with longer engagements until the employer and employee have reached a mutual understanding of their relationship.

A distinction also needs to be drawn between the employee's induction to the event organisation and their induction to the current event. The weight given to these two elements depends on the kind of event, the stage at which the employee joins and the type and expected duration of their role. In events, the new-employee induction is crucial: it can safeguard lives and ensure the health and welfare of customers, colleagues and the employee themselves, primarily because of the intrinsic dangers associated with many event sites and venues. Please see Chapter 8 for more information.

Virtual induction is practised by several events companies, which post important familiarisation and training materials for specific events on websites and company intranets for use by new and existing employees. These sites provide crucial event information about company policies and procedures, employee duties, site plans and so on. This supplements the usual induction, which informs new employees of the procedural and legal guidelines they must follow and gives them an opportunity to ask questions. In many events, the concept will be explained in relation to the employee's role. Event organisers will often pair new workers with those who are more experienced in order to familiarise them with an event.

5.6.2 Organisational culture and events

During this induction phase, the employee will gain an impression about various cultural norms they will be expected to observe during their time working on events. Schein (2010: 7) writes about culture in organisations and observes: 'Cultural forces are powerful because they operate outside of our awareness. We need to understand them not only because of their power but also because they help to explain many of our puzzling and frustrating experiences in social and organisational life.'

The organisational culture of an events company and gives each of its events a specific 'personality'. According to Schein, organisational culture is mainly made up of the factors developed in the following table:

Table 5.1 The factors comprising organisational culture

Beliefs and assumptions

What does the organisation do?
What business(es) is it in?
What does it seek to achieve in the future?
Who are its stakeholders?

What do its stakeholders want from the business?

What are the standards of behaviour of the people associated with the organisation?

How do the personal and professional values of the people align with those of the organisation?

How does the organisation view 'progress'?

Norms

How do the people associated with the organisation commonly:

- behave?
- interact?
- communicate?
- implement/react to change?
- How do these norms match corporate guidelines and expectations?
- What is the relationship between the groups in the organisation, the national cultural groups, the organisational culture and the corporate culture?

Signs

- Organisations often display outward indications of how they work, such as employee uniforms or visible price or service promises. How do such tangible signs relate to or contradict each other?

It is important to understand the organisation's culture because, whenever a new employee joins, they will very quickly reach their own conclusion about it, based on their assessment of these factors.

In addition to generic, organisational principles, the combined influences of other types of culture found in an organisation should also be considered, such as group culture. For example, members of an event banquet service staff team are likely to have their own set of assumptions, values, norms and signs that are additional to those of the parent organisation, or of the event they are working on. Group culture distinguishes its members to some extent from other groups and such distinctions can cause conflicts between them. When other cultures, such as national cultures or ethnic cultures, are combined with group cultures, the culture of the event itself and the corporate culture of the parent organisation, the HRM implications for the event manager can be challenging.

5.6.3 Team building

Event team building is also more complex than functional HRM suggests. Goldblatt (2010) highlights some of the complexity of leading and managing event teams, particularly from an outsourcing perspective.

Many event managers make the decision to outsource the skill sets required for particular events. Many new to the industry, such as events students, prefer instinctively to retain direct control over the more creative aspects of an event, such as design and production, often intending to outsource some of the more 'mundane' tasks, such as cleaning. However, in practice more experienced event managers understand that the distinctiveness of the event might depend upon the effective delivery of 'wow' factors and other creative, staging aspects which require expertise that is rarely found within the skill set of the existing team. There are other factors in play which also contribute to this perspective, including legal and safety restrictions, and the required capital and talent investment. These factors may be outside the scope of many general events management organisations, particularly for irregular use for individual events.

The construction, management and leadership of event teams, particularly in the context of these discussions regarding group culture, can prove challenging for any event manager and is another contributory factor that makes management in this industry distinct from that of other areas of management practice. For a wider discussion of event leadership and organisation structure, refer to Chapter 2.

Some event organisations take a psychological approach to the construction of teams. Psychometric tests can be used to assess the personality traits of individuals as early as the selection stage of the HRM process. Whether event managers favour this option will mainly depend on their own experiences with regard to predicting future employee performance.

In a team-building context, the most effective approach will be taken depending on the planned purpose of the team in question. Event teams can provide basic event delivery, such as customer service or various staging provisions. Others might be responsible for relatively complex problem-solving activities. The psychological characteristics, skill sets, and competencies of employees performing these roles will vary according to their specific planned context.

The combination of the above characteristics of individuals within the team should also be considered. Pfeffer (1998) found teams to be much more effective than individuals at organisational problem-solving. In the context of creative design, the more diverse the team, the longer the decision-making process, but the more effective the final result. According to the Gorge Group study (1994), excellence in team problem-solving performance was based on the creation of synergy between members, the building of commitment towards a common goal, the fostering of independence, constructive debates and mutual concern and respect for each other.

It should also be stressed that teams in the events industry are increasingly virtual in nature, particularly in vast, international parent companies. This enables the principles above to be facilitated through the use of information technology media, as discussed earlier in this chapter. It is therefore possible for event specialists in the field to be supported by members of a virtual 'back office' of personnel, many of whom they may never meet in person.

5.7 Developing effective communication with event workers

Boxall and Purcell (2008) focus on the management of the 'employee voice' in organisational decision-making through the promotion of employee involvement strategies. This approach is collectively influenced in the events industry by the involvement of trade unions and professional associations, whose scope and power will vary widely depending on the country concerned.

Effective communication, according to the Gorge Group (1994), is based on the organisation:

- proactively building a shared understanding
- focusing on the needs of others and predicting their questions
- communicating most effectively outside meetings.

5.8 Event employee learning and development

The events organisation should facilitate various degrees and types of employee development in order to maximise performance. The specialised field of HRM views these activities as the facilitation and promotion of cultures and processes that allow employees to learn. Formal training programmes certainly have their part to play in increasing the effectiveness of event employees, particularly in mandatory, operational management areas, such as safety. However, the genuine differentiation of event offerings may hinge on the promotion of a learning organisation where people are encouraged to keep learning and improving and are supported with the resources to do so. For example, the official London 2012 Olympic Games volunteering programme, while a vehicle for the achievement of much of the social legacy portion of the bid, successfully encouraged volunteering by promising that volunteers would gain skills in return for their activities in the lead-up to and during the Games.

5.8.1 Reflective practice

Kolb's learning cycle can be applied to the events industry as shown in Figure 5.1. This adapted model is an ideal starting point for the development of the learning events organisation as it focuses on problem-solving.

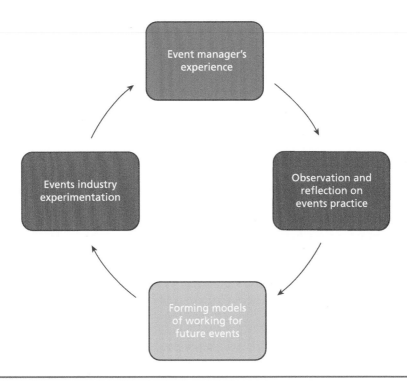

Figure 5.1 Kolb's learning cycle
Adapted from Kolb 1984

Another key HR function is to conduct a formal, organisational programme of learning and training for events by:

1 identifying the development need
2 designing the development activity
3 carrying out the development activity
4 evaluating the success of the development activity.

These four areas constitute the 'people development strategy' of the organisation, within the wider context of the business strategy, in relation to the business environment.

The identification of the development need will take place via various formal and informal systems. As Bowdin *et al.* (2011) point out, this can be linked to the appraisal systems of the organisation, although this approach will not be practical for most events organisations, with temporary and short-term workers. Certainly on-site, employee observations, customer complaint logs and other management information systems are useful indications.

Designing and carrying out the development activity will involve the planned use of methods of learning and development, which may include items in the following list, also developed from Torrington *et al.* (2009):

● off-job methods, such education and training courses
● on-job learning methods, such as coaching, mentoring, peer relationships, individual or group self-development
● e-learning methods.

Evaluation of the learning is likely to be continual and will rely on the accurate assessment of behavioural or attitudinal changes in line with the initial objectives set following the needs analysis. There are also employee-centred assessment methods, such as self-administered questionnaires, which are designed to measure the satisfaction derived from the learning process.

5.9 Motivating, maximising performance and retaining employees

Motivation of employees is too vast a topic for the scope of this chapter. In 'Maslow's hierarchy of needs' motivation model, reviewed briefly in Chapter 1 in relation to general event-attendees' motivation, it can be seen that employees' motivation results from unfulfilled human needs and suggests a human tendency to pursue the satisfaction of needs in a hierarchical order towards self-actualisation. Festinger's (1957) *Theory of Cognitive Dissonance* states that such dissatisfaction will result in psychological discomfort which the individual will seek to overcome.

However, in the context of Maslow's hierarchy, the modifying theory of Herzberg's 'two-factor theory' demonstrates that event employees are likely to view aspects of work differently according to whether they were:

● motivators (e.g., challenging work, recognition, responsibility) that give positive satisfaction, arising from intrinsic conditions of the job itself, such as recognition, achievement, or personal growth; or
● hygiene factors (e.g. status, job security, salary and fringe benefits) that do not give positive satisfaction, although dissatisfaction results from their absence. These are extrinsic to the work itself, and include aspects such as company policies, supervisory practices, or wages/salary (Hackman and Oldham 1976).

To overcome the simplifications of Maslow's and Herzberg's theories, Vroom's 'valency expectancy theory' proposed that the degree of effort an employee would exert to satisfy a need depended directly on the expectation that their efforts would achieve their predicted goals. It is expressed as:

Force (F) = Valency (V) × Expectancy (E)

In order to supplement these models' contributions to the wider understanding of employee motivation in an events context, more research has been conducted into the motivation of a particularly important group of event workers: volunteers.

5.9.1 Event volunteers and motivation

Many events survive because of the availability of a pool of willing and often repeat volunteers. However, as Bladen (2009) found, there are significant gaps in understanding as to the motivation of this crucial human resource. It is recognised that repeat volunteering will be based to some extent on the favourable evaluation by volunteers of their initial experiences. This is particularly crucial because, as Bowdin *et al.* (2011) state, event organisations that use large numbers of volunteers tend to recruit far more than were needed and then shed the unsuitable ones. This process, if practised by repeat event organisers, could jeopardise the sustainable future of such events. Additionally, researchers should examine such attitudinal factors as potential predictors of volunteers' future behaviours. Some volunteers are altruistic and desire to benefit others with little expectation of reward for so doing (Flashman and Quick 1985; Cuskelly *et al.* 2006). However, some repeat volunteers may be egoistic, doing so out of a self-interested desire to benefit themselves, while core – or 'career' – volunteers continue to volunteer because of the intrinsic rewards associated with the volunteering experience itself (Stebbins 1996).

> **Study activity**
>
> Have you ever volunteered for an event? What were your reasons for doing so? Were they mostly based upon altruism or egoism? Why?

5.10 Remunerating staff

Remuneration relates to the total benefit to a person for working on an event and is more inclusive a concept than simply 'pay' for a job done. The events industry provides tangible benefits in the form of money paid to workers, though most volunteers can expect little or no payment for their services, except perhaps reimbursement for certain 'out-of-pocket' expenses, such as travel to the venue. Event managers need to consider their chosen reward strategy for remunerating their employees carefully. Certainly, if the motivation of the staff depends on rewards, then the reward package must be sufficiently substantial to attract applicants and retain them once they become employees. The largest pressure for many events is that such a strategy is not only costly, because of the vast numbers of staff needed, but also self-defeating, because with such high labour costs many events would cease to be sustainable.

There is still much debate about the roles of and rewards granted to volunteers. There are substantial ethical concerns about the long-term sustainability of volunteering in the events industry. Many volunteers are students, who view their participation in events as work experience with a view to future employment. However, there is also the question of whether students should be expected to work for free as a standard part of their training while the event organisations profit from their efforts.

When setting payment levels, employers must consider the market rate for that type of employment. There are minimum-wage restrictions in the UK, the USA and Australia, as well as other considerations when setting pay levels. Other industry payment methods such as a bonus or commissions are less common. In many countries, it is routine to consult trade unions, although this is unusual in the UK events industry. There are also restrictions regarding the equal payment of workers, particularly based on gender. It is still reportedly legal and fairly frequent in the UK, the USA and Australia that female employees tend on average to earn less than their male colleagues, often for the same work.

CASE STUDY 5.2

Race for Life UK

Cancer Research UK is a registered charity in England, Wales, Scotland and the Isle of Man which was formed on 4 February 2002 by the merger of The Cancer Research Campaign and the Imperial Cancer Research Fund.

Cancer Research UK's Race for Life is a series of women-only events that raise money for research into all two hundred types of cancer and is recognised as one of the UK's largest fundraising event bodies.

Cancer Research UK's website defines its mission with the strapline 'Let's beat cancer sooner' and every year the results of the thrust of this mission are evident as statistics grow ever more positive. This work is accomplished by implementing a strategic plan with the following aims: to beat cancer by funding research and clinical trials, to employ doctors and nurses and provide cancer information to the public; to develop evidence-based policy with a policy development team informing Central Government on its decisions related to cancer and research; and to encourage the public to give their time, either by becoming an ambassador to make the government listen (for example, ambassadors helped to secure a £23 million government investment into radiotherapy on the NHS in England) or by volunteering at or taking part in an event.

(Cancer Research UK 2013)

The charity has set a goal to see three-quarters of cancer patients surviving the disease by 2034, so it needs finance and, as it receives no government money, it procures that finance through fundraising, with the biggest share coming from its Race for Life department. The first Race for Life event took place in 1994 in London. Strategy consultancy expert Jim Cowan (2010) had the original idea for Race for Life:

> Through my involvement in organising other running events I had noticed that the percentage of female participants was generally extremely low and although there were/are other societal issues and, although not enjoying

competitive sport is not limited solely to women, I came up with the idea of a less challenging distance (5km, which was very rare back then) and removing the 'testosterone' of competition by making the event female-only.

Thus the then Imperial Cancer Research Fund engaged Mr Cowan to organise and act as race director for the first event, where 750 participants raised £48,000. The following year the race was extended to six venues and had 4,500 participants who raised a further £210,000.

Nowadays Race for Life UK is the largest women-only mass participation event in the world. Over the past 20 years more than 7 million women have taken part in these internationally recognised UK events, raising over £513 million, not including the estimated amount raised in 2015 of more than £50 million, to fund the charity's life-saving work.

HR focus

Cancer Research UK is driven by a single cause. When asked in a Cancer Research UK recruitment video why she did what she did, an employee answered: because the people she is surrounded by 'are utterly inspirational', and that she is 'surrounded by people who are challenging the frontiers of science', while another said that they 'all work really hard because (they) know what (they) are doing is really important'. That kind of motivation has created within the whole organisation a uniquely enthusiastic and hard-working body of staff.

The Events Assistant scheme, in order to staff the Race for Life UK events adequately, actively uses this inspiration as a motivation on its recruitment drives by stating on its website: 'In the fight against cancer, every moment counts and with our scheme you will play an integral role in the successful planning and delivery of Race for Life' (Cancer Research UK 2016).

In 2016 nearly 300 Race for Life UK events are planned. The event season runs from May through to September at nine regions across the UK so structuring and then organising the Race for Life events requires more than just a financial and professional investment. It requires dedicated resources, a considerable amount of time and a strong commitment from each team member. It is not just a matter of securing and deploying staff. Instead, it involves a complex understanding of the diverse conditions of each event, the intricate infrastructure and, crucially, the emotional issues to ensure the events run smoothly and participants continue to feel motivated. While an organisation could recruit a large team and train each person to perform their individual role/s, Race for Life UK understands what it means to truly bring together a workforce and a set of volunteers who are not only trained for each specific job function, but who also understand the much bigger picture at hand. As a professional organisation, they have a strong understanding of the training requirements in order to ensure that all events employees and volunteers have the skills necessary to deal with all the health and safety issues, medical and pre-event preparation training and complex administration tasks and their implications.

(Cancer Research UK 2016)

1   Using this case, and the Industry Voice section, discuss some of the challenges facing an organisation such as Race for Life UK in managing event human resources.
2   Consider your up-to-date CV, or employment résumé. What changes could you make to the way you would present yourself to such a company to make yourself more employable?
3   Practice writing a cover letter to Race for Life UK or another organisation of your choice, introducing yourself as a potential applicant and describing your background as it benefits your potential employer.
4   Imagine you have been called for an interview. Write down some questions you are likely to be asked by the interviewer and your possible responses to them.

Industry voice

Kezia Stephens, Director of Content and Communications Online #Calpemocion

The most challenging event I have ever worked on was #Calpemocion. I wouldn't consider it my most successful, although it was the most successful event to promote tourism that Spain has ever held, and the part I was responsible for (social media) was a huge success; the most successful for social media in fact in the whole history of tourism events in Spain. As professionals we measure success in different ways, and on a personal level, as far as designing events to create emotional experiences is concerned, I know I have achieved more at other events that I have managed. Yet #Calpemocion was a huge success, and for the part I was responsible for, which gave it its prestige and its place in history, the management of human resources in this case was the key.

#Calpemocion was a macro tourist event at which 50 of the most influential bloggers in Spain, in sectors such as tourism, social media and communication, marketing, fashion, and events, were invited to enjoy a programme of activities over four days, with the primary goal of promoting the destination, Calpe, on the Costa Blanca.

One of the main events of the programme was the conference 'Experiences as Destination', which was directed by Domènec Biosca (Tourism Merit Medal granted by the Spanish government), had over 600 attendees, and achieved more than 50 million online impacts. It was Trending Topic three times in Spain and once in Europe, above the Eurovision Song Contest which was held on the same evening at the same hour. I was in charge of the communication strategy.

Implementation of the strategy and management of social platforms requires a skilled and experienced team. Results are crucial; there is no room for mistakes, and on that evening the window of the conference was short, and the competition for trending, with the Eurovision being held at the exact same time, fierce.

Staffing at the event as a whole required expertise, because the bloggers were constantly sharing every last detail of every moment on Twitter, Facebook, and all their social media platforms. That's what they were there for, the mission of the event was such. So the careful management of all the human resources was of vital importance. Staff were chosen to represent Calpe as a professionally run, slick tourist destination, and that mission was accomplished, and reflected in the incredibly positive feedback on social media.

5.11 Summary

This chapter has analysed the human resource challenges of managing events and it should be noted that there are significant differences between management of the human resources associated with events and the management of ordinary employees in other industries, due to the temporal, project structure of the event organisation. Therefore, the process of event recruitment and selection also tends to differ significantly from that found in other businesses, and these differences are compounded as the scale and duration of the event being managed increase. Also, the complexities of managing event employees and volunteers relate closely to the pulsating nature of the organisation and therefore require constant review throughout the event cycle so that short-term changes can be made in response to the usual fluctuations in customer attendance and the various transitions through the stages of the event cycle. Through employee retention methods, employee learning and development can be facilitated in conjunction with the strategic requirements of the event and its organisers.

Further reading

Cuskelly, G., Hoye, R. *et al.* (2006) *Working with Volunteers in Sport: Theory and Practice*, London: Routledge. Focused on sporting events, this book gives a thorough introduction to volunteering in events, including useful references to the research in the field.

Schein, E. (2010) *Organizational Culture and Leadership*, John Wiley & Sons: San Francisco. This book is a good overall introduction to this important topic.

Van der Wagen, L. (2007) *Human Resource Management for Events: Managing the Event Workforce*, Oxford: Elsevier. A thoughtful and practical overview of HR in events, this book has the added advantage of being thoroughly events-related.

References

Bitner , M. J. (1993) Managing the Evidence of Service, in E. E. Scheuing and W. F. Christopher (eds) *The Service Quality Handbook*: 358–370.

Bladen, C. (2009) Towards an Olympic Volunteering Legacy. Proceeds of the 2008 People, Place, Enterprise: The Olympic Legacy Conference, University of Greenwich.

Bladen, C. and Kennell J. (2014) Educating the 21st Century Event Management Graduate: Pedagogy, Practice, Professionalism and Professionalization, *Event Management* 18: 5–14.

Booms, B. and Bitner, J. (1981) Marketing Strategies and Organizational Structures for Service Firms, in Donnelly, J. and George, W. (eds) *Marketing of Services*, Chicago: American Marketing Association.

Bowdin, G., Allen, J., O'Toole, W., Harris, R. and McDonnell, I. (2011) *Events Management* (4th edn), Oxford: Elsevier.

Boxall P. and Purcell J. (2008) *Strategy and Human Resource Management*, Basingstoke and New York: Palgrave Macmillan.

Coyne, B. and Coyne, E. (2001) Getting, Keeping and Caring for Unpaid Volunteers for Professional Golf Tournament Events, *Human Resource Development International*, 4 (2): 199–216.

Cuskelly, G., Hoye, R. *et al.* (2006) *Working with Volunteers in Sport: Theory and Practice.* London: Routledge.

Elstad, B. (2003) Continuance Commitment and Reasons to Quit: A Study of Volunteers at a Jazz Festival, *Event Management*, 8 (2): 99–108.

Flashman, R. and Quick, S. (1985) Altruism is Not Dead: A Specific Analysis of Volunteer Motivation, in: L. Moore (ed.) *Motivating Volunteers*, Vancouver: Vancouver Volunteer Centre.

Getz, D. (2007) *Events Studies,* Oxford: Butterworth-Heinemann.

Goldblatt J. (2010) *Special Events*, John Wiley & Sons.

Gorge Group (1994) Getting Results in Network Organisations, Presentation at the ASTD annual conference, Anaheim, cited in Walton.

Hackman J. R. and Oldham, G. R. (1976) Motivation Through Design of Work, *Organizational Behaviour and Human Performance*, 16: 250–279.

Kolb, D. A. (1984) *Experiential Learning Experience as a Source of Learning and Development*, New Jersey: Prentice Hall.

Maslow, A. H. (1943) A Theory of Human Motivation, *Psychological Review*, 50 (4): 370–396.

McCurley, S. and Lynch, R. (1998) *Essential Volunteer Management* (2nd edn), London: Directory of Social Change.

Pfeffer, J. (1998) *The Human Equation*, Boston: Harvard Business School Press.

Pilbeam, S. and Corbridge, M. (2010) *People Resourcing: HRM in Practice*, New Jersey: Financial Times/Prentice Hall.

Stebbins, R. A. (1996) Volunteering, A Serious Leisure Perspective, *Non-Profit and Voluntary Sector Quarterly*, 25 (2): 211–224.

Toffler, A. (1990) *Powershift: Knowledge, Wealth, and Power at the Edge of the 21st Century*, New York: Bantam Books.

Torrington, D., Hall, L. and Taylor, S. (2009) *Human Resource Management* (7th edn), London: Pearson Education.

Tyson, S. and York, A. (2000) *Essentials of HRM* (4th edn), Oxford: Butterworth-Heinemann.

Van der Wagen, L. (2007) *Human Resource Management for Events: Managing the Event Workforce*, Oxford: Elsevier.

Walton, J. (1999) *Strategic Human Resource Development*, Harlow: Pearson Education.

Websites

Cancer Research UK. (2013) *A Voice for Radiotherapy*. Available at: www.cancerresearchuk. org/support-us/campaign-for-us/our-campaigning-successes/a-voice-for-radiotherapy. Accessed 8 January 2016.

Cancer Research UK (2016) *Volunteer – Support our events – Race for Life – Cancer Research UK* Race for Life – Cancer Research UK. Available at: http://raceforlife.cancerresearchuk. org/support-our-events/volunteer/index.html. Accessed 10 June 2017.

Cowan, J. (2010) *Race For Life | Cowan Global Website*. Cowanglobal.wordpress.com. Available at: https://cowanglobal.wordpress.com/tag/race-for-life/. Accessed 7 January 2016.

Festinger, L. (1957) *Theory of Cognitive Dissonance*. Available at: www.simplypsychology. org/cognitive-dissonance.html#leon. Accessed 7 July 2017.

Chapter 6

Event finance

Robert Wilson

Robert Wilson is a Principal Lecturer in Sport Business Management at Sheffield Hallam University, UK. His subject specialisms are financial reporting, management accounting and economic decision-making in the sports and leisure industry, and his main research interests are in the financing of professional team sports and the economics of major events.

Contents

6.1 Aims

By the end of this chapter, students will be able to:

- appreciate why financial skills are an important part of the event manager's portfolio of skills;
- articulate key financial terminology that is often applied to events;
- understand the meaning of budgeting in operational, tactical and strategic events management contexts;
- analyse budgeted against actual performance using recognised evaluation techniques;
- understand sources of event funding and how to secure such funding;
- monitor and evaluate an event's financial performance.

6.2 Introduction

This chapter examines the importance of event finance and places it in a context that should be easily understandable for any event manager to apply to their event, whether that event is a major undertaking like the Olympic Games or a local community fare or farmers' market. For all events, it is essential that the overall governance is underpinned by sound financial management so that the event runs successfully (from a financial viewpoint at least). Without needing to be a fully qualified accountant or having specific training in finance all event managers should be able to answer two fundamental questions. First, is the selling price higher than the cost? In other words, will the event bring in more money than it pays out? Or, is the event going to make a profit? If you are managing a small community not-for-profit event it is simple to modify this question to; is the event operating within the resources allocated to it? If the answer is 'no', then the event will struggle and could prove to be unsustainable.

The second question all events manager must answer is; can this event continue? In financial terms, this question relates to the event's ability to pay its creditors (people that it owes money to for goods and services). Many events will never take place due to an inability to meet these obligations because they have not considered cash flow and have run out of money to pay its creditors before the event can generate revenue. Being unable to meet these obligations is not uncommon and is the reason why you see businesses, organisations and events management companies going bankrupt. Event managers must ensure that they can pay their bills as they fall due and understand how to negotiate payment dates that fit in with income streams. Moreover, the sustainability of events is an increasingly important component of an event plan and you will need to demonstrate how you can generate the income to meet your expenses.

Before we start, however, it is important that we establish some ground rules; put simply, finance is not simply about numbers and you do not have to be a skilled mathematician to understand finance or manage money. Instead, you need to understand the guiding rules and principles that help to compile and structure a set of financial documents. As students or managers who work within the events industry, it is important that you appreciate the importance of financial management and responsibility and that you can communicate key financial information to both the internal and external stakeholders. The net result of these skills, coupled with those you have considered already, and will consider later, and elsewhere in this book, will enable you to set up, run and manage successful events.

A successful event cannot happen without sufficient financial support and, by definition, financial management. The most significant, and perhaps most routine error, in committing to an event is to do so without securing the necessary financing (or funding) at a very early stage. This will be a worry for any event manager from beginning to end and can ultimately mean the event is presented in a less than satisfactory way, which hinders success and event sustainability planning.

Many event managers shy away from managing money and financial performance because they are scared of the associated terminology. They will often focus on sexier components, such as marketing or volunteer training, rather than managing the basic functions of financial control. Financial viability, however, should be the key issue of any event planning process and if the expenses far outweigh the income streams, then managers should not be afraid to cancel their event. In not doing so, they compromise the future of similar events, acquire a poor image for their organisations and reduce the ability for bidding groups to bring other events to the region.

Unfortunately, the events industry has lagged behind other business sectors from a financial management point of view. For the most part, event marketing, planning and strategy have dominated events management education and led to a growing maturity in such areas. Financial management has often been overlooked, anecdotally because individuals claim to have a fear of numbers. There are still many event managers and graduates with events management degrees who struggle to understand even the basics of a budget or cash flow statement, let alone have the confidence to make informed judgements on the financial health of their event. However, as Wilson and Joyce (2008) point out, every organisation – ranging from multimillion-pound operations through to small, local, voluntary sports events – needs to manage money and make routine financial decisions. Therefore, if organisations have to do this, the chances are that successful managers will have to understand, communicate and use financial information too.

6.3 Financial terminology

Understanding the nature and application of finance is often a question of understanding the terminology that financial experts use. Demystifying this terminology is the first step in managing finance effectively since it will help you to understand what things mean and why they are important. Understand this and you will be able to apply it later on in the chapter.

Essentially, there are two types of accounts: financial and management. Depending on the nature of a user's information needs (explored in more detail later in the chapter), the style of the accounts and financial documents may be quite different. From the section above, you should have noticed that financial information can look two ways. When looking backwards – into the past – it is normal to examine financial accounts as they are prepared for external use and are based on historical information; they are also required by law. A set of financial accounts will, for example, illustrate the past financial position and financial performance of an organisation.

> Financial accounting **is the term used to describe the system for recording historical financial transactions and presenting this information in summary form.**

However, should a manager wish to be more proactive and examine future trends and issues, they will need to examine more forward-looking (future) accounting information. Such information will not be found in financial accounts, hence there are management accounts, that is, accounts that look forward and are based on providing information for managers to help with the planning, decision-making and control of organisations. Unlike financial accounts, management accounts are not a statutory requirement. It is important that managers understand the distinction between these two types of accounts since they dictate where they should look for information. These two types also structure the remainder of this chapter. Financial accounting and reporting are beyond the scope of this chapter because we are examining the tools that you can use to manage event finance. Consequently, we will focus on management accounting and how to plan, make decisions and control event finance.

> Management accounting **is the term used to describe more forward-looking financial data for planning, decision-making and control purposes.**

In reality, event managers should appreciate that they will plan their operations, consider the implications of their decisions and control their organisation in such a way that they reach (in most cases) their organisation's objectives. In order to plan and make effective decisions, a manager will have to adopt the principles of good management accounting, for example budgeting, break-even analysis and cash flow forecasting – some of which will be explored towards the end of this chapter.

Before we continue, it is worth outlining more key terminology that you may encounter when moving through the following sections:

- income statement or profit and loss account – a summary of financial performance and therefore actual income and expenditure over a period of time;
- balance sheet – a snapshot of a company's financial position at a specific point in time;
- cash flow – a forecast of funds coming in and out, presented over a period of time;
- assets – those things of value that a company owns, such as buildings, equipment and vehicles;
- debtor – an individual or organisation who owes the company money or service, such as someone to whom you have lent money;
- liabilities – the opposite of assets, such as a credit card company;
- creditor – an individual or organisation to which you owe money or service;
- depreciation – the loss in value of assets over time, for example, a computer will be worth less after it has been used.

6.4 Financial planning and control

The concept behind financial management is not the simplistic idea that you need to manage profit, but, more importantly, how to monitor, evaluate and control the income and expenditure for an event. It is vital for event managers to understand the changing values of the events industry and recognise that many events are provided to achieve social objectives, which operate at a loss, and which will normally require a government or local authority subsidy to operate. This does not mean, however, that proper financial planning and controls are not important. It is vital that event managers have an understanding of the costs of the products and services that they offer, in order to operate as effective business entities to generate profits, or ensure that taxpayers' money is not being wasted on frivolous plans or ideas.

Many events will rely on funding from national, regional or local government, funding from quangos (such as Sport England or the Arts Council), sponsorship or flexible credit terms from suppliers. However, using money from a third party is normally based on the simple assumption that the organisation's future returns will be sufficient to cover the borrowing or meet other objectives. Problems, however, often occur when organisations fail to meet their financial obligations. Consequently, an organisation's ability to pay its debts as they fall due usually means the difference between financial success and financial failure. If event managers are to make effective plans and decisions, they need to control their organisation's finances.

Exercising sound financial planning and control is of fundamental importance in running a successful event. A lack of knowledge regarding the cost of the event will almost certainly lead to failure. It is essential to plan, budget and monitor finances throughout the planning and execution of an event to avoid any implications with cost variation or changing economic conditions.

Before an event progresses too far into the planning process, it is essential to assess its financial viability. This will mean setting out a financial plan to balance the cost of running the event against any existing funds and prospective income. Several draft budgets may need to be compiled before producing the final version. Initially, the budget will be based on estimates, but it is important to confirm actual figures as soon as possible to keep the budget on track and to exercise something resembling financial responsibility (Running Sports 2007).

If a decision is made to go ahead with an event, it will be a managerial one and therefore possibly subjective. However, such a decision can be strengthened by a thorough understanding of the finances involved and the ability of the event to meet its financial obligations. What is more, the decision that determines whether an event is financially viable will ensure that effort (and money) is not wasted. Earlier chapters stressed the importance of project management and event design and production, and these stages are vital for the operational success of an event but they will yield success only if they have sufficient financial resources available.

CASE STUDY 6.1

Delivery of the Grand Départ 2014, Stage 2

Location: York and Yorkshire
Event type: Elite competition
Attendees: approximately 200,000 in York, 18.6 million around the world

Background

The UK, via Welcome to Yorkshire, won the rights to stage the opening three stages of the Tour de France 'Grand Départ' with the intention of hosting the 'grandest ever grand départ'. Delivered in July 2014, the first two stages (stage 1 starting in Leeds and finishing in Harrogate; stage 2 starting in York and finishing in Sheffield) took place on Yorkshire roads with stage 3 continuing between

Cambridge and London. Over the three days an estimated 4.8 million people lined the route; 3.3 million of those in Yorkshire and the remaining 1.5 million in Cambridge, Essex and London.

Local planning

In October 2013 York City Council (the host of the start of stage 2) agreed the following objectives for the delivery of the event:

- to deliver a safe and enjoyable event in York, which enhances the reputation of the city;
- to maximise the economic benefit opportunity in the short, medium and long term;
- to secure a long-lasting legacy across their communities, culture, cycling infrastructure and health.

Welcoming the Tour de France to York is understood to have captured the imagination of the city. The route was designed to showcase the best landmarks and the racecourse provided a perfect start location. The council provided spectator hubs in Rowntree Park, the Designer Outlet and Monks Cross. The city itself was adorned with yellow bikes (to depict the leader's jersey), banners and bunting.

Event delivery

To ensure a safe and enjoyable event in York alongside one that enhanced the reputation of the city was expected to be complex. The project in York was managed by a core project team of existing council staff and specialist input was utilised when required. The team had to work closely with the Tour de France Hub 2014 Ltd (the delivery organisation set up to coordinate the three stages), Welcome to Yorkshire and UK Sport, because of the need to work across geographical boundaries to ensure the event felt like the same event over three days. Other additional staff and teams were engaged in preparation, business continuity and volunteering with about 1,000 Tour Makers deployed across the city.

Proposals in the build-up to the Grand Départ Weekend included the 100-day festival, Grand Soirée, Grand Departy Concert, Bike Stories, city centre street entertainers and big screens, with a range of spectator hubs with family-friendly activities on the day of the event. Planning for the weekend was modelled on the basis of at least 250,000 visitors coming to the city early, with 28,000 heading for the race start at the racecourse and a detailed traffic management programme was put into place months before the event. These plans were tested before that weekend.

To secure a long-lasting legacy, the council also engaged community groups, schools and local businesses through smaller cycling events, children's races and other themed activities, with more than 10,000 people visiting the J'Adore Bishy Rue Street Party on 6 July, which has subsequently been recognised as a national 'Best Street' and won the Local Community Pride award. Additionally, 400 local families were invited to a community event at the Tour de Tang Hall.

For the first time ever the Grand Départ was preceded by a 100-day festival attracting 800,000 people to nearly 1,500 performances across the region. York had highlights of the Yorkshire Festival 2014, including the Bike Story, What's yours? and the Tour de Brass festival which celebrated Yorkshire's rich history of brass bands. Other examples include:

- Plant the city yellow – 3,000 packets of seeds were distributed across the city to residents, businesses and organisations;
- Dress to impress city walls community banners project – 60 banners representing 50 organisations and 500 participants;
- Bike Story in schools – a theatre education programme that engaged 23 schools and more than 3,000 pupils;
- Road through York – large-scale, 300 square metre community collage, created by more than 200 participants.

A cycling legacy was also high on the agenda with the launch of a Cycle Yorkshire website, Twitter feed, educational pack for teachers and a Cycle Yorkshire ride route being created.

However, the delivery of these activities, and the stage start itself, needs to be paid for and it is certainly not a straightforward task trying to find out the real costs behind the Tour since the organisations involved pay different amounts.

Costs and financials

The Tour is run by Amuary Sport Organisation (ASO), a commercial operation which charges a staging fee to the towns and cities wanting to host a start or finish stage. The fee varies, according to how big the stage is, making the start more expensive. York City Council paid £500,000 to host the start of stage 2, with other operating costs and all the activities on top of that. Sheffield, the host of the finish for stage 2, paid £200,000.

In total, according to Tour de France Hub 2014 Ltd, local councils on stages 1 and 2 paid £10.6 million to host and deliver the event, with £3.5 million of that being tied up in bid costs. Putting on the Grand Départ stage 1 cost £3.2 million and stage 2 cost £3.9 million. It is possible to break these figures down by delivery partner, however, and establish the direct costs to the City of York.

York City Council Cabinet set a budget for the Tour de France of £1.664 million to cover the cost of the event, funded from a variety of existing council budgets. When compared against actual delivery costs of £1.815 million the event can be seen to have exceeded its budget. Whether this is good value, or not, really depends on the success of the non-financial measure and objectives stated by the council. A summary of the full event budget can be found in Table 6.1 (the terminology is explained later in the chapter).

Table 6.1 Stage two start, York 2014 budget

Budget heading	Budget	Actual	Variance
	£'000	£'000	£'000
Event costs	564	568	4
Highways	200	200	0
Project management	221	222	1
Marketing and communications	100	67	−33
Legacy	99	25	−74
Regional contributions	480	481	1
Events and festivals	0	252	252
Total expenditure	**1,664**	**1,815**	**151**
EIF	500	500	0
DIF	200	200	0
Contingency	473	473	0
Capital contingency	200	200	0
TdF grant	291	204	−87
LCR TdF rebate	0	189	189
Total funding	**1,664**	**1,766**	**102**
Balance	**0**	**−49**	**−49**

This demonstrates that the event was broadly managed within budget once the unearned income (funding) is added. The largest item of unplanned expenditure was the additional cost relating to the events and festivals programme, which was not included in the original budget. This includes the cost of a music concert at Huntingdon Stadium (£187,000), the net cost of camping (£33,000) and the cost to support community events (£23,000). This adds up to a total deficit of £49,000 for the event.

6.5 Users of event finance information

Financial information is useful to a wide variety of stakeholders. These will often span several sectors and each will have a slightly different need for the information. For example, the Board of Directors of Intercontinental Hotels Group PLC will want to see how much profit they have made from trading activities and how each arm of the business is performing so that they can make future investment decisions and consider returns to shareholders. York City Council will want to know how much subsidy they have to provide in order to keep all of their leisure services running, so that their council taxpayers get value for money. The Chairperson of the Cheltenham Swimming and Water Polo Club will want to ensure that enough money is being received through subscriptions and funding to cover their running costs.

Study activity

Who do you think are the most important audiences for financial information:

1 in a private commercial organisation;
2 in a local authority event team; and
3 in a voluntary event organisation?

Generally, information relating to the finance of an organisation is of interest to its owners, managers, trade contacts (for example, suppliers), providers of finance (such as, banks and funding bodies), employees and customers. All of these groups of people need to be sure that the organisation is strong, can pay its bills, make a profit if it is commercial, and remain in business. An indicative list of users and their areas of interest is illustrated in Table 6.1.

6.6 Budgeting and events

Budgeting is subject area that takes its roots from the field of management accounting since it helps management to plan, make decisions and exercise control. It can be shown to be part of the overall planning process for a business, by defining it as 'the overall plan of a business expressed in financial terms'. These plans might involve trying to achieve a predetermined level of financial performance, such as a set profit over the year, or having sufficient cash

Table 6.2 Users of financial information and their information needs	
User groups	*Areas of interest*
Event managers	Managers require financial information so that they can make present and future plans for the event and see how effective their decisions have been.
Trade contacts (e.g. suppliers)	Suppliers and other trade contacts need to know if they are going to be paid on time by the event organiser.
Providers of private finance (e.g. banks etc.)	Banks and other lenders of finance need to ensure that any loans and interest payments are going to be made on time, both before they lend money and during the repayment period.
Providers of public finance (e.g. government agencies, quangos etc.)	Funding bodies will want to ensure that their funds are being used for the appropriate purpose and that those funds are helping to meet their performance objectives.
Her Majesty's Revenue & Customs (UK), Internal Revenue Service (USA) or the Australian Taxation Office etc.	The tax authorities require information about the profits/surplus of the event so that they can work out how much tax the organisation owes. They also need details for VAT and employees' income tax.
Employees/Volunteers	Organisations' employees and volunteers often wish to know whether their jobs are safe and that they are going to be paid on time or that the event is likely to run.
Spectators	It is common for spectators to know if goods/ services purchased are going to be delivered/ provided.

resources to be able to replace the equipment in a gym. Organisational business planning can be summarised as an analysis of four key questions:

1 Where are we now?
2 How did we get here?
3 Where are we going?
4 How are we going to get there?

To illustrate the link between general business planning and budgeting, the question 'Where are we now?' can be modified to 'Where are we now in *financial* terms?' Similarly the question 'Where are we going?' can be modified to 'Where are we going in *financial* terms?' To diagnose where a business *is* in financial terms requires the ability to be able to 'read' an income statement (or profit and loss account), a balance sheet and a cash flow statement. It is difficult to predict where a business is going (as it is to predict the future), but techniques such as compiling an expected income statement (profit and loss account), balance sheet and cash flow can help to focus attention on the business essentials. Furthermore, the process of planning ahead using budgets can help to test whether what you wish to achieve and the accompanying financial consequences are compatible or 'internally consistent'. The concept of internal consistency is covered in the next section, but this section closes by clarifying that the meaning of budgeting is the overall plan of a business expressed in *financial* terms.

6.7 Budgeting as a logically sequenced planning process

A key point about budgeting is that it is an ongoing process rather than a time-limited, one-off event. The mechanics of drawing up the numbers involved in a budget are only a small part of the overall budgeting process. By bearing in mind that budgeting is designed to help an organisation with planning, decision-making and control, it is possible to appreciate that budgeting is a continuous part of business life. This point can be reinforced by viewing budgeting as steps in a logically sequenced planning process, as shown in Figure 6.1.

Figure 6.1 can be reinforced by a commentary on each of the nine stages of budgeting.

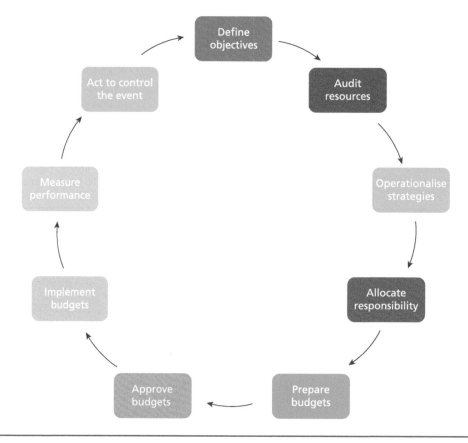

Figure 6.1 The budgeting process

6.7.1 Define your business objectives

The first question to ask when involved with any financial business planning is 'In monetary terms, what are we trying to achieve?' This question should provide a clue that most sane business people would not answer, 'Making a loss'. Losses are made in business but it is inconceivable to imagine that managers set out deliberately to make losses. Losses usually occur when there is a mismatch between what was planned and what actually happened. Organisational objectives vary according to the nature of the business. A community sports club which exists for the benefit of the members may desire nothing more than to break even or to make a small surplus to maintain its existing facilities. A more complex organisation, such as a professional football team, needs to balance the requirements of producing a successful team on the pitch (utility maximisation) with the requirements of being a commercial franchise (profit maximisation). Whatever the objectives of an organisation, they need to have certain qualities that enable them to be measured. These qualities are contained within the MASTER mnemonic.

- Measurable – e.g. a profit of £3 million in the financial year, or simply to break even;
- Achievable – the organisation must have the capability to attain its objectives; capability means staff, other resources and competitive advantage;
- Specific – objectives must be specific e.g. £3 million profit, not 'to do well this year';
- Time limited – objectives must have a stated date for being achieved;
- Ends related – objectives must relate to achieving outputs (ends) rather than describing means (how);
- Ranked – ideally, objectives should be ranked in priority order.

An example of an objective meeting the MASTER mnemonic might be:

Our first priority is to achieve a net profit of £3 million in the financial year 1 April 2009 to 31 March 2010. This target is considered to be attainable as the organisation has increased its capacity and the market is expanding.

6.7.2 Audit resources

The audit of resources is a 'reality check' on the objectives. Its purpose is to ensure that the objectives and the resources required to achieve them are internally consistent. As an example, Sheffield United need around 15,000 spectators per home match to break even. With a stadium capacity of nearly 31,000, it is clear that 15,000 people can be accommodated at a home match as long as they can be attracted to the match in the first place.

Where there is a discrepancy between the objectives and the resources available to achieve them, two courses of action are possible. First, the objectives can be changed so that they are compatible with the resources. Second, the gap between the resources available and the resources required can form the basis for prioritising capital investment, such as increasing the capacity of a stadium, or identifying training and development needs to ensure that staff have the skills to deliver what is required of them.

6.7.3 Operationalise strategies

Having defined what you want to achieve and confirmed that you have the resources to deliver the objectives, the budgeting process evolves to consider the day-to-day tactics to be used to meet the objectives. In small-scale events these might include the marketing plans, funding requirements, customer care protocols and opening hours. If organisational objectives can be regarded as *what* we wish to achieve, then operational strategies can be regarded as *how* we plan to achieve the objectives. Thus, a football club aiming for average match-day turnover of £300,000 might set out to achieve it via operational strategies for spectators, corporate hospitality customers, programme sales, half-time draw tickets, catering and beverage sales, merchandising sales and car parking.

6.7.4 Allocate responsibility

Successful achievement of objectives does not happen by chance, nor as a result of a mechanical exercise. Events management is primarily a service industry and the most important people in determining the extent to which objectives are met are an organisation's staff. In order for people to see where their contributions fit into an organisation's overall plan, they need to have agreed responsibility for particular areas of work. Agreed responsibility is particularly important in situations where staff can be rewarded, or indeed penalised, on the basis of their performance. Remember that this could be particularly difficult when managing volunteers. For example, a basic performance volunteer responsible for the health and safety of and could be assessed on the basis of the event running smoothly without incident. If it is known and clearly stated who is going to do what and by when, then there is the basis for a meaningful comparison of actual performance with planned or expected performance.

6.7.5 Preparation of budgets

It is worth noting that the actual preparation of budgets does not occur until the mid-point of the budgeting process. This is important because it underlines that budgeting is not an isolated process and is integral to overall business planning. When preparing a budget there are two important considerations: namely *how much* income or expenditure, and *when* will the income or expenditure occur? To illustrate the point, if a major festival is expecting 52,000 admissions at an average price of £25, then the answer to 'How much income will be generated?' is £1,300,000. However, it is unlikely that a festival will average 13,000 admissions per day for four days. There will be peak times, such as during the weekend, and off-peak times, such as on a Thursday when people are at work. Thus, in order to make sure that the appropriate level of resource (for example, staff) is in the right place at the right time, it will be necessary to plan the predicted level of activity on a day-by-day basis. Doing such an exercise will enable event managers to plan ahead for situations where expenditure is greater than income and there is insufficient cash to meet the shortfall. Having identified situations requiring management attention, strategies can be put in place to deal with them, such as negotiating an overdraft facility at the bank, rescheduling expenditure on capital items, or simply arranging late payment to creditors. The important point to note is that the process of budgeting identifies potential problems in advance, so that pre-emptive action can be taken.

It is unlikely that at the first time of asking the figures produced in the preparation of budgets will deliver the outcomes required. Therefore, managers may be asked to revise their budgets in such a way that the desired outcome is achieved. In practice, there are five ways in which a budget can be revised.

1 Increase revenue and keep costs constant. This could be achieved by increasing prices, increasing throughput, or a combination of the two methods. The key assumption here is that any increase in price will not be offset by a reduction in demand.

2 Decrease expenditure and keep income constant. This could be achieved by making savings on non-essential expenditure or reducing the quality of the service on offer (for example, fewer staff on duty).

3 Increase income *and* decrease costs, as 1 and 2 above are not necessarily mutually exclusive.

4 Alter the financial outcome required. It may be the case it is not possible to bring the required outcomes and the budget into line by using 1, 2 and 3. Therefore, rather than alter income and expenditure, management may decide to alter the financial outcome required. This approach can work both positively and negatively. If staff provide managers with a budget that exceeds the required bottom line and the assumptions underpinning the budget are correct, then it would make sense to increase the overall budget target accordingly. A much more likely scenario is that the targeted outcome cannot be met by revisions to income and expenditure, so managers decide to settle for a reduced financial outcome; for example, an annual profit of £2.9 million rather than £3 million.

5 Change the overall business objectives. It may well be the case that it is impossible to arrive at an acceptable solution to a budget using steps 1–4. Under these conditions it may be that the required outcomes and the organisation's capabilities are not compatible. The only remaining alternative is to change the organisation's objectives. As an example, private contractors managing local authority events are often required to meet social as well as financial objectives. Occasionally, pursuit of these differing aims may be mutually incompatible, in the sense that programming activities for priority groups at certain times prevents revenue maximisation. Every use of resources has an opportunity cost; that is, the price of the best alternative foregone. Thus in order to make the budget balance, it may be that some priorities which are no doubt desirable and equitable have to be sacrificed to the cause of wider business interests. For this reason, it is important that where possible objectives are ranked (see 'R' in the MASTER mnemonic in Section 6.7.1).

The significance of preparing a budget, comparing it with business objectives and taking corrective action where appropriate indicates the importance of achieving internal consistency. Using the budgeting model described thus far ensures that what an organisation wishes to achieve in overall terms and the financial consequences of doing so are consistent. If potential problems can be identified at the planning (input) stage, pre-emptive action can be taken by drawing up plans to deal with adverse circumstances. Clearly, this approach has a greater chance of success and is more desirable than trying to deal with situations reactively as they materialise, without prior warning. The process of modelling the financial consequences of various scenarios until an acceptable outcome is achieved is known as an 'iterative' approach, or in less scientific terms 'trial and error'.

6.7.6 Approval of budgets

Once an acceptable match has been achieved between an organisation's business objectives and the financial consequences of those objectives, then a line needs to be drawn under the preparation of budgets stage. The point at which this line is drawn is at the approval of budgets stage, which effectively puts an end to the various iterations of the budget and leads to the formal adoption of the budget the organisation wishes to pursue. It is recognised good practice for the approval of a budget to be formalised in the minutes of a board or committee meeting. Furthermore, budgets should be approved in advance of the financial period to which they relate. The wider significance of a budget being approved formally is that those who have compiled it and those whose performance will in part be judged by it know exactly what their responsibilities are. This, in turn, has two benefits. First, if you know what is expected of you, then evaluation of performance can be objective rather than subjective. Second, expectation generates accountability, which, in turn, gives managers the focus to concentrate on those things that are important in terms of meeting the organisation's objectives.

6.7.7 Implementation of budgets

As a logical consequence of a budget being approved, it can be implemented with effect from the date to which it applies. For example, if an organisation's financial year operates from 1 April to 31 March, then it would be a reasonable expectation for the budget to be approved by the committee or board at least a month before the new financial year started. A less than ideal situation would be an organisation entering a financial period without an approved budget, which would be the managerial equivalent of a boat sailing without a rudder. However, for one-off events it may be necessary to write up and implement budgets outside normal financial periods so that they reflect the demands of the event itself.

6.7.8 Measurement of performance

To reinforce the notion of budgeting being integral to overall business planning, it is vital to realise that the budgeting process does not end once the preparation and implementation phases are over. When the budget is operational, it is essential that periodically (at least monthly, or weekly in some cases), a check is made between how the organisation is actually performing compared with how it planned to perform. One of the greatest motivators in life is feedback and the same is true in budgeting. Management accountants use the mnemonic CARROT as a way of categorising the features of good-quality information for feedback purposes. Each component of CARROT is explained below:

- Concise – information fed back to managers needs to be to the point;
- Accurate – feedback is used for planning, decision-making and control purposes, so it follows that feedback should be error free;
- Reliable – similar to 'accurate', the same results of an actual versus budget comparison should be obtained if different people carried out the analysis; that is, the source information is robust;
- Relevant – different levels of management require different levels of information; therefore, feedback should be presented in terms that are relevant to the intended recipient;
- Objective – feedback should be concerned with verifiable factual evidence and not with individual interpretation of findings;
- Timely – there is a trade-off between timeliness and accuracy, but feedback should be received in sufficient time for it to be of value in terms of planning, decision-making and control purposes.

Measurement of performance is not an end in itself and is only valuable as an exercise if it is used to add value to the process of management in an organisation.

6.7.9 Taking action to control the event

If we accept that rational decisions require information that meets the requirements of the CARROT mnemonic, the final stage of the budgeting process is to use the information to inform the direction of the organisation. It is highly unlikely that there will be a perfect match between budget and actual comparisons, so the first decision to make is whether or not overall variance is within a tolerable range. If variances are tolerable, then significant changes in policy will be unlikely. By contrast, if variances are considered to be so significant that the organisation is 'out of control' (in financial terms), then proactive management action may be needed. On a positive note, if performance is considerably ahead of target, it may be prudent to revise targets upwards. If, however, actual versus budget comparisons reveal a significant shortfall in performance, then corrective action may be needed. Such action might include extra marketing to increase sales, reducing prices to stimulate sales, improving the quality of sales to boost repeat business, or, more predictably, cutting costs to try to maintain profit margins.

In concluding this section it is worth making three points relating to the assertion that budgeting is a logically sequenced planning process.

Budgeting is a process designed to help managers make sensible decisions about running their organisations. It helps to inform decisions, but clearly budgeting is not in itself a decision-making process. Compiling a budget is an iterative process. It is unlikely that the first draft of a budget will produce an acceptable result. Various scenarios will be modelled and differing assumptions will be tested until an acceptable solution is found. Figure 6.1 is a simple model of an ideal process; in practice, the numerous iterations will result in a more complicated picture. However, the basic point is that each step of the model is a reality check on the previous step, which is designed to ensure that an organisation's overall plans and the financial consequences of those plans are internally consistent.

Although Figure 6.1 implies a step-by-step approach to compiling a budget, in reality some steps are seamless. For example, defining your objectives (step 1), conducting an audit of resources (step 2) and devising operational strategies (step 3) are likely to be interrelated and to occur simultaneously.

6.8 Common methods of budgeting

In this section, 'methods of budgeting' refers to types of budgeting processes and behavioural aspects of budgeting. In terms of budgeting processes, there are two common ways in which budgets tend to be compiled. The most frequently used budgeting process is 'continuation' budgeting (or business as usual) and the other, somewhat rarer, process is 'zero-based budgeting' (ZBB). Continuation budgeting refers to situations whereby the business objectives of an organisation do not change significantly from one financial period to the next. Under these circumstances, it makes perfect sense to continue with essentially the same business objectives and hence the same approach to budgeting. An example of a continuation budget might be a voluntary swimming club's open meet whose main aim is to break even and to provide a service to the members. These types of budgets will be rarely used for one-off events but may be considered for events that occur as part of an annual calendar of activity. If the club's basic operations lead to a situation whereby the selling price is higher than the cost, then, apart from increasing spectator tickets and secondary spending prices to keep up with inflation, there is no point in wasting time and resources on a more complicated approach to the event's finances.

Continuation budgeting is also referred to as 'incremental' or 'decremental' budgeting. Incremental budgeting refers to a situation whereby an organisation increases its income and expenditure, usually by the rate of inflation, in order to pursue its existing policies. Decremental budgeting refers to a situation whereby an organisation agrees either a standstill level of funding (a cut in real terms) or an absolute decrease in funding. When faced with a decremental budget, managers are faced with the problem of deciding whether to pursue existing policies with less resources; to reduce funding to all policies by the same relative amount ('the equal

Table 6.3 Open swimming meet continuation budget

INCOME	This year	Inflation	Next year
Spectator tickets	1,450	3%	1,494
Other ticket sales	250	3%	258
Sponsorship	1,700	3%	1,751
Catering	220	3%	227
Merchandising	130	3%	134
Total income	**3,750**	**3%**	**3,863**
EXPENDITURE			
Volunteer kit	700	3%	721
Pool hire	2,500	3%	2,575
Marketing activities	136	3%	140
Administration	342	3%	352
Total expenditure	**3,678**	**3%**	**3,788**
PROFIT/(LOSS)	**72**	**3%**	**74**

misery' approach); or to cut funding to some activities in order to preserve the more highly ranked priorities (see R in the MASTER mnemonic). An example of a simple continuation budget for a swimming club's open meet is shown in Table 6.3.

The basic assumptions in Table 6.3 are that the club will pursue the same policies from one year to the next and will increase income and expenditure by the rate of inflation (in this case 3 per cent). Thus, all that has happened to the numbers in the budget is that they have increased by 3 per cent . There are some advantages and disadvantages to using continuation budgeting, which are outlined below.

6.8.1 Advantages of continuation budgeting

● Continuation budgeting is intuitively simple and easy to understand.
● It is an effective use of resources if business objectives, infrastructure and strategies have remained unchanged.
● It is quick and easy to update figures and budget templates that are readily to hand.
● It requires less staff resources and therefore costs less than zero-based budgeting.

6.8.2 Disadvantages of continuation budgeting

● The overall rate of inflation within a country does not necessarily equal the rate of inflation within a particular industry; therefore, the use of the headline inflation figure to increase budgets is somewhat crude.
● Continuation budgeting does not encourage growth in real terms. In Table 6.3, the net position is that the business stands still. Businesses need to grow in real terms to remain competitive and to have the resources to maintain their operating infrastructure.

- Changes may occur within the market place that demand a response, such as the application of internet technology and e-marketing. By not taking advantage of business opportunities as they present themselves, standing still may actually be going backwards, relative to your competitors.
- There is the danger that if income and expenditure budgets are not occasionally challenged, then targets are 'soft' rather than a fair test of an organisation's capabilities. Managers can allow for 'slack' (unnecessary expenditure) in budgets, which can be 'rewarded' when budgets for the next year are confirmed without detailed scrutiny.

Study activity

What are the benefits and drawbacks of using a continuation budget for an annual music festival (such as the Glastonbury Festival)?

Budget – the business or overall plan of an organisation expressed in financial terms.

Cash budget – an analysis of how the cash available to an organisation is expected to change over a given period of time.

Continuation budgeting – budgets compiled on the basis of no change in policies or priorities: business as usual.

Variance – the difference between actual performance and planned performance.

Zero-based budgeting – a method of budgeting that starts with the priorities of an organisation and allocates resources to those priorities according to their order of importance.

Although continuation budgeting is by far the most commonly used budgeting technique in all industries (not just events), if an organisation is facing a fundamental change to its operating circumstances or if you are planning a one-off or new event, a more analytical approach may be needed. Rather than starting with last year's budget (or one that you have found elsewhere) and updating it, the zero-based budget starts with a blank piece of paper and challenges every item of income and expenditure. An example of zero-based budgeting questions might be:

1 What is the purpose of this expenditure?
2 On what exactly will this expenditure be made?
3 What are the quantifiable benefits of this expenditure?
4 What are the alternatives to this proposed expenditure?
5 What would be the outcome of cutting this expenditure completely?

In order for funds to be allocated to a given item of expenditure, a robust defence would have to be made for the expenditure through these five questions. If some expenditure was not defendable, it might be cut and reallocated to more deserving areas of an organisation's activities. As an example, consider the case of the large festival we considered earlier. As part of its agreement with volunteers, it runs its own laundry to wash and iron volunteers' kit. The laundry will make use of staff, space, equipment, energy and consumables – all of which cost money. Furthermore, in the long run, equipment will need to be replaced and service contracts will have to be in place in case machinery breaks down. If commercial laundry facilities were available locally, which could match the quality of service provided in-house at a cheaper price, not only would the club save money but it could also use the released staff, space and other resources on more important business objectives. Alternatively, it may be even more cost-effective simply to buy additional kit and benefit from discounted prices. Clearly, using the zero-based approach would be a more rigorous way of questioning existing business practices than simply accepting that the club has always provided an in-house laundry and will continue to do so.

The purpose of zero-based budgeting is the allocation of resources in a systematic manner which is consistent with an organisation's wider business objectives. It makes an implicit assumption that people within an organisation act rationally and prioritise business objectives rather than personal agendas. Sometimes this can be an ambitious assumption. Compared with continuation budgeting, zero-based budgeting is resource-intensive and therefore can be wasteful if there has been no significant change in business objectives and operating procedures. Consequently, it is dangerous to make sweeping generalisations about one budgeting process being better than another. As in many instances of using applied management techniques, the best methods to use are the ones most appropriate to the circumstances faced by an organisation. If a business is stable with no major changes on the horizon, continuation budgeting might be the best method to use. By contrast, if a business requires a major strategic overhaul or if you are planning a new or larger event, zero-based budgeting might be the best method to use. Like many things in life, compromise can help to keep most of the people happy for most of the time. Thus, a business could use continuation budgeting most of the time, but once every three or five years a zero-based approach could be used to challenge the status quo and reallocate resources to where they are most needed.

Study activity

What are the benefits and drawbacks of using a zero-based budget for an annual music festival?

In addition to being familiar with methods of budgeting, such as continuation or zero-based approaches, it is important to realise the human dimension of budgeting. Events management is a people business and ultimately the extent to which business objectives are realised depends on the extent of staff motivation towards meeting targets. One of the great de-motivators in life is having targets imposed on you from above (top down) without consultation. Equally, for management, there is nothing more depressing than letting staff set their own budgets and finding out that the so-called 'bottom up' budgets do not deliver the organisation's overall business objectives. The compromise approach is for a participatory budgeting style whereby all staff whose performance will in part be judged by meeting the budget have some influence in the compilation of the figures by which they will be judged. There are no hard and fast rules about when to use 'top down', 'bottom up' or 'participatory' methods. Good managers need to have a broad range of skills and techniques. Furthermore, these skills and techniques should be used in a context-sensitive manner, contingent upon the particular circumstances of the business and its operating environment.

6.9 Applying budgeting to worked examples

Event organisers should report a summary of their financial transactions in two, or sometimes three, standard formats:

- the income statement (previously called the profit and loss account, or income and expenditure statement in the case of non-profit organisations);
- the balance sheet (if the event is running through an established company); and
- the cash flow statement.

The income statement is a measure of an organisation's financial performance; the balance sheet is a measure of financial position; and the cash flow statement illustrates how the cash available to an organisation has changed over a given period of time. In financial terms, the answers to the questions 'Where are we now?' and 'Where are we going?' can be seen by constructing an income statement, balance sheet and cash flow statement to show the change between the start point and the end point. In this section, examples of the income statement and cash flow statement are modelled, and issues relating to them are discussed. (Should you wish to read about the balance sheet, you should follow up some of the additional activities at the end of this chapter.)

6.9.1 The income statement

Table 6.4 repeats the first two columns from Table 6.3 and shows how a swimming club might produce a summary of its income statement for its event. The key message emerging

Table 6.4 An income statement

INCOME	This year
Spectator tickets	1,450
Other ticket sales	250
Sponsorship	1,700
Catering	220
Merchandising	130
Total income	**3,750**

EXPENDITURE	
Volunteer kit	700
Pool hire	2,500
Marketing activities	136
Administration	342
Total expenditure	**3,678**
PROFIT / (LOSS)	**72**
PROFIT / (LOSS)	**21,000**

from Table 6.4 is that the club is planning to make a surplus (profit) of £72 during the year (or event).

The problem with Table 6.4 is that a year is a long time and it is unlikely that income and expenditure will occur at the same rate throughout the year. Indeed, as this statement reflects the event, it is likely that it reflects only the final position and the budget does not show when profits or losses will occur. Many events are seasonal and will have peaks and troughs in terms of their level of activity. This, in turn, has implications for other areas of management, such as staff scheduling and cash flow management. If the data in Table 6.4 were to be allocated over twelve months on the basis of when such income and expenditure were predicted to occur, the monthly budget would appear like the example shown in Table 6.5. Remember that this is a relatively small swimming event and you may well have to include much more data – the principles are the same though.

Two important points emerge from Table 6.5. First, simply by looking at the profit or loss per month, it is clear that the events position in the calendar is a factor in the events' financial fortunes. Income is received from sponsors in February and again during the event in April in the form of spectator and other ticket sales, while expenditure exceeds income in October, November and December and again in March and May. This negative cash position must be managed. Second, a simple table of figures is not particularly helpful to somebody reading the budget. It would be much more helpful if the numbers were explained by a series of notes such as the examples given below.

- Income: Spectator ticket sales will occur in April and we expect 580 spectators to purchase tickets at an average price of £2.50 (£1,450). (Last year, 500 sales @ £2.50 = £1,250.)
- Expenditure: Pool hire costs are based on a discounted rate and are paid in May, after the event has taken place. Costs are £2,500. (Last year, pool hire was £3,700.)

In practice, it would be expected that all items of income and expenditure would be qualified by a written explanation. By providing a brief written commentary to the key figures and assumptions that underpin the budget, it is possible for those people who look at it to have a much clearer idea of the organisation's plans. If the club planned to make a profit of £72 (financial performance), it follows that the club's overall financial position would increase by £72.

For most sports managers, budgeting tends to start and end with a budgeted income statement, sub-analysed on a monthly basis (as shown in Table 6.5). This is a perfectly acceptable level of skill for most events managers. However, for those with ambitions to have full responsibility for all aspects of an organisation's financial performance, skills are also needed to be able to produce and act upon budgeted income statements (balance sheets) and cash flow statements.

This review of budgeting concludes with an example of measuring actual performance against budget.

6.10 Comparing actual and budgeted performance

The ultimate purpose of budgeting is to assist managers in the planning, decision-making and control of a business. To achieve this aim, periodic comparison of actual performance compared with planned or budgeted performance is required. Table 6.6 shows how such a comparison might be presented to the managers of an organisation.

Table 6.5 Swimming meet budget sub-analysed by month

INCOME	Aug	Sept	Oct	Nov	Dec	Jan	Feb	March	April	May	June	July	Total
Spectator tickets	0	0	0	0	0	0	0	0	1450	0	0	0	1450
Other ticket sales	0	0	0	0	0	0	0	0	250	0	0	0	250
Sponsorship	0	0	0	0	0	0	1700	0	0	0	0	0	1700
Catering	0	0	0	0	0	0	0	0	220	0	0	0	220
Merchandising	0	0	0	0	0	0	0	0	130	0	0	0	130
Total income	**0**	**0**	**0**	**0**	**0**	**0**	**1700**	**0**	**2050**	**0**	**0**	**0**	**3750**
EXPENDITURE													
Volunteer kit	0	0	0	0	0	0	0	700	0	0	0	0	700
Pool hire	0	0	0	0	0	0	0	0	0	2500	0	0	2500
Marketing activities	0	0	0	136	0	0	0	0	0	0	0	0	136
Administration	0	0	100	100	42	0	0	100	0	0	0	0	342
Total expenditure	**0**	**0**	**100**	**236**	**42**	**0**	**0**	**800**	**0**	**2500**	**0**	**0**	**3678**
PROFIT / (LOSS)	**0**	**0**	**-100**	**-236**	**-42**	**0**	**1700**	**-800**	**2050**	**-2500**	**0**	**0**	**72**
Cumulative	**0**	**0**	**-100**	**-336**	**-378**	**-378**	**1322**	**522**	**2572**	**72**	**72**	**72**	

Table 6.6 Actual versus budget comparison

INCOME	Actual	Incurred	Total	Budget	Variance	Direction	Note
Spectator tickets	1,450		1,450	1,350	100	F	1
Other ticket sales	250		250	0	250	F	
Sponsorship	1,700		1,700	1,800	−100	U	2
Catering	220		220	200	20	F	
Merchandising	130		130	100	30	F	
Total income	**3,750**	**0**	**3,750**	**3,450**	**300**	F	3
EXPENDITURE							
Volunteer kit	700		700	600	100	U	4
Pool hire	2,500	0	2,500	3,000	−500	F	5
Marketing activities	136		136	140	−4	F	
Administration	342	50	392	400	−8	F	
Total expenditure	**3,678**	**50**	**3,728**	**4,140**	**−412**	F	
PROFIT / (LOSS)	**72**	**−50**	**22**	**−690**	**712**	F	6

The columns in Table 6.6 are explained below:

- 'Actual' income and expenditure refers to entries made to an organisation's accounting system which are supportable by documentary evidence, such as invoices, receipts, staff time sheets and so on. 'Actual' figures are drawn from the financial accounting systems and can be supported by an audit trail of evidence.
- 'Incurred' (or 'committed') expenditure refers to expenditure which relates to the financial period in question that we know has been made, but has not as yet been billed for. This sort of data can be picked up from such documentation as purchase order forms. In order to produce timely budget reports, it is sometimes not possible to wait until all of the paperwork relating to expenditure in a period has been received. Thus, in order to reflect a more realistic picture of events, the 'Incurred' column is used to log known expenditure that is not formally in the account books. The 'Incurred' column tends to be used for expenditure only; it would be unusual to have incurred income.
- 'Total' is simply the sum of the 'Actual' and the 'Incurred' columns.
- 'Budget' refers to the approved budget for a given financial period.
- 'Variance' is the difference between the 'Total' column and the 'Budget' column.
- 'Direction' is a reference as to whether the variance on any given line of the budget is favourable (F) or unfavourable (U). One characteristic of good information is that it is relevant to the intended recipient. For non-finance specialists, spelling out whether a variance is favourable or unfavourable is a helpful aid to understanding the underlying meaning of the figures.
- 'Note' is a cross-reference to a written qualitative explanation of a variance. Numbers in isolation do not explain a variance, so it is sometimes useful for a written explanation to accompany some of the more significant variances.

To illustrate how qualitative explanations can help to explain the meaning of variances, below are examples of the notes that might have accompanied the actual versus budget comparison in Table 6.6. It is written in the form of a report and can easily be cross-referenced to Table 6.6.

EVENT BUDGET REPORT
To: Swimming Committee
From: Event Manager
Date: 10 September 20XY
Re: Actual v Budget Notes

- Note 1: Spectator ticket sales – Spectator ticket sales (580 at £2.50) were 40 ahead of target (540 at £2.50). More spectator ticket sales have been achieved by encouraging people who attended the event in the past to return this year.
- Note 2: Sponsorship – Following the renegotiation of last year's agreements with our club's partners, we were able to secure £1,700 in sponsorship (£100 below our target). This unfavourable result was due to one company having to reduce its involvement because of market pressures.
- Note 3: Total income – Total income is £300 ahead of target, following strong spectator ticket sales. However, it is not all net gain (see Note 6 below).
- Note 4: Volunteer kit – The increase in event size necessitated an increase in the number of volunteers and therefore an overspend of £100 against budget. Our club policy is to reward these volunteers for their time with an event T-shirt and we purchased twenty additional items at a cost of £5 per item.
- Note 5: Pool hire – Pool hire costs were £500 below budget due to an improved discount from the facility. We have reached an agreement to pay this set fee for the next five years.
- Note 6: The bottom line – The event had been due to record a loss of £690 following an agreement at the last Annual General Meeting. However, strong ticket sales and a significant reduction in pool hire costs (due to the five-year agreement) means that the event has made a small surplus of £72. This surplus will be reinvested into the swimming club to provide support for transport costs for away galas.

Signed
Event Manager

Any chairperson/director reading this report would be able to grasp the basic point that the event performed ahead of budget and had secured future discounts for the benefit of the club. At this stage, the actual versus budget comparison would be noted and no action would need to be taken, other than to congratulate and encourage those responsible for delivering the better-than-anticipated performance.

Study activity

Why is it important to compare budgets with actual performance and how frequently should a manager do this for: (1) small events, (2) annual events, and (3) major events?

6.11 Summary

The purpose of this chapter was to demonstrate the importance of financial management within an events management context. While any detailed analysis was beyond the scope of the chapter, provision is made to equip managers with the necessary skills to communicate, in basic terms, the financial sustainability of an event. The cyclical process of planning, decision-making and control, coupled with the analytical techniques that can be applied to management accounting information, should enhance the toolbox of skills that any event manager possesses. The importance of this process should not be underestimated in both profit and not-for-profit events, regardless of size or stature.

The main objective of all events should be to operate within their own resources so that they can be sustainable and so that people can appreciate their value. The tools identified in this chapter, including budgeting, should help this process. Furthermore, using financial and management accounting information as two sides of the same coin – which is rarely acknowledged – will help to provide managers with the necessary discipline and confidence for planning, making effective decisions and exercising financial control.

The income statement, balance sheet and cash flow statement equip managers with information that can determine the financial performance and position of an organisation and demonstrate the difference between profit and the typically scarce resource of cash. In addition, it can be determined whether or not the event should be held and whether you or your competitors can pay their debts as they fall due.

It is not possible within one chapter to cover all event finance information and budgetary techniques. However, you should have grasped the idea that financial management is important enough to be considered an integral part of any event. Other skills are required to come up with a marketing campaign or a training and development plan, but only those who understand finance can establish whether or not they are financially viable, worthwhile or even necessary in the first place. The best way to ensure that you develop the full range of financial management skills is to achieve a thorough understanding of the theoretical concepts involved and some tangible experience of event finance in practice.

Further reading

Ferdinand, N. and Kitchin, P. (2012) *Events Management; An International Approach*: Chapter 7, Financing Events, Sage. London. For more information on general event funding and financial planning.

Masterman, G. (2014) *Strategic Sport Event Management*: Chapter 5, Financial Planning and Control, Abingdon: Routledge.

Owen, G. (1998) *Accounting for Hospitality, Tourism and Leisure*, London: Pitman Publishing. A general view of accounting in leisure.

Wilson, R. (2011) *Managing Sport Finance*, Abingdon: Routledge. For guidance on recording and reporting financial information and for more detail on performing a thorough financial health analysis.

References

Running Sports (2007) Managing Events: What Do I Need to Know about Organising an Event? Available at: www.runningsports.org/club_support/all_resources/quick_guides/managing_events.htm. Accessed 7 November 2011.

Watt, D. C. (1998) *Funding, in Event Management in Leisure and Tourism*, Harlow: Longman.

Wilson, R. and Joyce, J. (2008) *Finance for Sport and Leisure Managers: An Introduction*, Abingdon: Routledge.

Chapter 7

Event marketing

Contents

7.1 Aims

By the end of this chapter, students will be able to:

- describe practical event market analysis methods and considerations and explain marketing planning components;
- explain basic customer-focused event marketing terminology and the role of new media in event marketing;
- evaluate the relevance of event marketing as an effective relationship-building tool;
- describe the role of event sponsorship and understand the process of attracting suitable event sponsors;
- explain how to manage the sponsorship process and sponsor relationships as well as current issues facing event managers in relation to sponsorship.

7.2 Introduction

There have been significant challenges for the development of effective event marketing analysis, planning, implementation and control methods. This chapter will highlight the crucial and changing role of the sponsor in modern events, where connection is made between the development of the relevance of the media to modern events, the scope for communication of sponsorship messages to specific audiences and the significant cost-recovery potential to event managers. In addition to the advantages of sponsorship to events, some of the main challenges facing this important activity will be explored.

It is important to understand what marketing can bring to the discipline of events management and to be clear about what 'event marketing' means. (Event experience is an important part of event marketing, and this was covered in Chapter 3.) Event marketing is: 'the process by which event managers and marketers gain an understanding of their potential consumers' characteristics and needs in order to produce, price, promote and distribute an event experience that meets these needs and the objectives of the special event' (Bowdin *et al.* 2011: 367). Bowdin *et al.*'s definition emphasises the fact that events should be seen as 'special' and that each event merits its own distinct marketing plan. However, this definition does not emphasise the need to build up longer-term relationships with event consumers, who are at the heart of everything to do with selling events.

Marketing should certainly not be seen as a bolt-on activity, nor viewed as merely the creative part of the event planning process. Perhaps an all too familiar view is that marketing commences once the event has been booked and the starting date set; but in this instance, what many event managers understand to be marketing is actually advertising. In fact, advertising is only part of the marketing process. Marketing must be viewed as a discipline that is important *before* the event takes place and as one that is used *during* the event and *after* it has finished, when it is crucial to gauge how well the event was received and to what extent sponsors could see value in the coverage that they paid for. It is also the responsibility of everyone involved with the running of the event, not just of the marketing department or team. Certainly, it is important to make it clear to everybody involved in an event that customer satisfaction should be at the heart of everything that event organisers do, and that this must be captured and used in future planning.

The event attendee looks for a 'lifestyle experience' (Allen *et al.* 2011) and something that they will remember as interesting, memorable and exciting. This is sometimes known as the '3Es' of event marketing – entertainment, excitement and enterprise (Hoyle 2002). The event attendee wants to be entertained by the event, anticipates feeling some excitement as a result of the element of celebration at the event, and expects event organisers to innovate or show enterprise.

Event marketers should differentiate between events that target consumers – B2C – and those that are aimed at business or trades – B2B – as these groups may have different motivations for attending. In B2C, the event attendee is a private consumer who is attending for personal motives, such as to see a favourite musician or to attend a festival. B2B customers are more likely to attend principally for business reasons, such as those who visit an internationally renowned event like the Nuremberg Toy Fair in Germany. The task of the event marketer becomes more complex when some events attract both business customers and private customers who are interested in the event's theme. For instance, the model train section of a toy fair attracts professional buyers as well as hundreds of enthusiasts who are keen to see the latest developments in their hobby.

7.3 Event marketing planning

The most effective way for an event manager to coordinate the marketing activities for their event is to develop them within a marketing plan. The key purpose of the marketing plan is to identify the current situation in which event organisers find themselves and then to map out a path for the events management team to follow. As with any plan, the event marketing team should then undertake the necessary evaluation to see if they have achieved their goals. Using McDonald's established marketing plan (see Figure 7.1), these main areas of marketing planning are:

- To set goals.
- To analyse the current situation.
- To create the marketing strategy.
- To allocate marketing resources and to monitor or evaluate the plan.

It is critical that the people responsible for marketing an event are clear about the goals that need to be set for it. The event's mission, or that of the events management organisation, should remind the staff working on it exactly what its purpose is. The mission of a corporate event organiser might merely entail becoming a key player in its market. The award-winning event company Mike Burton Group Ltd sets out to 'exceed expectations' and to 'live up to promises', and this mission seems to have served it well for the past thirty-five years. The simplest mission statements are often the most effective to communicate to an events team. Setting corporate objectives are also targets that the event organisers can use to guide the direction of their business. These might entail being the most recognised brand in the sector within five years, or to have the highest satisfaction levels of volunteers in the industry.

After setting the mission statement, the next stage is to analyse the current situation of the event through the use of market research. This looks at the capabilities of the organisers and how they are positioned in the market, and evaluates their marketing strengths. The main tool in this exercise, as shown in Figure 7.2, is a SWOT analysis. The 'internal analysis' shows the strengths (S) and weaknesses (W) of the organisation, while the 'external analysis' illustrates those factors which present the greatest opportunities (O) – such as market data which show increased attendances at music events – and threats (T) – such as the introduction of new safety legislation that might demand increased expenditure.

The next stage is to set marketing objectives in quantifiable terms – for example, using research data to show why people attend an event – which are used to clarify what the

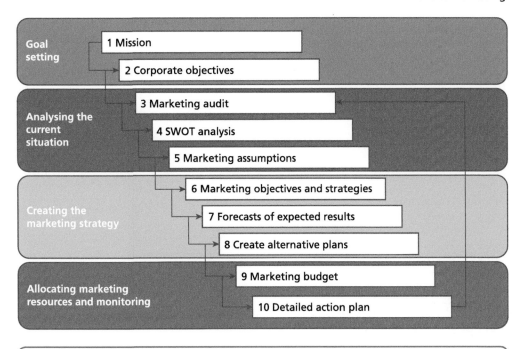

Figure 7.1 McDonald's marketing planning process
Source: Adapted from McDonald and Wilson 2011

marketing team has to achieve. These might specify the levels of customer satisfaction or enjoyment expected at an event, or the level of awareness resulting from marketing activities. A typical example of a marketing objective might be to receive positive feedback about the event from more than 75 per cent of all attendees, or to achieve 40 per cent of sales from previous event attendees. Once the marketing objectives have been identified and the budget determined, a detailed action plan will list exactly what needs to be done, by whom and when.

7.3.1 Expectations of event attendees

As the event market becomes more competitive, and more events take place, it is critical to understand the demands and expectations of attendees. To what extent has the organiser considered the concept of entertainment inertia, and that a percentage of their target group might choose not to attend because their diary is already full with other events? Can this potential consumer justify giving up time and money to attend another event (Wakefield 2007)? Is this an important event in the lives of those attending, with a reputation for delivering enjoyment or excitement, or is this merely one of a group of events from which some of our target group have to choose?

An attendee's expectation of an event is unlikely to be based solely on the experience of the performer or enjoyment of the event theme. Level of service, or service quality, is also important. The issue of service quality is well established, and researchers such as O'Neill and Wakefield have shown links between service quality and customer satisfaction, even though many of these event experiences are also considered to be 'intangible' and therefore hard to measure (O'Neill *et al.* 1999). Event managers have increasingly turned to SERVQUAL

	Strengths	Weaknesses
Internal	1 Established longer than competitors' events 2 Strong brand image 3 High levels of customer feedback 4 High customer loyalty – 60% return to event in following year	1 Low volunteer retention – only 30% 2 Low use of web-based applications
	Opportunities	Threats
External	1 To set up an additional event in a new venue 2 To sell 200 more tickets to overseas visitors 3 To increase sponsorship revenue by 20%	1 New safety regulations for events 2 Leading competitor has grown more than current industry average 3 Key target group has reduced spending power

Figure 7.2 SWOT analysis

customer service software, which considers people's expectations of service and measures this against their experience of service delivery. However, one can assume that there is a level of expectation of quality of service for most event attendees. In some cases, just asking the question, 'How easy is it for people to get to my event?' might help the organiser to identify factors which could affect attendance (Wakefield 2007). While factors such as availability of parking space, ease of access, refreshments, toilets, signage and the helpfulness of event staff might not be considered crucial, it is a straightforward exercise to gauge attendees' attitudes to these points through a carefully constructed questionnaire (O'Neill *et al.* 1999).

7.3.2 Market research for events

The main aim of conducting market research is to try to reduce the risk of running an unsuccessful event and to help meet the objectives of the event organisers (Goldblatt 2011). Without doubt, the main research tool used in event research is the questionnaire. A well-constructed and piloted questionnaire allows a sample of people to give important feedback about all aspects of the event, and it can be the basis for producing meaningful research data to help guide decision-making. The questionnaire should not be seen as the only tool in the armoury of the market researcher, but it does have a significant role to play in events management. For the event manager, engaging in market research should become an important part of their role. Published market research reports for the events industry are limited, but there is nothing to stop event organisers building up their own market research data. This will not only help organisers to make more informed decisions about events but will be an important aid in attracting sponsorship. It is important to seek feedback that is reflective of attendees' views. Citing a Tweet from an attendee which suggests that this is the best event that they have ever attended is fine if it is representative of the general view of attendees, but should not be used simply because it makes the event organiser look more effective in the evaluative reports that they write.

Event managers can also use market research to help them predict the likely attendance at a new event. Using the Market Breakdown Calculator (MBC), a technique applied by many

Table 7.1 Using the Market Breakdown Calculator to calculate likely attendance at a wedding fair
Source: Holden and Wilde 2011

Variable	% Value	Population	Source of information
Population within 50km of event venue	100%	1,000,000	National statistics
Females	51%	510,000	National statistics
Females 18–35	30%	153,000	National statistics
Females 18–35 not married but in a relationship	40%	61,200	National statistics
ABC1 – Middle class	65%	39,780	Secondary data
Number of people likely to react to adverts (adverts shown four times)	20%	7,956	Advertising industry averages
Actual number who will follow up this interest	40%	3,182	Industry experience
Likely to bring two other people	× 2	6,364 visitors	

entrepreneurs to test the validity of their latest venture, is a good way to estimate the likely demand for an event by using market research, and it allows the event manager to input some of their own experience and knowledge of that particular event market. In Table 7.1 the MBC shows how to measure the likely attendance at a wedding fair, which is targeted predominantly at brides-to-be. It is expected that most of the attendees will be female; live within 50 kilometres of the venue; be aged between 18 and 35; have had the opportunity to see four adverts promoting the event; have been in a relationship for more than six months; will be in one of the higher socio-economic groups; and will probably bring at least one other person with them. Of course these variables will be different for other events. For example, for an event attendee to travel 50 kilometres in the USA is a *local* distance, whereas in other countries this might be considered a long journey.

Using this method, the overall population of the targeted area is calculated and the key criteria for the target group are established. Then, by a process of elimination, the number of those who are unlikely to attend is subtracted. This initial calculation shows that there are likely to be 3,182 in the target group, each of whom might bring one other person to the event, making a segment size of 6,364 visitors. Of course, this is only one of the likely target groups, and the process can be repeated for other segments, with calculations revised when new research data become available. Market research data can be used with the MBC and, while many of the calculations are only estimates, the outcomes are better than complete guesswork. Using a spreadsheet allows the variables to be easily changed. If there is another wedding fair running simultaneously in the area, the event organisers must try to calculate what impact such competition will have on their event. This technique is particularly helpful when it demonstrates that a target group might be only 6,000 people and the event organiser has in mind that it might be nearer 30,000. It does not mean that the event will not be successful; it just helps to set more realistic targets.

7.3.2.1 Observation as a research method

Attending an event and taking notes about customer behaviour or their interaction with the event is another way of researching events. This is often called 'participant observation'. To use this research technique, rather than asking attendees about their experiences, researchers attend an event as if they themselves were attendees, record their observations of attendees' behaviour, and then listen for comments made by participants that might give further insight into their views of the event. However, it is important to be aware of the ethical guidelines concerning this type of research, and researchers should not do anything that might impact on people's enjoyment of the event or research in such a way that might endanger those attending or participating.

Researchers who attended the Coca-Cola Masters Surfing Event in Australia as observers were able to capture important information about the event experience. When supported by formal feedback through a questionnaire, this gave a more accurate impression of attendees' levels of satisfaction (O'Neill *et al.* 1999).

7.3.2.2 Secondary research

The key starting point for research data about the events market is published as secondary data in journal or book form. In some countries, this data might be available free through such institutions as business libraries. Industry bodies also produce annual reports on the events industry, and this data can be key in helping to develop marketing plans. Typical secondary reports for the events industry are Mintel's *Music Concerts and Festivals 2015* (available at www.oxygen.mintel.com) and Key Note's *Exhibitions and Conferences 2015* (available at www.keynote.co.uk).

7.3.3 Stakeholders

While consumers are the most important group for an event manager, there are other key people to consider – stakeholders. (These people will be covered in more detail in Chapter 9.) An event stakeholder is any group or individual with influence over the running of an event or someone who might be affected by the event. Allen *et al.* (2011) refer to the most important stakeholders as 'key players'. The event manager should consider what each of these stakeholders is seeking to gain from the event.

The importance of stakeholder groups varies from event to event, but many, such as the Planning Department at the local council, are important groups for a number of events as they are often required to grant permission before an event can take place. The key to successful stakeholder analysis is not only to identify the most important groups but to manage communication with them and consider which messages are sent to them, as shown in Table 7.2, where some key stakeholders are identified. This list is not exhaustive and serves only to demonstrate how many important stakeholders there are. This table can be adapted to any number of events and new stakeholder groups can be introduced. The local bank, for example, is important for helping the event organiser to secure funding to cope with the high levels of investment needed to launch the event. It helps the bank management to make their decision when they see how much publicity the event is receiving and how much the event is likely to impact on the local economy and community. Event sponsors are also key stakeholders. These are covered later in this chapter.

Study activity

Using the structure in Table 7.2, choose five stakeholder groups (one of which must be attendees) for a new three-day music festival that will take place on the outskirts of your town. At this event, 3,000 people are expecting to see ten bands, with around 1,500 of the attendees arriving by car, and as many as 2,000 camping in a nearby field.

Table 7.2 **Event stakeholders**

Stakeholder groups	Most appropriate means of communication	Current links with stakeholder (key people or groups)
Local government Planning Department	Written report to the Planning Department and a meeting to discuss the impact of the event in the chosen area	Planning Director Head of Planning Department Director of Cultural and Sporting Events
Governing body for the event	Letter Meetings Report of previous event	Supported by an association – International Festivals and Events Association (IFEA)
Local community	Local newspapers Radio stations Local television station Leaflets, letters and brochures Newsletters	Community leaders representing particular areas of town Police team responsible for local community
The media	Events management journals Local newspapers Local TV Websites Blogs Social media	Journalists in each publication with responsibility for events; specifically named correspondents Radio and TV news departments

7.3.4 Segmenting the events market and why people attend

While it might be assumed that many people are attending an event for the same reason, research shows that attendees often have different motivations and come from a range of backgrounds (Fink *et al*. 2002). How many people are attending an event for the first time, perhaps out of curiosity or as a result of promotional initiatives, and how many are regular attendees? By applying the principles of market segmentation, event managers can divide their attendees into clearly identifiable groups, ideally starting with their motivation for attendance. Capturing data about the social group, age and marital status is basic demographic information, but this is a useful starting point for segmenting events. Kahle *et al*. (1996)

looked at the reasons why people attend sporting events, but some of these reasons probably apply to other types of event as well. If event managers are able to identify specific segments and their motivations for attending, it should be possible to send tailored messages to each of these groups.

Kahle *et al.* (1996) discovered that fans attend sporting events because they enjoy the camaraderie of attending with like-minded people, and they sometimes feel obligated to attend as a result of a history of attending. It seems plausible that such reasons will motivate people who attend music or arts events, too. Some of the people who attend an event may well do so just because they like to go to a variety of events – they like to spend time with friends and enjoy the excitement of the build-up and the unpredictability. This is a significant segment, so it is important to capture their contact details.

Kim and Chalip (2004) developed a conceptual model to identify why people attend events. Their research focused on 'push factors', such as age, gender, education, income and previous attendance at events, and linked these to 'mediating factors', such as the attraction of the event and interest in the event. They found that both the perceived risk of attending and financial constraints impacted on the intention to attend.

Research will often show important reasons why people attend events and help event managers to make more informed decisions about their events. Nicholson and Pearce (2001) looked at the Wildfoods Festival, which incorporated four different events, and found that the most important factor for attendance was because attendees were specifically interested in one of the activities on offer, such as food and wine tasting.

In many cases, attendees might just come along in order to meet new people. A feature of many developed countries is the mobility of labour, with people taking jobs away from the place where they grew up. Single people will therefore attend events on their own or as part of organised groups as a way of enriching their social lives (Melnick 1993).

7.3.5 Event objectives

Many events have set capacities for attendees and participants. Goal-setting for an event with a stadium capacity of 50,000 people is relatively straightforward and just a matter of working out who these 50,000 people will be. Many event managers use customer relationship management (CRM) databases to manage lists of existing customers. This also includes such areas as loyalty cards for event attendees in order to encourage attendance at future events. Football clubs in England and NFL franchises in the United States often have huge databases, sometimes containing details of more than 400,000 contacts, and these can be important starting points in helping them to sell out their venues.

A simple objective might be to achieve a 70 per cent level of satisfaction with the event, which can be measured by a survey of a sample of those who attended. An event organiser should be careful not to assume that most people who attended were happy if they have no evidence to back up this opinion.

7.3.6 Event marketing mix

The next stage of the event marketing plan – the marketing strategy phase in McDonald's marketing plan structure – is to consider the elements of the marketing mix and break them down into discrete components. For event marketing, these components are usually broken down into Booms and Bitner's '7Ps': product, place, price, promotion, people, process and physical evidence, although some researchers use only five categories (Hoyle 2002). The latter include the make-up of the event product and the range of activities built into the event;

the place or location which is most appropriate to deliver the right event experience; the pricing levels which represent value for money for those attending while maximising revenue; the promotion or publicity that can be generated in the media to help publicise and make stakeholders aware of the event; and knowing how to position the event in the minds of potential attendees so that they might consider attending it again in the future.

Events also have different characteristics, such as intangibility, inseparability, variability and perishability (Blythe 2009). Research by Lovelock and Gummerson (2004) found that most writers on services marketing referred to the four characteristics of intangibility, heterogeneity, inseparability and perishability. An event is not a physical product – it is intangible – so it is difficult to promote without an understanding of the event experience that appeals to attendees. Booms and Bitner (1981) suggest that the event attendee therefore requires some physical evidence of their event experience. One way of addressing the issue of intangibility is to provide merchandising, such as T-shirts at music events, which act as tangible reminders of the event or the creation of social media content to remind attendees of aspects of event experience. The event itself is produced and consumed at the same time, so these are inseparable, which means that planning the event experience is also critical. The event production is variable since the experience of the attendee at a music festival or show is not guaranteed, and in a sporting event the outcome is uncertain. Finally, most events are perishable, because empty seats cannot be sold and potential revenue is lost once the event has begun.

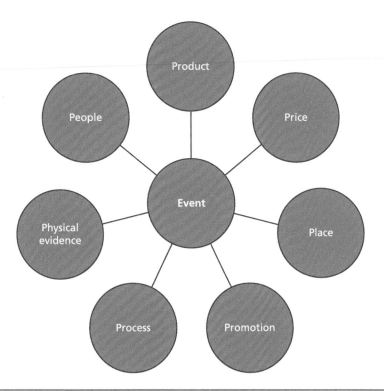

Figure 7.3 Event marketing mix
Source: Adapted from Booms and Bitner 1981

7.3.6.1 Event attributes and branding

Developing a recognisable brand and improving brand image are critical for event planners. These should not be seen as separate activities but as parts of the overall marketing plan. Blythe (2009) suggests that a consumer receives the following benefits from a brand:

- self-image
- quality
- cost
- expected performance
- differentiation from competing brands.

Consumers of prestigious events have an expected level of performance and quality, which are usually differentiated from competing events, where its cost reflects the status of the event and the event helps to improve aspects of their self-image. The physical evidence of the brand comes in the form of the brand name and logo, which are often an attendee's first view of the event in publicity material, so event organisers should invest in the outward appearance of these to items.

7.3.6.2 Event pricing and break-even analysis

Pricing strategies should reflect the objectives of an event organiser and should offer the potential customer value for money, while also taking the pricing of competitor events into consideration. An important starting point for price setting is to establish the break-even point. This is the point at which all the costs of the event are matched by the total revenue. If the total cost of the event is £10,000, and the typical cost of a ticket is £10, the break-even point is the sale of 1,000 tickets. Hitting this target as early as possible will allow the event manager to relax, at least a little. (See Chapter 4 for more on ticketing.)

The week-long Docklands Comedy Festival in London, which attracts a number of well-known celebrities, is free to attend since it is entirely financed by the sponsorship of large banks that are based in the area. This is also the case for the Nuremberg Classic Music Party in the Park, a biannual classical music concert that is free to enter for over 10,000 people because it is entirely financed by local businesses. Attracting sponsors to cover the costs of running an event is an increasingly important component of event marketing and is an area that appeals to organisations looking to develop firmer relationships with their local communities.

7.3.6.3 Demand-oriented pricing

Demand-oriented pricing takes into account the various market segments that are attracted to events, allowing the attendee more options to purchase. This requires a more sophisticated approach to pricing and a better understanding of how people buy. The different levels of price might reflect the position of the seats at the event or built-in extras, such as free gifts, discounted refreshments, free car parking and free event literature. Event marketers should always try to add value when they review their pricing, rather than take the riskier option of discounting. Price reductions serve to devalue the event and can ultimately lead to a fall in total revenue, presenting the event manager with the task of investing more money to try to generate new attendees and thereby make up for the resulting shortfall in revenue.

This approach to adding value is also referred to as 'upgrading' (Wakefield 2007). The customer who paid £30 for a ticket to last year's event might be happy to pay £35 this year if they get a better seat, a free drink in the bar and a 20 per cent discount voucher to purchase merchandise. More importantly, this represents another sale to an existing customer and possibly increases their loyalty to the event. Increasingly, consumers expect to be able to purchase tickets online, so these should be made available, but again with added value. Online ticketing is a quicker way of generating extra sales without the cost of employing ticket sellers, and for certain groups of event attendees this is their preferred purchasing method. Moreover, setting up online payment is a relatively straightforward procedure for event organisers (Holden 2008).

7.3.6.4 All-inclusive pricing

This is sometimes referred to as a 'package price'. It offers the event attendee added value while maintaining revenue levels. For some people, the ticket price might be set at an acceptable level, but they might still be dissuaded from attending if they think they will not be able to buy affordable, good-quality food at the event. Such people's concerns might be alleviated with the offer of an all-inclusive ticket.

7.3.7 Event distribution channels

'Place' is where the event experience is delivered and also where the distribution of tickets takes place (Blythe 2009). This includes websites, which are now an essential support tool for most events. The main functions of an event website are to remind people about the event experience, to facilitate the sale of merchandise and to make it easier to purchase tickets. For loyal event attendees, the website should manage their expectations and update them with news and developments about the event, performing the role of an online newspaper or magazine, or replacing the products that event managers use to publicise their events. The event manager can also use social media networks and email to disseminate information to potential customers.

7.3.8 Event promotion

A perceptual map is an important technique in the positioning of an event. It requires an understanding of how consumers view events, and also takes into account their attitudes to competitors' events.

In Figure 7.4 the hypothetical Premier Arts Festival (PAF) is positioned using eight variables, which represent the attendee's view of the event experience and also take into account the views of competitors' events. Questionnaires can provide the data needed for this analysis. In Figure 7.4 the PAF ranks lower on all-inclusive tickets and its range of additional services than all of its competitors. These results show the event marketer areas where improvements need to be made.

Advertising represents an additional cost for an event marketer, so it is essential to understand what impact this has and how its effectiveness can be measured in order that realistic targets might be set. In Figure 7.5 the impact of placing an advert for a wedding fair in a wedding magazine is evaluated. The advert is placed every month for six months. The target group of 60,000 women therefore have six opportunities to see (OTS) the advert, making a total maximum reach of 360,000, assuming that nobody sees the advert more than once. If only 5 per cent of this group do anything as a result of seeing the advert, then this represents 18,000 people. If the total cost of six adverts is £36,000, the cost of reaching each of these people is £2. Similar calculations can be used for other forms of advertising, but the most important consideration is that advertising does not have the impact that novice event managers often expect it to have.

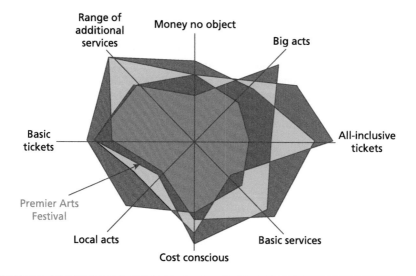

Figure 7.4 Perceptual map for an arts festival

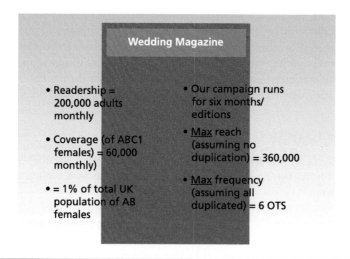

Figure 7.5 Measuring the impact of adverts

Study activity

As the event director for the NSCAA, suggest five or six marketing objectives that you would set for next year's convention.

Convention of the National Soccer Coaches Association (NSCAA)

Location: Philadelphia, USA
Attendance: 8,500

The NSCAA national convention is one of the biggest events in the soccer (football) calendar. It has been held for more than sixty years. Such is the scale and importance of the event that the dates are already set for the next ten years. It has 8,500 visitors (out of a total of 26,000 registered football coaches), many of whom are actively coaching football teams and are therefore in regular contact with around 500,000 players. The convention attracts 300 companies, predominantly from the USA, who hire around 700 booths, which has increased yearly over the past ten years. The organisers' aim is to provide an environment where those attending can have fun, excitement and learning opportunities, which involves attracting the most appropriate exhibitors. They create the perfect platform for attendees to observe coaching classes and to mix with important people from the world of football coaching. Usually, at least three high-profile soccer coaches or administrators are recruited to put on shows.

The number of overseas visitors to the convention is increasing, as the rest of the football world starts to wake up to the size of the youth football market in the USA. Trade exhibitors can demonstrate the latest in coaching equipment, footwear and clothing, technological innovations, as well as additional services, such as financial services, insurance and travel. Recent exciting changes include Major League Soccer's (MLS) Superdraft, where young players have the opportunity for trials with MLS teams.

The NSCAA generates additional revenue by selling advertising space in its publications. The *Soccer Journal* is sent to all 26,000 members and an online magazine called *The Technical Area* is emailed twice a week to members. Advertisers can also purchase mailing lists that allow them to target all members, providing the NSCAA with additional revenue. Exhibitors are also encouraged to join the corporate membership programme, which offers additional benefits and the chance to network with current members, such as Adidas.

Away from the daytime convention, the NSCAA attracts sponsors to host evening activities at clubs and restaurants, with partners including hotels, restaurants and bars. Rooms are provided for NSCAA committee meetings, and awards ceremonies are hosted to recognise achievement in football coaching.

The convention is usually held during the second or third week in January – in the middle of the traditional break for most clubs based in the north of the USA – which helps to ensure high attendance figures. With increasing numbers of participants, exhibitors and attendees, the convention looks set to continue its growth and enhance its reputation as an important part of the US football market.

7.3.9 E-marketing and internet marketing

It is important to clarify the meaning of the terms 'e-marketing' and 'internet marketing', as they are often used interchangeably. According to Chaffey *et al.* (2006: 252), internet marketing is 'achieving marketing objectives through applying digital technologies', which include websites, email, wireless or mobile and digital television. E-marketing refers to all of these too, but also to 'digital customer data and electronic customer relationship management systems'.

The fast pace of development in e-marketing and web-based technologies continues to present ever more opportunities and threats to event marketers. However, whenever an event manager decides to use any of these new applications, they must do so because they see it as a means of improving the overall consumer experience, not just because it is administratively more efficient or a lower-cost option than traditional methods. The challenge for the event marketer is to use these applications to improve overall marketing performance without creating distance from customers (Holden 2008).

The areas that event managers should focus on when developing their e-marketing plan include:

- Information strategy – knowing what information the customer needs and providing it.
- Production/delivery strategy – knowing how the product or service (including information) can reach the customer, despite their dealing with the marketing team from a distance.
- Organisational strategy – what needs to happen in the business to enable everything else to happen for the customer.
- Assessment strategy – a way of monitoring success and failure.
- Marketing strategy – focusing on customers to steer all of the above in the direction the company needs to follow in order to achieve its aim. (Adapted from Holden 2008)

Managers must ensure that the information needs of attendees are identified, and must then focus on the production and delivery of the event so that customer needs are satisfied. It is also vital to ensure that the whole event team is aware of the benefits of these applications and that evaluation techniques are used to assess the success or failure of the event. The final component is to build e-marketing activities into the overall marketing plan.

The World Wide Web (WWW) enables users of the internet to share information in the form of text, pictures or sounds, and it is a perfect vehicle through which event managers may communicate with key stakeholders (De Pelsmacker *et al.* 2010). For many international event attendees, the internet is usually their first point of contact when seeking information, so it is important for the event organisers to present their event in a professional manner. Web-based applications have built-in measurement tools, such as Google Analytics™, which show how many people have visited a website, the amount of time that each visitor spends on a web page and if any of the site visitors have requested further information or purchased anything. When a website is visited and the contents of a banner advert are accessed, this is called the 'click-through', so the 'click-through rate' is the proportion of website visitors who click on an advert (Chaffey *et al.* 2006).

Google Analytics™ has several other useful features:

- Advanced segmentation – This enables the event manager to segment their visitors by region, by number of visits to the site, by revenue generated per customer, and so on.
- Analytics intelligence – Here, any significant changes in data are noted and automatically pointed out to the site manager.
- Custom reports – All data on Google Analytics™ can be used to produce reports that present data in a more professional format.

- Advanced analysis tools – Extra tools enable the analysis of data using multiple dimensions and features that filter data (www.analyitcs.google.com).

If an event website is used to sell advertising space, payment will usually be based on how many people click-through the advertiser's banner advert. It is important for the event manager to ensure that their website appears near the top of search engines, such as Google, a process called 'search engine optimisation'. Clearly, more organisations are now using web technology, as the number of adverts that appear online is growing by as much as 20 per cent per year, perhaps encouraged by the built-in feedback that web technology provides (De Pelsmacker *et al.* 2010). Selling sponsorship on the event website is also possible, with the rate paid based on the number of visitors to the site, the time spent on the site and any data that show the type of visitors to the site.

> ### Study activity
>
> How might social networking sites, such as Facebook and Twitter, be used to support the activities of an event's marketing manager? You should focus principally on promotion, pricing, brand image and working with stakeholders.

As the vice-president of the Phoenix Suns NBA basketball team stated at the Sports Marketing Association Annual Conference in 2005, 'I sometimes think that the internet was invented for our business.' More than ten years after this comment, many marketing experts still share the same view and are embracing the opportunities presented by digital technologies, and the need to keep up with new developments is paramount. The fact is that the internet helps event managers to sell and distribute their tickets and provide information to stakeholder groups. Web-based applications are still evolving but they are already essential tools for event managers (Holden 2008). Consumers now expect events to have their own websites or pages and Twitter feeds and increasing numbers of people are purchasing tickets online. For instance, when the O2 Arena in London announced that 20,000 tickets were available for a Tina Turner concert, they sold out online in less than an hour, with many bought by overseas customers. In total, sales were over £1 million. The Olympic Delivery Authority (ODA) sold the majority of its tickets for the London Olympics online in special auctions, with 1.3 million people applying for only 30,000 tickets that were available for the men's 100-metre final alone (Topping *et al.* 2011). Efficient ticketing systems not only benefit customers but enable the event manager to process money from ticket sales more effectively.

7.4 Event sponsorship

The events business provides some of the best examples of how sponsorship works, with some of the biggest sponsorship deals linked to major events. According to BDS (2010), sponsorship is: 'a business relationship between a provider of funds, resources or services and an individual, event or organisation which offers in return rights and association that may be used for commercial advantage in return for the sponsorship investment'. According to the International Events Group (IEG) in 2015, $859 million were spent on the sponsorship of festivals, fairs and annual events in the USA, out of a total sponsorship market of $21.4 billion.

As more companies research their sponsorship activities, they forge better relationships with their sponsors. Some sponsorship managers have changed their job titles to 'relationship manager'

Image 7.1 **Virgin Racing media launch**
Credit: Jeff J. Mitchell/Getty Images

or 'partnership manager', to demonstrate the increased importance of their role. The practice of sponsoring events is well established. For instance, car manufacturers frequently supported early motor races by providing cars, expert mechanics or tyres at reduced cost because their association with the event helped to promote their core business to participants and spectators.

As the events market grows, so event managers must learn about the increasing cost-recovery possibilities that sponsorship presents. While sponsorship is a key function for some companies, the fact remains that the majority have not thought to use it as a marketing tool because they have not been approached by event managers.

7.4.1 Attracting sponsors

The first consideration for event managers who are looking to secure sponsorship is to ask how much money they might secure. Clearly, their goal is to try to get as much as possible in order to make the event more viable and ultimately more successful. The value of any sponsorship deal is subject to the following:

- How much coverage will the event receive in the media (press, radio, television, web)?
- Who will be taking part in the event?
- Who will attend the event?
- What, in particular (value), might the sponsor gain by supporting this event?
- What help could be provided to make the partnership a success, such as the number of staff who might be allocated to look after the sponsor at the event?

Finding the answers to these questions will depend on securing data from events through market research. Some of this data will be generated by the event organiser's own activities, while the rest might be found in secondary sources.

Increasingly, sponsors are interested in reaching people by electronic media, and an event organiser who is able to provide a list of contact details for attendees might stand a better chance of securing a deal. Perhaps one of the most important target groups for sponsorship is the media itself, with radio stations likely to be the most cooperative (Skinner and Rukavina 2003). Inviting media partners to be sponsors, even if this is only sponsorship in kind, means that they are much more likely to promote the event. This is invaluable in helping to raise the profile of an event and making it a more attractive proposition for other potential sponsors.

Media coverage is almost certainly the biggest driver of sponsorship deals for events, because it delivers a much bigger potential audience for the sponsor. While perhaps 100,000 people might attend an event and see the names of sponsors on billboards, the television audience – numbering in the millions, sometimes across many countries – has a much greater chance of increasing awareness of the sponsor's brand. For instance, the Guinness Rugby World Cup was shown in around 150 countries to a combined television audience of around 3 billion (Rines 2002), and this level of exposure is obviously of interest to major sponsors. However, even without media coverage, and for any size of event, an understanding of how the event audience might be attractive to the sponsor can help to maximise the value of the sponsorship deal.

There are different levels of sponsorship, with the most important being title sponsorship. Here, the sponsor's name is inserted before the event title, such as the Pedigree Chum United Kingdom Dog Show. Other levels of sponsorship enable more sponsorship partners to be recruited. In addition to the main title sponsor, different sponsors might be secured for specific parts of the event. These will receive less coverage and fewer benefits. Finally, minor sponsors might provide catering and refreshments.

An event organiser should always ask the question, 'What can I do for my sponsor(s)?', not 'What can the sponsor(s) do for me?' The organiser of a relatively new music festival is likely to view their 5,000 customers simply as lovers of music, and perhaps as passionate supporters of the event, but these people will have other interests and leisure activities, and they will consume many other products and services. A well-maintained database might highlight that they are predominantly middle class and that they are interested in travel and holidays. These event attendees would therefore be of great interest to a travel company that sells adventure holidays. A mail-out to these music lovers – as an official sponsor of their music festival, with an enclosed discount voucher – might easily generate 50 leads. If the company subsequently managed to sell just five holidays as a result, that would probably more than recoup the money it paid in sponsorship. Of course, this promotion would also increase awareness of the sponsor's core business and might well lead to future enquiries, making it even more financially beneficial. If the event organiser were to provide a hospitality package for the holiday company, enabling it to introduce some of its best clients to one of the bands, this would add even more value to the deal.

7.4.2 Developing the event sponsorship plan

Securing sponsorship for an event starts with a sponsorship plan to highlight what the event can offer a sponsor and the likely cost of the deal. A useful starting point is to produce a list of the costs of the event to see where it might be better to secure sponsorship in kind. Hiring a hall to put on the event might eat into the budget, so securing a sponsorship in kind with an organisation that has the use of a hall would be a good idea. Another example is Lucozade's sponsorship in kind of the London Marathon. The company provides the thousands of drinks that are handed out to runners during this gruelling event.

It is crucial to research potential sponsors. This type of investigation should uncover important information that will enable the event manager to find areas of mutual interest, but it might also prevent potentially embarrassing associations. As the number of sponsorship deals increases, more companies now issue guidelines on what they expect from a sponsorship deal (Stotlar 2005). These guidelines usually show that a company has experience in the sponsorship market, so they are very useful for any event organiser who is in the process of drafting sponsorship proposals.

Study activity

List the key factors that you would need to present to a drinks company if you wanted them to sponsor a musical event that will attract an audience of 5,000 people, mainly female and between the ages of 18 and 30. What would you expect the level of sponsorship to be for your event?

7.4.3 Setting event sponsorship objectives

Having researched potential sponsors, the event manager can begin to develop appropriate objectives for the proposed sponsorship plan, which will outline the benefits of the sponsorship

Image 7.2 **Budweiser advertisements at a baseball game**
Credit: John Grieshop/Getty Images

deal. In many cases, the person dealing with the proposal in the sponsor's organisation will not be the ultimate decision-maker, so providing them with a clear list of potential benefits should make their job of convincing their boss to approve the deal that much easier.

Sponsorship objectives must be realistic, and where possible should be measurable. For instance, if the aim is to raise awareness of the sponsor's name, a pre-event survey will show what current awareness levels are, and then subsequent surveys can be carried out during and after the event to provide evidence of the sponsorship's effectiveness.

Some potential sponsorship objectives are:

- To increase awareness levels of a company's products/services (Rines 2002).
- To demonstrate new or improved products to clients in an exclusive environment (Rines 2002; Skinner and Rukavina 2003).
- To improve the company's image (Sneath *et al.* 2005).
- To incentivise the workforce (Rines 2002; Stotlar 2005).
- To motivate/recruit/retain the workforce (Rines 2002; Skinner and Rukavina 2003).
- To develop better working relationships with distributors (Rines 2002).
- To improve relationships with the press (Rines 2002).
- To increase global exposure (Stotlar 2005).
- To increase sales (via product sampling) (Stotlar 2005).

More than one of these can be achieved in one deal. Perhaps the most popular objective is to increase levels of awareness of the sponsor's brand, but sponsors increasingly expect more than just this (Rines 2002).

Attendees are more likely to view a company more favourably as a result of its sponsorship of an event. For example, as many as 57 per cent of attendees said that their opinion of a motor manufacturer had improved after a six-day charitable event in the USA that attracted over 750,000 spectators (Sneath *et al.* 2005). Increasingly, evaluation services are being offered by specialist agencies, who can help to provide the data that event organisers need to provide to potential sponsors, but of course the cost of hiring agencies has to be included in the marketing budget.

7.4.4 Preparing the sponsorship proposal

In order to inform new potential sponsors of what they might gain from sponsoring an event, the management team must draw up a sponsorship proposal. This will communicate to the potential sponsor the precise benefits of sponsoring the event and how much cash or sponsorship in kind they will be expected to provide. It should also explain why they will achieve a much better return on their investment through sponsorship than they would from traditional advertising or sales promotions (Solomon 2002). A survey in the United States showed that around 55 per cent of all new sponsorship deals were secured as a result of a cold call to a potential sponsor (IEG Survey 2001, cited in Stotlar 2005). Ideally, a sponsorship proposal should cover the following areas (adapted from Solomon 2002):

- Exclusivity – Proposed sponsor to be the only one from their product category.
- Television – Specify the minimum amount of TV coverage for the sponsor.
- Signage – State how many signs the sponsor will be allowed to place at the event.
- Entertainment – Indicate how many hospitality options and free tickets are included in the deal.

- Display/merchandise – Indicate which merchandise options are available to the sponsor.
- Promotions/public relations – List the sponsor's access to event promotions and PR activities.
- Advertising – Detail how the sponsor's logo will be used in event advertising.
- Cost – How much the deal is worth and when the money should be paid.

These categories are the minimum that a potential sponsor will require; they should be comprehensive enough to protect both the sponsor and the event organiser; and they will form the basis of the sponsorship contract. Increasingly, sponsors demand exclusivity and are not prepared to share sponsorship with a company from the same industry. A sponsor will pay more for an event with media coverage, so a guarantee of a minimum level of media exposure might need to be specified. Sponsors often insert clauses into their contracts which specify minimum levels of media coverage. Therefore, the amount of space that will be in view of the media must be included, particularly if the names of other sponsors are going to appear in view at the same time. The total number of entry tickets to be included as part of the deal must be clarified in order to enable the sponsor to plan exactly who will benefit from them. Sponsors generally expect to be able to hand out publicity about their company, and in some cases give out samples, so the proposal must state exactly what they will be entitled to do. Using the sponsor's name in any advertising, promotion or public relations activities must be considered so that the sponsor gains more value from the deal.

When the drinks company Allied Domecq sponsored the Royal Shakespeare Company in 1995, its aim was to improve its image by linking with such a high-profile and prestigious company. It was also able to put on a special event in New York, where it entertained key stakeholders, including diplomats and politicians. This helped the company to develop better relationships with its stakeholders but in a more relaxed and stimulating environment, while showing that it had a working relationship with one of the most celebrated arts organisations in the world (Skinner and Rukavina 2003).

7.4.5 Creative sponsorship strategies

Some of the biggest sponsorship deals are now struck over naming rights of venues. For instance, the Sheffield Events Arena was sponsored by a local radio station and is now called the Hallam FM Arena and the major event arena in Los Angeles is named the Staples Center, after the office supplies company.

Increasingly, though, companies are looking to develop more innovative sponsorship strategies. When the National Westminster Bank sponsored cricket in England, it used a corporate social responsibility strategy to try to position its brand at the heart of the community. It designed a 'Cricket Community' road show, which invited local children to try cricket for the first time, with research showing 85 per cent of people thought that it had encouraged more children to take up sports. The amount of publicity that these events generated was important, but the fact that the bank was involved in such a project also helped to change the perception of some of its stakeholders.

It is important to manage relationships with sponsors. Early sponsorship deals were secured as a result of personal preferences within the sponsoring company, rather than for commercial reasons. When a local engineering firm sponsored an annual music festival, it was often as a result of a decision made by a director of the company who wished to support his partner's favourite event, rather than for sound commercial reasons. Of course, an engineering firm might receive considerable benefits by sponsoring such an event, but such an investment needs to be made as a result of effective research.

Many successful sponsorship deals now involve 'activation' – an amount of money that a sponsoring company invests above its initial sponsorship payment. According to Performance Research, after making a £1 million sponsorship payment, a company might find it beneficial to invest another £3 million to promote and support their sponsorship of an event (cited in Stotlar 2005: 38).

Companies often use sponsorship agents to help them to find the best match. Fiona Green, a sponsorship consultant with over twenty years' experience in the field, brokers deals between companies and potential sponsors. When representing an organisation that is interested in sponsorship, she compiles a list of events and compares these with the potential sponsor's objectives. She then contacts the managers of the most appropriate events to see if they can strike a deal. Such is the importance of this process that sponsorship agents are never mentioned once they have linked up a sponsor with a new partner.

7.4.6 Evaluating event sponsorship

Evaluating the effectiveness of sponsorship shows sponsors that their main objectives have been met, and, hopefully, exceeded. However, a budget for these activities must be agreed in advance. For larger sponsors, these services are usually provided as part of a comprehensive package by companies like the International Events Group (IEG). Smaller sponsors might also contract out some of their evaluation, but invariably they carry out their own research as part of their overall market research activities.

One of the most important techniques for assessing the impact of a sponsor's activities is to measure the amount of publicity generated, as shown in Table 7.3. The most frequently used measurement is the advertising equivalency of publicity (AEP). The exposure of the sponsor's brand on television is measured against the cost of buying the same amount of time in a TV advert. If, for example, Euronics sponsors the Ideal Homes Exhibition, which is then featured on television, the amount of time that the sponsor's name appears is recorded. According to the IEG, this is based on the amount of time that the brand name appears in shot, as long as it is at least 75 per cent visible (Lagae 2005). If the brand name appears in a prime-time television show for thirty seconds, then the AEP is the same as a thirty-second advertising slot during that programme. If the cost of placing a thirty-second advert is £40,000, then the AEP is £40,000. If this appears in five different countries, calculations must be made for each of those markets. Similarly, if the brand name appears in a half-page story in a magazine, and the cost of a half-page advert is £5,000, then the AEP is £5,000. Clearly, the simple appearance of a brand name does not have the same impact as an advert, but it is a recognised form of measurement. Keeping cuttings and files from press articles and social media coverage and presenting them to the potential sponsor is one way of showing them how they will benefit from event sponsorship.

Other evaluation techniques include interviewing important stakeholders, such as participants, to test their view of the sponsorship and their attitude to the brand. For larger groups, a survey will also provide important feedback. Sponsorship packages that direct participants to a website can be measured by the number of visitors to that website and the degree of movement around it.

When Guinness sponsored the Rugby World Cup in 1999, one of its principal objectives was to create a consistent global identity, which it believed sponsorship could deliver more cost-effectively than advertising. The cost of advertising in all countries exposed to the event was much higher than creating similar levels of exposure through sponsorship (Rines 2002).

Table 7.3 Sponsorship evaluation techniques

Aims of sponsoring events	Techniques for measuring the impact of sponsorship
To increase awareness levels of product/ service and company (Rines 2002)	Survey to measure percentage recall of the sponsor's involvement with the event, based on prompted brand awareness Media exposure measurement based on time on television and radio and the number of column inches in publications
To demonstrate new products or improved products to clients in an exclusive environment (Rines 2002; Skinner and Rukavina 2003)	Feedback from participants or attendees to gain their views about new products shown
To improve company image	Collect press cuttings and record the number of mentions as well as the audience or readership of the media where cuttings appear
To incentivise the workforce (Rines 2002; Stotlar 2005)	Staff attitude survey or interviews about proposed sponsorship
To motivate, recruit/retain the workforce (Rines 2002; Skinner and Rukavina 2003)	Staff surveys and interviews as part of appraisal
To develop better working relationships with distributors (Rines 2002)	Formal and informal feedback from distributors who attend the event Measure the increase in sales, or sales leads, as a result of sponsoring the event
To involve the local community	Interview key stakeholders Survey local community
To create a global identity (Rines 2002)	Measure the impact of media coverage on a global basis

Study activity

What are the main threats that an event manager will face when trying to secure sponsorship for the first time?

7.4.7 Building loyalty and sponsor networks

Even though the sponsorship market is growing, unfortunately, for event managers, sponsors do not always continue to sponsor the same event. If the principal aim of the deal was to increase awareness of the brand and this has been achieved, a sponsor might choose another marketing communications activity that will help to generate new sales leads. Others do not renew their deals if the sponsorship has not delivered the expected benefits. Event managers must take this into consideration and develop effective working relationships with their sponsors. As a minimum, they should produce an annual report with feedback about the impact of the sponsorship deal, and collaborate with the sponsor throughout the year.

Other, more innovative ideas are to hold a party for the sponsor to celebrate the relationship and to give gifts, such as signed photographs or other tangible mementos of the event (Skinner and Rukavina 2003). It is also important, if possible, to sign long-term agreements with sponsors, or to renew contracts if the partnership has been beneficial. In some cases, encouraging staff and participants to buy the sponsor's products is a simple way of rewarding the sponsor for their investment.

7.4.8 Ethical and legal considerations in event sponsorship

Event organisers are under increasing pressure not to associate with controversial sponsors. When tobacco companies were banned from advertising on television in the 1970s, they turned to the sponsorship of major events, predominantly sports, in an attempt to ensure that their brand names received continued media exposure. However, now, while Formula One teams are still sponsored by tobacco companies, they are not allowed to show the sponsor's name or logo when they compete in France (Stotlar 2005). This legislation also extends to the large fleets of vehicles that are used to transport team equipment from event to event. There is also more pressure on event organisers not to work with sponsors from the booming online betting industry, and there has even been some discussion about accepting sponsorship from fast-food companies. While these companies are not yet affected by legislation, it is important to monitor current opinion and to be clear about how this type of sponsorship impacts on brand image.

Event organisers should also be aware of ethical considerations when choosing their sponsors. While a local school might be happy to receive £20,000 to help in the staging of its annual swimming gala, is it acceptable for a local fast-food outlet to sponsor the event, given the current problem of childhood obesity? It is sometimes difficult to find the right answers to such questions, especially when large sums of money are involved, but the event organiser should always be aware of the danger of negative publicity.

Ambush marketing represents a threat to sponsorship agreements, and event managers must be prepared to protect the interests of their sponsors. An ambush marketer creates marketing communications at or near an event to convince stakeholders that they are an official sponsor, even though they are not. Thus, an organiser must take steps to prevent attendees from displaying the brand names of non-sponsoring organisations. Event personnel might be instructed to confiscate any non-sponsor branded items, to stop them from being filmed by television cameras or photographed by the press inside the venue. This created a stir at the World Cup in Germany in 2006, when Dutch football supporters were instructed to remove branded dungarees that had been handed out by a non-sponsor, leaving the fans to watch the match in just their underpants.

A few years later, the major computer game manufacturer Nintendo chose not to attend the Nuremberg International Toy Fair, but it ambushed the event by driving a mobile promotional van through the centre of the city during the week of the event.

Sustainability at UK rural music festivals – sustainability as a way of selling sponsorship for festival and event managers

Keep Me Local: Sustainable Festival Services – by Edmund Bell-King

Festival organisers and other event managers are under increasing pressure to tackle issues of sustainability and this case study considers a new Keep Me Local Limited (KML) sustainability service that is being offered to UK festival promoters. These services are primarily designed to assist festival promoters and their UK brand partners to capture event-goer mindshare and to encourage sustainable personal behaviour before, during and after rural music festival events. From the point of view of raising the awareness of events and as part of the overall marketing plan, it is essential to present a more sustainable festival or event.

The UK summer rural music festival market has grown rapidly over the last twenty years. However, this growth has come at an environmental cost. Rural festival venues generate significant logistical, supply chain and travel-related carbon emissions and attendant air pollution.

UK festivalgoers generate their own external and festival-related emissions, particularly through their personal travel to and from the event. If looked at holistically, travel-related energy use is, by far, the largest single emissions factor related to the carbon generated around rural UK music festivals. This is not surprising since locating a music festival at a rural venue leads directly to higher personal travel emissions because the use of carbon-efficient, high-capacity, end-to-end transport nodes is simply not always an option for those deciding to travel to rural locations. Indeed, festivalgoer travel-related emissions are rarely calculated or reported on as part of a Festivals Carbon Management Plan, being seen by promoters as an 'externality' to the event itself. However, the necessary travel by festivalgoers is directly related to the decision to attend a festival, which makes this the primary reason for the generation of emissions in the first instance. Therefore, it seems logical that festivalgoer travel-related emissions should be attributed to the overall carbon emissions footprint of each festival, and so should be included in the Carbon Management Plan.

Once festivalgoers arrive at a rural festival, they are essentially living 'off-grid' for the duration of the event. Accordingly, they will indirectly generate additional carbon emissions through their use of energy for power, provided by the festival promoters. Energy for power use is for both personal maintenance, such as, eating, drinking and shower and toilet use, as well as for tent lighting and recharging of personal electronic devices; a must for most festivalgoers.

While some of the local power sources available at rural festivals are increasingly using solar-powered technology, many still use diesel generators to provide primary or back-up 'base-load power' to ensure that all the likely festivalgoers' power needs are met.

In terms of charging personal electronic devices, many festival promoters have now put marketing agreements in place with brand partners to sponsor festivalgoer device-charging. Some brands have more recently started to 'gift' portable charging units to festivalgoers. However, these are mostly manufactured abroad and tend to have a lower specification; the quality of manufacture and usable lifespan may be shorter and more variable than expected. Taking this into account, it not surprising that these gifted units are seen by many festivalgoers as 'disposable' items, post-event, generating additional e-waste for the event promoter to have to deal with after everyone has gone home.

Finally, the logistics involved to supply heating and serve food and drinks at rural festivals also has carbon-related emissions. While these emissions are included in a Festivals Carbon Management Plan, their point of origin and traceability through the supply chain, to the extent to which their 'food miles' contribute to festival emissions, cannot currently be tracked by festivalgoers. Ideally, festivalgoers should be made aware of the provenance of all food and drink they consume at a festival. Certainly, as things currently stand, little effort has gone into seeing if connecting local food and drink supply chains could reduce the overall footprint of these rural music festivals.

The recent growth, and often, unsustainable nature of many festival activities, both internal and external to the event, create potential unnecessary emissions. This opaqueness has attracted an ever-increasing level of concern and criticism, voiced both in the media, and by festivalgoers themselves. In response, both the industry association and individual festival promoters have started to seek new ways to engage with and educate festival audiences to encourage more sustainable behaviour before, during and after the event experience. They are also becoming more transparent themselves in terms of carbon emissions when embarking on event planning and management. The KML Sustainable Festival Services includes:

1 A highly sustainable (zero-emissions, zero e-waste) free device-charging service that is both a simple and fast charging option for festivalgoers. This service neatly eliminates the device power-down recharging headache for festivalgoers, who are, effectively, living 'off-grid' for the duration of their stay at rural music festivals with limited access to normal power outlets.
2 The service also offers sponsoring brand partners engagement opportunities with pre-registered festivalgoers, before they have even attended an event, by inviting them to become carbon neutral in terms of their travel and event attendance emissions to and from the festival of their choice.
3 Brand and retailer engagement with both individuals and self-aggregating groups attending rural festivals, via a KML/brand-sponsored gamification

app that gives prizes and rewards to individuals or groups for sustainable activities, such as personally going 'festival carbon neutral' by supporting the ColaLight Project. To enable this, the app allows pre-registered festivalgoers to calculate and offset their likely means of travel and routing with a standardised festival emissions footprint. Offsetting of combined travel/festival emissions is provided through the purchase of carbon credits from the ColaLight Project via the KML carbon management module from their device.

Keep Me Local will also offer key brand partners/festival promoters an audience engagement app experience that has sustainability gamification at its core. Subscribing brands will be teamed up with UK Festival Association partners to deliver a festival-specific sustainability app experiences across multiple UK music festivals. Clearly, this will receive exposure overseas since a number of attendees at these festivals will attend from other countries. What follows is one suggestion for addressing sustainability.

Recharging options

Festivalgoers can recharge their batteries with a brand-sponsored charging-unit and pay a small fee as a contribution, which at only £2 per day could generate as much as £40,000 at major festivals. This money would then be given to crowd-funding projects such as ColaLight and this can be match-funded by the brand partner. Each time a user recharges, their social media account will be updated and a message of thanks for their donation can be sent. This also enables them to be considered for a prize draw.

Clearly, these projects offer the festival and event organiser a chance to tackle issues of sustainability and encourage attendees to consider what their impact is at the event. A small donation for recharging reduces the impact on the environment and enables brand partners to communicate directly with festival and event attendees, while also benefiting the environment. Of course, this may vary in different countries, but it is certainly an issue that event managers should explore before it becomes legislation.

Study activity

1 How would you incorporate sustainability into your marketing objectives for an event?
2 How would you incorporate sustainability into your marketing activities and how much should it feature in your promotional activities?
3 How could you use sustainability as a way of attracting more sponsorship for your event?

Industry voice

Deepak Trivedi, Global Sports Management Consultant

I have worked in the sports industry for over fifteen years with high-profile and world-class, global sporting events. My career has focused primarily on the sport of tennis, though I have also worked within basketball, soccer and had leadership roles for both London 2012 and Rio 2016 Olympic Games. I currently serve on the board of directors for Tennis in New York and am the vice chair for the New York Open. In addition, I serve as a consultant on the International committees for several sports governing bodies and institutions.

The organisation of world-class sporting events is more important than it has ever been. There are now more sports products, services and brands then there have ever been before. Sporting events have become opportunities to build themselves as a brand in the eyes of the consumer and, therefore, establish themselves in order to build a successful and sustainable legacy.

This means that, in effect, the way that the event is organised is as important as the event itself. The event has to ensure that it aligns itself with the appropriate sponsors that match the events values and brand association. This should be viewed as an opportunity, for example, the US Open tennis event has many high-end sponsors, such as Emirates Airlines and Ralph Lauren. These are brands that share similar values and appeal as the event's attendees.

The management of volunteers is crucial in sporting events management. Most sports events, both domestically and internationally, use volunteers as part of the human resources element. However, there are many challenges that exist when events use volunteers. It is essential to ensure that volunteers remain motivated and stimulated in their work, with job rotation where possible to keep their work interesting, and ensure that they are trained to understand the service values of the event. As is the case with paid workers, they are also effectively event 'ambassadors' and therefore a representation as the 'face' of the event.

The service element is key. Think about the first moment you walk through the gates at one of Disney's theme parks . . . what happens? You are revived by loud, cheerful, energetic Disney ambassadors with smiles the size of Snow White's castle! Why? Because it works! They are setting you up for an unforgettable day, full of amazing memories with those nearest and dearest to you. Every person you encounter is part of your memorable experience. Service industries have set the benchmark when it comes to this. Consider the legendary, luxury hotel chain . . . The Ritz Carlton. Their corporate credo 'We are ladies and gentleman serving ladies and gentlemen' has set the tone for all guest and associate interaction. The second you walk into a lobby of a Ritz Carlton hotel, you 'feel' the service culture and commitment to excellence that is synonymous with their brand. And, it keeps customers coming back!

The sports industry has learned from these examples. Sports fans, too, want more experiences! This helps to appeal to the wide-ranging and more interactive fans who are attending more sporting events. Organisations and events are consciously and consistently identifying opportunities to use sponsorship, volunteer engagement, fan experience and a commitment to delivering service values to create the event's identity, image and culture. Many of today's factors, such as the widespread emergence of social media, developments in superior technologies and the changing nature of the typical sports fan, are constantly causing the event marketing and management landscape to evolve. However, there needs to be a committed, strategic approach to how these factors are incorporated within the events if event organisers and management are to achieve their desirable outcomes.

7.5 Summary

To gain an understanding of what event consumers require from an event experience, it is necessary to investigate what role the event plays in their lives, and which emotions are associated with that experience. Events are about lifestyle, excitement and escapism from day-to-day life; they must be memorable and an important ingredient in the lives of attendees. This requires a new approach to research and marketing planning to ensure that organisers cater for both consumers and key stakeholders, who can contribute to the success of the event. Event managers must ensure that research is at the heart of everything they do when planning an event. They must work hard to develop the event's brand image and must be willing to improve factors that impact on service quality. More attention needs to be paid to pricing and promotion, as well as to new technologies that can improve overall customer satisfaction. There are a bewildering number of social media options available and these should feature in your marketing activities, and event managers should be fully conversant with how to use them or else employ people who can.

Growing numbers of event managers are now dependent on sponsors for funding, so they must find ways to improve relationships with these companies. An ability to attract sponsorship might well be the difference between success and failure, so more resources must be devoted to sponsorship evaluation and innovative sponsorship strategies that will make potential sponsors even keener to invest in events.

Further reading

Fink, J. S., Trail, G. T. and Anderson D. E. (2002) Environmental Factors Associated with Spectator Attendance and Sport Consumption Behaviour: Gender and Team Differences, *Sport Marketing Quarterly*, 11: 8–19. This important article explores sports fans' consumption during sporting events and features the previously under-researched area of female attendance at events.

Holden, P. R. (2008) *Virtually Free Marketing*, London: A & C Black. This is an important textbook that covers the significant issues relating to social media; an increasingly crucial area in events management.

McDonald, M., Mouncey, P. and Maklan, S. (2014) *Marketing Value Metrics: A New Metrics Model to Measure Marketing Effectiveness*, London: Kogan Page.

O'Neill, M., Getz, D. and Carlsen, J. (1999) Evaluation of Service Quality at Events: The 1998 Coca-Cola Masters Surfing Event at Margaret River, Western Australia, *Managing Service*

Quality, 9 (3): 156–165. This is one of the first articles to consider the importance of service quality as part of an overall marketing plan in events management, with clear suggestions for future research in this area.

References

Allen, J., O'Toole, W., Harris, R. and McDonnell, I. (2011) *Festival and Special Events Management*, New Jersey: John Wiley & Sons.

BDS (2010) Sponsorship. Available at: www.sponsorship.co.uk/in_sponsorship/in_sponsorship. htm. Accessed 31 October 2011.

Blythe, J. (2009) *Principles and Practice of Marketing*, Hampshire: Cengage Learning.

Booms, B. and Bitner, J. (1981) Marketing Strategies and Organizational Structures for Service Firms, in J. Donnelly and W. George (eds) *Marketing of Services*, Chicago: American Marketing Association.

Bowdin, G., Allen, J., O'Toole, W., Harris, R. and McDonnell, I. (2011) *Events Management* (4th edn), Oxford: Butterworth-Heinemann.

Burton, M. (2011) Mike Burton Events Management Company. Available at: www.mikeburton. com. Accessed 14 June 2011.

Chaffey, D., Ellis-Chadwick, F., Johnston, K. and Mayer, R. (2006) *Internet Marketing: Strategy, Implementation and Practice*, London: Prentice Hall.

De Pelsmacker, P., Geuens, M. and Van den Burgh, J. (2010) *Marketing Communications: A European perspective*, London: Prentice Hall.

Goldblatt, J. (2011) *Special Events: A New Generation and the Next Frontier*, New Jersey: John Wiley & Sons.

Holden, P. R. and Wilde, N. P. (2007) *Marketing and PR*, London: A & C Black.

Hoyle, L. H. (2002) *Event Marketing: How to Successfully Promote Events, Festivals, Conventions and Expositions*, New York: John Wiley & Sons.

Kahle, L. R., Kambara, K. M. and Rose, G. M. (1996) A Functional Model of Fan Attendance Motivations for College Football, *Sport Marketing Quarterly*, 5 (4): 51–60.

Kim, N. and Chalip, L. (2004) Why Travel to the FIFA World Cup? Effects of Motives, Background, Interest and Constraints, *Tourism Management*, 25: 695–707.

Lagae, W. (2005) *Sports Sponsorship and Marketing Communications: A European Perspective*, London: Prentice Hall.

Lovelock, C. and Gummerson, E. (2004) Whither Services Marketing? In Search of a New Paradigm and Fresh Perspectives, *Journal of Service Research*, 7 (1): 20–41.

McDonald, M. and Wilson, H. (2011) *Marketing Plans: How to Prepare Them, How to Use Them* (7th edn), London: John Wiley & Sons.

Melnick, M. J. (1993) Searching for Sociability in the Stands: A Theory of Sports Spectating, *Journal of Sport Management*, 7, 1: 44–60.

Mintel (2006) *Sponsorship*, London: Mintel International Group Ltd.

Mintel (2009) *Sports Sponsorship*, London: Mintel International Group Ltd.

Nicholson, R. E. and Pearce, D. G. (2001) Why Do People Attend Events: A Comparative Analysis of Visitor Motivations at Four South Island Events, *Journal of Travel Research*, 39: 449–460.

Rines, S. (2002) Guinness Rugby World Cup Sponsorship: A Global Platform for Meeting Business Objectives, *International Journal of Sports Marketing and Sponsorship*, 4: 449–465.

Skinner, B. E. and Rukavina, V. (2003) *Event Sponsorship*, New York: John Wiley & Sons.

Sneath, J. Z., Zachary Finney, R. and Close, A. G. (2005) An IMC Approach to Event Marketing: The Effects of Sponsorship and Experience on Customer Attitudes, *Journal of Advertising Research*, December: 373–381.

Solomon, J. (2002) *An Insider's Guide to Managing Sporting Events*, Champaign: Human Kinetics.

Stotlar, D. (2005) *Developing Successful Sports Marketing Plans*, Morgantown: Fitness Information Technology.

Topping, A., Collinson, P. and Walsh, F. (2011) Olympics: Man Gets £11,000 of Tickets after Bidding for £36,000, *Guardian*. Available at: www.guardian.co.uk/sport/2011/jun/01/olympics-man-wins-tickets-bidding. Accessed 12 June 2017.

Wakefield, K. L. (2007) *Team Sports Marketing*, Oxford: Butterworth-Heinemann.

Chapter 8

Event health, safety and risk management

Contents

8.1 Aims

By the end of this chapter, students will be able to:

- understand key health, safety and risk management terminology;
- evaluate the health, safety and risk legal and moral obligations associated with managing events;
- explain the process of risk management at events;
- analyse in detail three of the key risks associated with events.

8.2 Introduction

Within the events industry, the perception of health, safety and risk issues is changing fast. In the past, there has been a tendency to view health and safety issues as 'red-tape' bureaucracy that merely ticks regulatory boxes while creating extra work for the already stressed event manager.

However, over the past fifteen years, the importance of health, safety and risk has been accentuated by many high-profile event disasters that could, conceivably, have been prevented if correct health, safety and risk procedures were in place. These issues have been covered extensively in the media and have resulted in governments and industry bodies seeking to regulate against future problems by increasing legislation.

The difficulty of balancing health and safety requirements with the provision of exciting events is becoming a significant challenge as laws and regulations grow at the same speed as innovations and experience opportunities. The industry strives to juggle both aspects, driven by the desire to put on a good but safe show. As the UK events management industry bodies AEO, BECA and EVA (2002: 9) suggest: 'There is no great mystery in managing Health and Safety on-site, but there is a skill in managing it well – especially whilst retaining the all-important WOW! factor.'

There are three elements to managing health and safety matters correctly: first, the management of health, safety and risk prevents or reduces accidents and near misses on-site; second, correct management prevents litigation, claims, fines, imprisonment and bad press for the event organisation; and third, risk assessment and health and safety compliance are often legal requirements.

8.2.1 Guiding principles

For industry professionals, the essential principle to understand is that health, safety and risk management is a key part of event planning. It should be factored in from the very start of the process and should be considered during every part of the planning process.

There are four key principles relating to health and safety that every event organiser should bear in mind. These are summarised in Figure 8.1.

8.2.2 Impacts of health, safety and risk-related incidents

Health, safety and risk-related incidents at events can have wide-ranging and often disastrous impacts. Without proper attention to health, safety and risk management, event organisers expose their audience, their colleagues and their contractors to injury and loss of life.

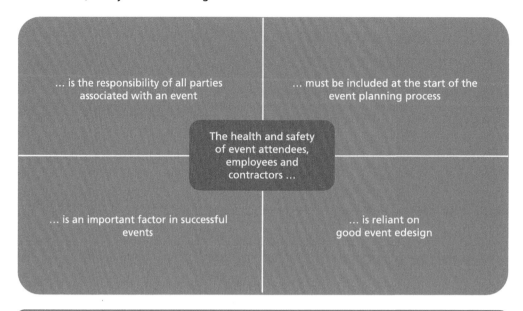

... is the responsibility of all parties associated with an event

... must be included at the start of the event planning process

The health and safety of event attendees, employees and contractors ...

... is an important factor in successful events

... is reliant on good event edesign

Figure 8.1 The importance of health and safety at events

A small-scale incident, such as a person tripping and falling, can result in a loss of event focus since the audience is distracted by the incident. This loss of focus will affect the audience's perceptions of the event and may result in issues with stakeholders, who will be unhappy with the shift in focus, away from their key messages. Such small-scale incidents can therefore impact on the future effectiveness of an event, so their importance should not be dismissed.

Study activity

You are an event manager of a small-scale local event. During the event, a child trips over a cable and breaks her leg. The local newspaper runs the story and questions the safety of your event.

Write a list of ways in which you can respond to this incident, which will help you to recover some of your reputation for running a safe event. Whereas small-scale incidents can have serious ramifications, it is the large-scale incidents that will cause the most problems for the event organisation. It is important to remember that these health, safety and risk-related incidents can also have devastating and ruinous results. The media may report the incident, resulting in negative publicity, changes in the local mood towards the event and a shift in worldwide perceptions. One example of this was the 2010 tragedy at the Love Parade in Germany, which resulted in 19 deaths, worldwide negative publicity and the eventual dissolution of the event. (For news reviews and footage of this disaster, see the YouTube sources list at the end of the chapter.)

Another large-scale event disaster was the Shoreham air show crash that took place in South East England in August 2015. A vintage jet aircraft crashed while doing a display over land, killing 11 people and injuring 16 others. This tragedy led to the Civil Aviation Authority announcing certain restrictions on displays over land, which resulted in the cancellation of or fundamental changes to displays at airshows across the UK.

A large-scale event disaster occurred when the *Marchioness* leisure boat sank in 1989. The boat was hosting a private party with 131 people on board when it collided with a large dredger. The pleasure boat sank almost immediately and 51 people drowned. According to Hartley (2002), the long-awaited public inquiry blamed almost everyone involved, including the Department of Transport, the captains of both vessels, the companies that managed them and the police. This inquiry eventually led to the Department of Transport carrying out a comprehensive Formal Safety Assessment of River Thames passenger vessels (later extended to all operating environments for domestic passenger ships in the UK). This covered every aspect of their safety, including 'their encounter risk with large ships and bridges, fire risk, stability, subdivision, freeboard, visibility, life-saving appliances, means of escape, manning, passenger numbers, trading areas and safety management' (Maritime and Coastguard Agency 2005: 1).

8.2.3 Key areas of health, safety and risk for the average event

This textbook demonstrates that every event is unique and needs particular attention and consideration. However, it is useful to note some key areas of event planning that need a particular focus from a health, safety and risk perspective. These can range from significant aspects of event planning – venue and site design – to circumstantial issues, such as refreshments and sanitation (HSE 2014).

Some of the key areas for event organisers to consider are:

- control of hazardous substances
- communication procedures
- crowd management
- electrical installations and lighting, including special effects and pyrotechnics
- facilities for people with special needs
- fire safety
- food, drink and water
- noise and vibration
- major incident (emergency) planning
- medical, ambulance and first-aid management
- performers, TV and media
- sanitary and waste facilities and management
- structures and barriers
- transport management
- venue and site design and management. (List adapted from HSE 1999: 3)

Later in this chapter, three specific risks of particular interest to event managers will be discussed in detail.

As well as the individual areas that need health, safety and risk management, it is important that event organisers consider the event phases and the safety implications for each. These phases can be represented as the build-up (pre-planning); load-in (set-up of the event); show (the event itself); load-out (dismantling equipment); and breakdown (dismantling the venue or the final processes of leaving the venue, as appropriate). These phases and the safety implications for each are shown in Figure 8.2.

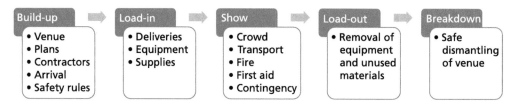

Figure 8.2 Event safety phases

8.2.4 Legal requirements

The regulations, laws and legislation that event organisers are required to adhere to vary from country to country, but it is essential that organisers understand their legal obligations. An event organiser must understand the laws and regulations in both the country where their organisation is based *and* the country where the event will take place – often, there are marked differences between the two. It is essential that anyone involved in events management is clear on the legal responsibility that they have in relation to compliance with health and safety legislation because, in the majority of cases, this responsibility will rest with the event organiser (HSE 1999: 167).

CASE STUDY 8.1

Government responsibilities: The Colectiv Nightclub, Bucharest, Romania

On 30 October 2015, a fire broke out at a Romanian nightclub after a spark from a pyrotechnics show ignited foam décor. Forty-five people died and dozens of others were injured. It is believed that up to 400 people may have been inside the club for the rock concert. Reports from concert goers suggested that there were only two exits and only one of these was initially open, with the audience having to break the second door down in order to escape.

The club's owners and city hall clerks, as well as the owners of the company that installed the fireworks that caused the fire were all either arrested or under investigation.

In an unexpected twist, the tragedy sparked protests in Bucharest, and led to the resignation and arrest of the local mayor. Protesters said that the mayor had granted a permit for the club, despite the fact that it had not being authorised by firefighters. This outcry in turn led to large-scale protests, which claimed that the government was corrupt. The result was the resignation of the prime minister and his government less than a week after the fire.

(www.bbc.co.uk/news/world-europe-34684973;
www.theguardian.com/world/2015/nov/07/romanian-prosecutors-
arrest-local-mayor-over-bucharest-nightclub-fire)

Legal issues are the foundation of all elements of event planning. The importance of operating within the rules set by government and local authorities must never be underestimated. Readers should consult the Event Operations chapter (Chapter 4), which covers legal issues relating to duty of care, responsibilities of event organisers, contract law and so on.

8.3 Health and safety legislation

Health and safety legislation changes continually, and it is often difficult to keep up to date with the latest amendments and additions to laws and regulations. It is essential, however, that event managers do so. Figure 8.3 gives some useful links to resources that contain the latest health and safety regulations around the world. Please note that these resources change frequently and may be out of date by the time of publishing. Up-to-date resources are easily found.

Study activity

Identify the key health and safety acts for your country. In pairs, discuss the key requirements of these acts in relation to the events industry.

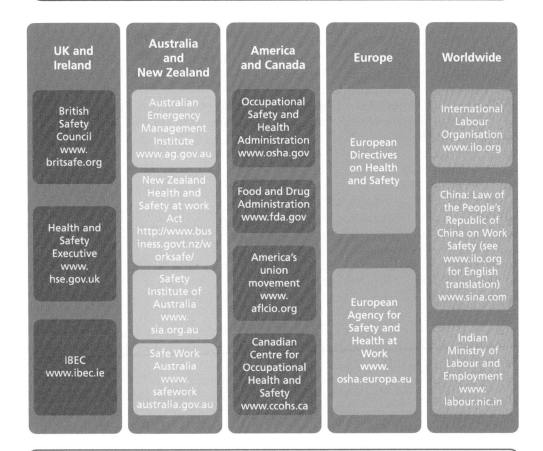

UK and Ireland	Australia and New Zealand	America and Canada	Europe	Worldwide
British Safety Council www.britsafe.org	Australian Emergency Management Institute www.ag.gov.au	Occupational Safety and Health Administration www.osha.gov	European Directives on Health and Safety	International Labour Organisation www.ilo.org
Health and Safety Executive www.hse.gov.uk	New Zealand Health and Safety at work Act http://www.business.govt.nz/worksafe/	Food and Drug Administration www.fda.gov		China: Law of the People's Republic of China on Work Safety (see www.ilo.org for English translation) www.sina.com
	Safety Institute of Australia www.sia.org.au	America's union movement www.aflcio.org	European Agency for Safety and Health at Work www.osha.europa.eu	
IBEC www.ibec.ie	Safe Work Australia www.safeworkaustralia.gov.au	Canadian Centre for Occupational Health and Safety www.ccohs.ca		Indian Ministry of Labour and Employment www.labour.nic.in

Figure 8.3 International resources for health and safety legislation

8.3.1 Regulations, licences and permits

Many of the myriad licences, permits and regulations that events operate within and around are related to health and safety. As already noted, these will differ from one country to the next, but they all have similar requirements. It is essential that the event manager checks these in detail at the start of the planning process. It is the responsibility of the event company to ensure that they have researched and are in compliance with the relevant requirements.

Many of the regulations, licences and permits relate to environmental issues (such as noise control); licences for temporary or personal activity; licences for premises; fire regulations; ambulance, medical and police provision; highways and traffic control; and general workplace health and safety. In the UK, guides issued by organisations such as the Association of Events Organisers (AEO), the Association of Event Venues (AEV) and the Event Supplier and Services Association (ESSA) are key resources. In particular, *The Guide to Managing Health and Safety at Exhibitions and Events* (AEO, BECA and EVA 2002) and the AEO, AEV and ESSA *E-Guide* (2010) should be read by event managers, as should the Health and Safety Executive's 'Events health and safety' website. The Emergency Management in Australia is a useful tool for event managers operating there, and other countries have similar resources that are equally easy to find. The AEO, BECA and EVA (2002: A1) guide lists UK regulations that need to be considered during the build-up, show and breakdown phases of an exhibition (these can be related directly to all other events; similar regulations exist in other countries):

- Health and Safety at Work etc. Act, 1974
- Management of Health and Safety at Work Regulations 1999
- Workplace (Health, Safety and Welfare) Regulations 1992
- Personal Protective Equipment at Work Regulations 1992
- Provision and Use of Work Equipment Regulations 1998
- Lifting Operations and Lifting Equipment Regulations (LOLER) 1998
- Manual Handling Operations Regulations 1992
- Fire Precautions (Workplace) Regulations 1997, as amended 1999
- Health and Safety (First Aid) Regulations 1981
- Reporting of Injuries, Diseases and Dangerous Occurrences Regulations (RIDDOR) 1995
- Electricity at Work Regulations 1998/EVA Regulations for Stand Electrical Installations
- Health and Safety (Signs and Signals) Regulations 1996
- Noise at Work Regulations 1989
- Building Regulations
- Building Standards (Scotland) Regulations
- Environmental Protection Act 1990/Environment Act 1995.

Additional codes of practice and guides to consider include:

- The Licensing Act 2003
- Guide to Fire Precautions in Existing Places of Entertainment and Like Premises 1990
- *Event Safety Guide* (a guide to health, safety and welfare at music and similar events which has now been turned into multiple webpages)
- NOEA's Code of Practice for Outdoor Events
- Temporary De-mountable Structures Guidance on Design Procurement and Use 1999
- Specific local authority regulations (your venue will be able to advise you about these)
- Health and Safety in Construction – HSE Publications HS(G)150.

This list is not exhaustive, and changes are often made, but it demonstrates the large number of issues that the event manager needs to consider at the start of every event. There is concern that the sheer volume of health and safety regulations is strangling some sectors of the industry – in particular, small-scale local community and cultural events. For instance, organisers of local street parties often find the myriad rules, regulations and legalities intimidating. They fear that they might face the cost of acquiring licences and permits, and worry about navigating the legal system, so it is hardly surprising that they frequently come to the conclusion that it is not worth the effort.

CASE STUDY 8.2

Licences and permits for street parties: The Big Lunch

Image 8.1 **The Queen's Diamond Jubilee, 2012 – street parties and celebrations were held throughout the UK**
Credit: Tim Graham/Getty Images

The UK has a long history of celebrating important occasions with our neighbours by hosting street parties. Some of the most notable street parties in the UK include those held on VE Day in 1945 and on the occasion of Queen Elizabeth's coronation in 1953, and in recent years to celebrate various royal weddings. However, such parties have declined in number, largely because of the significant increase in local council regulations relating to health and safety. In response to this, in 2009 an initiative called 'The Big Lunch' aimed to reignite interest in street parties. The organisers of the Eden Project launched this new scheme with the aim of getting as many people as possible to have lunch with their neighbours, encouraging acts of community spirit, engagement and fun (Big Lunch 2011).

They use the internet as a resource for local communities to try to make the organisation of a local street party as simple as possible. The website provides details about the type of insurance required, and tells communities how and when to approach their councils. It advises organisers to hold their events in private or community gardens to avoid the need for road closures, and gives guidance on whether there is a need for risk assessments and health and safety certificates. This advice falls in line with the industry view that local community events should be kept simple: small, private parties and local community events do not need risk assessments and certificates, but if anyone can attend or if tickets are sold, the other processes and requirements outlined in this chapter may come into play. In 2011, over a million people took part in The Big Lunch; by 2015 this had risen to 7.29 million.

For further information on The Big Lunch, see the YouTube sources or visit www.thebiglunch.com.

8.3.2 Health and Safety at Work etc. (HSW) Act 1974

This is the primary piece of legislation for health, safety and welfare of people at work within the UK and is an example of national legislation that affects the events industry. In Australia and the USA, similar legislation is the Occupational Safety and Health Acts. If there is no such legislation in the country where the event manager is operating, they should follow the procedures and requirements outlined in the HSW in order to develop their own code of practice.

The HSW sets out general principles of managing health and safety at work, and enables the creation of requirements through such regulations as the Control of Substances Hazardous to Health Regulations 2002 (COSHH) and the Management of Health and Safety at Work Regulations 1999 (MHSW). It explains the general duties that employers have to employees and members of the public, and the duties that employees have to themselves and to each other.

In the UK, this is the most important legislation to which the events industry must adhere. It makes it mandatory for all employees to conduct a risk assessment of their work activity (Upton 2008). It is, therefore, essential that each event manager and company has a grasp on the document and its key points. Specialist legal support should be sought, if necessary, and students working or living in other countries should be familiar with their own key pieces of legislation.

8.3.3 The Management of Health and Safety at Work Regulations (MHSW) 1999

The Management of Health and Safety at Work Regulations 1999 generally make employers' legal obligations with respect to health and safety much more explicit. Like the HSW, they apply to every work activity: 'The MHSW regulations have been put in place in order that you take care of all those you work in conjunction with – employees, contractors, clients or customers. The aim of the regulations is to reduce damage by assessing all potential risks and to create action plans for emergencies' (HSE 2003: 2). These regulations require employers to review risk assessments periodically, to ensure that they are familiar with hazards and risks in the workplace, to improve safety procedures at every opportunity and to ensure work is organised and training is offered (HSE 2003).

The regulations state that organisations have a legal duty to put in place suitable arrangements to manage health and safety. The HSE advocates a common-sense, practical approach that should be part of the everyday process of running an organisation – as such, they suggest organisations adopt the Plan, Do, Check, Act approach, which integrates health and safety into good management practices, rather than treating it as a stand-alone process. This approach can be summarised as:

- Plan – determine your policy and/or plan for implementation
- Do – identify the risks, organise for health and safety and implement your plan
- Check – monitor the performance and investigate after incidents
- Act – review the performance, act on lessons learnt. (HSE 2014)

8.3.4 Corporate manslaughter law

Legally, the event organisation often has responsibility for the safety of its employees. In the UK, this is covered by the Corporate Manslaughter and Corporate Homicide Act 2007. Event organisers operating in other countries should check their own laws on corporate responsibility in detail. These laws specify that adequate safety practices and procedures must be in place, and they allow for conviction if it can be proved beyond reasonable doubt that a company was homicidally reckless about risk (Slapper 2007). During events, this applies to the accidental death of both employees and attendees.

In 2008, there was a stampede of 2,000 people at the launch of a sale event at a Wal-Mart store in America, and an employee was trampled to death. The employee's family sued Wal-Mart in a wrongful-death lawsuit which claimed that the company had engaged in specific marketing and advertising techniques specifically to attract a large crowd and create an environment of frenzy and mayhem. In America, a wrongful-death case alleges that a person was killed as a result of another's negligence or other form of liability. The lawsuit was settled when Wal-Mart agreed to improve its crowd control for its day-after-Thanksgiving events,

Study activity

For non-UK students

Find the relevant corporate responsibility law or Act for your country and make a note of its exact name. Now, do the same for control of hazardous substances and safety at work legislation. Finally, identify the governing body for health and safety and note any other specific health and safety regulations for your country.

For UK students

What are the major differences between the Health and Safety at Work etc. Act 1974 and the Management of Health and Safety at Work Regulations 1999? Discuss your findings with another student.

and 'the world's largest retailer also agreed to set up a $400,000 victim's compensation fund, donate $1.5 million to the community and provide 50 jobs annually to high school students in the area' (Robideaux 2009; see also the YouTube sources).

8.4 Health and safety management

The information and advice in this section is based on *The Event Safety Guide* (HSE 1999) and from the Health and Safety Executive website on Event Health and Safety – both are essential reading for all events management students and organisers.

8.4.1 Key elements of successful health and safety management

As we have seen, legislation and regulation of health and safety have become paramount to the successful and safe delivery of any event. Once the event concept is developed, but *before the event manager proceeds any further*, it is essential that they turn their full attention to the management of health and safety before, during and after the event. This process begins with the creation of a health and safety policy.

AEO, BECA and EVA (2002: A2) advise the following procedures for the creation of a health and safety policy (they are concerned c hiefly with exhibitions, but their advice is relevant industry wide):

> Your policy and arrangements for managing Health and Safety on-site at your exhibition must be written down formally. Your Health and Safety Policy should be broken down into three major sections:
>
> 1 The policy statement
> 2 Organisation of the health and safety
> 3 The arrangements for the management of health and safety.

It is a legal requirement that employers with five or more employees produce a written health and safety policy. For UK students, templates of these policies can be found at www.hse.gov.uk.

Even if you are not required to have a health and safety policy, all event organisers should have, as a minimum, a safety plan. A safety plan identifies the following:

● Scale, type and scope of the event
● Type and size of audience
● Location
● Duration of the event
● Time of day and year the event will be held.

Using this information, event organisers can create risk assessments (see 8.6 for details).

Study activity

In groups of three or four, devise your own event concept, and, from that, create a safety plan. You will use this plan to create a risk assessment later in the chapter.

Once a safety plan or policy has been created, the event manager must ensure that it is put into practice. This involves the dissemination of the relevant parts of the policy to all relevant stakeholders, including all staff, the local authorities and government, suppliers, the venue and the customers. Once these stakeholders have been briefed, the event manager must monitor the ongoing delivery and performance of the health and safety policy and ensure that all aspects of it are implemented correctly, efficiently and within all legal requirements and available guidelines. The last part of the management of any health and safety policy happens after the event has finished. At this point, the policy should be fully reviewed and audited in order to assess its performance and management. Do not underestimate the importance of this. If the health and safety policy is not managed effectively, the event manager and their organisation may be held liable for any accidents or issues that arise during the event.

8.4.2 Responsibilities

In order to be clear on the importance of ensuring health and safety policies and procedures are in place, it is useful to have an understanding of the responsibilities of both the employee and the employer/event organisation.

8.4.2.1 Employer

An event employer must consult employees or a health and safety representative on (among other things) any changes that affect health and safety at work; the information to be given on the likely risks and dangers arising from event work and the measures to reduce or eliminate these risks; what to do when dealing with a risk; and health and safety planning.

General employer duties also include: making the workplace safe; ensuring machinery is safe; and giving the necessary information, instruction, training and supervision for health and safety. In particular, an employer must assess the risks to health and safety and arrange to implement the health and safety measures identified as being necessary by that assessment. They must also appoint a competent person to assist with health and safety responsibilities, and consult the safety representative about this appointment; cooperate on health and safety with other employers sharing the same workplace; set up emergency procedures; provide adequate first-aid facilities; and ensure that the workplace satisfies health, safety and welfare requirements (HSE 1999).

8.4.2.2 Employee

It is important to note that event employees' health, safety and welfare at work are protected by law in most countries. However, an employee also has a responsibility to look after themselves and others around them. This responsibility includes the need to identify potential issues and recognise problems within the health and safety provision. These problems can be small, such as identifying a loose panel on a stage set and informing someone so that it does not cause injury. Or they can be large, such as noticing that the planned layout for crowd flow may cause a crush and ensuring the relevant amendments to the plan are carried out. At the very least, if there is a problem, event employees should discuss it with their employer or, if there is one, their safety representative.

8.5 Risk management

Risk management involves an organisation or employer looking at risks in the workplace and implementing policies and procedures to minimise them. It is not solely concerned with health and safety. In fact, risks can arise in any area of the business, including financial, business planning and strategies, employee relations, and sales and marketing. In events, the management of risk will therefore relate to the overall event strategy, with organisers required to carry out several other forms of risk management based on specific issues, such as finances and return on investment, marketing and PR, sponsorship/ticket revenue strategy and environmental impact.

In particular, risks are now frequently assessed in terms of the Triple Bottom Line (TBL), which refers to the social, economic and environmental aspects of activities. These aspects are usually assessed in the evaluation of an event to determine the outcome for various stakeholders (Hede 2007), and it is becoming increasingly common to include them in a risk assessment that reviews external risks to the event. In other words, a TBL risk assessment will ask questions relating to the social, economic and environmental risks and impacts associated with the event, assess how these risks affect the wider public, and gauge the extent to which the event organisation is accountable for them. (A TBL approach to risk management is also often related to sustainability, which is covered extensively in Chapter 14.)

Another key aspect of risk management is that risk is not solely a negative concept. A good risk management strategy will highlight opportunities as well as potential problems. Risk management theory has moved away from the idea that the process is about crisis management. Instead, it is now widely agreed that the identification of risk can lead to greater understanding of a company's relationships, working practices, decision-making processes and overall output. It is therefore important for the event manager to understand the fundamental purpose of risk management and how it should be used across the events business.

However, the major focus for an event manager when considering risk management in an event context is the consideration of specific risks that usually relate to operational issues. Allen *et al.* (2008: 588) define risk as 'the likelihood of the special event or festival not fulfilling its objective', and this chapter will focus on the operational risks that might result in such an eventuality.

8.6 Risk assessment

A risk assessment focuses on risks that really matter and pinpoints the (usually straightforward) solutions to ensure that risks are controlled. Risk assessments protect workers and businesses and ensure compliance with the law. As the Health and Safety Executive (2011: 1) points out, 'The law does not expect you to eliminate all risk, but you are required to protect people as far as "reasonably practicable."' Carrying out a risk assessment is an absolute necessity for all event managers, even when the legislation does not require one.

An event risk assessment is an examination of elements that could cause harm to people. In other words, it is the identification of things that could go wrong (Tum *et al.* 2006). Every event will have many elements of risk: for instance, bad weather can create havoc at an outdoor event; overcrowding of one area can cause a crush; heavy consumption of alcohol may result in behavioural problems; a loose piece of wire may cause a trip; and so on. Every event should therefore have a risk assessment that enables the organisers to gauge whether they have taken adequate precautions to prevent harm to employees, visitors and suppliers. Organisers are legally required to assess the risks in the workplace and implement a plan to control those risks (HSE 2011).

As Tarlow (2002) points out, risk assessment is not only a way of identifying potential risks and attempting to eliminate or reduce them – it should also form the basis for contingency plans and emergency procedures.

8.6.1 Definitions

There are several key words that events industry professionals use when referring to health, safety and risk. It is important that the definitions of these words are clear and properly understood.

- *Hazard* – Anything which has the potential to cause harm to people. This could be a dangerous property of an item or a substance, a condition, a situation or an activity.
- *Risk* – The likelihood that the harm from a hazard is realised and the extent of it. In a risk assessment, risk should reflect both the likelihood that harm will occur and the severity of it.
- *Risk assessment* – The formal assessment of the relevant hazards and the potential severity of the outcome.
- *Risk control* – Methods employed to reduce risk to acceptable levels.

8.6.2 Carrying out an event risk assessment

A risk assessment should identify the period of time for which it will remain valid. It should take account of the views of employees and safety representatives and should follow the five steps outlined by the Health and Safety Executive (shown in Figure 8.4). Broadly, in an event context, these steps equate to identifying and assessing hazards and implementing preventative measures.

The record should be retrievable for use by the employer in reviews and for safety representatives, other employee representatives and visiting inspectors (HSE 2003). A risk assessment template can be seen in Table 8.1. Included are some typical examples of potential hazards to illustrate how to complete the form.

Risk assessments should not be overcomplicated. Often, the risks are well known, and appropriate control measures are easy to apply. An event manager does not usually need to be a health and safety expert to complete a risk assessment – they should simply have a good understanding of what is involved. However, larger and more complex events may require some expert help. A variety of risk assessment organisations can assist here, while local authorities and governing bodies are often able to advise, too.

- Step 1 • Identify the hazards
- Step 2 • Decide who might be harmed and how
- Step 3 • Evaluate the risks and decide on precautions
- Step 4 • Record your findings and implement them
- Step 5 • Review your assessment and update if necessary

Figure 8.4 Five steps to risk assessment
Source: HSE 2011

> **Table 8.1** A sample risk assessment document

Event Name				
EVENT DETAILS	Location	Date	Running times	Expected audience numbers
DURATION	Site build	Live event	Break	
PERSONNEL	Organiser	Venue contact	Sponsors/exhibitors	AV suppliers
	Entertainment/ artist	Staging/set designers	Catering	Other suppliers
RISK ASSESSMENT	Completed by	Signature	Date	

IDENTIFICATION OF HAZARDS

What is the hazard?	*Who might be harmed and how?*	*Existing measures to control risk*	*Level*	*Further action required*	*Responsibility*
Slippery floor	Staff and visitors might slip on wet floor left by caterers or caused by spillages in food hall.	General good housekeeping. Suppliers and cleaners briefed thoroughly to mop floors regularly, and immediately after a spillage.	Low	Food hall monitored every 30 minutes by nominated personnel.	Event manager
Transportation around site	Movement of vehicles around event site requires transport to use the same pathways as pedestrians. Accidents may occur.	Some designated roads for vehicles. Pathways clearly signposted for pedestrians. Routes positioned to enable easy access to work areas.	High	Separation of pedestrians from transport pathways by fencing.	Site manager/ event manager
Risk of verbal or physical abuse	Unhappy visitors may abuse staff, entertainment or artists.	Managers on hand to intervene and security to be called if necessary.	Low	N/A	Event manager/ HR manager/ supplier managers

What is the hazard?	Who might be harmed and how?	Existing measures to control risk	Level	Further action required	Responsibility
Manual handling of boxes, event material and equipment	During set-up and breakdown of event, staff may be at risk of injury.	Porters employed to do most movement of materials. Materials as far as possible to be delivered to the correct room/ building to avoid second handling.	Low	Staff will not set up on their own – always working in pairs. Trolleys provided to transport material.	Operations manager
Fire evacuation of main room/ building	All	Staff briefed on fire evacuation procedures. Fire evacuation procedures explained to student staff when they first arrive on-site for the event. Basic fire evacuation procedures explained to visitors during the introductory talk.	High	Ensure that all staff running event have received information and training on fire evacuation procedures (usually given during induction).	Operations manager

As Shone and Parry (2010) point out, the risk that is inherent in much of events management is not chiefly related to safety. It often relates to whether suppliers will provide their services, whether the audience will turn up or whether the marketing will deliver the expected results. Such risk factors, often identified during the screening process, do not need to be included in the risk assessment document. Nonetheless, contingency plans should be in place as part of the overall event plan.

Study activity

Think of the last event you attended and, using the information from the sections above:

- Describe five potential hazards at the event and the level of risk they represented to attendees, employees and/or contractors.
- Suggest which controls could be introduced to ensure that these risks are reduced to acceptable levels.
- Link the risks you have identified to the relevant legislation.

8.7 Specific event risks

Event organisations are usually concerned with a number of particular risks. It is important to note, however, that the three specific event risks listed here by no means comprise an exhaustive list. Event organisations will need to consider many more issues when compiling a risk assessment. These include the use of volunteers, communication procedures, emergency planning (including medical, ambulance and first-aid management), environmental impacts, recording and reporting of incidents, smoking, the protection of children and facilities for special needs. Of course, each event is unique and therefore demands a particular and individual risk assessment process.

8.7.1 Alcohol and drugs management

The management of alcohol, drugs and smoking makes up an important aspect of the control systems that need to be implemented in order to maintain a safe and comfortable atmosphere at an event. These elements are highly unpredictable, which means they represent a risk, so they should be managed as such. Many events have been cancelled or fined due to problems caused through the provision of alcohol or the consumption of illegal drugs in the audience. Sometimes, even the threat of such activities is enough to disrupt an event. For instance, in 2010, the district administration in southern Goa revoked a 'no-objection' certificate that had been granted to a music festival that was due to take place on Agonda Beach, citing concerns over potential drug-dealing. (See YouTube sources.)

For many events, provision of alcohol is part of the organisational plan. Different types of events will, of course, involve different levels of consumption. A weekend musical festival with a primary target audience of 18–25-year-olds will probably need to think carefully about the management of the likely heavy consumption of alcohol, whereas a classical music concert in a park will probably be dealing with much lower consumption. Nevertheless, both events demand consideration and planning.

It is important to note that alcohol is defined as food under the law, so its provision must meet the relevant food safety legislation, regulations and codes of practice. In order to ensure that the provision of alcohol is kept within legal, and safe, limits, Bowdin *et al.* (2010) suggest implementing alcohol risk management procedures that include limiting ticket sales, closing hotels early, increasing security and roping-off certain areas. In addition, the following prevention strategies should be employed:

- Ensure that security are well trained and correctly briefed.
- Ensure that no under-18s are served.
- Serving staff should be fully trained to refuse service, recommend soft drinks and slow down service, if necessary.
- Use a drink ticketing system.
- Provide adequate access to food.
- Implement crowd management procedures.

The risk of drugs at events has increased steadily in line with the proliferation of drugs in society generally. In the UK, much of the current anti-drug legislation and many of the drug policies have their roots in attempts to regulate the illegal raves that were prevalent in the 1980s (Lenton *et al.* 1997). While this particular cultural moment has passed, there is still a strong correlation between dance events and drug use. Students interested in how drug use impacts upon events will find much of interest in research that centres on rave culture and dance events (a good starting point is the aforementioned article by Lenton *et al.*).

It is important to note that many drugs are illegal, so the prevention of drug-taking should be paramount to event organisers. Strategies for searching guests, refusing entry and involving the police, where appropriate, are essential. However, most events in the UK and Europe with a profile audience who may be open to the use of drugs now operate a controlled drug policy, which, as well as putting into place prevention strategies, ensures that harm-reduction measures are in place. Lenton *et al.* (1997) suggest three main strategies to minimise the drug-related harm suffered by youngsters at dance events: information campaigns; guidelines issued to nightclub owners and/or rave promoters; and the employment of outreach workers. Figure 8.5 incorporates these strategies alongside other practical solutions to provide a robust drug control policy that should minimise harm. In addition, Case Study 8.3 discusses a more controversial method for ensuring that audience members do not come to harm from illicit drug use at events.

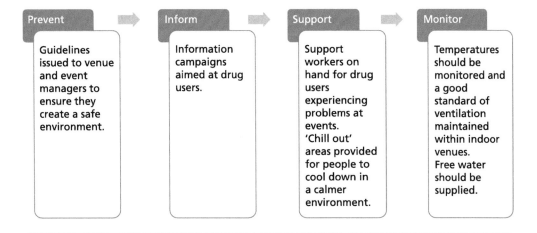

Prevent

Guidelines issued to venue and event managers to ensure they create a safe environment.

Inform

Information campaigns aimed at drug users.

Support

Support workers on hand for drug users experiencing problems at events. 'Chill out' areas provided for people to cool down in a calmer environment.

Monitor

Temperatures should be monitored and a good standard of ventilation maintained within indoor venues. Free water should be supplied.

Figure 8.5 Drug control strategies to minimise potential drug-related harm

CASE STUDY 8.3

Drugs and prohibition – different strategies to prevent harm or death from drugs at events

In Europe, event organisers – and particularly for music festivals – have in recent years begun to move towards a hard reduction model. They have not stopped trying to prevent drugs from entering their events – searches upon arrival are still commonplace at a festival, as are arrests and confiscation of illegal substances – but they have acknowledged that these preventative measures are largely ineffective. They have, therefore, moved towards creating a safer environment for audience members by minimising the risk of taking drugs. Drugs 'cut' with other, far more dangerous, substances are a leading cause of death at festivals and so festival organisers have attempted to tackle this by offering a drug-testing service in which attendees can have their drugs checked for content. Accompanying these testing facilities are 'amnesty bins', in which attendees can dispose of illegal substances without fear of recrimination. These areas also allow festival attendees to discuss drug use in a safe environment, offering the chance to change consumer behaviour at the point of consumption.

In Europe, it is recognised that these strategies, which aim to educate attendees and reduce harm, are working. In countries, such as Australia, where no drug-testing service exists, there has been a renewed call for such initiatives to be introduced at events after five people died at various music festivals due to drug use in a one-year period.

(www.release.org.uk;
www.sbs.com.au 7 December 2015)

8.7.2 Fire safety

Uncontrolled fire at events can cause problems that range from minor injury or property damage to panic, stampedes and death. Fire prevention and evacuation procedures are essential parts of the risk assessment process.

In 2003, the heavy-metal band Great White started a fire with their stage pyrotechnics. These pyrotechnics ignited the highly flammable soundproofing in the club where the band was performing, and 96 people died as a result. The band's tour manager, Daniel Biechele, pleaded guilty to 100 counts of involuntary manslaughter and spent four years in prison. One of the club's owners received a similar sentence, while the other received a ten-year suspended sentence, three years' probation and 500 hours' community service. In 2008 it was reported that a total of $175 million had been offered to the victims' families by various defendants (*USA Today* 2008; Challis 2009). Another example of fireworks creating a tragedy at an event can be seen in Case Study 8.1.

Events are subject to fire prevention regulations. In the UK, this is covered by the Regulatory Reform (Fire Safety) Order 2005. Event managers should ensure that they understand the fire regulations and requirements of whichever country is hosting their event. These regulations usually establish minimum requirements that will provide a reasonable degree of safety from fire in buildings or other structures. They cover such areas as the number and functionality of fire exits, the storage of flammable liquid, the extinguisher or sprinkler systems and the use of open flames and cooking devices (Silvers 2004). They also outline the regulations relating to safe capacity of spaces and evacuation procedures.

In order to understand the provision of fire safety, it is essential that event organisations follow these general principles:

- People can walk unaided to safety; particular provision should be in place for those less able to walk unaided and for disabled visitors.

- The route out of the venue should be clearly recognisable and accessible no matter where the fire breaks out.
- When fire breaks out, people often try to leave the way they entered. Where this is not possible (perhaps because the fire has broken out there or smoke is causing visibility issues), people should be able to find an alternative route to safety (HSE 1999: 22).
- Stewards and staff must be trained to usher people to safety. There is often resistance from guests who have underestimated the risk and do not want to use another exit.

Large-scale events or those involving pyrotechnics or other designed elements that present a fire hazard will require a site inspection by a fire warden or fire marshal. The event manager will be present during this inspection, and the installation of extra fire extinguishers or fire exit signs may be necessary. Equipment may need to be moved and venues may be required to install sprinkler systems (Silvers 2004) or to make provision for extra fire wardens on-site during the event.

Finally, while it is much less likely that people will be trapped by fire at an outdoor event, the risks should still be managed and controlled as they are for indoor events. Fire warning systems are required for outdoor structures, such as marquees; campsites should have fire watchtowers; and campers should be provided with safety advice.

> ### Study activity
>
> Remember the event you created in groups earlier in the chapter? Revisit the safety plan, and using the information provided above, carry out a risk assessment that considers all the major hazards your event might encounter. Use a template from the internet to create your risk assessment.

8.7.3 Managing crowds safely

As Abbott and Abbott (2000) suggest, crowd management and crowd control are two distinct but interrelated concepts. The former relates to the facilitation and movement of crowds during the normal circumstances of an event, while the latter relates to the steps that must be taken when a crowd starts to behave unexpectedly. Therefore, crowd management is proactive, while crowd control is reactive. Crowd management is carefully planned and implemented via the risk management and risk assessment processes prior to an event, and 'a well-conceived crowd management plan hopefully will eliminate the need for extensive crowd control' (Abbott and Geddie 2001: 269).

8.7.3.1 Key issues of crowd management

CROWD ANALYSIS

The most important of aspect of crowd management involves making an accurate estimate of the number of attendees (Bowdin *et al.* 2010; Silvers 2004). When doing this, event managers should bear in mind the capacity of the venue, and they should be able to forecast the expected turnout. This forecast should be based on several factors: attendance in previous years, numbers who visit similar events, proposed level of publicity, number of advanced ticket sales, and so on. Allowance should always be made for much larger numbers turning up on the day, especially for events that are not based solely on advanced ticket sales.

At the end of the 1990s, the Glastonbury Festival suffered a few years of over-attendance,

Image 8.2 **The Glastonbury Festival 2016**
Credit: Simone Joyner/EyeEm/Getty Images

and these additional attendees (who gained entry without tickets) caused numerous safety problems. These problems became so severe that the festival was prosecuted in 2000 for having too many people on-site, and the local authority felt that it could no longer issue a public entertainment licence. The festival organisers then took the following year off to review the situation and devise workable solutions that complied with safety regulations, allowed proper crowd management and did not impact on Glastonbury's core philosophy and creativity. They set up a Licensing Working Group and liaised closely with industry experts, the police and the local authorities to implement various highly effective measures. (See Glastonbury Festivals 2002, a report that is strongly recommended for students interested in crowd management and crowd safety. A shorter discussion of the festival's crowd management techniques can be found in Glastonbury Festivals 2011.)

CROWD BEHAVIOUR

It is important to have an understanding of the type of attendee the event will attract. A rock concert that encourages dancing and generally boisterous behaviour will have a very different crowd management plan from that of a toy exhibition, which will attract mainly families. The Health and Safety Executive (HSE 2000), therefore, advises that it is important to know the age range and social mix of attendees, which will allow event managers to anticipate likely behaviour and make the appropriate arrangements.

Abbott and Geddie (2001) highlight the importance of circumstances that may trigger crowd problems. Their list includes: cancellation, no-shows, congestion, lack of parking, the use of special effects, and the presence of obscene or violent performing acts. Other factors, such as weather, noise levels and the presence of rival groups, should be carefully considered in the crowd risk management process.

Thus, event managers must be fully aware of the type of event they are staging and how their audience might react. This is not as simple as deciding that a concert for 70,000 young adults will need detailed crowd management plans whereas a classical music event for 15,000 middle-aged adults will not – a loss of crowd control can occur in the most unlikely places, as the Wal-Mart stampede tragically proved in 2008. Similarly, religious festivals often suffer crowd-related tragedies. For instance, 147 worshippers died in a crush in a Hindu temple in 2008 (BBC 2008); and more than 450 people died in a stampede at a water festival in Cambodia two years later (Sky News 2010). There have also been many serious incidents during the Muslim Hajj: in 1990, 1,400 pilgrims died in a stampede in a pedestrian tunnel; in 1994, 270 people were crushed to death; in 1997, 350 people died in a fire; in 1998, 180 pilgrims died in a crush; in 2004, stampedes resulted in the deaths of 250 people; and in 2006, at least 362 people died in a similar fashion (Al-Bab.com 2011; BBC 2001; and see Case Study 8.4).

However, a key point for organisers to remember is that crowd disasters are usually created because of management issues, and not because of the manner in which a crowd behaves. In order to militate against crowd disasters, event organisers should be planning for crowds not to be too tightly packed. Work by the Fire Safety Engineering Group at the University of Greenwich (2016) and the *Guardian* (2015) indicates that moving crowds with a density of up to four people per square metre are safe, because individuals within them have room to make decisions and the crowd will not move like a fluid mass. However, when the density of the crowd becomes higher – around six people per square metre – bodies are too tightly packed together and individuals can no longer choose where they go. This creates pressure waves, which can travel through the crowd, resulting in a loss of control. When the crowd is this dense, they become prone to two types of accident – a progressive crowd collapse, where one person falls and adjacent people fall on top, due to the sudden gap and the pressure from the other sides. This often happens when crowds are moving through confined spaces (see Case Study 8.4). The second type of crowd disaster is when people are 'squeezed' to the extent that they can no longer inflate their lungs, and die gradually of asphyxiation. This is known as a 'crowd crush' and happens when people push into a confined area – Hillsborough is an example of this, as is the disaster at the Love Parade in Germany.

> Crowd forces can reach levels that are almost impossible to resist or control. Virtually all crowd deaths are due to compressive asphyxia and not the 'trampling' reported by the news media. Evidence of bent steel railings after several fatal crowd incidents show that forces of more than 4500 N (1,000 lb) occurred.
>
> (Crowd Dynamics 2011)

Silvers (2004) provides a useful list of definitions to explain potential reactions of a crowd in unforeseen circumstances:

- *Crowd crush* – The crowd is compressed into ever-smaller areas because there is no portal or escape, and this compression quickly becomes critical. An example was the Hillsborough Stadium disaster in 1989 (see YouTube sources).
- *Crowd collapse* – Individuals at the front of a crowd fall over, and those behind consequently lose their balance and fall on top. An example of this is the 2015 Hajj tragedy.

- *Crowd craze* – This is rarer than other crowd reactions and typically occurs when the crowd rushes or pushes forward, towards an individual or a desired object.
- *Crowd panic* – The frenzied desire to escape a real or perceived danger. Panicking crowds often trample those who have fallen and are lying on the escape route. In the aforementioned Cambodian water festival disaster, the crowd seems to have panicked because of rumours that people were being electrocuted and that the bridge on which they were standing was starting to collapse (see YouTube sources).
- *Crowd surge* – This often occurs at concerts. In the 2009 Mawazine Festival in Morocco, the 70,000-plus crowd surged forward to see singer Abdelaziz Stati. This resulted in at least 11 deaths and 40 injuries.

The general principles are that the event manager must know the type of crowd expected to attend and must have the right precautionary (and often calming) measures in place before the event starts. These measures can range from ensuring the visibility of security staff and personnel, to removing audience members who are displaying inappropriate or unruly behaviour. No two crowds are the same, so it is difficult to predict how one will behave in unexpected circumstances, but event managers should still have an understanding of a crowd's basic sociological behaviour and how that crowd might react. For further information on this topic, see numerous relevant articles in the journal *Events Management*, Abbott and Abbott (2000), Abbott and Geddie (2001), the HSE's *Managing Crowds Safely* (2000) and Crowd Dynamics (2011). A particularly valuable resource is the Fire Safety Engineering Group (2016).

8.7.3.2 Crowd control planning

In order to implement a successful crowd management plan, event managers also need to assess the factors that make up a crowd control plan. This will consist of the steps and procedures that should be taken once a crowd has lost control, and it will outline the measures that should be implemented at different stages of the event (Abbott and Geddie 2001).

Abbott and Geddie (2001) suggest that there are three stages in a crowd control plan – pre-crisis, crisis and post-crisis. During the pre-crisis stage, the event manager will consider certain preventative tactics to avoid crowd control problems (such as staff training, facilities management and the use of a control centre to aid communication). A crowd-related risk assessment will be produced at this stage. To help with this, the event manager should consider what might go wrong, who might be harmed and what the best response would be (see Table 8.2).

The second stage – the crisis stage – begins when the preventative measures fail. During this stage, practical crowd control measures, such as clear evacuation procedures and calm personnel, are essential – as is a proactive response before the situation escalates. For instance, overcrowding should be dealt with before the crowd starts to panic.

The final stage – the post-crisis stage – involves the review and evaluation of the strategy after the event. A full review should be completed by the organiser to ascertain whether security and personnel all responded effectively and efficiently, and to identify key issues or problems that may arise again in the future.

CASE STUDY 8.4

Crowd safety: the Hajj

Muslims consider pilgrimage to the holy city of Mecca, Saudi Arabia – known as the Hajj – as the most significant demonstration of their faith and unity. As the world's largest annual pilgrimage, the Hajj attracts more than 2 million people every year. The size and scale of the event have resulted in a string of major accidents, which have raised serious concerns over the management of the annual pilgrimage.

The worst accidents have occurred near Mina, where the pilgrimage traditionally ends with the 'Stoning of the Devil' ceremony. All pilgrims must pass through a small area in a single day in order to participate in the symbolic stoning of the devil – and this has caused major crowd safety implications.

At the event in 1990, panic broke out among the crowd inside a tunnel – more than 1,400 people died. In 2006, a stampede after the lunchtime prayers led to the deaths of 362 people. After this tragedy, the Saudi Arabian government took steps to manage crowds at this crucial point in order to reduce the risk of future fatalities. Their plan included the construction of a further two levels, resulting in a total of three balconies from which pilgrims could throw their stones, enabling freer and faster passage. Tens of thousands of personnel were hired to promote safety and provide stewarding and safety-related services to attendees. Hundreds of closed-circuit television cameras were installed along the route to monitor crowd movement, allowing the timely correction of bottlenecks of pilgrims as soon as they arose, and to enable stewards to clear groups of people as they gathered.

In addition to improving safety at the Stoning of the Devil ceremony, the organisers have focused on the health of attendees. Over forty ambulances are now on hand to attend to victims of heatstroke, those experiencing breathing problems due to overcrowding and poor ventilation, and those who have been hit by rebounding stones. Cooling equipment has been installed inside the galleries on each balcony to maintain air circulation and reduce the temperature.

These modern measures, designed to reduce the risk of death and injury, were implemented in order to bring one of the world's oldest festivals into line with health, safety and welfare legislation as well as the progressive practices of the modern, international events industry. However, In 2015, panic broke out when two groups of pilgrims preparing for this last major rite of their trip collided at the intersection of two narrow streets. Eyewitness reports suggest that this crush resulted in the crowd continuing to 'surge' behind, with more and more people being pushed into the tragedy. As the problems became apparent, more issues arose when people attempted to escape in a variety of directions. Official numbers from the Saudi government suggest that more than 700 people died. The Associated Press count indicates the death count was actually 2,177. Early indications suggest that this disaster was a progressive crowd collapse (see 8.7.3 for details).

(CNN, 9 December 2008; *Independent*, 20 October 2015;
Guardian, 24 September 2015)

Table 8.2 Crowd management risk assessment checklist

Are the numbers controlled and predictable?

Are visitors likely to be familiar with the venue?

What are the characteristics of the predicted crowd – age/gender/family structure?

Is the event likely to generate high emotions?

How will performers affect this?

Might there be aggressive behaviour/drug/alcohol use?

Are gatecrashers likely?

Study activity

The Stoning of the Devil ceremony requires the organisers of the Hajj to balance religion, culture, tradition and safety. In pairs, discuss what you think the organisers' priorities should be and pinpoint five of the key challenges they face in managing this crowd.

Review questions

1 What is the guiding principle for health and safety management in the events industry?
2 Name the three most important laws, legislations or regulations that are in effect in your country. What are the key points of these directives and how would you comply with them?
3 Silvers (2004) suggests there are five ways in which a crowd might react in unforeseen circumstances. Name them, and describe the differences.

Industry voice

Oliver Gardiner, Managing Director, Vespian Security

Within my role as a crowd manager and head of event security, I must take into consideration the expectations and motivation of all those attending and organising an event. When a customer, contractor, organiser or artist attends an event, they expect to be safe, treated fairly and with respect, that they will enjoy themselves and that they will have access to help and assistance, if required. These expectations encapsulate many aspects of an event site and its organisation – from toilets, queuing, pricing and crowd safety to medical assistance, conditions underfoot and entertainment programming.

Great crowd management and security are about a friendly, customer-focused approach and an accurate understanding of the event and audience demographic that is attracted to it. Depending on the demographic, the expectations of the crowd at different events could be poles apart, as would be the solutions to managing those crowds correctly. If insufficient numbers of security and crowd management staff are placed in certain locations, crime and disorder, or a crowd safety incident, could go unnoticed, resulting in complaints, poor press on social networking sites, minor or serious injuries, or even death. The importance of a safely managed event, where everyone is able to return home safely with themselves and their belongings intact, must not be underestimated.

No two days are ever the same, and no two events are identical. An important part of the modern crowd manager's roles and responsibilities is to be able to adapt plans and systems at a moment's notice to achieve the end goal, no matter what the situation may be.

8.8 Summary

This chapter has demonstrated the centrality of health, safety and risk issues in the event planning process. The guiding principle is that health, safety and risk management should be built into the planning process from the very start. The health, safety and welfare of event attendees, employees and contractors are the responsibility of all parties associated with events and should be paramount in all decision-making.

Health and safety is governed by much legislation and regulation, and event managers need to be confident that they understand the myriad licences, permits and regulations required to stage an event (no matter what size) and that they are operating within the relevant laws. If there is any doubt, seek professional advice.

This chapter has also focused on the management of health and safety, particularly on the design of an event to ensure that hazards and risks are minimised. Without due care and attention to the management of health and safety, and the assessment of potential risks, event organisers expose themselves to potential claims, fines and even criminal prosecution, should things go wrong. When things do go wrong at events, they often do so with catastrophic results. Identifying what may be a hazard, and the likelihood of that hazard causing problems for the staff or attendees, is therefore an essential part of the risk management process. The risks associated with events management are wide-ranging and atypical – every event is unique and should be assessed as such. This chapter has outlined the key risks and has looked at some of them in more detail, but a successful event manager will understand that the information presented here is far from exhaustive.

While health, safety and risk management can cause some restrictions to event design, the experience will not be compromised if it is handled skilfully. Consequently, the delivered event will be both excellent and safe.

Further reading

Allen, S (2014) Is it Safe? *Australian Leisure Management*, issue 2015. In this article, Steve Allen explains why it is essential for Australia to keep up with the world's best practice in leisure management.

Berlonghi, A. E. (1995) Understanding and Planning for Different Spectator Crowds, *Safety Science*, 18: 239–247. This paper provides summaries of different factors for distinguishing and assessing crowds within the context of special event planning. It relates the practicalities of events management to academic theories.

Health and Safety Executive (2014) Running an Events Safely. Available at: www.hse.gov.uk/event-safety/running.htm. An essential guide to health, safety and risk management for event organisers. The website has a UK focus, but it can be used as a starting point for key areas of consideration for event organisers around the world.

Health and Safety Executive (2016) Managing Crowds Safely, Norwich: HSE Available at: www.hse.gov.uk/pubns/books/hsg154.htm This booklet aims to provide practical guidelines on managing crowd safety in a systematic way by setting out an approach that can be used by organisers of any event or venue. Guidance is targeted at all owners and operators in all public venues where the HSW Act applies. The venue may be used regularly (for example, shopping centres and sports grounds) or occasionally (as for fireworks displays and agricultural shows). The guide is aimed at organisers, but will also be of interest to venue staff and contractors.

Silvers, J. (2012) *Professional Event Coordination* (2nd edn), New Jersey: John Wiley & Sons. A very practical look at events management, with clear and sound advice on aspects of risk assessment, the identification of hazards, the provision of security, the emergency services and communication procedures. Recommended for those new to events management in practice.

Worksafe Victoria (2007) *Crowd Control at Venues and Events: A Practical Occupational Health and Safety Guide* (2nd edn), Melbourne: State Government Victoria. A useful 44-page guide that will help both crowd control agencies and host employers (venues and events) to fulfil their responsibilities in relation to the Occupational Health and Safety Act 2004. It identifies common safety problems and suggests solutions to ensure crowd control is conducted as safely as possible. Finally, it provides numerous recommendations and tools to ensure the health, safety and welfare of crowd control staff as well as other staff and patrons.

References

Abbott, J. L. and Abbott, S. M. (2000) The Importance of Proper Crowd Management and Crowd Control in the Special Events Industry, in J. Allen, R. Harris, L. K. Jago and A. J. Veal (eds) *Events beyond 2000: Setting the Agenda, Proceedings of the Conference on Evaluation, Research and Education, Sydney, July 2000*, Sydney: Australian Centre for Event Management, University of Technology.

Abbott, J. L. and Geddie, M. W. (2001) Event and Venue Management: Minimizing Liability through Effective Crowd Management Techniques, *Event Management*, 6: 259–270.

AEO, BECA and EVA (2002) *The Guide to Managing Health and Safety at Exhibitions and Events: 'The Red Book'* (2nd edn), Berkhamstead: AEO, BECA and EVA.

AEO, AEV and ESSA (2010) *E-Guide 2010*. Available at: www.aeo.org.uk/files/eguide_2011_version1.pdf. Accessed 4 November 2011.

Al-Bab.com (2011) The Hajj Pilgrimage to Mecca. Available at: www.albab.com/arab/background/hajj.htm. Accessed 9 June 2011.

Allen, J., O'Toole, W., Harris, R. and McDonnell, I. (2008) *Festival and Special Event Management* (4th edn), Queensland: John Wiley & Sons.

BBC (2001) Hajj Perils, Ancient and Modern. Available at: http://news.bbc.co.uk/1/hi/world/middle_east/1203697.stm. Accessed 9 June 2011.

BBC (2008) Scores Die in India Temple Crush. Available at: http://news.bbc.co.uk/1/hi/world/south_asia/7643373.stm. Accessed 9 June 2011.

The Big Lunch (2011) About the Big Lunch. Available at: www.thebiglunch.com. Accessed 9 June 2011.

Bowdin, G., Allen, J., O'Toole, W., Harris, R. and McDonnell, I. (2010) *Events Management* (3rd edn), Oxford: Butterworth-Heinemann.

Challis, B. (2009) After the Great White Tragedy: Where Now with the Crowd Safety Legislation?, *Music Law Updates*, December. Available at: www.musiclaw updates.com/articles/ARTICLE%2009GreatWhite.htm. Accessed 9 June 2011.

Cornish, S. C. (2010) An Examination of the Crowd Management of Traditional Events: Prospects for the 21st Century, *Journal of Crowd Safely and Security Management*, 2 (1): 6–14.

Crowd Dynamics (2011) Available at: www.crowddynamics.com. Accessed 14 February 2011.

Fire Safety Engineering Group (2016) Available at: www.fseg..ac.uk. Accessed 7 January 2016.

Glastonbury Festivals (2002) *The Report of the Licensing Working Group*. Available at: www.glastonburyfestivals.co.uk/_assets/pdf/educational-resources/3TheReview. pdf. Accessed 9 June 2011.

Glastonbury Festivals (2011) *Crowd Control*. Available at: www.glastonbury festivals.co.uk/_assets/pdf/educational-resources/10CrowdControl.pdf. Accessed 9 June 2011.

Guardian (2015) How Crowd Disasters Happen. Available at: www.theguardian.com/world/2015/oct/03/hajj-crush-how-crowd-disasters-happen-and-how-they-can-be-avoided. Accessed 7 January 2016.

Hartley, H. (2002) A Party on the River: The 1989 *Marchioness* Disaster: Regulation of Safety on the River Thames and the 'Political Economy' of Risk, *World Leisure Journal*, 44 (4): 30–43.

Health and Safety at Work Act (1974) Available at: www.legislation.gov.uk/ukpga/1974/37/contents. Accessed 9 June 2011.

Health and Safety Executive (HSE) (1999) *The Event Safety Guide*, Norwich: HSE.

Health and Safety Executive (HSE) (2000) *Managing Crowds Safely: A Guide for Organisers at Events and Venues*, Norwich: HSE.

Health and Safety Executive (HSE) (2002) *COSHH: A Brief Guide to the Regulations*, Norwich: HSE.

Health and Safety Executive (HSE) (2003) *Health and Safety Regulations: A Short Guide*, Norwich: HSE.

Health and Safety Executive (HSE) (2009) *Working with Substances Hazardous to Health: What You Need to Know about COSHH*, Norwich: HSE.

Health and Safety Executive (HSE) (2010) Example Risk Assessment for a Village Hall. Available at: www.hse.gov.uk/risk/casestudies/villagehall.htm. Accessed 12 February 2010.

Health and Safety Executive (HSE) (2011) *Five Steps to Risk Assessment*, Norwich: HSE.

Health and Safety Executive (HSE) (2014) *Managing for Health and Safety*, Norwich: HSE.

Hede, A. (2007) Managing Special Events in the New Era of the Triple Bottom Line, *Event Management*, 11: 13–22.

Lenton, S., Boys, A. and Northcross, K. (1997) Raves, Drugs and Experience: Drug Use by a Sample of People who Attend Raves in Western Australia, *Addiction*, 92 (10): 1327–1337.

Maritime and Coastguard Agency (2005) *Formal Safety Assessment & Research Projects of Domestic Passenger Vessel Standards*, London: HMSO.

NFPA (2011) Nightclubs/Assembly Occupancies. Available at: www.nfpa.org/itemDetail.asp?categoryID=633&itemID=21073&cookie%5Ftest=1. Accessed 9 June 2011.

Robideaux, C. (2009) Wrongful Death Suit Settled Involving Wal-Mart 'Black Friday' Stampede. Available at: www.youtube.com/watch?v=Wsa4BYcwII0. Accessed 9 June 2011.

Shone, A. and Parry, B. (2010) *Successful Event management* (3rd edn), Hampshire: Cengage Learning.

Silvers, J. (2004) *Professional Event Coordination*, New Jersey: John Wiley & Sons.

Slapper, G. (2007) Corporate Manslaughter Law is a Vast Improvement, *The Times*. Available at: http://business.timesonline.co.uk/tol/business/law/article2097907.ece. Accessed 28 December 2010.

Sky News (2010) Cambodia: 456 Dead in Festival Stampede. See, Tarlow, P. E. (2002) *Event Risk Management and Safety*, Chichester: John Wiley & Sons.

Tum, J., Norton, P. and Wright, J. N. (2006) *Management of Event Operations*, Oxford: Butterworth-Heinemann.

Upton, M. (2008) *Safe Event Management*, paper presented at Theatre Managers Association Conference, 10 June. Available at: www.crowdmodelling.com/2008_upton.pdf. Accessed 4 November 2011.

USA Today (2008) RI Club Fire Released from Prison. Available at: www. usatoday.com/news/nation/2008-03-19-4281531984_x.htm. Accessed 23 June 2017.

YouTube sources

Deputy Collector Revokes Permission Granted for Chakraview Music Festival in Agonda. Available at: www.youtube.com/watch?v=Yevh3NNYnmI. Accessed 9 June 2011.

German Love Parade Raw Video Footage from Associated Press. Available at: www. youtube.com/watch?v=4WnV74PW4bo&feature=related (images and comments may be disturbing). Accessed 9 June 2011.

German Love Parade Stampede Kills 18. Available at: www.youtube.com/watch?v=YwxBRrY8Vco. Accessed 9 June 2011.

Sky Sports News: Hillsborough Disaster 20th Anniversary. Available at: www.youtube. com/watch?v=pPAD1Q2jzVI. Accessed 9 June 2011.

Stampede Kills 378 during Cambodian Festival. Available at: www.youtube.com/watch?v=3_VqI2TY-H0. Accessed 9 June 2011.

The Big Lunch 2011. Available at: www.youtube.com/watch?v=jG6KorBRRkc. Accessed 24 June 2017.

Wal-Mart Stampede Death Lawsuit. Available at: www.youtube.com/watch?v=Wsa4BY cwII0. Accessed 9 June 2011.

Other useful resources

Bucharest nightclub fire. Available at: www.bbc.co.uk/news/world-europe-34684973; www.theguardian.com/world/2015/nov/07/romanian-prosecutors-arrest-local-mayor-over-bucharest-nightclub-fire. Accessed 24 June 2017.

Event Safety Guide – webpages available at: www.hse.gov.uk/event-safety/running.htm. Accessed 24 June 2017.

Health and Safety Executive (2016) *Managing Crowds Safely*, Norwich: HSE. Available at: www.hse.gov.uk/pubns/books/hsg154.htm. Accessed 24 June 2017.

Shoreham Airshow Crash (2017) *Anniversary of Shoreham Airshow Crash*. Available at: www.shorehamairshow.co.uk/. Accessed 24 June 2017.

Strategies to prevent drug-related harm or death at events – available at: www.release.org.uk; www.sbs.com.au 7 December 2015.

Chapter 9

Sporting events

Contents

9.1 Aims

By the end of this chapter, students will be able to:

- review the development of the sports industry to its present role;
- understand the processes involved in sporting event business management;
- discuss the challenges posed by current issues affecting sporting events;
- understand the legacies of particular sporting events.

9.2 Introduction

This chapter will highlight the specific nature of sporting events and their major contribution to the development of events management as a worldwide industry. The issues of political influence, legacies, economic impact and how to bid for sporting events will also be discussed, in light of the current difficulties facing major bodies such as FIFA and the Lawn Tennis Association (LTA), as will the extent to which the event manager can prepare to deal with these issues. The motivation of attendees at sporting events, the development of sponsorship and the role of television in sporting events will also be reviewed. Particular practical emphasis will be placed on the management of participants, event safety in relation to challenges of crowd behaviour and management of such issues as violence, racism, drugs and alcohol.

The history of sporting events is unclear, as the first events began more than 2,000 years ago. There is evidence of these occurring in ancient Greece, China and Egypt, with the first Olympic Games held in 776 BC (Masterman 2014). The first modern Olympics took place in Athens, Greece, in 1896. Football – now perhaps the biggest global sport – was first played in its current format in Sheffield in 1860, when Sheffield FC, the oldest football club in the world, met Sheffield Hallam FC, the second-oldest club in the world, at Sandygate Lane, the oldest football stadium in the world. They competed for the Youden Trophy, sponsored by Thomas Youden, a local theatre owner, at a cost of £2 (equivalent to £170 today; Sheffield Hallam FC website).

That first football game in Sheffield exhibited some of the key components of a modern sporting event. The sport of football was given a set of rules by the Sheffield FA, which enabled competition to take place within a clearly laid-out formula. Each team or participant had the opportunity to win a prize – donated by a benefactor or sponsor – and they were overseen by a referee. Spectators either paid to watch or were invited to attend, hospitality and catering were laid on for them, and the media – at this stage simply the local newspaper – was present to record the event. In the following years, as the number of teams grew, so did the competition, the number of spectators and the revenue from the sale of refreshments.

9.3 Overview of the sports industry

The scale of sporting events varies from the small local event, attracting only a handful of competitors and in some cases no spectators at all, to the mega-event that is open to billions of people around the globe. As illustrated in Table 9.1, sporting events vary in terms of number of participants, total media coverage, value of sponsorship deals, total running costs, management type and the distance travelled by the participants. However, all of these events, whether a one-day local wrestling competition or a one-month international basketball tournament, usually feature an individual or team winner, some form of prize and arbitration

Table 9.1 Typology of sporting events

Size of event	Characteristics of the event
Local	For example, school sports day
	Restricted to local entrants
	Usually well established
	Small-scale sponsorship and local media coverage
	Costs are usually covered by entrants and donations of facilities made by the local community
Regional	For example, regional baseball tournament
	Restricted to counties or states
	Usually linked to a regional sports organisation
	Sponsorship usually offered by a sponsor with direct interest in sports
	Media coverage might (occasionally) include television
	Most costs are covered by entrants and/or their sports team
National	For example, national ice-skating championships
	Open to all clubs/individuals based in one country
	Organised by a national sports body and financed by the entrants
	Sponsorship linked to a recognised national brand
	More media coverage than a regional event
International	For example, Berlin Marathon
	Open to a number of countries but cost to entrant determines the level of international involvement
	Majority of participants come from host country and nearest neighbours
	Organisers mainly part time, with support from volunteers
	More media interest but still mainly national media coverage
Global event (mega-event)	For example, Olympic Games
	Participants travel from many countries, so most cover considerable distances
	Organising committees are usually full time or on long contracts, with high volunteer involvement
	Sponsorship is high due to increased media coverage on a global basis
	Revenue-generating opportunities are considerable

of the event. In all events, it is the spirit of sport and taking part that are the most important factors, and, as Masterman (2014: 3) points out, there is 'wider significance to society than just the staging of a sporting event'. Such are the growth and increasing value of the sporting events industry that continuing political intervention and political comment in the future are almost inevitable. Governments have long used sporting events to make political statements, such as the US government boycotting the Moscow Olympics, and many people are prepared to stake their political and personal reputations on bidding for lucrative sporting events. Thirty years ago, a mega-event might generate a few million pounds in revenue, but now the bidding process alone can easily stretch into the tens of millions. This has led to accusations of bribery and corruption being levelled at both those who wish to host events and members of awarding committees. This has escalated to such a level at FIFA that the very future of the organisation has been brought into question and the FBI have launched a major investigation.

All of this illustrates that the sporting events industry is a fast-growing and lucrative business. Sporting events management is still a relatively new academic research area, with very few books covering the topic, although there are increasing numbers of events management degrees offered at university level. Somewhat more academic journal articles have been written on the subject, but most of these tend to focus on the US sporting events industry. In 2014, according to the Office of National Statistics, 800,000 tourists attended football matches in England, which represents a significant impact on the finances of sport, and on the sporting events themselves.

This industry has boomed over recent decades. In the United States, the overall sports market – which includes participation in sports, taking part in events and attending as a spectator – was estimated at between $44 billion and $73 billion in 2005 (Humphreys and Humphreys 2008) and Price Waterhouse Cooper estimated that the global sports market was worth $145 billion dollars a year in 2015, and growing on average by 3% per year. This not only establishes sports as an important contributor to the general economy in terms of employment and revenue generated but suggests that sports, and sporting events, impact on the lives of a significant number of people. A key turning point in this development of sports as a profitable business was the 1984 Olympic Games in Los Angeles – the first modern Games not to incur a huge loss for the host city. Profits were achieved through the greater involvement of sponsors, lucrative broadcasting contracts and other outside investment. All of this was in stark contrast to the Montreal Olympics in 1976, which incurred such huge losses that the city government was still paying off the debt thirty years later.

There is frequent discussion about European football leagues and the fact that just a handful of teams in most countries win the majority of the league titles and cup competitions, and that these leagues and cups are not competitive for most teams as they lack outcome uncertainty. American sporting events organisers take this problem very seriously, to such an extent that they have devised a system to overcome it. In order to maintain competitive leagues and retain the interest of all fans throughout the season, the National Football League (NFL) manages professional teams' recruitment of new players by ensuring that the best college players sign for the teams that finished lowest in the divisions. This 'draft pick' was introduced in an attempt to ensure that all teams are competitive and have a chance of winning at least their regional division (Cousens *et al.* 2001).

9.3.1 The impact of sporting events

Considerable emphasis is now placed on sporting events' impact and legacy. These topics will be covered in more detail in Chapter 14, but their importance in the sporting events industry merits further attention here. Sport England, a key governing body for the development of sports in England, has produced several reports that consider the impact of sporting events on the wider community. They currently spend £324 million per year to maintain and develop sports participation, which a significant amount spent on the preparation of participants for sporting events.

9.3.1.1 The social impact of sporting events

There are a number of ways in which a sporting event can impact on a local community, either positively or negatively. The key negative impact is inconvenience for local residents (Small 2007), with specific problems including increased traffic congestion, extra people in the area during the event and the possibility of crowd disorder or even hooliganism. These have been issues for decades, but recently more individuals and communities have started to argue that the benefits of hosting sporting events outweigh the negative aspects. An example follows that illustrates this change in attitude.

In the 1970s, Sheffield United Football Club applied to Sheffield council to redevelop part of its ground. The proposal included building a hotel, expanding leisure facilities, increasing the overall capacity of the stadium and introducing new corporate hospitality viewing areas. These extensive plans were rejected by the city council, which ruled that an increase in traffic and numbers of people attending the stadium would affect the quality of life of local residents. The latter were already unhappy about the disruption caused by sporting events in the area, which numbered only about twenty-five each year. Thirty years later, the football club submitted much-revised plans, but with the same aim of developing the stadium to include more facilities. This time, they have been accepted, and it is hoped that the development will regenerate what has now become a rundown area of the city. It will certainly create much-needed jobs for a local community with high unemployment. The current stadium already has a hotel and several office suites that are rented out to local companies, and these have created jobs and have generally improved the local environment.

Obviously, objections from the local community can seriously threaten the success of a sporting event. The London Olympics drew fierce opposition from the residents of Greenwich – an important stakeholder group – who felt that the equestrian events – which were held in their Royal Park – would cause disruption for at least six months before the main event in August 2012 and that the park would be closed during this time. This is a far from unusual reaction and this was further emphasised when pictures appeared in the national press of banners with the word LOCOG printed on them, displayed outside local business, which is the logo of the London Organising Committee of the London Games, with the slogan 'Licence to Kill Off Greenwich', as a protest at the amount of business that they lost during the equestrian events held in Greenwich. While governments generally promote the positive social impacts of major sporting events, local residents are still often sceptical (Preuss and Solberg 2006).

Some sporting event organisers attempt to overcome such opposition by claiming that local residents will have the opportunity to meet people from other countries and other cultural backgrounds, and that the event will benefit other local cultural activities. For instance, a car-racing event in Florida was promoted as a sports tourism event, because it was expected that attendees would stay on after the race and take part in local cultural activities. However, research found that most people who attended the main event did not take part in other events in the area, so there was no significant social benefit (Pennington-Gray and Holdnak 2002; Maennig and Zimbalist, 2012).

9.3.1.2 The economic impact of sporting events

The economic impact of a sporting event is usually a key part of the bidding process for staging it. Barget and Gouguet (2007) estimated the net social benefit of hosting a prestigious new tennis tournament in France. After deducting all of the costs associated with the tournament, and measuring the reactions of local people, the net social benefit was €215,000 (£195,000). There are two schools of thought, and much debate, among sports economists and event planners about the economic impact of sporting events. For instance, some researchers have highlighted

Image 9.1 **Equestrian Events at London Olympics with Greenwich in the Background**
Credit: Alex Livesey/Getty Images

'time switchers' – people who are displaced when an event takes place in a major location (Preuss 2005). If an event takes place in Barcelona in August and attracts many visitors, other people who would normally visit the city in the summer might well avoid it because they have no interest in the sporting event. Their revenue is not only 'displaced' for that year but they may never return in the future either. Event planners often ignore this consequence of hosting a sports event. They are more likely to make a calculation based solely on the number of visitors to their event multiplied by the average amount of money that those people will spend when they are in the city. To that can be added the jobs created by building the new facilities. For example, the Olympic Village in London was used to provide housing for local people after the event, and regenerated what was deemed to be a deprived area. However, those opposing the event might well suggest that the government should build houses and regenerate the area anyway, as part of their general responsibility to the community, without the need for an Olympic Games.

To sum up, a city will usually gain some social and economic benefits from hosting a sporting event. However, there will almost certainly be costs, too, and these should always be considered when planning such an event.

9.3.2 Sporting event legacies

The legacy of a sporting event is now one of the key criteria for sporting events bids, and it is frequently discussed by politicians and the media. Barcelona gained improved transport links and benefited from other regeneration projects as a direct result of hosting of the 1992 Olympics. However, the Olympic Stadium itself now stands empty. It was handed over to the football club Español after the Games, but they have now moved to their own purpose-built stadium, a fact that has been largely overlooked by sports marketing academics. The future of London's Olympic Stadium has been the subject of much legal wrangling and challenges in the courts, with several rival football clubs bidding to make it their new permanent home. The stadium was eventually taken over by West Ham United, but the cost of remodelling what was a new stadium added an extra £200 million to the bill, and the rent that West Ham pay has also caused considerable discussion and is not without controversy. Manchester City Football Club's move into the city's Commonwealth Games Stadium was less problematic and ranks as one of the more successful conversions of a mega-event stadium after a games.

Study activity

Look at the World Cup and Olympics in Brazil and say what you think are the advantages and disadvantages of hosting these games for the Brazilian government.

9.3.3 Bidding to host sporting events

In the previous sections, dealing with the impact and legacy of sporting events, reference was made to the potential social and economic benefits of hosting a sporting event, as well as the influence of local and national governments. There is now increasing competition to host such events, with governments from all over the world putting in bids. The competition is so fierce for events, such as the Olympics, the European Football Championships and the FIFA World Cup, that several million pounds have to be invested in the bidding process alone. New bidding procedures have emerged in an attempt to guarantee fairness in the selection of hosts, and therefore bidding teams should pay more attention to making successful bids.

Countries now set up organising committees to prepare complex bids for high-profile events, while multi-venue events – such as the FIFA World Cup – also generate strong *internal* competition between cities who want to host some of the games. This means that sports clubs and their local authorities now invest heavily in trying to become a designated host venue. When the Football Association (FA) in London coordinated its bid to host the 2018 or 2022 World Cup, fifteen potential host cities tendered bids to host matches, meaning that three were likely to be unsuccessful if England were awarded the competition. These were complex bids requiring teams of experienced people from football clubs, sporting associations, local councils, area development agencies, industry figureheads and sponsors, each of whom spent up to six months working on the project. (For further information, see the FA website.)

Of course, the vast majority of bids for sporting events end in failure for the bidding committee (Emery 2002: 317), meaning that deprived areas are not regenerated and the region does not gain a reputation as a major sporting venue. As a result of the high failure rate of bids, any sporting events people who have been involved in successful bids are highly sought after and rewarded, not only in their host countries but overseas. For instance, Mike Lee was part of the successful bid teams for both the 2012 and 2016 Olympics, and then helped Qatar secure the 2022 World Cup (see *Guardian* website).

Given the increase in the number of bids to host sporting events, bidding teams need to look closely at the factors that contribute to a winning bid, and need to incorporate these elements, where possible, in their own bid. Of course, it could be argued that the bidding process varies according to the sporting event, but a review of the literature suggests that a number of factors are universally helpful to all bids. Recent successful bids have hired well-known personalities in an attempt to influence the key stakeholders that make up the team which awards the event. For instance, the British government recruited footballer David Beckham to lobby individual members of the International Olympic Committee (IOC) during the 2012 bidding process. Gold medal-winners Dame Kelly Holmes and Sir Steve Redgrave were also part of the lobbying group, but Beckham was the key weapon. Prime Minister Tony Blair introduced him to individual IOC members who had not yet decided how they would vote, and many of these men and women were said to have been 'star-struck' in Beckham's presence. With the final vote so close, Beckham's influence may well have helped to secure the Olympics for London.

In a survey of 135 people from twenty-one countries who had been involved in bidding for a variety of 'hallmark' sporting events, eight key factors for success were identified (Westerbeek *et al.* 2002; see Table 9.2). These provide a useful starting point for any group that is interested in compiling a bid for a sporting event.

A bidding host city or sporting body must address all of these issues when making a presentation. They comprise a checklist for the bidders but also for the committees charged with choosing the successful applicant. While the cost of facilities is not necessarily the most important factor, it is becoming harder for countries without a strong infrastructure to be

---

Table 9.2 Key success factors when compiling a bid for a sporting event
Source: Adapted from Westerbeek *et al.* 2002

Success factors	Issues to address
Accountability	To what extent does the bid represent the views of the community whose tax revenues will be spent on the event, and how strong is the reputation of the bidder in this sport?
Political support	Are the key decision-makers in the sporting bodies, local council, local government and national government known? Does the event promise to leave a legacy for the bid city?
Relationship marketing	Are there enough people with influence in their sport, or established event managers, who can influence key stakeholders?
Ability	What evidence is there to show that the bidder can successfully manage this type of event? Experience counts.
Infrastructure	Where will all the spectators, competitors and employees stay during the event, and how good are the arrangements for transporting them to and from the venues?
Bid team composition	Can a bid team be assembled that represents the sport and will be able to deal comfortably with important decision-makers?
Communication and exposure	How well known is the potential host city and does it have a reputation for hosting events?
Existing facilities	Given the escalating costs of providing new facilities for events, are there existing facilities that can be utilised for the event?

successful in bids, as the costs of providing the necessary facilities are unlikely to be covered by sponsorship revenues and government grants. The typical cost of a new stadium for a mega-event can easily reach £750 million, but some of this outlay can be recouped if it is handed over to a new owner or tenant once the event has finished. This also has the benefit of making the venue available for future bids for other events.

While this research was conducted into bidding for mega-events, those wishing to host smaller events can learn from it, too. The principal reason for staging a sporting event should be to promote and develop sport, so this should always be stressed in a bid. This could help to secure the support of local politicians who wish to promote healthy lifestyles among the community. In turn, this might persuade other key stakeholders to offer their support or funding. Any potential benefits to the local economy should also be calculated and presented to stakeholders, as should any research which indicates that the local community is in favour of the event.

9.3.4 Venue design

If a bid has been successful, the first thing to consider is the design or development of the stadium (or stadiums) where the events will take place. Over the last ten years, greater emphasis than ever before has been placed on venue design. The economic viability of a stadium has become a key factor in this design process, with owners keen to ensure that their investment continues to generate revenue on a regular basis.

Table 9.3 provides some examples of recently built or redeveloped sports stadiums that now operate as multi-purpose event arenas. These innovative approaches have generated

Table 9.3 **Features of new and redeveloped sports stadiums**

Club or organisation	Country	Extra features at venue
Arizona Diamondbacks	USA	Replaceable stadium floor to cater for events that cannot take place on grass or AstroTurf
Wembley Stadium	England	Sliding roof to reduce the impact of inclement weather, and hosts a full-time sports university
Sapporo Stadium	Japan	Sliding roof and interchangeable floors to suit different sporting events
Emirates Stadium	England	Assisted housing for local people employed in key services, conference facilities and museum
Phoenix Suns	USA	Nightclub, café and shops
Leyton Orient Football Club	England	Apartment blocks in corners of the stadium, medical centre and training facility shared with local community
Sheffield United Football Club	England	Offices that can be converted into hospitality areas on match days, car parks used for the city's Park and Ride scheme, new hotel and conference facilities
Charlton Athletic Football Club	England	School/college that converts to hospitality area for events, including gym and crèche
New York Yankees	USA	Extra space for non-sporting major events, including conference facilities and hospitality

considerable additional revenue for the stadiums' owners. Charlton Athletic and Leyton Orient secured public funds for their redevelopment projects by incorporating a school and a health centre, respectively, in their new facilities. The New York Yankees' new stadium is another wonderful example of a multi-purpose stadium. With 1.3 million square feet, it can cater for a range of non-sporting events that generate additional revenue on an almost daily basis. The Staples Center in Los Angeles is the home to four sports franchises and hosts a number of high-profile concerts and other key events. It is not uncommon for four different events to take part every weekend and the event organisers pride themselves on their ability to switch from one key event to another in just a few hours.

Study activity

You have been asked to design a new 30,000-seat sports stadium in your home market and incorporate as many features as possible that will help the owners to maximise customer experience and increase revenue-generating opportunities. Assuming that an average ticket costs £20 and that a sold-out venue will therefore generate around £600,000, list the additional features that you intend to introduce in your design, and say how much they will contribute to turnover. For example, if you incorporate a coffee bar that serves around 1,000 people a week and generates an average of £2 per person, then that makes a weekly turnover of £2,000, or about £104,000 a year. Outline the potential advantages and disadvantages for each of your design features.

CASE STUDY 9.1

The design of a new multi-purpose stadium in the Gujarat province in India by StadiArena

Location: StadiArena, Gujarat, India
Event venue: sporting events and other events
Attendees: up to 25,000

This case study looks at the design of a new multi-purpose stadium in Ahmenabad, Gujarat, India, using StadiArena innovative design to convert part of the outdoor stadium into an indoor arena using the latest technology www.youtube.com/watch?v=ByYs5RL0l5E.

It is believed to be the first venue of its kind in the world and the first ever multi-purpose stadium to be built in India. While this sort of design incurs additional costs, compared to a traditional-style stadium, the flexibility that this conversion allows the venue means that they will be able to use it every day of the week and it can accommodate a range of different activities. By being able to section off one end of the main stand, the football stadium can still be used, while the other end of the stadium can host a sporting or cultural event. The designers of the stadium have also made use of the stadium roofs, by placing tennis courts on top of one of the stands. According to StadiArena, the brief for this stadium was to 'create a sporting arena with the potential to generate revenue 365 days a year', according to Paul Fletcher, the industry voice in this chapter and the founder of StadiArena. The StadiArena patented technology means that the stadium can be converted from an outdoor arena to an indoor one at the push of a button and the seats from one end of the stadium start to retract to create additional space.

This multi-purpose stadium will host a range of both sporting and cultural events, and will also feature retail outlets, offices, banquet halls and a hotel. The vision was to create a sporting arena with the potential to generate revenue 365 days a year.

9.4 Managing the sporting event: managing participants

The role of the participant in sporting events is sometimes taken for granted, yet in an increasingly competitive sporting event environment, there is increasingly strong competition for future competitors.

At the Regensburg Marathon in Bavaria, Germany, many of the publicity stands are occupied by promoters of other marathons, such as Munich and Berlin, who are keen to sign up participants for their rival events. A keen German runner might have the choice of six different marathons in his region in a single year. Sporting event participants should therefore be treated in a way that makes them want to return and take part in future events, so there is a need to manage their experience and convince them to participate again. In other words, while it is important to cater to the needs of the media, spectators and sponsors, *participants* should certainly not be neglected. Below is a list of the factors that an events management team should take into consideration when managing participants:

- Develop a player-friendly event so that participants have a positive experience. They are more likely to come to the next event if they enjoy themselves.
- Think about the timing of the event and how this fits into the participants' timetables. Avoid clashing with a competitor's event.
- Consider whether the family and friends of the participant should be looked after, particularly if they are supported by a large number of people. These may be asked their opinion of the event and could well be influential.
- Organise a player-friendly party, either at the beginning or at the end of the event. This will add to the participants' experience and will influence how they view the event.

- Can they be given souvenirs or gifts, or at the very least photographs, as reminders of the event?
- Use contracts to protect the event and the participant. These can have incentives and bonuses built into them, and help to clear up misunderstandings. They might also have a clause that allows the event manager to withdraw a competitor should their behaviour away from the sport have a detrimental impact on the event. (Adapted from Cousens *et al.* 2001)

9.4.1 Managing participants' drugs and alcohol consumption

The first attempt to address the problem of drug use in sports came in 1967, with the founding of the Olympic Committee Medical Commission, which was established after rumours of drug-taking in the Olympic Games (Beckett and Cowan 1979).

One of the biggest issues facing sporting event organisers today is the high percentage of athletes who take medicine or supplements prior to competing. In a survey carried out for the 2004 Olympics, 75 per cent of the athletes admitted taking supplements or medicines three days before competition, with as many as 20 per cent of these competitors taking five or more supplements (Ambrose 2004: 502). In March 2016, Russian tennis player Maria Sharapova was found guilty of taking a banned drug, which was previously not on the list of banned substances and which she had been taking for ten years. The problem of drug-taking has become such an issue in cycling that the reputation of the sport has been seriously tarnished, which makes it less appealing to major sponsors who are unwilling to be associated with an activity that might impact on their brand image.

The English FA has taken the lead in attacking the use of drugs to enhance sporting performance (in a sport where drug-taking is not considered to be a serious problem) by introducing random drug testing in mobile units for its affiliated players.

Alcohol abuse is much easier to identify, and many sports clubs now carry out random tests on players to see if they are under the influence of alcohol.

9.4.2 Safety at sporting events

While most sporting events proceed without complications, they are potentially very dangerous places for both attendees and employees. It is the duty of the event manager to ensure that everyone at the event remains safe.

For many people, the sporting event provides an escape from the monotony of day-to-day life and an opportunity to get excited by their favourite team or athlete. Some relish the chance to let off steam by shouting, cheering and singing. In such an environment, passions can run high and lead to catastrophe.

Recent disasters at sporting events are etched in the memories of those who attended. In 1985, around 50 people died in the Heysel Stadium, Belgium – a stadium that was due to be rebuilt since it was deemed unsuitable for modern sporting events. Just a couple of weeks earlier, 55 people had died in a stadium fire in Bradford, England. Then, in 1989, 96 people were crushed to death at Hillsborough in Sheffield (Dickie 1995). After this tragedy, the British government commissioned the Taylor Inquiry to look into stadium safety. Its final report recommended that all major stadiums should be all-seater and a host of other safety guidelines were issued. Many of these were followed, with all clubs in the top two divisions of English football replacing their terraces with seats. However, similar reforms have not been implemented elsewhere. As late as 2009, many supporters died at a stadium in the Ivory Coast when a wall collapsed on top of them. This occurred despite FIFA devoting much time and energy towards improving safety at football grounds. Its guidelines are helpful in the management of both large- and small-scale football matches, and they should also be considered by organisers of other sporting events (see the FIFA website).

Another safety concern at sporting events is the threat of terrorist attack, which we witnessed in a recent bomb at the French National Football Stadium in 2015. Most organisers now manage this very carefully and efficiently inside the stadium, but terrorists are constantly developing their strategies in response. Both the Togo football team and the Sri Lankan cricket team have been attacked en route to matches, illustrating the importance of protecting competitors outside as well as inside the venue.

Study activity

Look at FIFA's safety guidelines (on the FIFA website) and suggest which of these regulations might also be useful in a basketball or athletics event. Pick what you think are the five most important regulations.

9.4.3 Crowd management

One of FIFA's guidelines on stadium safety states that 'the match organiser must take all reasonable measures to ensure that the consumption of alcohol does not interfere with the spectators' safe enjoyment of the match' (FIFA website). Nevertheless, in a survey of football supporters in Scotland, it was found that around 20 per cent of all casualties recorded at matches were related to excessive drinking (Crawford *et al.* 2001).

Of course, the problem of alcohol consumption at sporting events is not restricted to football in Scotland. It presents a serious dilemma for the majority of sporting event managers, particularly as sponsorship revenue may well come from major brewers. For instance, InBev signed a six-year sponsorship deal with the NFL that is reputed to be worth around $1.2 billion. To counteract criticism of such links with brewers, some sporting event organisers have introduced alcohol-free areas in an attempt to isolate any drink-related problems that might arise.

9.4.4 Violence and racism at sporting events

While the majority of sporting events take place without any spectator violence, organisers must always be sensitive to the threat of it. As far back as 1910, Swedish fans invaded the pitch to attack opposition players (Andersson 2001), and since then there have been numerous examples of violence at football matches throughout Europe, although the number of incidents has fallen significantly over the past ten years. There are still serious problems at football matches in Argentina, where the *Barras Bravas*, the name given to hooligan gangs, are responsible for vicious assaults on rival fans (Duke and Crolley 1994). Such is the level of violence that the Argentinian government has frequently suspended the football league in order to penalise the clubs, who otherwise seem to have little interest in rectifying the problem. While many event organisers will argue that hooliganism is a societal problem rather than a sporting problem, they need to be aware that people often cite violence at football matches as a reason for not attending any live sporting events.

Another recurring problem at some sporting events is racism. Black footballers have been subjected to racist chants and taunts from opposition supporters, especially in Eastern Europe and, more recently, Spain. Nor is this problem confined to football in Europe. Tennis players Serena and Venus Williams suffered racist abuse at the Indian Wells Tournament, California, in 2001. As a result, they refused to play in the event for the next two years – a boycott that had a significant impact on the success of the tournament (Spencer 2004).

Many clubs and organisations are taking positive steps to tackle this issue through anti-racism campaigns. The 'Kick It Out' campaign was English football's attempt to convince fans to reject racism and the racist groups that have long tried to recruit new members at matches. Meanwhile, Atlético Madrid has specifically encouraged immigrants from South America to support the club, thereby broadening the ethnic mix of its fan base. It is estimated that up to 500,000 people have arrived in Madrid from South America in the past few years, and a television advertising campaign has urged these new arrivals not only to come along to Atlético's matches but to integrate with the wider community.

CASE STUDY 9.2

Golf in a coliseum and a powerful environmental message

Location: Scottsdale, Phoenix, Arizona, USA
Event type: golf tournament
Attendees: 600,000 over days, including 22,000 spectators on hole 16
The drama of the event: the 'coliseum' hole

Golfers are not renowned for their exuberance when playing in golf events, in fact the etiquette of golf guides players in how they must behave as competitors, with many restrictions on their dress, their behaviour around other golfers, and how they should portray the game of golf. This game is more than 300 years old and steeped in tradition and has been an established sporting event in the USA, Australia and the United Kingdom. Traditionally, it was played by the aristocracy and the cost of equipment and green fees at courses, has meant that many people have been excluded from the game. However, it is popular on television and attracts key sponsors. Many of its players earn millions of dollars every year, and in South Korea hundreds of female golfers dedicate their lives to the game in golf academies, with many of the top 20 female golfers in the world originating from there.

The Phoenix Open, sponsored by Waste Management has become one of the most talked-about events on the golf circuit, even though the tournament is not a 'major.' In 2015, around 600,000 people attended the event over five days, with more than 205,000 people attending on Saturday, a new record for golf event attendance. However, the success of the event is perhaps not just down to the number of key golfers who play, but also to the fact that the most important objective of the event is to ensure that fan experience is addressed. Additionally, it is important to make sporting events more sustainable and educate consumers as to how to they can reduce their own personal impact on the environment by carefully managing waste disposal and water usage. The fans who attend the tournament still respect golf etiquette, but that does not prevent them from turning up in fancy-dress costumes and from cheering success on the course.

The main focal point of the tournament is the 16th hole, which they now refer to as the 'coliseum' hole. This is a short par 3 hole and, in order to create a better atmosphere, the hole is completely surrounded by temporary stands that hold as many as 20,000 people, creating this coliseum effect. When players shoot for the hole, they are applauded and cheered for success and poor shots are met with a groan. Many of the players enter into the spirit of the event and encourage audience participation. Once the golfers have played their shot, the caddies then race each other to the hole, carrying a full bag of clubs, roared on by the appreciative crowd.

This is typical of the approach of a number of USA sporting event managers who are not prepared to try new ideas in order to maximise fan experience. The sponsors, who as their name suggests are a waste disposal company, use the event to promote green issues in a fun way in the hope that this gets the message across to their consumers. On one of the days, fans are encouraged to turn up in a green top, to show their support of recycling, and the sponsors make a donation to environmental projects for every green top that is worn at the tournament.

While most golf tournaments are only set up to run on the days of the sporting activity, the Waste Management Open has pre-tournament fun activities for spectators and celebrity guests to attend, which makes it also very popular with participants and their families. Spectators are encouraged to make charitable donations and the 2016 tournament was estimated to have made $8 million for charities.

The Waste Management tournament also uses a golf tournament to communicate key messages to important stakeholders about the need to preserve energy and reduce the amount of non-recyclable waste that they consume as packaging. The success of the closed hole has without doubt made golf and sporting event organisers look at ways of making their golf days and sporting events more enjoyable.

9.5 Sporting events marketing

Sporting events marketing attempts to unravel what motivates people to attend sports fixtures, matches and tournaments. While there are examples of research into sporting event attendees, which date back to the 1970s and 1980s, it was only during the late 1990s that the first specialist publications in sports marketing started to appear. This fact always surprises people in the sports industry, who assume that this is a well-established and thoroughly researched subject. Perhaps 90 per cent of all research papers on sports marketing focus on US sports, such as baseball, American football, ice hockey and basketball, and they look at collegiate as well as professional events. NASCAR, arguably the most popular motor sport in the United States, also features regularly in publications. This should come as no surprise, as the NASCAR merchandising market is vast; generating a staggering \$2 billion each year (Lowry 2004, cited in Amato *et al.* 2005). The Sports Marketing Association (SMA) was launched in the United States in 2002, in recognition of the growing importance of sports marketing among practitioners and as an academic subject.

The main difference between the marketing of normal goods and services and the marketing of sporting events is that the outcome of the latter is uncertain, meaning that the attendee could view it as either the best or the worst event ever. However, the focus remains the same, with the aim of the organiser being to satisfy a range of customers in the expectation that satisfied customers will choose to return in the future. A sports event marketer must therefore identify the service needs of attendees, understand those needs, and continue to satisfy them. The organisers must be aware of their relationship both with customers, who pay to attend the event, as well as with other stakeholders, such as sponsors and broadcasters who pay for television rights.

Image 9.2 Scottsdale golf event USA – 22,000 spectators on one hole and a record attendance of 205,000 spectators on one day
Credit: Maddie Meyer/Getty images

In trying to understand why people attend sporting events, factors influencing attendees can be broken down into three broad categories: front room, back room and circumstantial, as shown in Table 9.4 (Tomlinson *et al.* 1995). Using these various factors, researchers attempted to gauge the attitudes of sports fans attending events. It is important to consider all of the reasons why people attend such events in order to satisfy their needs and requirements. While it is assumed that the main reason for attending an event is love of the sport, Table 9.4 shows that

> **Table 9.4** The factors that affect attendance at a sporting event
> Source: Adapted from Tomlinson *et al.* 2005

Front room	Back room	Circumstantial
Does the general atmosphere appeal to the attendee?	Is there a tradition of going to games?	Are they attending with family or friends?
Are the right food and drinks available?	Is it an evening game? (May have different atmosphere to a daytime game)	Are they interested in live sporting action?
Is the venue clean?	How easy is it to get to the stadium?	Do they prefer to attend at certain times of the season?
Is the stadium well-designed?	What is the parking like?	Does the team have a chance of winning?
Is there any pre-match entertainment?	Is the game live on television?	Has the team played well recently?
Is there off-field entertainment?	Will star players be appearing?	Are there other games on television?
How will the other fans behave?	Is there community support for the team?	Are there other sports teams nearby?
Is there a band?	Are there facilities for children?	Is the weather good for this event?
How good are the seats?	What is the transport like for the event?	Has the team won a high percentage of their games? Is this game a special event? Is the opposing team successful?

many other factors also influence attendance. This table therefore provides a useful checklist for sporting event organisers. When Tomlinson *et al.* (1995) carried out their research, they found that back-room factors had the largest negative impact on attendance.

While seeing their team win is important for sporting events customers, the other factors are equally important – and perhaps even more important – to compensate for the team losing. A typical example is the quality and value of the food and drink that are available. Clearly, with attendances of over 50,000 people, and at an average of around £4 per head in additional expenditure, the potential revenue from refreshments alone can be as much as £200,000.

One of the key challenges for sporting event marketers is to ensure that customers receive high levels of service and that the issue of queuing is taken seriously. Research undertaken in the United States has found that service quality, the physical environment and waiting times all affect attendees' enjoyment of the event (Hightower *et al.* 2002). At the very least, then, sporting event managers should look for innovative ways to reduce attendees' queuing times. For instance, upgraded tickets could include food and drink in the purchase price, and these items could then be delivered to the attendee's seat during the event. Consequently, that person would not have to waste time queuing for food, and the queue would be shorter for those who did not choose to buy the upgraded ticket. A number of organisations have also developed apps which allow attendees at events to order and pay for their food and drink before the intervals, which reduces the queues.

Tomlinson *et al.*'s research (1995) challenges the traditional view that fans' motivation to attend is based primarily on the performance of their team. Other researchers, such as Wakefield and Sloan (1995), also challenge this view, suggesting that people are motivated by the experience of the event, being with similar people and pure escapism. This area is still ripe for research, and sporting event organisers will benefit from an increased understanding of why people attend their events.

Fan festivals and events prior to the start of an event are innovative ways to attract more attendees. For instance, the Women's United States Soccer Association held an interactive fan festival – 'Soccer Sensation' – in which fans were able to meet players and take part in soccer activities (Jowdy and McDonald 2003). The main objectives of this type of 'experiential branding' are to raise customer awareness and to improve relationships between players and supporters. On this occasion, the event also raised cash through sponsorship, which meant it was able to sell tickets for future matches at discounted prices.

Study activity

To what extent does the televising of sporting events affect attendance at live sporting events? Consider two sporting events that are televised and list the main area where you think that this might impact on live attendance at the event.

9.5.1 Types of attendees at sporting events

The crowds at sporting events are often made up of groups of like-minded people, and a sporting event organiser should be able to identify these distinct groups using the principles of market segmentation. Most of these people will insist that they are unique individuals and do not resemble any of their fellow attendees, but research has shown that that is rarely the case.

As can be seen in Table 9.5, there are four broad categories of sports attendee: the most devoted, who attend frequently; the moderates, who attend an average number of games; the less frequent, who attend occasionally; and the 'new fans', who are relatively recent attendees at sporting events. All of these fans might claim to be loyal, but they consume sporting events differently, so attempts to communicate with them should be different, too. This basic level of segmentation is a starting point for developing marketing strategies. For instance, those fans who attend only three or four games each season, out of a possible twenty-five, might be encouraged to attend just two more games each year. Meanwhile, those who already attend every game could be offered the opportunity to upgrade their tickets. Different marketing techniques might then be devised to increase the attendance of those who usually watch events from private hospitality boxes, the increasingly important family market, and the growing number of female sports fans. Compiling a database of attendees will help sports event organisers to categorise them more accurately, and will therefore enhance the efficiency of their marketing initiatives.

Table 9.5 Classification of sports fans by frequency of attendance

Type of fan	Author/researcher
Most loyal: high or vested, devoted, fanatical, dysfunctional, frequent, season-ticket holders, hard core, old, genuine, traditional	Branscombe and Wann 1991, Sutton *et al.* 1997, Hunt *et al.* 1999, Arnett and Laverie 2000, Tapp and Clowes 2002, Rodriguez *et al.* 2003, Malcolm 2002, Amato *et al.* 2005, Stewart *et al.* 2003
Fans showing average support: medium or focused, local, enthusiast, moderately frequent attendance	Branscombe and Wann 1991, Sutton *et al.* 1997, Hunt *et al.* 1999, Arnett and Laverie 2000, Rodriguez *et al.* 2003
Occasional fans: low or social, temporary, casual, infrequent, sporadic spectator	Branscombe and Wann 1991, Sutton *et al.* 1997, Hunt *et al.* 1999, Tapp and Clowes 2002, Amato *et al.* 2005, Arnett and Laverie 2000, Rodriguez *et al.* 2003
New fans: usually watch major teams/stars, corporate, temporary	Redhead 1997, King 1997, Giulianotti 2002, Sandvoss 2003, Rodriguez *et al.* 2003, Tanaka 2004, Stewart *et al.* 2003, Hunt *et al.* 1999, Crespo *et al.* 2003

Study activity

How does an economic downturn affect the running of a major sporting event, such as the Olympic Games?

CASE STUDY 9.3

The cost of converting a major sporting event venue

Location: London, England
Event type: Olympic Games
Attendees: 80,000 (converted to 60,000 after the event)

This case study considers the costs of converting sporting venues after they have been used for a major sporting event; a key factor for the organisers of these events, and in particular, London 2012, which was estimated to cost around £9 billion to set up – an event that has widely been reported to have been successful. In contrast, during the construction of stadiums for the 2014 World

Cup in Brazil, many Brazilian citizens took part in street protests, questioning the cost of hosting the World Cup and the Olympic Games. It was suggested that the resources should have been allocated to key areas, such as health and education, rather than on building stadiums that would not be utilised fully once the events had finished. With this in mind, the London Organising Committee for the Olympic Games (LOCOG) was set up to manage the Olympic Games and, after the games, the London Legacy Development Corporation (LLDC) was tasked with finding suitable tenants for the £700 million main stadium, which hosted mainly athletics events.

Many industry specialists were critical of the fact that the stadium was built without the support of a London football club, or any other sports. People were unaware of the *costs* of refurbishing the stadium for new tenants or owners. The LLDC negotiated the use of the stadium with three different football clubs and, eventually, West Ham United were offered the tenancy. When Tottenham Hotspur Football Club bid to take it over, even though it was not close to their existing stadium, they talked about demolishing the existing structure in order to construct facilities that were more in line with those needed by a football club. The reason for this suggestion is due in part to the high cost of land in London and so their plans would have made use of the land and converted more of it into revenue-generating facilities. When West Ham eventually signed the agreement to move into the stadium in September 2016, the question of how they were going to finance this move became a key talking point. It was assumed that they would have to pay a significant fee and high rent in order to take over such a large venue that offered them the opportunity to increase their stadium capacity, from 34,000 to 60,000, and significantly improve their hospitality facilities.

Many of the details of the agreement between West Ham United and the LLDC were withheld by the LLDC, but under the Freedom of Information Act (2000) they were forced to reveal more. Many people were surprised that it cost in the region of a further £300 million to refurbish a stadium that was £700 million in construction, taking the total cost to around £1 billion. There was criticism of the deal with West Ham who were to take over a 60,000 capacity stadium at a rent of only £2 million per year or £40,000 a week, and objections also that their contribution to the redevelopment was no more than £20 million from a total bill of £300 million. The sale of their current ground was estimated to generate around £200 million in revenue, as the site would lend itself to the development of new apartments to be sold on a rising London property market.

The conversion of a stadium for a major event to a new-use venue after that event is a key ingredient of a legacy strategy and likely to receive support from major stakeholders. However, the cost of that conversion has now come under greater scrutiny and there is an implication that many no longer see this as a successful handover to a new tenant. This also means that future plans to host major sporting events will be more closely examined in the future since criticism will be aimed at the Olympic Games Committee whose task is to evaluate the legacy potential of their events *before* awarding the Olympic Games.

Study activity

Choose a sport, such as football, American football or cricket, and identify six key market segments that you think a club should target. You should indicate what percentage of the total supporter base each segment might represent.

Industry voice

Steve Sutherland, Sports Marketing and Events Consultant, formerly Marketing Manager of the Football League, assistant to the Chief Executive of Charlton Athletic Football Club

Steve Sutherland has witnessed dramatic changes in the sports industry over the last thirty years and he has been involved in many major events. Now, in his new role as a sports marketing consultant, he has advised Greenwich Borough Council when it hosted a number of high-profile events in the 2012 Olympics, secures funding and sponsorship on behalf of football community trusts, and advises companies as to how they can use sponsorship to communicate more effectively with their stakeholders.

Steve recognises the extent to which new technology has changed the events industry:

> It seems incredible now, but my first experiences in events were in the pre-internet days when Twitter and Facebook were still some twenty-five years away. These were the days when not many football clubs or other sports clubs had computer databases. Information on supporters or businesses was kept in paper form in flip-files, and database marketing was no more sophisticated than sending letters to supporters once a year about renewing season tickets. When I was given a car phone in 1991, it felt really high-tech.
>
> I'm proud of the fact that the very first club to launch a club-branded credit card was Charlton Athletic, when I did a deal with a company called Transnational Financial Services in 1990. Now all clubs have exactly the same product.

Steve was also involved in some of the first TV deals when he was marketing executive at the Football League, just before the Premier League was launched: 'At that time, the collective deal for four football divisions was a mere £11 million and the sponsorship deal with Barclays was just £2 million.'

The events industry changed dramatically after the Taylor Inquiry issued its report on the Hillsborough tragedy, as Steve recalls:

> This effectively forced football clubs to invest in their stadiums to make them safer and more customer-oriented, and there were major developments in

the modernisation of professional football. Football clubs, which formed part of a multimillion-pound events industry, were also forced to review crowd safety and policing. Faced with mounting police bills, football clubs like Charlton Athletic started to train their own stewards. In fact, Charlton is still a leader in steward training courses and has advised other clubs.

Steve is currently one of the leading authorities on sports and corporate social responsibility (CSR). He advises companies on how to invest in community-based sporting events and still works closely with the Charlton Athletic Community Trust (see the CACT website):

> Football clubs are now extremely sophisticated with regards to their marketing practices, with the result that sponsors and advertisers still flock to become involved in the sport. Clubs now play a significant part in their local communities, recognising that the iconic status of the football club can be a force for good, and the more enlightened ones even recognise that community marketing boosts interest in the club and attendances on match days as well.

Steve was also behind the pioneering Valley Express service, an initiative that was copied by other event organisers. As he points out:

> Finding a parking space at the Valley, home of Charlton Athletic Football Club, was problematic and impacted on local residents, so we set up the Valley Express, a subsidised bus service that picked up fans within a 70-mile radius of London. With 3,000 fans on these buses, about 15 per cent of a typical gate, traffic congestion was greatly reduced at the venue.

Steve feels that the events industry has much to gain from becoming more involved with community projects:

> From my time at Charlton Athletic and at the British Amateur Boxing Association, where I was also a CSR consultant, I have noticed that working with children in deprived areas helps to get them off the streets and into gyms, which, in turn, helps to teach them about respect and discipline. There is an opportunity for the sporting events and the wider events industry to get involved with CSR programmes, as the power of a tracksuit over a suit or a uniform cannot be overstated.

Furthermore, Steve is clear about the positive effect of hosting regular sporting events in a local community, such as Charlton:

> Without a doubt, if the football club is thriving, then the local economy will be too. Charlton Athletic is a significant local employer, not just of full-time staff but large numbers of match-day staff as well, in catering, security and

maintenance, and each week many thousands of people flock to the area and frequent the local bars, restaurants and shops.

Charlton was also one of the first football clubs to develop strategic partnerships with other organisations in order to increase income:

> For a stadium to survive, it is vital to develop facilities and work in partnership in order to generate non-event revenue. We formed a strategic alliance with Greenwich Leisure Limited and grant funding enabled us to build a gym in the West Stand. We then obtained a European grant to operate classes, and a full-time college was set up at the club. For a stadium to thrive, it has to be used every day of the week, and whether that's for hospitality, seminars, presentations, product launches, classrooms or medical matters, strategic alliances are vital in achieving this. The latest project is a new drop-in medical centre, built with grant funding from Greenwich NHS.

Finally, Steve offers advice to people who would like to work in the sporting events industry:

> Football clubs do advertise key positions, so relevant qualifications are important. But most jobs in football go to people who are known to the club. So I would recommend volunteering or becoming a match-day worker in security or catering, or even taking a level-one coaching course and getting work as a part-time coach in the community department.

9.6 Summary

This chapter has highlighted the significant growth in the sporting events industry; in terms of participation, media attention, overall revenue generation and the importance of staging events to local and national governments. Consideration has been given to the impact of sporting events and the legacies left by some of them, as well as the process involved in making a successful bid for an event. Politicians' involvement and influence have also been discussed, as has the relationship between sports and politics.

The chapter has shown that sporting event arenas have changed significantly over the past twenty-five years to meet higher consumer expectations and to compete with other events. More emphasis is being placed on comfort and additional services, both for fans and for those using the facilities when the main sporting event is not taking place. Examples of good practice in stadium design have been given, as have suggestions for how sporting event managers might incorporate these into their future plans. We have seen that significant improvements have been made in customer care and event safety in recent years, but also that crowd violence may still pose problems for event organisers. Managing the experience of participants has also been identified as an important consideration for staging events in a more competitive sporting event market. Finally, we have highlighted the need for more research into why people attend sporting events. What remains clear is that the sporting events industry is vibrant, with increasing revenues, rising attendances and ever-expanding television viewing figures.

Further reading

Emery, P. R. (2002) Bidding to Host a Major Sports Event: The Local Organising Committee Perspective, *International Journal of Public Sector Management*, 15 (4): 316–355. An article that provides insight into the bidding process for major sporting events and offers a useful framework for those who want to find out more about the subject.

Masterman, G. (2014) *Strategic Sports Management* (Olympic edn), Oxford: Butterworth-Heinemann. This is the leading book on sporting events management from a European perspective.

Tomlinson, M., Buttle, F. and Moores, B. (1995) The Fan as Customer: Customer Services in Sports Marketing, *Journal of Hospitality and Leisure Marketing*, 3 (1): 19–36. This article, one of the first to focus on customer service in the sporting events industry, used research to identify the most important service factors from a spectator's perspective.

References

Agrawal, J. and Kamakura, W. A. (1995) The Economic Worth of Celebrity Endorsers: An Event Study Analysis, *Journal of Marketing*, 59: 56–62.

Amato, C. H., Okelshen-Peters, C. L. and Shao, A. T. (2005) An Exploratory Investigation into NASCAR Fan Culture, *Sport Marketing Quarterly*, 142: 71–83.

Ambrose, P. J. (2004) Drug Use in Sports: A Veritable Arena for Pharmacists, *Journal of the American Pharmacists Association*, 44 (4): 501–516.

Andersson, T. (2001) Swedish Football Hooliganism 1900–1939, *Soccer and Society*, 2 (1): 1–18.

Arnett, D. B. and Laverie, D. A. (2000) Fan Characteristics and Sporting Event Attendance Examining Variance in Attendance, *International Journal of Sports Marketing and Sponsorship*, 23: 219–238.

Barget, E. and Gouguet, J.-J. (2007) The Total Economic Value of Sporting Events: Theory and Practice, *Journal of Sports Economics*, 8 (2): 165–182.

Beckett, A. H. and Cowan, D. A. (1979) Misuse of Drugs in Sport, *British Journal of Sports Medicine*, 12: 185–194.

Branscombe, N. R. and Wann, D. L. (1991) The Positive Social and Self-Concept Consequences of Sports Team Identification, *Journal of Sport and Social Issues*, 152: 115–127.

Bush, V. D., Bush, A. J., Clark, P. and Bush, R. P. (2005) Girl Power and Word-of-Mouth Behaviour in the Flourishing Sports Market, *Journal of Consumer Marketing*, 22 (5): 257–264.

Cousens, L., Babiak, K. and Slack, T. (2001) Adopting a Relationship Marketing Paradigm: The Case of the National Basketball Association, *International Journal of Sports Marketing and Sponsorship*, 2: 331–355.

Crawford, M., Donnelly, J., Gordon, J., MacCallum, R., MacDonald, I., McNeil, M., Mulhearn, N., Tilston, S. and West, G. (2001) An Analysis of Consultations with the Crowd Doctors at Glasgow Celtic Football Club, Season 1999–2000, *British Journal of Sports Medicine*, 35: 245–250.

Crespo, A. H., Garcia de los Salmones, M. M., Agudi San Emeterio, A. and del Bosque, R. (2003) Analisís de los Factores de la Calidad Percibida en los Espectaculos Deportivos Aplicación al Fútbol Professional, paper presented at the Congreso Mundial de Gestión Económica del Deporte, Barcelona, 14–15 May.

Dickie, J. F. (1995) Major Crowd Catastrophes, *Safety Science*, 18: 309–320.

Duke, V. and Crolley, L. (1994) *Argy-Bargy at the Match: Football Spectator Behaviour in Argentina*, European Studies Research Unit Working Paper, University of Salford.

Duke, V. and Crolley, L. (2001) Fútbol, Politicians and the People: Populism and Politics in Argentina, *International Journal of the History of Sport*, 18 (3): 93–116.

Emery, P. R. (2002) Bidding to Host a Major Sports Event: The Local Organising Committee Perspective, *International Journal of Public Sector Management*, 15 (4): 316–355.

Giulianotti, R. (2002) Supporters, Followers, Fans and Flaneurs: A Taxonomy of Spectator Identities in Football, *Journal of Sport and Social Issues*, 261: 25–46.

Hamilton, G. (2004) Watch Boca Juniors Play River Plate in Buenos Aires, *Observer*, 4 April.

Hightower, R., Brady, M. K. and Baker, T. L. (2002) Investigating the Role of the Physical Environment in Hedonic Service Consumption: An Exploratory Study of Sporting Events, *Journal of Business Research*, 55: 697–707.

Humphreys, B. R. and Humphreys, B. R. (2008) The Size and Scope of the Sports Industry in the United States, IASE/NAASE Working Paper Series, No. 08-11.

Humphreys, B. R. and Ruseski, J. E. (2008) Estimates of the Size of the Sports Industry in the United States, paper presented to the International Association of Sports Economists, Gijon, Spain, 8–11 August.

Hunt, K.A., Bristol, T. and Bashaw, R. E. (1999) A Conceptual Approach to Classifying Sports Fans, *Journal of Services Marketing*, 136: 439–452.

Jowdy, E. and McDonald, M. A. (2003) Relationship Marketing and International Fan Festivals, *International Journal of Sports Marketing and Sponsorship*, 4: 295–312.

King, A. (1997) The Lads' Masculinity and the New Consumption of Football, *Sociology*, 31 (2): 329–346.

Lowry, T. (2004) The Prince of NASCAR, *Business Week*, 3871: 90.

Maennig W. And Zimbalist, A. S. (2012) *International Handbook on the Economics of Mega Sporting Events*, Cheltenham: Edward Elgar Publishing.

Malcolm, D. (2002) Football Business and Football Communities in the Twenty-first Century, *Soccer and Society*, 1 (3): 102–113.

Pennington-Gray, L. and Holdnak, A. (2002) Out of the Stands and into the Community: Using Sports Events to Promote a Destination, *Events Management*, 7: 177–186.

Preuss, H. (2005) The Economic Impact of Visitors at Major Multi-sport Events, *European Sport Management Quarterly*, 5 (3): 281–301.

Preuss, H. and Solberg, H. A. (2006) Attracting Major Sporting Events: The Role of Local Residents, *European Sport Management Quarterly*, 6 (4): 391–411.

Redhead, S. (1997) *Post-Fandom and the Millennial Blues: The Transformation of Soccer Culture*, London: Routledge.

Rodriguez, D., Wigfield, A. and Eccles, J. S. (2002) Changing Competence Perceptions, Changing Values: Implications for Youth Sport. Research report, National Inst. of Child Health and Human Development (NIH), Bethesda, MD.

Sandvoss, C. (2003) *A Game of Two Halves: Football, Television and Globalization*, London and New York: Routledge.

Small, K. (2007) Social Dimensions of Community Festivals: An Application of Factor Analysis in the Development of the Social Impact Perception (SIP) Scale, *Event Management*, 11: 45–55.

Spencer, N. E. (2004) Sister Act VI: Venus and Serena Williams at Indian Wells: 'Sincere Fictions' and White Racism, *Journal of Sport and Social Issues*, 28 (2): 115–135.

Stewart, B., Smith, A. C. T. and Nicholson, M. (2003) Sport Consumer Typologies: A Critical Review, *Sport Marketing Quarterly*, 12: 206–216.

Sutton, W. A., McDonald, M. A. and Milne, G. R. (1997) Creating and Fostering Fan Identification in Professional Sports, *Sport Marketing Quarterly*, 61: 15–22.

Tanaka, T. (2004) The Positioning and Practices of the 'Feminized Fan' in Japanese Soccer Culture through the Experience of the FIFA World Cup Korea/Japan 2002, *Inter-Asia Cultural Studies*, 51: 52–62.

Tapp, A. and Clowes, J. (2002) From 'Carefree Casuals' to 'Professional Supporter', *European Journal of Marketing*, 3611 (12): 1248–1269.

Wakefield, K. L. and Sloan, H. J. (1995) The Effects of Team Loyalty and Selected Stadium Factors on Spectator Attendance, *Journal of Sport Management*, 9 (2): 153–172.

Westerbeek, H. M., Turner, P. and Ingerson, L. (2002) Key Success Factors in Bidding for Hallmark Sporting Events, *International Marketing Review*, 19 (3): 303–322.

Wilde, N, (2009) Interview with Orlando Salvestrini, President of Marketing, Boca Juniors, *International Journal of Sports Marketing and Sponsorship*, 10 (3): 2–5.

Wong, L. L. and Trumper, R. (2002) Global Celebrity Athletes and Nationalism: Fútbol, Hockey and the Representation of Nations, *Journal of Sport and Social Issues*, 26 (2): 188–194.

Websites

Charlton Athletic Community Trust: www.cact.org.uk.

FA: www.thefa.com/TheFA/England2018.

FIFA: www.fifa.com/mm/51/53/98/safetyregulations.

Guardian: www.guardian.co.uk/football/2010/dec/02/mike-lee-qatar-world-cup-bid.

Managing sporting events: www.helpforclubs.org.uk.

New York Yankees: www.newyork-yankees.mlb.com.

Olympic Games: www.olympic.org.

Phoenix Suns: www.nba.com/suns.

Sheffield Hallam FC: www.theoldestfootballgroundintheworld.com/history.

Sport Business magazine: www.sportbusiness.com.

Chapter 10

Mega-events

Contents

10.1 Aims

By the end of this chapter, students will be able to:

- define and categorise mega-events;
- analyse individual mega-events across different periods of their existence;
- evaluate the relationship between mega-events and urban regeneration;
- evaluate the relationship between mega-events and tourism.

10.2 Introduction

Mega-events, like the Olympic Games and the World Expos, have become increasingly important in the global economy as governments compete to bring them to their cities in order to catalyse economic, social and cultural change. These events attract attendances in the millions and the largest of them command television audiences that number in the billions. This chapter is intended to introduce the concept of the mega-event and to highlight key challenges in successfully managing this diverse group of events. A definition and typology of mega-events will be given, which shows that the 'mega' category can relate to audience size, economic impact, visitor numbers and/or socio-cultural significance. Emphasis will be placed on understanding the pre-, during- and post-event periods and the relationships between mega-events, tourism and urban regeneration.

10.3 Defining mega-events

The term 'mega-event' refers to those events that take place for a global media audience and/or that have significant, long-term impacts on economies and societies.

For the purposes of distinguishing between different kinds of events and for moving on to think about how these events are planned and delivered, we can place mega-events on a scale of large events, depending on their socio-economic and media impacts.

Mega-events are distinguished by the immense scale of their audiences and their social and economic impacts, as shown in Figure 10.1. Included in the total audience are both large numbers of attendees at the 'live' event and even larger numbers of people who watch the event via various media, especially television. Increasingly, these media audiences are being extended and developed through the use of streaming media and media archives. While 3.2 billion people watched the matches of the 2014 FIFA World Cup in Brazil , and 695 million viewers watched the final match on television in their homes, it is estimated that more than 280 million people watched matches on their mobiles, tablets and computers (FIFA 2011).

Events on this scale are infrequent but usually periodical. The Summer and Winter Olympic Games, for example, take place on four-yearly cycles. The World Expo, a global cultural fair, moves between countries on a five-yearly basis, and the most recent one attracted more than 20 million visitors over a five-month period, with 2.7 million visiting in the first month (see Case Study 10.1).

Roche (2000: 1) defines mega-events by referring to their significance and appeal, describing them as 'large-scale cultural (including commercial and sporting) events, which have a dramatic character, mass popular appeal and international significance'. Roberts (2004) emphasises the stand-alone character of mega-events, suggesting that they are out-of-the-ordinary events,

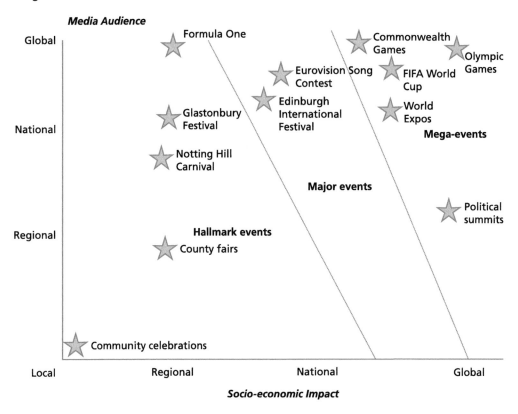

Figure 10.1 Media and socio-economic scales of large events

The Milan World Expo 2015

Location: Milan, Italy
Event type: mega-event
Attendees: 20,000,000

On 31 March 2008, the International Exhibitions Bureau in Paris awarded the 2015 World Expo, after a competitive bidding process. The World Expo in Milan ran for 184 days, from 1 May until 31 October 2015. The event was themed with the concept 'Feeding the planet: Energy for life'. The Expo took place on a 1km^2 site to the north of the city, which hosted 5,000 events in a mixture of temporary spaces and specially constructed new venues, including pavilions and other contributions from 145 countries.

Image 10.1 **Malaysian Pavilion at the Milan Expo 2015**
Credit: Ernesto Ruscio/Getty images

Hosting the Expo cost the Italian Government around 1.3 billion euros, with an additional 0.3 billion euros from private investors, and 1 billion euros from international country participants. As well as showcasing the cultures of the participating countries, the Milan Expo also promoted its themes of sustainability and food security, in particular. The *Milan Charter* was signed at the event by a number of heads of state and representatives from non-governmental organisations, setting out global principles for nutrition, food rights and environmental security.

(EuroNews 2015; Expo Milano 2015)

discontinuous in character and remarkable for their size. It has been pointed out that not all mega-events are mega in the same way and that events can be evaluated for their mega-nature according to four characteristics: visitor attractiveness, mediated reach, cost and transformative impact.

Discontinuity and drama are undoubtedly two key elements of mega-events that help us to understand their appeal and significance. However, these are relative concepts that vary between locations and cultures. Events such as the Glastonbury Festival, an annual UK music festival, stand out within their host communities as dramatic and a break from the normal routine, but Glastonbury's 2015 TV audience of just 18.7 million viewers (Gumble 2016) suggests that it is on a different scale to the most recent Olympic celebrations in Rio De Janeiro in 2016, which attracted an estimated worldwide audience of 3.7 billion (BBC 2016). Getz and Page (2016: 59) incorporate this relativity into his definition of the mega-event, explaining that they are 'those that yield extraordinarily high levels of tourism, media coverage, prestige, or economic impact *for the host community, venue or organisation*' (emphasis added). For example, the impact of the Glastonbury Festival, with its 135,000 attendees and 18.7 million viewers in a small rural community of just 8,932 people show the relative nature of the 'mega' in mega-events.

Within the category of mega-events, three major kinds can be identified that are characterised by their audience and/or significance at the global level: cultural, political and sporting mega-events.

10.3.1 Cultural mega-events

These mega-events focus on the development and/or promotion of regional or national culture. Typically, they involve the designation of an area or region as the event hub for a specific period of time and include a wide programme of cultural events across a variety of cultural forms. Examples include the Eurovision Song Contest, which involves a series of regional and national events and finally a single international event, and the European Capital of Culture programme.

The European Capital of Culture programme began in 1985 with certain cities designated by the European Union as the European Capitals of Culture; candidate cities had to bid for a chance to win the award in a competitive process. Successful cities host a year-long programme of cultural events that emphasise their particular distinctiveness, as well as their European connections. The European Commission describe the aims of the programme:

> to put cities at the heart of cultural life across Europe. Through culture and art, European Capitals of Culture improve the quality of life in these cities and strengthen their sense of community. Citizens can take part in the year-long activities and play a bigger role in their city's development and cultural expression.
>
> (European Commission 2017: 1)

In 2017, the cities of Aarhus in Denmark and Paphos in Cyprus have been awarded the title together, with the aims of considering new ways in which culture and cities can contribute to modern life, while recognising Europe's multicultural heritage, respectively. In 2018, Valletta, in Malta, will be one of the European Capitals of Culture, along with Leuuwarden in the Netherlands. The Valletta event will include five key special events in its programme, including: Opening and Closing ceremonies, the Valletta Pageants of the Seas, a newly written contemporary opera and a film festival, as well as community-focused events, such as carnivals, music festivals and public art (Valletta 2018 Foundation 2017).

Liverpool was awarded the title of European Capital of Culture in 2008 after winning a competitive bidding process against eleven other European cities. Winning this title helped to secure £4 billion in new investment for the city, and hosting the year-long cultural festival generated £800 million in revenue from 15 million visitors to cultural events and attractions. It is estimated that the worldwide television audience for the opening event was 300 million (Liverpool 08 2009). Istanbul won the Capital of Culture bid for 2010. The organisers announced the following aims, which illustrate the diverse expectations of mega-event impacts:

- From 2006 onwards the name of Istanbul will be associated with culture and the arts all over the world.

- As Turkey moves ahead with the process of its candidacy for the European Union, the projects that will be realised will demonstrate that Istanbul, the symbol of the country, has been interacting with European culture for hundreds of years.
- The city's cultural heritage will be managed in a sustainable manner and it will become even more of a magnet than ever before.
- Istanbul will achieve lasting gains in the fields of urban renewal, urban living and environmental and social development.
- New museums will be established to protect and display our cultural assets, and historical buildings will be renovated, given new roles and opened to the public.
- The people of Istanbul will embrace new artistic disciplines. Young, talented people will have the opportunity to become more closely involved in artistic creativity.
- Many jobs will be created, ranging from those in communications to organisation, education, design, management and creative fields.
- Those who come to Istanbul for cultural and artistic projects will visit the city's cultural riches, mosques, churches, palaces and museums.
- Cultural tourism will be invigorated and will develop. (Educated, cultured tourists spend three times more than ordinary tourists. This means that, as a European Capital of Culture, Istanbul will have great tourism potential.)
- Internationally, many people from the world of culture and the arts, together with members of the print and visual media, will visit Istanbul. This will make a positive contribution to Istanbul's promotion and branding. Being selected as a European Capital of Culture will give a boost to the city's economic relations with Europe as well as contributing to its cultural relations. With the renovation that will take place, the administrators and the common people will join together, hand in hand, sharing their knowledge and experience, to develop a long-term sustainable model for the future.
- Istanbul local residents will be proud of their city as they discover more of its beauty. (Istanbul 2010–2011)

10.3.2 Political mega-events

These events have increased in frequency and size with the progress of globalisation since the 1970s. Now, more than ever, political delegations and NGOs from the developed and developing world meet to debate and harmonise policies on global trade, security and the environment. These events, like the World Economic Forum and the parallel World Social Forum, have a global significance that transcends visitor numbers and budgets that would normally be associated with a major event, such as a music festival or sporting contest.

The United Nations Climate Change Conference Copenhagen 2015 (COP 15) is an example of this new kind of mega-event. This event brought together 40,000 delegates, including 147 heads of state and 3,000 accredited journalists and 5,000 other journalists for twelve days in an attempt to reach a new global agreement on the response to climate change. The event had a budget of 170 million euros and security was provided by 11,000 armed police. As well as the main conference session, large side-events, such as the 6th Annual Sustainable Innovation Forum, took place during COP 21, attracting around 1,500 delegates to watch more than 75 high-profile speakers (Sustainable Innovation Forum 2016). An increasingly common feature of these events is the large number of protesters and demonstrators who attempt to disrupt or influence them. At COP 15, held in Copenhagen in 2009, around 100,000 protesters took to the streets, provoking a large and costly police response. In Paris for COP 21, protests were smaller, due to security concerns following recent terrorist attacks, but hundreds of thousands of people around the world took part in associated demonstrations (BBC 2015).

Key to understanding the position of political events such as COP 21 as a mega-event, however, is its political and environmental significance. A total of 193 countries sent delegates, and the event brought together political leaders and decision-makers with global levels of influence. Millions more participated in the event at a distance through protests and demonstrations in other countries, with the aim of influencing the proceedings.

10.3.3 Sporting mega-events

Sporting mega-events are the most commonly analysed type in the events management literature. Tournaments such as the Olympic Games and the FIFA World Cup stand alone in terms of their attendance, media audience and commercial activity. New technologies of communication and digital media have played a part in the development of sporting mega-events as the world's premium media events. Since 1960, the amount paid by US broadcasters for the rights to broadcast from the Summer Olympics has grown from $390,000 for Rome to $894 million for Beijing, and £1.18 billion for London 2012 (Horne and Manzenreiter 2006). In 2014, the US Network NBC paid $7.75 billion for the rights to broadcast the six Olympic Games from 2022 to 2032 (Sandomir 2014). The budget for the Beijing Olympics in 2008 – by far the largest and most visually spectacular games yet seen – reached $40 billion and involved the creation of six new Olympic venues and the reconstruction of a large area of the city.

It is now customary for sporting mega-events to be justified in terms of their funding and public policy impacts by the development of a significant legacy from these events. This legacy will normally include post-games uses for the Olympic venues, improved infrastructure in the host city and an improved destination brand for the city in the international tourism market. Four years after hosting the 2006 Winter Olympics, Torino, in northern Italy, was the country's fourth most visited city, after Rome, Florence and Venice. This was achieved through the development of the local tourism industry during and following the Games period, the use of the Games as a catalyst for urban renewal and the increased media profile of this largely industrial town. This demonstrates the potential power of the Games to rebrand a host city through harnessing the vast investment and media audience that the world's largest mega-events generate.

Study activity

What events in your country would you class as mega-events? What are the impacts of these events at the local, regional and national levels?

10.4 Mega-event periods

Like all events, mega-events have a planning stage and have impacts that extend beyond the life of the event itself. Specifically for mega-events, we can talk about the pre-event period, the event period and the post-event period.

10.4.1 The pre-event period

10.4.1.1 Competitive bidding

The first stage in the pre-event period is when the decision is made to stage a mega-event or, more commonly, to *bid* to stage a mega-event. Of course, some mega-events are intimately

Figure 10.2 The Olympic host city selection process for London 2012
Source: Adapted from Theodoraki 2007

linked to particular places (such as Munich's Oktoberfest), but this process usually begins with the event owners – for example, the International Olympic Committee or the International Expositions Bureau – announcing that they will accept submissions from potential hosts. There are then several competitive stages during which the number of potential hosts is reduced until a winner is chosen. The stages include the submission of bid documentation, visits by the event owners and formal presentations. Each city will develop a bid file that will normally include:

- Guarantees from the host city to the event owner.
- A profile of the host city, including:

  o demographic information
  o information on the environment
  o economic information
  o political information.

- Plans for the content of the event.
- Plans for facilities, accommodation and transport.
- Plans for associated celebratory and educational events.

The period of competitive bidding will start well in advance of the actual event itself. The level of planning required to stage a mega-event and the resources required to make it a success mean that an 8–10-year lead-in period is not uncommon for successful Olympic bids (Girginov and Parry 2005). At the start of this period, a Bid Committee will be formed that brings together political figures, Olympic experts, planners, media professionals and a range of stakeholders in the Olympic planning process. This Bid Committee will eventually hand over to an Organising Committee for the Olympic Games (OCOG), which will then be the lead body for the delivery of the Games themselves.

It is not only the Olympic city candidature process that generates a frenzy of bureaucratic activity. The successful bid of Umeå, in Sweden, to become European Capital of Culture in 2014 took ten years from start to finish and involved 350 people and collaborations with six other European cities.

CASE STUDY 10.2

Qatar and the 2022 FIFA World Cup

Location: Qatar
Event type: mega-event
Attendees: 1,000,000+

On 3 December 2010, FIFA announced that the World Cup in 2022 would be held in Qatar, a wealthy micro-state on the Arabian Peninsula, in the Middle East. Five years later, in 2015, FIFA Officials were arrested by the US Government and are facing allegations of corruption in relation to awarding this mega-event to Qatar.

In 2010, Qatar won 14 from a possible 22 votes from the FIFA executive. In 2011, a whistleblower from within the Qatari bid itself, claimed that more than $1.5 million in bribes were paid to FIFA Executive Committee members in order to secure their votes for Qatar's controversial bid. Qatar has only recently begun to develop its sporting infrastructure and only has professional football on a very small scale. For most of the year, it is too hot to play football, with temperatures reaching as high as 50° Celsius. Because the country does not have the sports infrastructure necessary to stage an international tournament, the government has had to invest an estimated £200 billion into the construction of new stadiums and facilities and the construction phase has been beset by problems, including fatalities of construction workers and allegations of the use of slave labour. In June 2015, FIFA President Sepp Blatter resigned amid allegations of corruption over the 2022 event and pending criminal prosecutions of FIFA executive members.

In the majority of cases, the hosting of mega-events is associated with improvements of the image of the hosting country. This would normally lead to an increase in international tourism, overseas investment and political benefits. However, in the case of Qatar 2022, Brannigan and Giulianotti (2015) have argued that the disputes surrounding the event have actually damaged the reputation of the country by linking it to controversies over corruption, human and minority rights and the financial aspects of global sport.

(Booth 2015; ABC News 2015; Brannigan and Giulianotti 2015)

10.4.1.2 Resources

A major task facing any city planning to host a mega-event is to assemble the required resources for making it a success. It is estimated that the costs of hosting the Athens 2004 Olympic Games rose to $12 billion, far in excess of the possible contribution from the Olympic movement of $4.3 billion. Despite this huge cost, recent research suggests that the overall economic impact of hosting the games on the Greek economy was positive (Foundation for Economic and Industrial Research 2015). This has serious implications for our understanding of the pre-event period, during which mega-event hosting cities must seek to acquire sufficient resources to produce the event. Although host cities aim to achieve significant benefits and produce a legacy from hosting these events, assembling adequate resources is a key task of the pre-event period. This funding typically comes from two sources: direct public investment, and partnerships with the private sector.

Hosting a mega-event requires large amounts of public investment. From the beginning of the bidding and planning process, the potential host city starts to accrue costs for something which, at this stage, may not even take place. The cost of bidding includes marketing, PR, staffing, premises, travel and lobbying. If a bid is successful, the host city must identify and acquire the land required for developing the mega-event location and begin the long and costly processes of planning and consultation. This is followed by the huge capital investments required in infrastructure development to improve travel networks for coping with visitors, as well as the construction of venues for the event. In addition, the human and organisational capital required to coordinate and manage these processes places a drain on state resources at both the local and the national levels. In the majority of cases, these upfront costs will be met through direct taxation and, sometimes, a special levy on residents, with the justification that the benefits of hosting the mega-event will outweigh the costs, especially once its legacy is taken into consideration. Politicians and event organisers frequently justify the decision to host a mega-event using the 'public good' argument.

Getz and Page (2016: 59) set out the three criteria of the 'public good' that have to be satisfied in order to justify the massive public sector commitment to hosting a mega-event:

- Events fit into accepted policy domains (culture, health, economics and so on).
- Public benefits are substantial (it is worth our while to get involved), inclusive (everyone gains) and can be demonstrated or proved.
- There are rules and accountability for money spent and other actions taken.

Within these three points, the most contentious is the second – demonstrable public benefit. Assuming that the benefits can be anticipated, planned for and measured, then the decision to host a mega-event becomes a matter of performing a simple cost–benefit analysis: will the benefits of hosting the event outweigh, or at least match, the costs of producing it? The assumption that is implicit in all mega-event bids is that they will, but the dispersed and diverse impacts of mega-events make this difficult to assess. Mega-events always have a number of specific effects that occur at different points in the life of the event, as is shown in Figure 10.3.

The problem caused by this distribution of event impacts is that the tangible benefits of hosting a mega-event are predicted to take place *during* or *after* the event. (The exception to this is the area of tourism, which will be dealt with in a later section of this chapter.) The very long planning period for mega-events and the huge public resource commitment involved during the pre-event stage can, therefore, cause significant political difficulties for host cities and governments. (The issue of the public perception of mega-events is addressed below.)

Two categories of partnership are important for understanding the planning and resourcing of mega-events. First, there are the partnerships required between different agencies, departments

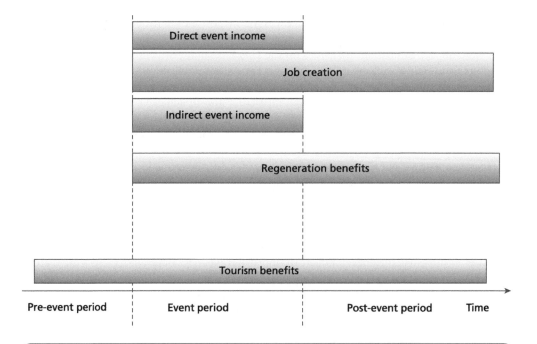

Figure 10.3 The distribution of mega-event impacts over time

and companies in the public and private sectors that are involved in delivering the event. Second, there are the partnerships between the event owners and hosts, on the one hand, and private companies, on the other, which take the form of sponsorship arrangements. The most significant sponsorship deals often allow companies to brand themselves as 'official partners' of the mega-event. These two types of partnerships can be termed *delivery partnerships* and *commercial partnerships*, and both help to generate the resources needed to stage a mega-event. Delivery partnerships generate extra resources for a mega-event during the pre-event period in two distinct ways: through planning and construction.

Planning partnerships tend to be embodied in particular organisations or forums. A planning partnership makes use of resources that are dispersed through different public bodies and other organisations. In particular, it brings additional organisational resources, experience and in-kind benefits to the planning of a mega-event, as well as additional human capital in the form of experts and administrative support. An example is PODIUM – the Further and Higher Education Unit for the 2012 Olympic Games. This public body

> functions as a platform on which to build the engagement of the Further and Higher Education sectors with the 2012 Games. The Unit works directly with a number of stakeholders including colleges, universities and the London Organising Committee of the Olympic and Paralympic Games (LOCOG), seconding the Unit's Head into LOCOG's Culture, Ceremonies and Education team for two days per week. Other stakeholders include: London Higher, the Olympic Delivery Authority, Government Departments, Regional Development Agencies, Sector Skills Councils, the Association of Colleges, British University & Colleges Sport, Guild HE and Universities UK.
>
> (PODIUM 2009)

Construction partnerships are typically made between public and private sector bodies, to contract in the experience, capabilities and capital of the private sector in order to support the construction of venues and improvements to infrastructure, as well as other capital-intensive projects that would be difficult for the public sector to fund otherwise. For example, the $600 million Cape Town Stadium for the 2010 FIFA World Cup in South Africa was constructed by Murray Roberts and WHBO, which were contracted in by the Organising Committee. The project was not directly managed by the state, and the management of the stadium during the event and in the post-event period was handled by a consortium of partners from the private sector with specific stadium-management experience. The $780 million Fisht Olympic Stadium for the 2014 Winter Olympics in Sochi, Russia, was designed by the international form of architects, Populous. It was constructed by Buro Happold, a global engineering firm, who were appointed to follow a brief developed by the local Organizing Committee. The Organizing Committee set demanding specifications, including for sustainability and the future use of the venue as a stadium for the 2018 FIFA World Cup and as the eventual home for the Russian national football team in winter, when it is too cold to play. Buro Happold were awarded a contract of $157 million to manage these aspects of this huge engineering project (Frearson 2014; Buro Happold 2015). However, the involvement of the private sector does not in itself guarantee that financial targets will be met. The eventual costs of the Olympic Stadium and Athletes' Village in Sochi amounted to more than twelve times the budget.

Commercial partnerships add capital and commercial support to a mega-event, usually through sponsorship deals that offer a promotional benefit to the event partner. The highest category of these partnerships is that of 'official partner'. Official partners of mega-events are often granted permission to use the event logos and branding materials as part of their own promotional activity.

Liverpool 08 had twelve official partners, each making a cash or in-kind contribution to the event. For example, Hill Dickinson LLP was the first official partner announced for Liverpool's Capital of Culture programme, taking on the responsibility for 'all legal and contractual dealings with sponsors, partners, suppliers, event organisers and the myriad of other businesses involved in the multi-year programme building up to 2008 and in the legacy years following' (Hill Dickinson LLP 2007). Virgin Trains paid £2 million for the right to become an official partner of Liverpool 08, additionally agreeing to promote the mega-event on its trains and through its services.

Potential sponsorship deals began at £20,000 and were marketed by Liverpool 08 as a portfolio of opportunities:

> Depending on the level of investment, companies can get access to a spectrum of Culture Company assets, including:
>
> ● intellectual property (logos, designations, 'Look of the Capital of Culture')
> ● category exclusivity
> ● corporate use (letterheads, business cards, B2B promotions, website)
> ● consumer use (TV, radio, print, direct mail, outdoor, website, database use)
> ● sponsor recognition (banners, advertising, website links)
> ● tickets and hospitality (complimentary allocation and access to purchase additional)
> ● event creation and involvement upgrades. (Liverpool 08 2008)

10.4.1.3 Public perceptions of mega-events

Thus, the public perception of mega-events is affected by the distribution of event impacts. The majority of the benefits from hosting a mega-event occur late in the life of the event itself, and often well into the future, beyond the event and into the legacy period. Therefore, it is not surprising that public reaction to plans for hosting a mega-event based on predictions of these long-term and often intangible benefits can be negative or hostile. There is a widespread belief that the 'true' costs of a mega-event are often hidden from the public in order to avoid widespread alarm, an assumption that is supported by facts, like the dramatic 300 per cent rise in costs of the Sydney 2000 Olympics in the twelve months before the Games were held (Girginov and Parry 2005), or the 51% overspend on the costs of delivering the Rio 2016 Olympic Games, which cost the recession-hit country of Brazil $4.1 billion (Ahmed and Leahy 2016).

A key element of the management of mega-events in the pre-event period, then, is the marketing of the event – not to potential event tourists and attendees, but internally, to the population of the host city and country. This internal marketing is a key activity of the bidding team for any mega-event and, once the event has been won, it becomes a significant task for the Organising Committee.

For London 2012, this involved extensive consultation through roadshow and drop-in events in East London, focusing on the local employment and regeneration benefits of the Games. More widely across the UK, the focus was on the celebratory aspects of the Games, the increased tourism opportunities they should provide and the increase in sporting participation that they are expected to drive, especially among young people. Research into UK citizens' willingness to pay (WTP – a measure of the amount that individuals think is a reasonable contribution for them to make to the staging of an event) for the 2012 Olympics found that this decreased with distance from London, with Londoners' WTP £22 per year, Mancunians' £12 per year and Glaswegians' just £11 per year (Atkinson et al. 2008). With the vast majority of sporting activities taking place in one area of the country, the Cultural Olympiad programme of events associated with the Games was promoted as one of the main ways of spreading the benefits of hosting the Olympics around the country (Kennell and Macleod 2009).

It is important to note that public perceptions of the decision to host a mega-event are changeable and will be influenced by the actual manifestations or otherwise of benefits associated with the event. Research carried out by Guala (2009: 25) shows that public opinion regarding the Torino 2006 Winter Olympics was representative of that measured for similar events:

> pride and optimism at the beginning, then uncertainties and concerns two or three years before the games . . . then happiness and success during the games and shortly after; one year after the games a more realistic judgement is registered, but always positive about the experience and [the future].

Study activity

Look at the websites of the IOC, the International Expositions Bureau and FIFA. Examine the successful bids of the most recent host countries. What similarities and differences can you find between them? Should all mega-event bids be judged by the same criteria?

10.4.2 The event period

During a mega-event, the organisers will be required to carry out a vast number of functions. The Athens Organising Committee identified 53 separate areas of responsibility during the 2004 Olympic Games. Broadly, these functions can be broken down into a number of interrelated areas common to all mega-events (see Figure 10.4). The Beijing Organising Committee for the Olympic Games (BOCOG) had twenty-five departments, each with a separate management function.

It is not only host cities of the Olympic Games that have to deal with this sort of logistical complexity. The most recent of Munich's annual Oktoberfest beer festivals attracted 5.6 million visitors over 16 days. There were 700 booths or small stalls and 14 large tents, each capable of holding 10,000 people. During the event, 6.9 million litres of beer are drunk, and more than a quarter of a million traditional German sausages are eaten (Oktoberfest.net 2016). Each Oktoberfest contributes approximately $1.4 billion to the regional economy of Munich and Bavaria. To deliver such an annual mega-event successfully, there is a need for a complex functional structure that integrates political oversight, departmental responsibility and management functions (see Figure 10.5).

We look at the management issues associated with all events elsewhere in this book, but it is useful here to look at three areas of management that are of particular significance to mega-events during the event period: volunteers, global media and security.

10.4.2.1 Volunteers

Mega-events make use of volunteers on a huge scale. Without their contributions, mega-events as we have come to understand them could not take place due to the huge investment in human capital that would be required to employ a paid workforce. During Beijing 2008, an estimated

Figure 10.4 Mega-event organisers' responsibilities in the event period

1 million volunteers were involved in producing and managing the Games. The organisers of the 2006 Melbourne Commonwealth Games recognised the important contribution made by volunteers by nominating all 14,500 of them as 'unsung heroes' of the event. Every one was named individually in the official event documentation. London 2012 made use of 70,000 volunteers, known as the 'Gamesmakers', who were widely credited with making a significant contribution to the atmosphere of the event, and who were involved in every aspect of attendees' experiences, from arrivals at the major airports, through to stewarding and leading cheers within the event venues during the sport itself.

During a mega-event, volunteers can be used in all aspects of staging. These volunteers will be drawn from diverse sections of the population and, although the headline-grabbing volunteer programmes for mega-events publicise opportunities to meet famous people, the majority of volunteer opportunities will be in customer service or behind-the-scenes roles. Many mega-event hosts seek to link volunteer programmes to skills development and the creation of employment opportunities, both to attract applicants and to contribute to local economic development in the host community. Although it is unrealistic for every volunteer to expect to move directly from the event into paid employment, large-scale, long-term volunteering programmes aim to provide opportunities for people to develop their skills and to gain basic qualifications and work experience.

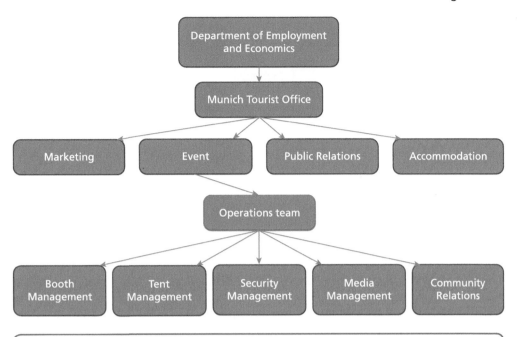

Figure 10.5 The functional structure of the Munich Oktoberfest
Source: Adapted from Shulenkorf 2005

Employment growth is a key element of the justification given by cities for hosting mega-events. Given the huge public investment involved, the success of this is a major factor in influencing public opinion. During the pre-event period of the 1992 Olympic Games in Barcelona, unemployment in the city halved, mainly thanks to the creation of 59,382 jobs that were directly connected to the Games. Immediately after the Games, unemployment rose again by 21,000, before falling back in 1995 (Brunet 2009). The investment generated by hosting the Olympic Games contributed significantly to the strong relative performance of Barcelona's employment market in the legacy period, but the city's experience demonstrates that the employment benefits of hosting a mega-event are not always straightforward or immediate.

This suggests that people must volunteer for reasons other than the hope of gaining direct employment. Indeed, volunteer motivation is a much-researched topic in events management literature. Getz (2007) reviews twelve recent studies and highlights what he judges to be the most important motivating factors:

- altruism
- social benefits
- career benefits
- a sense of challenge
- volunteering as a form of 'serious leisure'
- community pride.

Dickson and Benson (2013) studied the London 2012 Gamesmakers directly after their volunteering experiences and found that the main motivating factor was the chance to be involved in what volunteers perceived to be an event of great significance, agreeing in a survey

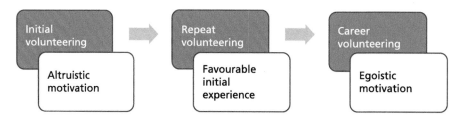

Figure 10.6 Bladen's developmental stages of volunteering
Source: Bladen 2009

with statements like 'it was the chance of a lifetime' and 'I wanted to help make the games a success'. When asked how their skills had developed as a result of being Olympic volunteers, the main areas identified by respondents were customer service skills (31 per cent); teamwork skills (29 per cent); communication skills (27 per cent); interpersonal skills (25 per cent) and the ability to work under pressure (21 per cent). Additionally, 82 per cent of volunteers said that they would be better able to volunteer in the future because of how their skills had developed and 57 per cent said that this would help them with future paid employment.

Bladen (2009) conceptualises the motivations of mega-event volunteers within a model of repeat volunteering. This model suggests that first-time or one-off volunteers are motivated primarily by altruism, while repeat volunteers are driven by the quality of the volunteering experience, and career volunteers see the intrinsic benefits of volunteering itself. So there is a progression from altruistic volunteering motivations to egoistic motivations, as shown in Figure 10.6, which implies that different management strategies will be necessary for managing different volunteers successfully. The sheer scale of the volunteer contribution at a mega-event means that event managers will be working with large groups of individuals at different points on this motivational journey.

10.4.2.2 Global media

Horne and Manzenreiter (2006) claim that the expansion of mega-events in the twentieth century can be understood only by reference to a 'sports–media–business alliance'. This is based on the development of new communications technologies, the professionalisation and commercialisation of sports and the economic opportunities offered to host cities by successful mega-events. This alliance is encapsulated in the relationship between the Olympics and global media. As Roche (2000) points out, the media audience for other mega-events is dwarfed by that of the Olympic Games; and indeed, for mega-events such as the World Expos, whose aim has always been to showcase global culture, the rise of television and new media has provided increased competition for their natural audiences. In contrast, the growth of visual media has helped to extend and deepen the sporting mega-event audience.

For the Olympic Games, broadcasting rights are sold by territory. In the United States, media companies bid competitively for the right to broadcast the Olympics inside North America. For the 2008 Games, NBC paid $894 million. European rights are sold to a collective entity, the European Broadcast Union, which then re-sells them at the national level. For Beijing 2008, European broadcast rights were sold for $443 million. By 2015, the rights deal for Europe had grown to $1.3 billion, and covered transmission and streaming across all television and digital formats to the European audience of 700 million people across 50 countries (International Olympic Committee 2015a). Broadcast rights account for 53 per cent of total income for the

> ### Table 10.1 US broadcast rights for the Summer Olympic Games
> Sources: Horne and Manzenreiter 2006, Dawson 2016

Year	Host city	Network	Amount $m
1960	Rome	CBS	0.39
1964	Tokyo	NBC	1.5
1968	Mexico City	ABC	4.5
1972	Munich	ABC	7.5
1976	Montreal	ABC	25.0
1980	Moscow	NBC	72.0
1984	Los Angeles	ABC	225.0
1988	Seoul	NBC	300.0
1992	Barcelona	NBC	401.0
1996	Atlanta	NBC	546.0
2000	Sydney	NBC	705.0
2004	Athens	NBC	793.0
2008	Beijing	NBC	894.0
2012	London	NBC	1181.0
2016	Rio	NBC	1226.0

Olympic Games, with sponsorship in second place at 34 per cent, ticketing at 11 per cent and merchandising at 2 per cent. Table 10.1 shows the growth in broadcast deals for the Olympic Games in the US from 1960 until the present day.

As well as broadcast rights, the media presence at the Olympic Games is managed through the use of an accreditation system. Individual journalists and media organisations are given official permission to report from inside the Games, are granted access to secure areas and are able to use an accredited media centre, which will have been specially constructed and equipped so that journalists can plug directly into global media networks.

The growth of new media and the diffusion of journalism into non-traditional networks, such as blogs and other forms of social media, have complicated the relationship between the organising committees for each Games and the media, and, at the same time when traditional broadcast deals have grown, reporting of the Olympic Games has become less and less controllable. In response to this, the Sydney 2000 Games was the first to include a non-accredited media centre, and this has been repeated in every Games since. These spaces provide facilities for *any* journalist and they are often used by those reporting on the non-sporting aspects of the Games, such as the cultural programme, local-activity and human-interest stories (Garcia and Miah 2004). During Beijing 2008, more than 12,000 journalists used the non-accredited media centre. The incorporation of these reporters provides two main benefits to the organisers of each Games, and to the Olympic movement as a whole. First, it creates a space in which new media realities of citizen journalism and online democracy can be brought into the organisation of the event in a managed way. Second, it helps to legitimise the system of charging for accredited media access to the Games, by creating a tiered system of privileged access to athletes, officials and facilities. For London 2012, a single media centre was built to accommodate 6,200 media representatives, who were a mixture of accredited and non-accredited journalists, all of whom had to apply for permission to use the centre and its high-specification facilities (Sports Journalists Association 2012).

10.4.2.3 Security

In order to understand the security implications of hosting a mega-event, it is necessary to examine why events are often targets for acts of terrorism or protests. Tarlow (2002) provides four reasons to explain why events become targets:

- *Location* – Events are necessarily held close to major transportation routes and population centres.
- *Economic* – Disrupting events can cause significant damage to tourism and other business activity.
- *Media* – The media will already be present on site, leading to increased reporting of any attack.
- *Anonymity* – The presence of large numbers of attendees at an event makes it likely that terrorists can remain anonymous in a crowd.

Mega-events stretch these criteria to their maximum impact, so it is likely that they will continue to be significant targets for terrorism and other forms of political protest.

The most infamous security breach at a mega-event took place at the 1972 Olympic Games in Munich. Palestinian terrorists killed 11 Israeli athletes during the Games and the tragedy was given widespread and instantaneous media coverage thanks to the presence of vast numbers of journalists at the Olympic site. The location of this terrorist attack had been chosen for precisely this high symbolic value.

Post 9/11, mega-event planners are even more conscious of the possibility of a terrorist attack at one of these high-profile, urbanised, global media events. Between the Los Angeles Games in 1984 and the Athens Games in 2004, security costs rose from $79.4 million to $1.5 billion (Boyle and Haggerty 2009). This is not a uniquely Olympic issue: planning for the FIFA World Cup in South Africa in 2010 made provision for the use of 40,000 police officers, 50,000 reservists and thousands of private security staff (Giulianotti and Klauser 2009). In 2009, an al-Qaeda plot to attack the Munich Oktoberfest was detected in advance by the security services, leading to the imposition of a 3.7-kilometre no-fly zone around the site and enhanced physical security in 2010. Following the ISIS attacks in Paris in 2015, security for the 2016 EUFA Football Championships in France was heightened, supported by the extension of an official national state of emergency to cover the period of the tournament; the deployment of more than 100,000 troops and police; the imposition of no-fly zones above training grounds and stadia; and the installation of drone-defence technology at all event venues.

In common with urban security management generally, attempts to manage the risk of terror are becoming more dispersed and anticipatory, with host cities relying heavily on techniques such as surveillance, behaviour and attendee profiling, as well as the increased use of private security firms. One of the legacies of Beijing 2008 for the mega-event field was its security innovations, including the use of official protest areas and unprecedented levels of monitoring and security clearance that were implemented to reduce the negative impacts of political protest and terror at the event. Although the presence of the Games in China has been hailed by some as helping to create a climate in which limited protest was allowed, in contrast to the pre-Games period in China, these protests were very tightly controlled. It is likely that future Games will follow this model of licensed protest. The 2010 Winter Olympic Games in Vancouver, Canada, saw an unprecedented level of security, with a security budget that rose from an initial estimate of $175 million to more than $1 billion by the end of the event. This money was spent on 17,000 security staff, a network of nearly 1,000 CCTV cameras and the establishment of secure zones for channelling both spectators and protesters. A newly formed Vancouver Integrated Security Unit brought together twenty different law enforcement agencies, armed with semi-automatic weapons, including border police, who carried out spot checks of citizens' immigration and citizenship status during the Games period (Boykoff 2011).

Cultural and sporting mega-events are high profile and require significant political support to take place, which situates them within the political arena. However, political mega-events acquire their significance through their political impact, and this impact also generates significant security concerns in their management. Protests associated with the meeting of the group of twenty industrialised nations (G20) and the World Trade Organisation (WTO) have contributed to the high profiles of these mega-events in the global consciousness and have proved extraordinarily expensive to police. Much of the publicity generated by such gatherings is negative, on account of the often violent security operations that are associated with them. The 2009 meeting of the G20 in London prompted the largest security operation seen in the UK for over a decade, with total security costs estimated at upwards of £10 million for the two-day event.

Study activity

How can mega-event organisers balance security concerns with the need to create exciting, dynamic events? As an attendee at a mega-event, what inconveniences would you be prepared to accept in the name of security and at what point would these deter you from attending?

10.4.3 The post-event period

The post-event period is the longest and most complex to analyse because it has no definitive end point, and because the impacts attributable to mega-events, or claimed by host cities, are numerous. It is therefore necessary to differentiate three separate time-frames within the post-event period (see Figure 10.7).

Immediately following the mega-event period, a number of short-term effects will occur. These will not necessarily be reliable indicators of the long-term impacts of hosting a mega-event, but they can include: a sudden and dramatic drop in local employment as event-related jobs, and volunteering opportunities, are wound up; problems of oversupply in the tourism market as the increased capacity developed for the event period is no longer needed; and the under-utilisation of expensively constructed mega-event venue and infrastructure projects. These consequences alone can make assessing the impacts of a mega-event problematic in the immediate post-event period. There will also be a period of delay in the winding-up of the event organisation, the processing of statistical information and the movement of capital flows associated with hosting the event, such as sponsorship money, merchandising income and ticket revenue.

The intermediate post-event period is when the impacts of hosting a mega-event can become clear. Within this time-frame, host cities can develop post-event management arrangements for facilities and governance frameworks for former mega-event sites. It is not uncommon for there to be large-scale political changes within a host nation or city during this period, as the

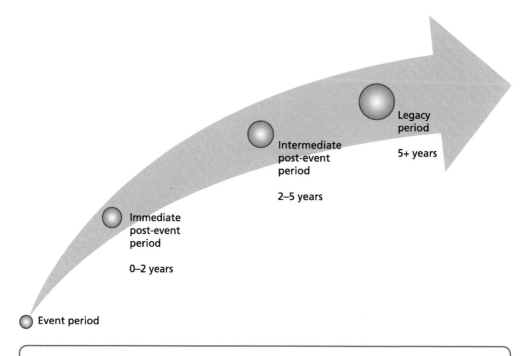

Figure 10.7 The post-event period

post-event period will extend beyond standard political electoral cycles. This will also have an impact on the post-event impacts of a mega-event since the financial, physical and social aspects of the event become part of the political discourse in the host city.

Five years after the 2004 Athens Olympics, all but one of the twenty-two Olympic venues were unused, and one of the core venue complexes had become notorious for hosting not prestigious sporting events but large groups of illegal squatters. It is now possible to assess the impacts of the Athens Games accurately, especially in comparison with its successor event in the Olympic calendar – the 2006 Winter Games in Turin – which successfully handed its venues to a management company and has integrated them into its regional and sporting development strategies. Other host cities have attempted to avoid their Olympic Stadiums becoming costly and embarrassing white elephants by handing them over to professional football teams capable of attracting the large crowds necessary to fill them.

For the 1992 Olympic Games in Barcelona, the Estadi Olímpic Lluís Companys was renovated and extended to accommodate the huge crowds expected for the Games. After the Games, the stadium was eventually given to RCD Espanyol, the city's second professional football team, who then moved out again in 2009 into a newly built stadium, with a smaller capacity that could be managed more sustainably, given the team's realistic weekly attendances.

Shortly after the 2012 Olympic and Paralympic Games in London, it was announced that the Premier League football club West Ham United would be moving into the stadium, which would retain its capacity to host athletics events, but would have its capacity reduced by 25,000 to 50,000. West Ham will pay £2.5 million per year for the use of the stadium, on a 99-year lease, which has been criticized by some as providing poor value for the public investment, since the total cost of converting the stadium for football use has been estimated at £701 million (Gibson 2016).

Image 10.2 **Estadi Olímpic Lluís Companys, Barcelona**
Credit: Tottenham Hotspur FC/Getty Images

The legacy period is the most politically charged aspect of the post-event period for a mega-event. Planners and politicians alike view the hosting of a mega-event as a way to fast-track processes of urban development and economic restructuring that would normally take place over much longer time-frames (Andranovich *et al.* 2001). Hosting mega-events provides a stimulus for the redevelopment of cities, the creation of new urban areas and the diversification of economies. Alongside these instrumental legacies of a mega-event are the intrinsic legacies that hosting high-profile examples of sporting and cultural practices is supposed to deliver: an increase in sports activity within the population, for example, or a rise in cultural participation. Set alongside further socio-economic targets, such as rises in employment, educational achievement and social cohesion, it is worth considering why these mega-events, if they are so beneficial to society, have not become the norm, rather than the exception, in development planning. A look at the history of some of these development goals associated with mega-events shows that these potentially high-impact events are also high risk: for every high-profile success story (such as Barcelona: see Case Study 10.3, below), there is a parallel story of cost overruns, poorly managed legacies and political problems. Issues of event impacts and legacy are dealt with in detail in Chapter 14. The main area in which the long-term benefits of mega-events are anticipated by planners is regeneration.

10.4.4 Mega-events and urban regeneration

As outlined above, many of the positive impacts claimed for hosting mega-events in the legacy period are linked to the concept of urban regeneration. This is a 'comprehensive and integrated vision and action which leads to the resolution of urban problems and which seeks to bring about a lasting improvement in the economic, physical, social and environmental condition of an area that has been subject to change' (Roberts 2000: 17). Mega-events, by virtue of the massive investment they attract and the policy focus that they generate, can provide a major stimulus to regeneration programmes and, in many cases, can become the main element of major regeneration schemes.

Strategies of regeneration have been explicitly employed throughout the UK and Europe since the Second World War as the need for physical reconstruction provided an opportunity for the reconsideration of urban form in response to new economic and social conditions. In the UK, successive governments have produced regeneration and development frameworks that have prioritised different economic sectors, institutional actors and policy outcomes. Table 10.2 summarises the variety of approaches to regeneration that have been adopted in the United Kingdom since the 1950s.

We can see from this historical overview that events have begun to take on a role in regeneration only since the 1980s. This period was one of major economic restructuring in Western economies as industrial production moved globally south and east to areas of lower costs, and the manufacturing bases of many cities were lost. This period of globalisation left many derelict industrial sites in its wake and, with this, a legacy of unemployment, skills loss and social problems. Increasingly, governments in the UK, the US and Europe turned to major projects, such as the hosting of mega-events, as a means for regenerating these former industrial areas and addressing their associated cultural, social, political and economic problems.

The contributions that a mega-event can make to regeneration are manifold. Although the tendency is to look to an increase in tourism as the main socio-economic impact of a mega-event, we can identify three strategies of integrating mega-events into urban regeneration, in a development of Evans's (2005) categorisation of cultural regeneration.

10.4.4.1 Mega-event-led regeneration

This strategy places a mega-event at the core of a regeneration strategy, as a catalyst for all other developments in the area. Such schemes use the event to brand the regeneration scheme and to promote its uniqueness and value. An example of a city that has pursued this policy consistently is Barcelona, which used the 1992 Olympics and then the 2004 World Forum of Cultures to drive the regeneration of the city (see Case Study 10.3).

10.4.4.2 Mega-event within regeneration

This category describes regeneration strategies where the event is embedded into a broader regeneration strategy, being only one element amid other, equally important components. An example of this is the role that the 2002 Commonwealth Games played in the regeneration of Manchester in the north-west of England. Although hosting the Games became a major impetus for the deepening and continuation of regeneration in the east of the city, their potential to contribute to existing regeneration policy in the city was identified by planners and politicians at the bidding stage (Carlsen and Taylor 2003). Hosting the Games provided an opportunity to leverage additional external funding into an area that has been undergoing significant regeneration developments since the 1980s (Smith and Fox 2007).

Table 10.2 The evolution of British regeneration policy

Sources: Roberts 2000, Bianchini 1993, McGuigan 1996, Diamond and Liddle 2005, Morgan 2002

Period	1950s	1960s	1970s	1980s	1990s	2000s
Policy type Major strategy and orientation	Reconstruction Post-war reconstruction and extension of older areas and cities, with some suburban growth	Revitalisation Continuation of 1950s themes	Renewal Focus on in-situ renewal and neighbourhood schemes; mainly peripheral new developments	Redevelopment Many major high-profile schemes; events begin to be incorporated into regeneration strategies	Regeneration Move towards more integrated and holistic policy approaches	Imagineering Flagship projects and mega-events play key roles in regeneration policy
Key actors and stakeholders	National and local government	Greater balance between public and private sectors	Growing role for private sector	Emphasis on private sector and special agencies and quangos	Partnership the dominant approach	Partnership approach continues
Funding	Majority public sector	Majority public sector with growing private sector	Resource constraints on public sector; greater private sector investment	Private sector dominant, often with public sector funding	Greater balance between public, private and third sector activity	Emphasis on the 'leveraging' of public sector funds to produce large impacts
Social content	Improvement of housing and general living standards	Social and welfare improvement	Community-based action; increase in empowerment	Community self-help, with selective state support	Emphasis on the role of the community	Neighbourhood empowerment and management become key policy concerns
Physical emphasis	Replacement of inner areas and some peripheral development	Continuation of 1950s themes	More extensive renewal of older urban areas	Major schemes of replacement and new developments; growth of flagship schemes	More modest than 1980s; growth of heritage approaches	Urban centre and fringe renewal
Environmental approach	Landscaping and some greening	Selective improvements	Environmental improvement with some innovations	Growth of environmental concern	Broader idea of environmental sustainability introduced	Climate change drives sustainability agenda forward

> ### CASE STUDY 10.3
>
> # Events and the regeneration of Barcelona
>
> **Location:** Barcelona, Spain
> **Event type:** mega-event
>
> Barcelona offers a high-profile example of the role that mega-events can play in strategies of urban regeneration. Potential host cities often cite its success in order to justify their own bids for mega-events, with many of them lauding the 'Barcelona Model' (Balibrea 2001).
>
> Until the 1970s, Barcelona was a major European industrial city, with a large Mediterranean port and manufacturing services for the automobile, pharmaceutical and textiles industries. Global economic restructuring in the 1970s, coupled with the restructuring of the Spanish state in the post-Franco period, led to a series of industrial and economic crises in the city, leaving it in a 'post-industrial' state, with many derelict former industrial spaces and buildings.
>
> In 1991, in response to this period of decline the Mayor of Barcelona, Pasquall Maragall, articulated his vision for a city that would be globally competitive: 'in urban competition, factors like the environment and cultural and education infrastructures count more and more. In a strategic sense we can say that cities are like businesses which compete to attract investments and residents, selling places which are suitable for industry, commerce and all kinds of services' (cited in Balibrea 2001: 213). Maragall oriented the city to a mega-event-led regeneration strategy. In 1986, the city was awarded the 1992 Summer Olympic Games, and this became the key driver of Barcelona's attempts to reinvent itself for the post-industrial era.
>
> The Olympic Village was constructed in the disadvantaged port area of Poblenou and the construction of the Olympic venues and public spaces was integrated into a major physical development programme. This included waterfront developments, a new ring-road for the city, the reclaiming of brownfield sites and the demolition of redundant industrial buildings. The new developments associated with this period of change were polycentric, with the aim of 'Monumentalising the outskirts and revitalising the historic centre' of the city (Balibrea 2001: 212) to produce a more sustainable arrangement of urban form. Tourism development was encouraged through the construction of new hotels as well as rail and airport improvements. Between 1986 and 2000, Barcelona's hotel capacity increased by 300 per cent.
>
> The cost of producing the Games themselves was $1.3 billion, but the associated physical investment totalled $8 billion, demonstrating the contribution made to the development of the city through hosting this mega-event (Brunet 2009).

Alongside these significant physical developments, a process of rebranding and managing the symbolic representation of the city took place during this period (Garcia 2004). Barcelona's local government seized on the opportunity to promote the city as a leisure and tourism destination, promoting Catalan culture and refurbishing key architectural landmarks, as well as implementing an ambitious cultural development programme, capitalising on the opportunity to reposition itself in the global tourism market. By 2006, Barcelona was voted Europe's most attractive city, and was the continent's fourth most-visited.

In 2004, Barcelona hosted the Universal Forum of Cultures, another global event, in this case under the umbrella of the United Nations. Although this drew only 3.5 million visitors against an expected target of 5 million, and cost $2.3 billion to produce, it provided an opportunity for the city to maintain the mega-event-led strategy of urban regeneration and to continue to develop through event-associated investments in infrastructure and tourism.

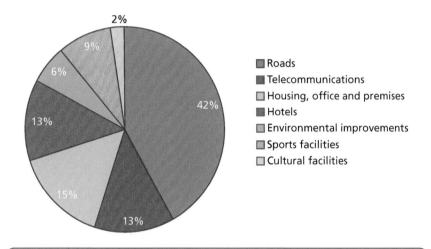

Figure 10.8 Investments in Barcelona, 2004
Source: Brunet 2009

Study activity

What steps can mega-event organisers take to win public support for hosting the event when the legacy benefits may not be immediately apparent?

10.4.4.3 Mega-event added to regeneration

This category describes a situation in which a mega-event becomes an addition to an existing regeneration strategy but is not fully integrated within it. In this category of mega-event planning, the benefits of the event will not be fully leveraged for regeneration purposes. Increasingly, the legacy benefits of hosting a mega-event are viewed as central to successful bidding and to gaining public support for the event, so contemporary events rarely fall into this category.

The two most recent Olympic Games to be hosted in the United States, Los Angeles 1984 and Atlanta 1996, can both be identified with this planning style, however. Both host cities emphasised the financial sustainability of their bids, with Los Angeles generating a $200 million profit that was then used to endow a sporting trust, but its Games had no positive impact on the overburdened mass-transit, housing and education sectors of the city. Although contemporary mega-events are less likely to suffer similar criticism, due to the recently developed expectation that all mega-events should contribute to sustainable development, events with poor legacies might fall into this category through bad planning or management. For instance, the Athens 2004 Olympics were poorly integrated into development planning and left the country with a debt of £7 billion (Baim 2009).

Smith (2007) offers ten key principles for the use of events in regeneration:

1 Embed event strategies within wider regeneration programmes.
2 Use the event as a coherent theme and effective stimulus for other regeneration projects.
3 Incorporate regeneration planning into the initial stages of event planning.
4 Promote shared ownership and understanding of the regeneration plans among all partners in the event and legacy planning process.
5 Design effective management and functional relationships between event managers and regeneration managers to deliver joint goals.
6 Allocate sufficient human and capital resources throughout the lifetime of an event to achieve its goals.
7 Design event regeneration projects that engage with, and meet the needs of, the most deprived members of a community.
8 Plan for an even geographical distribution of positive impacts across areas targeted for regeneration through an event.
9 Integrate physical and infrastructure developments with social and economic regeneration targets.
10 Ensure community representation from the planning stage onwards in the events management process.

10.5 Mega-event tourism

Mega-event tourism can be defined as tourism activity generated either directly or indirectly by the presence of a mega-event within a location.

The major direct economic driver associated with mega-events, and the most obvious manifestation of their impact in the event period, is tourism. The planned increases in tourism that accompany mega-events are related to the increased exposure that an event location will gain in the three event periods and also the opportunity that a mega-event provides for a host city to reposition itself within the global tourism marketplace. Forecasts for the Korea International Marine Expo in 2012 predict visitor numbers of 8.9 million (Lee *et al.* 2008), compared to average *national* annual tourist arrivals of just 7 million, clearly indicating the significance of mega-events in the tourism market place. Sochi airport, serving the 2014 Winter Olympics handled 3.1 million passengers in 2014, an increase of 30 per cent on the previous year, and will now be adding extra capacity and routes as a result of the increased international tourism profile of the destination (International Olympic Committee 2015b).

Tourism that is directly generated will include attendance at the event itself and visits in the pre- and post-event periods that are motivated by a desire to encounter the event in its development or legacy phases. From 2009, it was possible to book excursions and visits to the 2012 Olympic site in London, and this increasingly formed part of tourist itineraries in the British capital in the run-up to the Games.

Indirectly generated tourism activity will be related to the increased media profile of the host city and promotional campaigns mounted by both the city and the host nation to maximise the benefits of this increased global exposure. Typically, these campaigns will include the promotion of other events during the event periods, as well as other destinations in the host nation.

10.5.1 Pre-event period tourists

These tourists have been attracted to the destination due to the increased media coverage of the destination resulting from it becoming a mega-event host. Pre-event tourists may be motivated to experience the planning period of the event – perhaps to visit an event location or to participate in pre-event activities, such as handover ceremonies or cultural celebrations.

10.5.2 Event period tourists

Tourism flows in the event period can be positive, negative or neutral. Weed (2008) makes use of Preuss's (2005) nine categories of 'event affected people' to categorise movements of people associated with the mega-event period. These are summarised in Figure 10.9.

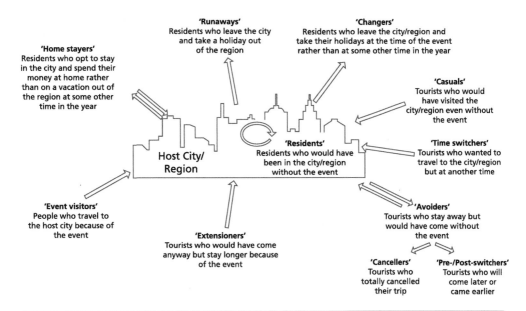

Figure 10.9 Mega-event tourism flows
Source: Weed 2008, adapted from Preuss 2005

This figure shows the complexity of mega-event tourism flows. The scale of the event means that it has implications for understanding the behaviours not only of event tourists directly but of all potential tourists to and from a host city during the event period. In fact, minimising the impacts of negative tourism flows associated with mega-events can be as crucial to the overall economic success of the event as maximising positive flows.

10.5.3 Post-event period tourists

Hosting a mega-event generates both tangible and intangible tourism legacies. The intangible tourism benefits include enhancing or developing the image of the city, and increasing and improving tourism industry skills within the local economy. The tangible benefits for the tourism industry include an increased accommodation supply, improved visitor facilities and transport infrastructure, and new visitor attractions. Many mega-event tourists are cultural tourists who seek new cultural experiences associated with a mega-event; many of these experiences come after the event thanks to the creation of new districts and cultural facilities. For example, the main attraction at the 2005 World Expo in Aichi, Japan, was a life-size reconstruction of a house inhabited by the characters of Hayao Miyazaki's animated children's film *My Neighbour Totoro*. This was reopened in 2006 and continues to be the most popular tourism attraction in the destination, having attracted more than a million visitors.

The tangible and intangible tourism benefits of hosting a mega-event can deliver a significant uplift in visitor numbers through enhancing the image of the destination, increasing its media exposure and enhancing the visitor experience.

CASE STUDY 10.4

The tourism impacts of the 2010 FIFA World Cup in South Africa

Location: South Africa
Event type: mega-event
Attendees: 3,180,000
£2.4 billion

The 2010 FIFA World Cup was hosted by South Africa. This was the first World Cup to be hosted in Africa, and the first mega-event of any kind to be held on the continent. £2.4 billion were spent on building six new stadiums for the event and improving tourist infrastructure to accommodate the 3.18 million spectators who attended matches. The combined television audience for the event was 3.2 billion with 909.6 million people watching the final alone.

One of the reasons that South Africa bid to host the World Cup was to improve the destination image of the country and to attract more tourists, both those from Africa and from more distant international markets where football is a popular sport, especially wealthy tourist markets in Western Europe and Asia.

During the World Cup itself, tourism to South Africa increased by 16.8 per cent when compared to the year before. This increase was due in large part to the

309,554 tourists who came to South Africa specifically to watch games during the competition and these tourists spent approximately $500 million during their stay. Of these tourists, 32 per cent of international arrivals were from Africa, 24 per cent were from Europe, 13 per cent were from Central and South America and 11 per cent from North America. Of these arrivals 59 per cent were visiting South Africa for the first time.

However, despite the immediate positive tourism impacts of hosting the World Cup, South Africa's tourism industry has suffered problems since the mega-event, despite an overall increase in tourism figures. Ferreira and Boshoff (2014) analysed Cape Town's hotel market after the event and found that the significant increase in hotel construction in the period leading up to 2010 had left the city with an oversupply of hotels, particularly in the luxury hotel sector. By the second quarter of 2011, hotel occupancy rates and revenue per room were at their lowest point since 2007, which had contributed to hotel closures and a number of properties in the city being put up for sale. Some five-star hotels had dropped their room rates so low that they were now cannibalizing the market for four- and three-star hotels, squeezing many small businesses out of the market. This research found that when cities host mega-events, consideration must be given to the future demand for tourism services in the destination, during the rush to develop new tourism infrastructure alongside event venues in the run-up to a mega-event.

Study activity

How can tourism agencies maximise the benefits of positive tourism flows and minimise the impacts of negative tourism flows during a mega-event period?

Industry voice

Clive Little, Director of Events and Programming, Olympic Park Legacy Company, London, UK

Delivering a strategic events programme

The Legacy Company was established in May 2009 by its founders – the Mayor of London and the British government – as a public sector, not-for-profit company which is responsible for the long-term planning, development, management and maintenance of the Olympic Park and its facilities after the London 2012 Games. The Queen Elizabeth Olympic Park, as it will be known after the Games, will be at the centre of London's growth in the twenty-first century. Its connections, sporting facilities, parkland, waterways and family housing will form a unique mix – building on the best of London's traditions to create a beautiful, active park, embracing East London, its diverse creativity and culture. It will anchor a new city district while linking into the surrounding neighbourhoods to promote convergence, regeneration and prosperity in East London.

Unlike the majority of London's major parks, such as Hyde Park and Regent's Park, the future Queen Elizabeth Olympic Park is situated in an area of relatively low population density by comparison. These central London parks are, to a much greater extent, self-activating parks, predominantly due to the population that immediately surrounds them but also due to their maturity, high profile and close proximity to major densities of international visitors.

Therefore, the role of events and programming is fundamental to the park's future success, not just in terms of animating the park and ensuring high levels of visitors but also to help ensure that the residential development platforms managed by the Legacy Company reach a peak value, thus maximising the financial return to the public purse. The demand for housing on these development platforms, in and around the park, will have a direct correlation to the events and programming taking place as part of a 'quality-of-life' mix.

In order to fulfil the ambitions for the park and live up to the Legacy Company's aims, as well as public and media expectations, the park needs to deliver an incredibly diverse range of events – from low-level community programming and profile-raising entertainment through to hosting world-class sporting events that build on the legacy aims.

The events and programmes we deliver at the park will be driven by our three key priority themes:

- Building local ownership and showcasing the cultural expression of the East End.
- Encouraging sports and healthy living.
- Attracting regional and international visitors.

Delivering the correct solution needs careful strategic, geographic and logistical consideration that continuously references back to our three priority themes, whilst also consulting, informing and feeding back into numerous planning work streams within the company.

Our planning process can be broken down and simplified to show the key (but not conclusive) elements that need consideration – as follows.

Assess the assets

- Which spaces across the park are suitable for hosting events?
- What are the legacy venues capable of delivering?
- Do we have the correct mix of indoor/outdoor space, especially with regard to seasonality issues?

Research the practicalities

- What limitations might arise due to noise issues (coming from or into the park)?
- Is there a ceiling in terms of total visitor numbers due to crowd control and flow?
- Assess what impact planning and licensing controls might have on the events programme.

Understand the market

- Undertake two major market research pieces, with one looking at the general events market and the other looking specifically at local and community programming.
- Launch a call for 'Expressions of Interest' (EOI) to ascertain what the external appetite is for events and programming at the park, from event organisers, sporting bodies, brands and so on.

Inform the design process

- Recommend ways of adapting or shaping the spaces and venues to ensure we have facilities that work well and efficiently for event organisers.
- Decide what events infrastructure should be facilitated (to add value for third-party hirers/partners).
- Ensure the park and its event spaces work well logistically and spatially.

Build the strategic events programme

- Use the market research and EOI process to inform and shape what the events programme will be.
- Ensure the programme reaches the correct volume, in the correct places at the correct time.
- Shape the programme to have synergy with the physical tone of the park. (The park is sectored into two core zones: the south park – active; and the north park — passive.)
- Ensure the programme offers the best revenue income for the park in order to increase the investment that can be made into local and cultural programming.

Investigate the best delivery methods

How can we deliver the events and programmes while reducing the risk to the company? Ensure that the events and programming budget offers best value through:

- Licence agreements/hire to third parties.
- Subsidising when an event delivers strongly in line with our key priority themes.

- Promoting events through the Legacy Company – most applicable to small-scale, high-frequency events or programmes.

By following an ordered planning phase, like this, the events programme and the park can be tuned to ensure the best fit between the two. Comprehensive planning work also gives us a solid set of data and information that can be used to focus energy on spaces and times that might otherwise be neglected.

Delivering the right programming for the park and its users is a hefty challenge but one that would inspire any event manager or programmer. Two hundred and 50 acres of public realm and a set of world-class Olympic venues are incredible assets, and they will offer the ultimate job satisfaction once animated successfully.

10.6 Summary

This chapter has defined and categorised a mega-event as a special kind of large-scale event that delivers global media and/or socio-economic impacts.

The time-frame of the mega-event has been split into three periods. The pre-event period is characterised by huge levels of speculative public investment and the battle to win public approval. The event period itself requires sophisticated organisation and functional apparatus to respond to the complexity of managing one of the world's largest events. Finally, the benefits of perhaps a decade of investment must be leveraged in the post-event period.

Mega-events have the potential to generate massive benefits for host cities and nations, but they can equally encumber both city and state with massive burdens. Embedding mega-events into broader strategies of urban regeneration and tourism development helps to increase the likelihood of positive outcomes while reducing the risk of negative impacts.

Further reading

www.bie-paris.org. The website of the International Bureau of Expositions, which is responsible for the awarding and regulation of World Expos.

www.olympic.org. The website of the International Olympic Committee, which contains archived information on all previous Olympic and Paralympic events.

Weed, M. (2008) *Olympic Tourism*, Oxford: Butterworth-Heinemann. Although this book focuses on Olympic tourism, it contains many models and useful references that will aid understanding of tourism flows associated with all mega-events.

References

ABC News (2015) FIFA corruption probe: Timeline of scandal from Qatar announcement to high-profile arrests. Available at: www.abc.net.au/news/2015-05-28/fifa-timeline-of-corruption-and-scandal/6502700. Accessed 6 February 2017.

Ahmed, M. and Leahy, J. (2016) Rio 2016: The high price of Olympic glory in *Financial Times*.

Andranovich, G., Burbank, M. and Heying, C. (2001) Olympic Cities: Lessons Learned from Mega-event Politics, *Urban Affairs*, 23 (2): 113–131.

Atkinson, G., Mourato, S., Symanski, S. and Ozdemiroglu, E. (2008) Are We Willing to Pay Enough to Back the Bid? Valuing the Intangible Impacts of London's Bid to Host the 2012 Summer Olympic Games, *Urban Studies*, 45 (2): 419–444.

Booth, R. (2015) 'We will be ready, inshallah': inside Qatar's $200bn World Cup, in *Guardian*. Available at: www.theguardian.com/football/2015/nov/14/qatar-world-cup-200-billion-dollar-gamble. Accessed 6 February 2017.

Baim, D. (2009) Olympic-driven Urban Development, in G. Poynter and I. MacRury (eds) *Olympic Cities: 2012 and the Remaking of London*, Farnham: Ashgate.

Balibrea, M. P. (2001) Urbanism, Culture and the Post-industrial City: Challenging the 'Barcelona Model', *Journal of Spanish Cultural Studies* 2 (2): 187–210.

BBC (2015) *COP21: Rallies call for Paris climate change action*. Available at: www.bbc.co.uk/news/world-34956825. Accessed 5 February 2017.

BBC (2016) *Rio 2016: The greatest show on Earth in stats*. Available at: www.bbc.co.uk/sport/olympics/37148372. Accessed 5 February 2017.

Bianchini, F. (1993) *Cultural Policy and Urban Regeneration: The Western European Experience*, Manchester: Manchester University Press.

Bladen, C. (2009) Towards an Olympic Volunteering Legacy, in J. Kennell, E. Booth and C. Bladen (eds) *The Olympic Legacy: People, Place Enterprise: Proceedings of the First Annual Conference on Olympic Legacy, 8 and 9 May 2008*, Greenwich: Greenwich University Press.

Boykoff, J. (2011) Anti Olympics, *New Left Review*, 67: 41–59.

Boyle, P. and Haggerty, K. (2009) Spectacular Security: Mega-events and the Security Complex, *International Political Sociology*, 3 (3): 257–274.

Brannigan, P. and Giulianotti, R. (2015) Soft power and soft disempowerment: Qatar, global sport and football's 2022 World Cup finals, in *Journal of Policy Research in Tourism, Leisure and Events*, 34 (6): 703–719.

Brunet, F. (2009) The Economy of the Barcelona Olympic Games, in G. Poynter and I. MacRury (eds) *Olympic Cities: 2012 and the Remaking of London*, Farnham: Ashgate.

Buro Happold (2015) *A Showpiece Stadium for the 2014 Winter Olympics*, London: Buro Happold.

Carlsen, J. and Taylor, A. (2003) Mega-events and Urban Renewal: The Case of the Manchester 2002 Commonwealth Games, *Event Management*, 8 (1): 15–22.

Dawson, J. (2016) 'Olympics TV Rights Costs Run Risk for NBCUniversal' in *Variety*. Available at: http://variety.com/2016/tv/news/nbcuniversal-olympics-2016-broadcast-costs-1201811506/. Accessed 6 February 2017.

Diamond, J. and Liddle, J. (2005) *Management of Regeneration*, Abingdon: Routledge.

Dickson, T. and Benson, A. (2013) *London 2012 Games Makers: Towards Redefining Legacy*, London: HMSO.

EuroNews (2015) 20 Million People Visited Milan Expo, a 'huge success'. Available at: www.euronews.com/2015/10/29/20-million-people-visited-milan-expo-a-huge-success. Accessed 4 February 2017.

European Commission (2017) *European Capitals of Culture: More than 30 Years*, Brussels: European Commission.

Evans, G. (2005) Measure for Measure: Evaluating the Evidence of Culture's Contribution to Regeneration, *Urban Studies*, 42 (5/6): 959–983.

Expo Milano 2015 (2015) *Review the Experience of the Universal Exposition*. Available at: www.expo2015.org/en/rivivi-expo/. Accessed 7 July 2017.

Ferreira, S. L. and Boshoff, A. (2014) Post-2010 FIFA Soccer World Cup: oversupply and location of luxury hotel rooms in Cape Town. *Current Issues in Tourism*, 17 (2): 180–198.

FIFA (2002) 41,100 Hours of 2002 FIFA World Cup TV Coverage in 213 Countries. Available at: www.fifa.com/newscentre/news/newsid=84258.html. Accessed 26 October 2011.

FIFA (2007) No.1 Sports Event, press release. Available at: www.fifa.com/mm/document/fifafacts/ffprojects/ip-401_06e_tv_2658.pdf. Accessed 4 October 2011.

FIFA (2011) *2010 FIFA World Cup South Africa: Television Audience Report*, London: Kantar Sport.

Foundation for Economic and Industrial Research (2015) *The Impact of the 2004 Olympic Games on the Greek Economy*, Athens: IOBE.

Frearson, A. (2014) Sochi Winter Olympics commence inside Populous-designed stadium, in *Dezeen*. Available at: www.dezeen.com/2014/02/05/fisht-olympic-stadium-sochi-2014-populous/. Accessed 6 February 2017.

Garcia, B. (2004) Urban Regeneration, Arts Programming and Major Events: Glasgow 1990, Sydney 2000 and Barcelona 2004, *International Journal of Cultural Policy*, 10 (1): 103–118.

Garcia, B. and Miah, A. (2004) Non-accredited Media, the Olympic Games, the Media and the Host City: The British Academy 2004 Project, *Culture @ The Olympics*, 6: 1–7.

Getz, D. (2007) *Event Studies*, Oxford: Butterworth-Heinemann.

Getz, D. and Page, S. (2016) *Event Studies* (3rd edn), Abingdon: Routledge.

Giampiccoli, A., Lee, S. S. and Nauright, J. (2015) Destination South Africa: Comparing global sports mega-events and recurring localised sports events in South Africa for tourism and economic development, *Current Issues in Tourism*, 18 (3): 229–248.

Gibson, O. (2016) West Ham's Olympic Stadium contract: club to pay £2.5m per season in rent, in *Guardian*. Available at: www.theguardian.com/football/2016/apr/14/west-ham-olympic-stadium-club-pay-per-season-rent. Accessed 6 February 2017.

Girginov, V. and Parry, J. (2005) *The Olympic Games Explained*, Abingdon: Routledge.

Giulianotti, R. and Klauser, F. (2009) Security Governance and Sport Mega-events: Toward an Interdisciplinary Research Agenda, *Journal of Sport and Social Issues*, 34 (1): 1–13.

Guala, C. (2009) To Bid or not to Bid: Public Opinion before and after the Games: The Case of the Turin 2006 Winter Olympic Games, in J. Kennell, E. Booth and C. Bladen (eds) *The Olympic Legacy: People, Place Enterprise: Proceedings of the First Annual Conference on Olympic Legacy, 8 and 9 May 2008*, Greenwich: Greenwich University Press.

Gumble, D. (2016) Adele, Coldplay and ELO Glasto performances set record high viewing figures, in *Music Week*. Available at: www.musicweek.com/live/read/adele-coldplay-and-elo-glasto-performances-set-record-high-viewing-figures/065161. Accessed 5 February 2017.

Hill Dickinson LLP (2007) Official Partners.

Horne, J. and Manzenreiter, W. (2006) An Introduction to the Sociology of Sports Mega-events, *Sociological Review*, 54 (2): 1–24.

International Olympic Committee (2015a) *IOC awards all TV and multiplatform broadcast rights in Europe to Discovery and Eurosport for 2018–2024 Olympic Games*. Available at: www.olympic.org/news/ioc-awards-all-tv-and-multiplatform-broadcast-rights-in-europe-to-discovery-and-eurosport-for-2018-2024-olympic-games. Accessed 6 February 2017.

International Olympic Committee (2015b) *Factsheet: Sochi 2014 Facts and Figures*, Lausanne: IOC .

Istanbul 2010 (2011) Benefits for Istanbul. Available at: www.en.istanbul2010.org/AVRUPAKULTURBASKENTI/istanbulakatkilari/index.htm. Accessed 28 April 2011.

Jonas, A. and Ward, K. (2002) A World of Regionalisms? Towards a US–UK Urban and Regional Policy Framework Comparison, *Journal of Urban Affairs*, 24 (4): 377–401.

Kennell, J. and Macleod, N. (2009) A Grey Literature Review of the Cultural Olympiad, *Cultural Trends*, 18 (1): 83–88.

Lee, C., Song, H. and Mjelde, J. (2008) The Forecasting of International Expo Tourism Using Quantitative and Qualitative Techniques, *Tourism Management*, 29: 1084–1098.

Lee, C. and Taylor, T. (2005) Critical Reflections on the Economic Impact Assessment of a Mega-event: The Case of the 2002 FIFA World Cup, *Tourism Management*, 26: 595–603.

Liverpool 08 (2008) Commercial Support. Available at: www.liverpool08.com/commercial/. Accessed 16 January 2010.

Liverpool 08 (2009) *Liverpool08 European Capital of Culture: The Impacts of a Year Like No Other*, Liverpool: Liverpool 08.

McGuigan, J. (1996) *Culture and the Public Sphere*, Abingdon: Routledge.

Morgan, K. (2002) The New Regeneration Narrative: Local Development in the Multi-level Polity, *Local Economy*, 17 (3): 191–199.

Persson, C. (2002) The Olympic Games Site Decision, *Tourism Management*, 23: 27–36. PODIUM (2009) About Us. Available at: www.podium.ac.uk/about-us. Accessed 16 January 2010.

Preuss, H. (2005) The Economic Impact of Visitors at Major Multi-sport Events, *European Sport Management Quarterly*, 5 (3): 281–301.

Roberts, K. (2004) *The Leisure Industry*, London: Palgrave.

Roberts, P. (2000) The Evolution, Definition and Purpose of Urban Regeneration, in P. Roberts and H. Sykes (eds) *Urban Regeneration*, London: Sage.

Roche, M. (2000) *Mega-events and Modernity: Olympics and Expos in the Growth of Global Culture*, Abingdon: Routledge.

Sandomir, R. (2014) NBC Extends Olympic Deal into the Unknown, in *New York Times*. Available at: www.nytimes.com/2014/05/08/sports/olympics/nbc-extends-olympic-tv-deal-through-2032.html?_r=0. Accessed 6 February 2017.

Shulenkorf, N. (2005) *Oktoberfest Munchen: The World's Largest Public Event*, Nordestet: Grin Verlag. See, Oktoberfest.net 2016. Accessed 7 July 2017.

Smith, A. (2007) Large-scale Events and Sustainable Urban Regeneration: Key Principles for Host Cities, *Journal of Urban Regeneration and Renewal*, 1 (2): 1–13.

Smith, A. and Fox, T. (2007) From Event-led to Event-themed Regeneration: The 2002 Commonwealth Games Legacy Programme, *Urban Studies*, 45 (5): 1125–1143.

Sports Journalists Association (2012) *Boris opens centre for non-accredited Olympic press*. Available at: www.sportsjournalists.co.uk/accreditation-details/boris-opens-centre-for-non-accredited-olympic-press/. Accessed 6 February 2017.

Sustainable Innovation Forum (2015) *Post Event Report*, London: Sustainable Innovation Forum.

Tarlow, P. (2002) *Event Risk Management and Safety*, New York: John Wiley & Sons.

Theodoraki, E. (2007) *Olympic Event Organisation*, Oxford: Butterworth-Heinemann.

Valletta 2018 Foundation (2017) *Bid Book Update*, Valletta: Valletta 2018 Foundation.

Vickery, J. (2007) *The Emergence of Culture-led Regeneration: A Policy Concept and its Discontents*, Centre for Cultural Policy Studies Research Paper No. 9, University of Warwick.

Chapter 11

Events in the public and third sectors

Contents

11.1 Aims

By the end of this chapter, students will be able to:

- analyse the differences between the private, public and third sectors in the events industry;
- evaluate the particular considerations associated with the planning and delivery of public sector events;
- evaluate the particular considerations associated with the planning and delivery of events in the third sector.

11.2 Introduction

Definitions of events often rely on management analysis and academic research with a 'for-profit' focus. However, a large proportion of UK events are carried out by and on behalf of the third sector of the economy and the public services. Such events, while often high budget and carried out by cash-rich organisations, may not embody the same characteristics of planning, design and management as their for-profit sector counterparts. Building on the key aspects of events management that are applicable to events in all sectors of the economy, this chapter highlights the particular characteristics of third sector and public sector events and the different nature and style of managing their success.

Getz (2012) identifies three groups of event organisers in each of the private, non-profit and government/partnership groups. However, the recent growth of social enterprise and changes in the relationship between public and private sectors that have intensified since the global economic crisis, which began in 2008 with the 'credit crunch', necessitate a redrawing of this model. We can now place organisations that produce events in the three categories, as shown in Figure 11.1.

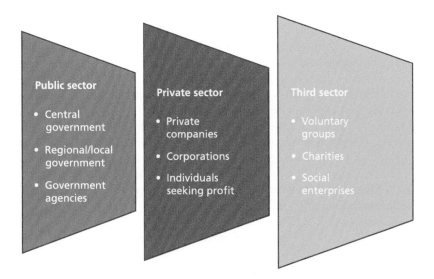

Figure 11.1 The three event-producing sectors

The private sector has been the focus of the majority of events management textbooks, dominating the literature with discussions of profitability and revenue management. In this chapter, we will explore events in the public and third sectors, both of which are increasingly using events in order to achieve their social, political and cultural aims.

11.3 The public sector

The public sector refers to those organisations that are either in the direct control of government at the national, regional or local levels, or receive their core funding from public finances. This sector, despite being encouraged to be more businesslike, is fundamentally different from the private sector when it comes to managing events in one major respect: accountability is to local citizens and the electorate rather than shareholders and/or investors (Wood 2009). The main impacts of this are in terms of how public sector organisations justify their involvement in events management and in how the events themselves are evaluated. Although it is tempting to suggest that public sector events will differ fundamentally from events in other sectors in terms of their content and design, recent moves towards greater private and third sector involvement in what have traditionally been areas of public sector monopoly – such as health, education and welfare – have blurred these distinctions.

CASE STUDY 11.1

The role of governments in the events industry

Event name: Japan: Meetings and Incentives
Event category: various
Venue and location: across Japan
Date: year round
Website: www.japanmeetings.org/

Japan Meetings and Incentives (JMI) is a part of the Japanese National Tourism Office, which was set up with government funding, specifically to promote Japan as a destination for the MINCE market [Meetings and conferences, Incentives, Networking events, Corporate hospitality, Exhibitions and trade shows]. JMI carries out activities, such as promoting the destination at exhibitions and fairs, marketing to event managers and lobbying on international event organisations' behalf to local and national government departments, in order to provide favourable conditions to attract the MINCE market to Japan.

In 2010, the Japanese National Tourism Office launched their Event policy, which had the aim of: Increasing the number of international events held in Japan by 50 per cent.

(JNTO 2015:Promotion of Meetings, Incentives, Conferences and Exhibitions (MICE) holding and attraction)

There has been a huge recent growth in the use of events by local and regional governments, but there are concerns that these are not always used in a strategic or effective way (Wood 2009). However, despite these concerns, it is clear that events strategy has become a new form of public policy, with the public sector involved in events that range from local, interactive gatherings to mega-events like the Olympic Games. The following sections will look at the strategic role that events can play in the public sector and how these can have the greatest impacts.

We can use the model in Figure 11.2 to categorise the different roles that the public sector plays in the events industry.

Figure 11.2 The role of the public sector in events management
Source: Adapted from Allen *et al.* 2008: 39–41

11.3.1 Venue management or ownership

In many locations, especially outside regional metropolitan centres, event venues can be publicly owned. Local government may be the owner of theatres, arts centres, community facilities, and parks and streets where events are staged. Public ownership of event venues usually either reflects historical patterns of ownership in an area or is a legacy of public sector investment that has been necessary to develop large event facilities. Increasingly, these venues are operated by specialist event organisations that are able to maximise return on the state's investment through the application of specialist management techniques in promotion, human resources and artist management.

For example, in Nashville, Tennessee, in the United States, the Bridgestone Arena is owned by Davidson County and the Sports Authority of Nashville. The day-to-day management and promotion of the venue have been contracted out to a specialist management company, Powers Management, which has the specialist arena and events management skills required to make a success of this 20,000-capacity venue. It is one of the most well-known event venues in America, having welcomed more than 13 million visitors since it opened (Bridgestone Arena 2016; Nashville Predators 2011).

11.3.2 Regulation

The public sector also has an interest in monitoring and regulating the negative impacts of events, which it does through licensing and the enforcement of statutes on, for example, noise pollution. In addition to this, the public sector is able to incentivise or disincentivise particular forms of activity through taxes. This can be done by central government through the manipulation of nationwide taxes, or through changes in local taxation by local government.

Image 11.1 **WWE Night of Champions 2014 at the Bridgestone Arena**
Credit: Chris Ryan/Getty Images

In 2010, a report by the British Visits and Events Partnerships called on the British government to bring VAT (sales tax) down to a level that would make the country's events industry more competitive with its European rivals (BVEP 2010). Typically, in Europe, sales tax applied to accommodation, facilities management, restaurants and bars is set between zero and 8 per cent, while in the UK it has recently been increased to 20 per cent.

11.3.3 Service provision

Using funds raised from taxation, local government will be responsible, to a greater or lesser degree, for the maintenance of public space, transport, utilities provision and the emergency services – all of which must be in place for the smooth running of an event. Liaising with local government departments on these issues is a key aspect of the management of large events and event venues.

11.3.4 Funding

The public sector can make direct and indirect funding contributions to events. Direct funding involves the finance necessary for the production of an event. For example, the Australian government provides funding of approximately AU$1.5 million per year to support the creation of work for Australia's major international festivals. This is delivered through the *Major Festivals Initiative*, which has the aims to:

- increase access for Australian audiences to new high-quality Australian performing arts productions of scale
- support the development of new Australian works that grow audiences
- expand appreciation of new Australian performing arts productions
- promote international awareness of the quality of Australian performing arts productions and Australian stories
- strengthen Australia's reputation as a sophisticated and artistic nation with a confident, outward-focused arts sector
- increase overall levels of presentation of new Australian performing arts productions of scale.

(Department of Communications and the Arts 2016:
Major Festivals Initiative)

Indirect financial support to the wider events industry is provided through state support for training for events professionals (for example, through higher education programmes) and business support services.

11.3.5 Event organisation

In some cases, public sector organisations are directly responsible for producing events. Although this function is often contracted out to specialist event organisers, some celebratory and commemorative events are still delivered directly by public sector bodies. As Pugh and Wood (2004: 61) state, 'the majority of local governments in Britain now have a substantial and varied events programme', but these events are usually supported only by departments with limited, non-specialist resources in terms of staff, funding and time (Wood 2009).

11.3.6 Marketing

Where events receive direct support from the public sector in terms of marketing, this is normally related to destination marketing and tourism promotion. Governments make use of events for destination branding by public sector bodies concerned with inward investment and tourism, as well as, more recently, to support other goals, such as the promotion of social cohesion and civic identity (Raj *et al.* 2013). Events, especially cultural events and festivals, have become core elements in destination marketing (Richards and Palmer 2010), and many towns and cities are now building events into their marketing strategies.

The fundamental test of whether the public sector should be involved in events, and whether their involvement has been constructive, is based on the 'public good' argument (Getz 2012: 88). This asks whether the contribution of government to an event will produce benefits for society as a whole or for targeted groups within it. This argument can be tested in the pre-event and post-event phases by asking the following three questions:

1   Does the event fit into the accepted policy domain of government?
2   Are the public benefits significant and inclusive?
3   Is the event managed sustainably in economic, social and environmental terms?

These relatively simple questions often demand complex responses, and local authorities, government agencies and other public bodies sometimes need to recruit external consultants to answer them. For example, in order to develop an events strategy to promote tourism and inward investment, the city of Birmingham in the English Midlands commissioned an external consultancy – Festival and Events International – to develop a strategic framework for events in the city and partnerships with other regional and local bodies. This took four months and involved a national and international benchmarking exercise to establish the extent to which the city's plans to get more involved in events were in the best interests of the public (FEI 2011). In some cases, government-supported events can have negative impacts, such as when the economic failure of the World Student Games in Sheffield in 1991 led to an increase in local taxation (Raj *et al.* 2013).

> ### CASE STUDY 11.2
>
> # The relationship of the public sector to the Roskilde Festival
>
> **Event name:** Roskilde Festival
> **Event category:** cultural
> **Venue and location:** Roskilde, Denmark
> **Date:** every June/July for five days
> **Attendance:** 100,000
> **Sponsors:** Tuborg
> **Website:** www.roskilde-festival.dk/uk/
>
> The Roskilde Festival was established in 1971 as an annual festival of rock music on the outskirts of Copenhagen, Denmark. Since then, it has grown into one

of the largest annual rock events in Europe. Every year, the festival attracts up to 100,000 visitors, and it is responsible for 20–25 per cent of annual tourism receipts in the Roskilde region.

In 2016, the headline acts included the Red Hot Chili Peppers, LCD Soundsystem and Wiz Khalifa. There are six performance areas in the festival. The smallest, tented space has a capacity of 2,000 and the largest, the 'Orange Stage', has a capacity of 90,000. There is an 80-hectare campsite attached to the festival. A peculiarity of the event is the 'naked run' that takes place every year, in which festivalgoers run naked around the boundaries of the site, with one male and one female winner receiving tickets to the following year's event.

The festival is produced by the Roskilde Charitable Foundation, a not-for-profit company with just six full-time employees, but which recruited 32,000 volunteers to produce the festival in 2016. Any financial surplus generated by the event is channelled back into cultural and sporting facilities in the region. Since 1992, this has totalled €36.3 million. Because of the foundation's charitable status, it is not liable for many state taxes and it does not pay sales tax.

The festival generates its own revenues from ticket sales and sponsorship, but it is involved in a number of partnerships with the public sector in areas such as tourism and economic development. The local authority is responsible for licensing the event and for providing policing and transport services. A local university, which specialises in events management now provides training for event staff in crowd control every year, and the regional tourist board has developed a collaborative ticketing arrangement where festival attendees can receive discounted rates in local accommodation and other regional attractions. In 2001, the Roskilde county and municipal councils awarded a €1.5 million grant for the development of 'Musicon Valley', a Silicon Valley-inspired music and technology development, with the aim of building on the success of the festival. This now contains 'Rock City', an entertainment, education and cultural tourism destination.

(Bærenholdt and Haldrup 2006;
Hjalager 2009; Roskilde Festival 2016)

Study activity

Read through Case Study 11.2. In what ways does the public sector support the Roskilde Festival? Make a list of the reasons why you think the public sector offers this support. Is such support in the best interests of the public?

11.4 Events in the public sector

Governments can use events to gain control of specific agendas in the public eye, build support for policies and programmes, and deliver on specific policy objectives. National governments take responsibility for major international and political events, occasions of state and national celebrations (Allen *et al.* 2008). Local government has responsibility for place-making, destination branding, generating inward investment, reducing out-migration and community cohesion, and it makes use of events to fulfil these duties.

Local authorities deliver a wide range of events for their communities, businesses and visitors, which may include:

- networking events
- conferences
- festivals and other celebratory events
- cultural events
- information and consultation events.

The first four of these are covered in the chapters on corporate and cultural events (Chapters 12 and 13, respectively). However, information and consultation events are specific to the public sector and have specific characteristics that are explored below.

11.4.1 Information and consultation events

These events are used by the public sector to inform the public about new projects or initiatives and to produce a dialogue with citizens that can inform the development of these areas. They can occur on a variety of scales, from small neighbourhood-level meetings to touring information roadshows.

Hiller (2000) emphasises that good public policy development must involve the community in a meaningful and ongoing way. This is especially important in the planning of large and mega-events as, even though the members of the community around an event are often conceived as key beneficiaries of its positive impacts, the idea to stage the event rarely comes from within the community, and the project may face objections and resistance. Hiller shows how far the public sector must go when addressing this community participation deficit through consultation. As part of the preparations for the 2022 FIFA World Cup, the government in Qatar organised a series of consultation events that visited five different shopping malls across the country, which were attended by around 30,000 people. The aim of the events was to learn more about progress in delivering the event, but also to listen to residents' opinions about the 2022 mega-event (Supreme Committee for Delivery and Legacy 2016).

Community consultation events can take any one of the four forms illustrated in Figure 11.3.

Information provision events are the most common form of community consultation. Limited forms of interaction are offered, but these events are useful for conveying large amounts of information to a wide audience. They can be repeated and can be mobile, at a low cost. For example, the government of the city of Toronto, Canada, ran three consecutive small events to inform local residents in areas affected by their new 'Tall Buildings Strategy' of the impact that this new planning policy would have on them. These three events took place in community facilities, including a church hall and a gym (City of Toronto 2011)

At public hearings, evidence is presented to the public, along with expert advice, and final decisions are taken by a representative body, such as a court or council. An example of this kind of consultation event was the public hearing held on World Water Day 2011 by the Environmental and Sustainable Development Commission of the House of Representatives, in Brasilia, Brazil. The hearing heard evidence from experts on the theme of water conservation and the convening panel then made recommendations to the Brazilian government on the basis of its deliberations (UNESCO 2011).

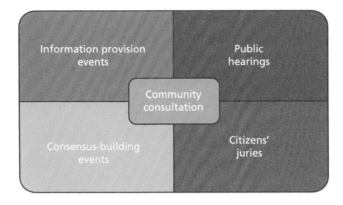

Figure 11.3 Forms of community consultation events

In consensus-building events, the public are brought into the decision-making process and can influence the outcome of the decision. For example, in 2010, Sport England, the governing body for sports in England, staged this type of consultation in twenty-three locations. Each one involved face-to-face discussions and an online survey. The aim of these events was to develop a consensus view on the future governance and support of athletics. Sport England stated that, 'The consultation roadshows had an additional aim. They weren't just about influencing England Athletics in the delivery of its core activities; they were also aiming to help clubs and volunteers themselves to share their own ideas for action and change' (Sport England 2011).

In a citizens' jury, selected members of the public are asked to represent the views of the community as part of the decision-making process. These have been used more widely in the United States and Germany than elsewhere (Carson 2001), but they are being utilised increasingly in a range of contexts as a cost-effective way of gauging public opinion. An example of this form of consultation met in 2002 in Baltimore, USA, with the support of the United States Environmental Protection Agency, to examine policy responses to the threat of climate change to the US Atlantic coast (Jefferson Centre 2002).

Communities are often also consulted in ways that do not make use of the interactive possibilities offered by events, such as through postal, telephone or web surveys.

11.4.2 The impacts of public sector events

Public sector events share sets of outcomes with all other forms of events (see Shone and Parry 2010), but these have particular implications in the public sector due to governments' responsibilities towards, and accountability to, their citizens (see Figure 11.4).

11.4.2.1 Economic implications of public sector events

Any event can have either positive or negative impacts. However, a private sector event normally has a direct economic impact – one way or the other – only on the event company that produces it. By contrast, a public sector event can have significant economic consequences, sometimes for many years after the event has taken place. In the case of small-scale events, these economic implications may be limited to individual departments or public bodies, but with large and mega-events, the consequences can be much more significant, sometimes

Figure 11.4 Aspects of public sector events

affecting national economies and the future delivery of public services. Among the potential negative impacts of a mega-event are consumer price and land price inflation, tax increases, the mismanagement of funds and the costs associated with corruption.

11.4.2.2 Developmental implications of public sector events

The public sector will usually be engaged in the development of particular locations when it supports or delivers events, ideally guided by the principles of sustainable development. However, although developmental goals – such as poverty reduction, educational attainment and public health improvements – often form part of the bid for hosting an event, there is growing scepticism in the literature about whether such developmental targets can ever be achieved in practice (Maenning and du Plessis 2009).

11.4.2.3 Political implications of public sector events

Staging or financing events to support a particular policy or political agenda can work in favour of the public sector or against it, depending on the success or failure of the event. In addition, a non-political event can have political implications if it is seen not to have produced good value for money in terms of public investment or to have caused controversy that reflects badly on the political decision to back it. Hosting always has political implications when there is public sector involvement, especially for major and mega-events.

Barker *et al.* (2001) analysed the impacts of hosting the America's Cup, a sailing competition and the oldest sporting trophy competition in the world, in Auckland, New Zealand. There were high expectations of the potential positive impacts of this event, to such an extent that the government appointed a minister to maximise them. The event was judged to have improved international trade relations, to have increased the potential of the country to attract overseas investment, and to have enhanced New Zealand's international image and reputation, which would strengthen its bids for future major events.

11.4.2.4 Social/community implications of public sector events

Many events are produced or supported by the public sector because of the positive impacts that they may have in such areas as community cohesion, social inclusion, local pride and identity. However, events can also have negative social impacts (as set out in Chapter 14), and these can lead to both financial problems for governments and reputational problems with political implications.

11.4.3 Public sector event financing

Governments around the world are becoming commissioners of services from the private and third sectors, meaning that they increasingly commission specialist event producers to deliver their events. This is in line with the more strategic marketing orientation in local government

---

CASE STUDY 11.3

Private companies delivering public sector events

Event name: NHS Institute for Innovation and Improvement Alumni Conference
Event category: public sector event
Venue and location: Excel, London, UK
Audience: 1,200 delegates
Website: www.worldevents.com/index.shtml

This one-day conference was held to celebrate 50 years of management training schemes in the National Health Service, the UK's publicly funded healthcare system. It had the dual role of bringing together professionals from within the NHS and promoting the NHS to a media and stakeholder audience.

The NHS commissioned a private sector event management company – World Events – to produce and manage this event. World Events provides international events management services, producing hundreds of events each year for both private and public sector clients:

> World Events is an international event agency. Founded in 1986, the company has 130 full-time staff and a further 100 trained staff who work with us on a part-time basis. Offices are located in Europe, USA and Asia with a revenue in excess of €46.7m/£39.8m/$57.7m. World Events is ranked in the top ten events management agencies in Europe and has won numerous industry awards for the work it has conducted for its clients.
>
> (World Events 2011)

For this event, World Events' role included:

- event design – developing a theme
- recruiting sponsors and exhibitors to help fund the conference
- marketing the event
- bookings using a bespoke web presence and online booking system
- sourcing keynote speakers and a facilitator
- operations management
- catering.

The event format involved keynote presentations, workshop sessions, debate and discussion. There was a significant use of technology during the event and it was produced to a very high standard in terms of décor and operations management. Delegate feedback was very good, with the following data recorded by World Events:

- 75 per cent got a good impression of the future vision
- 87 per cent were more likely to take part in activity post-conference
- 83 per cent would use the website to remain informed
- 80 per cent found the event useful and enjoyable.

Study activity

What are the benefits to the National Health Service of commissioning a private company to produce an event like the one outlined in Case Study 11.3? Do you think the public sector has the capability to produce outstanding events?

that was identified by Pugh and Wood (2004) when they looked at local authority events. These developments form part of a changing public sector paradigm in which government is seen as enabling and facilitating, rather than directly delivering, the full range of public services.

11.5   The third sector

Between the private and public sectors, and often bridging the two in practical terms, is the third sector. Known historically as the 'charitable' or 'voluntary' sector (Shone and Parry 2013), when it comes to events management, contemporary third sector organisations often still contain a strong voluntary and/or charitable component, but they may act in entrepreneurial, businesslike ways that do not conform to older stereotypes of village fête committees and well-meaning volunteer organisations.

Many third sector organisations channel public sector funding to the community level, delivering services in communities, and increasing numbers of them engage in forms of social enterprise – generating profitable business for socially sustainable ends. Such businesses have often evolved from charitable and voluntary groups that wished to avoid the constraints imposed by the regulation of charities and sought to develop a more entrepreneurial attitude to social change. Social Enterprise UK, a representative body for social enterprise in the UK, states:

> Social enterprises trade to tackle social problems, improve communities, people's life chances, or the environment. They make their money from selling goods and services in the open market, but they reinvest their profits back into the business or the local community. And so when they profit, society profits . . . The best government data estimates that there are approximately 70,000 social enterprises in the UK contributing £18.5 billion to the UK economy . . . and employing almost a million people.
>
> (SEC 2016)

For example, the Play House, in Birmingham, is an educational theatre company that operates as a social enterprise. Every year, the company produces more than 1,000 touring theatre events for schools and young people, and it typically involves around 25,000 people in its work. To achieve recognition as a social enterprise, it has demonstrated that more than 50 per cent of its income comes from trading, that at least 50 per cent of the company's profits are spent on socially beneficial purposes, and that, if it ceased trading, its assets would be distributed for socially and environmentally beneficial purposes. Meeting these requirements allowed the Play House to be awarded the government-sponsored 'Social Enterprise Mark', which allows potential funders and partners to have confidence in its social responsibility (Play House 2011; Social Enterprise Mark 2011).

11.6 Events in the third sector

Third sector organisations operate in the same social and economic climate as any other form of business, so it should come as no surprise that the third sector has embraced the growth in the planned events sector as vigorously as its private and public sector counterparts. Third sector organisations carry out three main roles in the events industry, as shown in Figure 11.5.

11.6.1 Venue management and ownership

Third sector organisations, such as charities, community organisations and social enterprise, can own and/or manage event venues. In the UK, local government will often retain legal ownership of a range of possible event venues, but the day-to-day management of these venues will be provided by a third sector organisation. This system ensures that the venue is run in accordance with the public sector's commitment to public value, but it removes many of the costs and complications of management from the public sector.

Other third sector organisations own venues outright and use them to generate income to help them meet their social, cultural or environmental goals. An example is the Impact Hub, in Johannesburg, South Africa. This venue was set up to support local third sector groups and to encourage innovation in social enterprise. It does this by providing networking, meeting and work spaces for social enterprises, along with an exhibition and event space

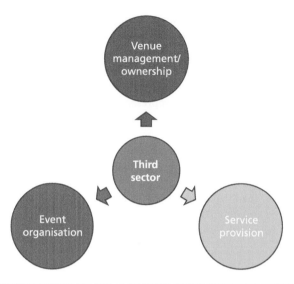

Figure 11.5 The roles of the third sector in events

Image 11.2 The Hub, Cape Town, South Africa
Credit: Gallo Images/Getty Images

with catering facilities. The Hub makes its spaces available for private hire in order to generate income, and also hosts its own events on such topics as climate change, social entrepreneurship and new technologies. They describe their activities with the following statement, clearly showing the entrepreneurial, international outlook of many contemporary social enterprise projects:

> Impact Hub Joburg forms part the world's largest network of inspiring workspaces, vibrant learning communities, and entrepreneurial incubation programs – from startup to investment ready and beyond. We foster social innovation through collaboration to create sustainable impact.

From Amsterdam to Johannesburg, Singapore to San Francisco, Impact Hub has evolved into a rapidly expanding, diverse global network of over 15,000+ members in 81 Impact Hubs in 50 countries on 5 continents. Each community is a wealth of innovative programs, events, and cutting-edge content.

(Impact Hub Johannesburg 2016)

11.6.2 Service provision

Third sector organisations can be involved with both indirect and direct service provision for events. Within communities, third sector groups can provide services relating to neighbourhood management, crime reduction, the maintenance of public space and youth work that help to create a stable and secure environment for events. In addition, they can provide direct services, such as catering, volunteers, and advice and consultations. In Manchester, Good Mood Food provides catering services for the local events industry, mainly for small- to medium-size business events and private functions. The firm is a social enterprise that offers training, employment and volunteer opportunities for individuals suffering from mental health problems, and it also campaigns to highlight the links between good food, health and mental well-being (Good Mood Food 2011).

11.6.3 Event organisation

Third sector organisations stage events to gain publicity for their social goals, to raise funds, and/ or for training and networking purposes. The third sector is very diverse, including everything from international non-governmental organisations (NGOs) to small local campaign groups. Because of this diversity, third sector organisations are involved in staging a wide range of events, including:

- cultural events
- networking events
- conferences
- community festivals
- fundraising events.

The last two categories in this list are characteristic of third sector events activity. Festivals are discussed in depth in Chapter 13, but fundraising events have a specific and prominent role within the third sector, so are explored in more detail here.

11.6.4 Fundraising events

Fundraising events, of which there are many different types, are extremely common within the third sector. Getz (2007: 26) suggests a list of events that commonly fulfil a fundraising function:

- gala dinners
- concerts
- entertainment shows
- sponsored endurance events
- celebrity sports
- auctions.

Webber (2004) provides a categorisation of fundraising events that helps to explain their various objectives (see Table 11.1).

However, as Webber goes on to show, such events, in themselves, are not very efficient in terms of income generation (see Table 11.2). Instead, they should be seen as part of a more strategic approach to fundraising that includes relationship-building and increasing awareness if their potential for charitable giving is to be fully exploited.

Table 11.1 Types of fundraising events
Source: Webber 2004

Fundraising event	Objective
Donor development	To generate additional income from existing supporters
Rewarding current supporters	To maintain the enthusiasm and engagement of current supporters
New support generation	To attract new supporters
Networking	To increase networking opportunities between supporters and potential supporters
Awareness raising	To develop awareness of the cause for which funds are being raised; to maintain awareness of the cause in the minds of supporters, public and the media

Table 11.2 **Productivity of different fundraising methods**
Source: Webber 2004

Fundraising method	Income raised per pound spent
Legacies	43.3
Committed giving	3.7
Memberships	2.7
Local fundraising	2.3
Fundraising events	2.2
Direct marketing	2.0
Not from individuals:	
Trusts	9.9
Corporate	4.7

CASE STUDY 11.4

A fundraising event for a social enterprise

Event name: Leonardo DiCaprio Foundation
Event category: third sector event
Venue: The Domaine Bertraud Belieu Vineyard, St Tropez, France
Date: July 2016
Audience: 250-plus
Website: http://leonardodicaprio.org/

Every year, the Leonardo DiCaprio Foundation, set up by the Hollywood actor, holds a gala event to raise money and awareness for the foundation's chosen causes:

> In 1998, Leonardo DiCaprio established his foundation with the mission of protecting the world's last wild places. LDF implements solutions that help restore balance to threatened ecosystems, ensuring the long-term health and well-being of all Earth's inhabitants. Since that time the Leonardo DiCaprio Foundation (LDF) has worked on some of the most pressing environmental issues of our day.
>
> (Leonardo DiCaprio Foundation 2016)

The 2016 gala event raised over \$40 million for charity, through both sales of tickets, which were available from £9,999, and a celebrity auction. The auction included:

- A Harley Davidson motorcycle signed by Leonardo DiCaprio, Robert De Niro and Martin Scorcese (\$673,000)
- A walk-on role in Leonardo's next movie (\$2.4 million)
- Two of Bono's (from the band U2) personal guitars, signed (\$1 million)
- A Damien Hirst sculpture (£6 million).

Study activity

Use the internet to identify a charity in which you have an interest. Put yourself in the place of an event manager seeking new business in the third sector. How would you pitch an event concept to fundraising managers in the charity you have selected? What can an event offer them that differs from other, more economically productive, forms of fundraising?

11.7 Other not-for-profit events

11.7.1 Political and state events

Political events are held by political organisations and governments. They include party conferences, protests, trade union meetings and policy launches. These vary in scale from national party conferences, to large-scale political protests (such as demonstrations against meetings of the G20), to local-level activist group meetings.

Van Wyk (2005: 468) defines a political event as:

carefully planned, organised, managed and implemented/hosted even by political office bearers either in government, interest groups, civil society members or outsourced to event managers. Furthermore, this event has a political or public nature with a political purpose and message, with the intention to reach as many people as possible by a variety of means such as hosting an event, marketing and the media, and the intention to reach a specific objective or a number of objectives.

State events are ceremonies that are held to mark occasions of national significance, such as the opening of parliament, the inauguration of a leader or the commemoration of a conflict. They possess their own intrinsic socio-cultural significance, but also have an economic impact, often attracting high numbers of tourists. Among the specific challenges posed by political and state events with very high media profiles are issues of media management, political and cultural relationships, crowd management and security.

Van Wyk (2005) illustrates the scale of such events by citing two examples of South African presidential inaugurations:

- 1999 – 55,000 attendees, including thirty heads of state from other countries and 5,000 foreign dignitaries.
- 2004 – 45,000 attendees, including thirty-five heads of state from other countries.

CASE STUDY 11.5

A radical political event

Event name: Mutiny
Event type: political event
Venue: Resistance Gallery, London, UK
Audience: 200
Website: http://jointhemutiny.wordpress.com/about/

Mutiny events are radical political gatherings that take place on a bi-monthly basis at the Resistance Gallery in Bethnal Green, London. They have been developed and are produced by a non-hierarchical, loosely affiliated group of individuals and are open at the planning stage to anyone who wants to contribute or become involved in the event. The aim of the Mutiny events is to create new ways for people to engage with the political situation in the UK and worldwide by bringing together journalists, performers, academics, poets, artists and musicians in events that mix entertainment and debate with very high levels of audience participation. They are examples of a new generation of political events that have emerged across the world as young people, in particular, move away from mainstream forms of political engagement and create forms of political practice that make greater use of creativity, participation and activism in their design.

> We want to change the world. We want to see an end to the carbon economy, to the global dominance of the American military complex and sweatshops abroad and call centres in the UK. At the same time we want to spend an evening with friends, enjoying a drink and the spectacle of alternative films and documentaries, performances and poetry, comedy and art installations.
>
> (Mutiny 2011)

The content of each Mutiny event is themed by discussion on topics that have included money, love, the media, fashion and education. The format changes for each event, but will typically involve a panel discussion, individual speakers, musical performances, an art exhibition, and a great deal of audience interaction and debate. In addition, Mutiny events make use of social media, including Twitter and Facebook, to involve people who are unable to attend in person and to collect feedback throughout the night from the audience.

Study activity

Using the internet, what examples of political events at the activist level can you find in your region? What can event managers learn from these events in terms of audience participation, marketing and social media? What could students of events management and professional event managers contribute to the growth and development of such events?

11.7.2 Faith events

Faith events are diverse in size and reach – from intimate meetings of a few individuals, to organised faith services and celebrations, to the largest single event in the world in terms of attendance: the Hajj in Mecca, Saudi Arabia. This annual religious pilgrimage is undertaken by approximately 3.4 million people every year (Raj *et al.* 2009).

Faith events often play a key role in the lives of individuals and families, marking significant life events, such as births, deaths and weddings. Other faith events form part of the official calendar of a country or culture, reflected in public holidays, such as Mexico's Feast of the Dead (Getz 2007) and Christmas. Typically, a formal faith event is followed by a more secular celebratory event, such as a wedding reception or meal. Pilgrimage is another type of faith event, where individuals follow a particular path to reach a sacred destination of importance to their faith.

In 2010, Pope Benedict XVI, the head of the Roman Catholic Church, visited the UK for the first time. His multi-event tour included Glasgow, Edinburgh, Birmingham and London. As this was an official state visit, the host country was expected to meet many of the costs of the tour, with the eventual cost to the public finances estimated at between £12 million and £20 million. There were three ticketed events, with an aggregate audience of approximately 225,000 people (*Guardian* 2010).

Industry voice

Leon Panitzke, Director, Verve Communications

Verve is a full-service communications company, with a focus on PR and communications. Events management is one of the things that we're involved with, but it's something that I've personally been focused on entirely for about three years now. We have eight full-time staff, so we're quite a small, specialist agency, with a main focus on working with the public sector. We work with local councils, some government departments and National Health Service (NHS) trusts. We also have a wide pool of associates, so when we have to ramp up for bigger events, we can draw on this talent pool. I'm a director of Verve, and have been since 2005, when the company was set up. As a director, I'm the main point of contact for our client, and it's also my job to project-manage the whole event, from start to finish. So I'll be involved from the outset, from the original brief, through to writing the project plan and liaising with all the partners and, because we're quite heavily involved with the public sector, one of my main jobs is pulling together quite complex partnerships.

An event that we managed for the London Development Agency (LDA), which was called the 'Personal Best' recognition ceremony, was for over 1,000 people at the O2. That came out of a conversation with a public sector colleague who said they were looking for some support for an event. They didn't have the budget to run an event along the same lines that they did two or three years ago, when the public finances were more generous (they'd run an event the previous year at Wembley Arena). So we worked with the LDA to put together a programme and we introduced a jobs and skills fair to the event, which they hadn't done before. That was an idea that came out of the initial meeting. I was involved in all aspects of the event from the proposal stage, then working with twenty-eight different London boroughs. We had five months to create the event from scratch, including involving a number of celebrities and politicians. It was a really good example of partnership working really well because, having to deal with that number of different public bodies was quite problematic.

A lot of the small-scale events that we do tend to be consultation exercises: for example, we worked on something called 'A Picture of Health for South East London', which is the biggest-ever consultation exercise carried out for the NHS in London. We carried out a consultation with over a million people, which is pretty massive, but the events themselves tended to be quite small scale and deliberative, with maybe 50 to a hundred people at public events. Obviously, the job there is to make sure that everybody who *should be* consulted *has been* consulted, and that it's not just a rubber-stamp exercise, because the process has to be robust enough to stand up to a judicial review, should that ever happen. Most of the consultation events we've done are about public bodies trying to engage stakeholders and talking to residents. For example, a health body wanting to close an A&E department is always going to cause outrage, so the organisation has to prove that they've carried out a full and proper consultation exercise.

We are definitely a private sector organisation, because we are a limited company, but I would say 95 per cent of our business at the moment comes from the public sector. We will now have to look at adapting to the new financial climate, as lots of the funding that's been there in the past for public sector organisations to put on events won't be around. We are looking at different funding mechanisms and different ways of doing business. Some of my public sector clients have had meetings with me recently to ask how they can actually make money from some of the events that they used to put on for free. A lot of private sector events companies will be looking at those financial models over the coming years.

11.8 Summary

In this chapter, we have seen that the rapid recent growth of the events industry in the private sector has been matched by that in the public and third sectors. The public sector carries out a range of roles in the events industry – from regulation, taxation and oversight through to event production and marketing. Increasingly, however, the public sector seeks to commission specialist event managers and event production companies to deliver events on its behalf.

Meanwhile, the third sector is growing in importance, both socially and economically, as the relationships between the state, the private sector and citizens develop in advanced economies. Organisations, such as social enterprises and charities, are active in the events industry, producing events and providing services for them. Other forms of not-for-profit event have their own specific characteristics and do not fit into the neat categories of private, public and third sectors. In this chapter, we have looked briefly at political, state and faith events as examples of these.

Future event managers will need to develop relationships not just with other private sector organisations but also with public bodies and those in the third sector. Increasing numbers of events management students will work in these sectors after graduation. In this area, both nationally and internationally, there are complex relationships of regulation, partnership and funding that impact on successful events management. Keeping abreast of local developments and national trends will therefore be a key skill for future event managers in all kinds of organisations.

Further reading

Raj, R. and Morpeth, D. (2015) *Religous Tourism and Pilgrimage Management* (2nd edn), Oxford: CABI. Covers an important area for events management in terms of visitor numbers and global reach that is currently under-researched in the events management literature.

Ridleyduff, R. (2015) *Understanding Social Enterprise: Theory and Practice*, London: Sage. This is a very useful introductory text for anyone seeking to understand or work within the growing field of social enterprise.

Shone, A. and Parry, B. (2014) The Events Business: Supply and Suppliers, in *Sucessful Event Management: A Practical Handbook* (3rd edn), Hampshire: Cengage Learning. Provides a useful analysis of the different sectors involved in delivering events and the relationships between them.

References

Allen, J., O'Toole, W., Harris, R. and McDonnell, I. (2008) *Festival and Special Event Management* (4th edn), Oxford: John Wiley & Sons.

Bærenholdt, J. and Haldrup, M. (2006) Mobile Networks and Placemaking in Cultural Tourism: Staging Viking Ships and Rock Music in Roskilde, *European Journal of Urban and Regional Studies*, 13 (3): 209–224.

Barker, M., Page, S.-J. and Meyer, D. (2001) Evaluating the Impacts of the 2000 America's Cup on Auckland, New Zealand, *Event Management*, 7: 79–92.

Bridgestone Arena (2016) *History*. Available at: www.bridgestonearena.com/arena-info/history. Accessed 12 December 2016.

British Visits and Events Partnership (BVEP) (2010) *Britain for Events*, London: BVEP.

Carson, L. (2001) Innovative Consultation Processes and the Changing Role of Activism, *Third Sector Review*, 7 (1): 7–22.

City of Toronto (2011) *Community Consultation Meetings Notice, March 2011*, Toronto: City of Toronto.

Create London (2010) *Create09 Festival Report*, London, Create London.

Department of Communications and the Arts (2016) *Major Festivals and the Arts*. Available at: http://arts.gov.au/funding/major-festivals-initiative. Accessed 21 March 2017.

Event Scotland (2009) *Scotland: The Perfect Stage*, Edinburgh: Event Scotland.

FEI (2011) *Birmingham City Council Events Strategy 2008–2012*. Available at: www.feiuk. com/Case_Study_02.asp. Accessed 17 January 2011.

Fifteen Foundation (2011) A Big Night out with Jamie. Available at: www.fifteen. net/ abignightoutwithjamie/Pages/default.aspx. Accessed 18 February 2011.

Getz, D. (2005) *Event Management and Event Tourism*, New York: Cognizant Communication.

Getz, D. (2007) *Event Studies: Theory, Research and Policy for Planned Events*, Oxford: Butterworth-Heinemann.

Getz, D. (2012) *Events Studies: Theory, Practice and Research for Planned Events*, Abingdon: Routledge.

Good Mood Food (2011) Good Mood Food. Available at: www.goodmoodfood. org/. Accessed 18 February 2011.

Guardian (2010) Pope's Visit: An Interactive Guide. Available at: www.guardian.co. uk/world/ interactive/2010/aug/25/popes-visit-interactive-guide-uk. Accessed 18 February 2011.

Hiller, H. (2000) Mega-events, Urban Boosterism and Growth Strategies: An Analysis of the Objectives and Legitimations of the Cape Town 2004 Olympic Bid, *European Journal of Urban and Regional Studies*, 24 (2): 439–458.

Hjalager, A.-M. (2009) Cultural Tourism Innovation Systems, *Scandinavian Journal of Hospitality and Tourism*, 9 (2–3): 266–287.

Hub Cape Town (2011) The Events. Available at: http://capetown.the-hub.net/public/events. html. Accessed 18 February 2011.

Impact Hub Johannesburg (2016) *Home Page*. Available at: http://johannesburg.impacthub. net/. Accessed 21 March 2017.

Jago, L., Chalip, L., Brown, G., Mules, T. and Ali, S. (2003) Building Events into Destination Branding: Insights from Experts, *Event Management*, 8: 3–14.

Jefferson Centre (2002) *Citizens Jury: Global Climate Change*, St Paul: Jefferson Centre. Maenning, W. and du Plessis, S. (2009) Sport Stadia, Sporting Events and Urban Development: International Experience and the Ambitions of Durban, *Urban Forum*, 20 (1): 61–76.

JNTO (2015) *Promotion of MICE Holding and Attraction*. Available at: www.mlit.go.jp/ kankocho/en/shisaku/kokusai/mice.html. Accessed 21 March 2017.

JNTO (2017) *Japan Meetings and Incentives*. Available at: www.japanmeetings.org/index.php. Accessed 21 March 2017.

Leonardo Di Caprio Foundation (2016) Home page. Available at: http://leonardodicaprio.org/. Accessed 21 March 2017.

Mutiny (2011) Join the Mutiny. Available at: http://jointhemutiny.wordpress.com. Accessed 18 February 2011.

Nashville Predators (2011) Bridgestone Arena. Available at: www.nashville corporate partnerships.com/bridgestone_arena/bridgestone_arena.html. Accessed 18 February 2011.

Play House, The (2011) About Us. Available at: http://theplayhouse.org.uk/about/. Accessed 17 February 2011.

Pugh, C. and Wood, E. (2004) The Strategic Use of Events within Local Government: A Study of London Borough Councils, *Event Management*, 9: 61–71.

Quinn, B. (2003) Symbols, Practices and Myth-making: Cultural Perspectives on the Wexford Festival Opera, *Tourism Geographies*, 5 (3): 329–349.

Richards, G. and Palmer, R. (2010) *Events Management: Principles and Practice*, London: Sage.

Raj, R., Walters, P. and Rashid, T. (2009) *Events Management: An Integrated and Practical Approach*, London: Sage.

Raj, R., Walters, P. and Rashid, T. (2013) *Events Management: Principles and Practice*, London: Sage.

Rosklide Festival (2016) *The Full Line Up is Ready with 179 Acts*. Available at: www.roskilde-festival.dk/news/2016/the-full-line-up-is-ready-with-179-acts. Accessed 21 March 2017.

SEC (2016) About Social Enterprise. Available at: http://sec2016.serc.res.in/. Accessed 7 July 2017.

Shone, A. and Parry, B. (2013) *Successful Events Management: A Practical Handbook* (4th edn), London: Cengage Learning.

Social Enterprise UK (2016) *Social Enterprise FAQs*. Available at: www.socialenterprise.org.uk/about/about-social-enterprise. Accessed 21 March 2017.

Supreme Committee for Delivery and Legacy (2016) Over 3,000 people consulted about World Cup plans in first 2022 roadshow. Available at: www.sc.qa/en/news/over-30-000-people-consulted-about-world-cup-plans-in-first-2022-roadshow. Accessed 21 March 2017.

Social Enterprise Mark (2011) The Play House. Available at: www.socialenterprise mark.org.uk/profile/theplayhouse. Accessed 17 February 2011.

Sport England (2011) England Athletics: Responding to Your Views. Available at: www.englandathletics.org/page.asp?section=1287andsectionTitle=Consultation. Accessed 22 June 2011.

Stokes, R. (2007) Relationships and Networks for Shaping Events Tourism: An Australian Study, *Event* Management, 10: 145–158.

Stokes, R. and Jago, L. (2007) Australia's Public Sector Environment for Shaping Event Tourism Strategy, *International Journal of Event Management Research*, 3 (1): 42–53.

UNESCO (2011) The World Water Day is Discussed in a Hearing in Brazil. Available at: www.unesco.org/new/en/brasilia/about-this-office/single-view/news/the_world water_day_is_discussed_in_public_hearing_in_brazil/. Accessed 22 June 2011.

Van Wyk, J. (2005) Managing Political Events, in D. Tassiopolous (ed.) *Event Management: A Professional and Developmental Approach*, Lansdowne: Juta.

Webber, D. (2004) Understanding Charity Fundraising Events, *International Journal of Nonprofit and Voluntary Sector Marketing*, 9 (2): 123–124.

Wood, E. (2009) An Impact Evaluation Framework: Local Government Community Festivals, *Event Management*, 12: 171–185.

World Events (2011) Our Company. Available at: www.worldevents.com/ourcompany/. Accessed 18 February 2011.

Chapter 12

Corporate events

Contents

12.1 Aims

By the end of this chapter, students will be able to:

- evaluate the function of events in a corporate context;
- recognise the role of corporate events in brand awareness, image enhancement, staff development, motivation and profile-raising;
- analyse a range of corporate events and their respective target markets;
- consider the strategic business objectives and motivations of corporate events management;
- examine the key contemporary issues faced in corporate events management.

12.2 Introduction

Corporate events are produced by or for businesses, with a primary purpose of supporting business growth. This distinguishes them from other forms of events, whose aims may be more cultural, political or sporting. Corporate events are broad, however, and can encompass many other kinds of events, which often have relationships with corporations without having the same strategic objectives as events focused on business. For example, some events are distinguished as important corporate events by the significance and size of the corporate sponsorship, branding and hospitality on offer, such as the international circuit of Formula One motorracing – clearly a sporting event, but one that relies heavily on corporate event aspects within its overall portfolio.

Getz (2007) goes as far as to say that events such as these have become 'corporatised': that is that some cultural events, for example, have become transformed by their relationship with corporate brands. Similarly, Masterman (2004) notes that corporate hospitality, advertising and branding are prevalent at many events. Although this chapter focuses on the more orthodox business-to-business (B2B) and business-to-customer (B2C) events of the corporate events industry, it is important to recognise the corporatisation of many events as a consequence and cause of the professionalisation of the events industry and of its economic significance.

As mentioned in previous chapters, businesses have been focusing on experiential marketing and the 'experience economy' for quite some time (Pine and Gilmore 1999). Companies seek to influence their potential consumers through the provision of memorable and enjoyable experiences, leading to a growth in a newer form of corporate event that can often appear to be cultural or non-corporate in nature, but which actually promotes specific products and services. 'Smirnoff Experience' is a set of music events, CD and digital music releases and other cultural events that were created to promote the traditional Smirnoff Vodka brand in new markets and to a new generation of consumers. In Bangalore, India, a Smirnoff Experience event was held to market the drink in a region where spirit brands are prohibited from direct marketing. EDM artists, including Nero and Rusko, performed to audiences of more than 5,000 people in a convention centre in an event that also featured the world's first ever projection-mapped stage. The event was successful in generating more than 2 million social media impressions for the brand and 50,000 new Facebook fans, as well as extensive mainstream media coverage (*Vice* 2014).

Traditional corporate venues, such as shopping centres and megastores, are also now animated through the staging of pop-up events in order to enhance the retail experience, promote products or attract new markets. For example, Disney used a series of pop-up events in shopping centres in the UK to promote their film *Home*. The events were held at 15 shopping

Table 12.1 Factors influencing the growth of corporate events

Internal	External
Increasing corporate visibility	Globalisation of markets
Driving sales	Municipal promotional strategies
Improving staff morale	Technological advances
Broker relationships between firms	Developments in travel

centres and included 53 days of activities that were enjoyed by 53,000 children. The events included themed kids-club activities, character appearances and branded fixtures and fittings (Intu 2016). At the extreme end of this is the Dubai Shopping Festival, launched in 1996 to promote the economic development of the Gulf state. The six-week-long festival is focused in the second-largest shopping mall in the world, the 6.5 million-square-foot 'Mall of the Emirates', and it has become a major feature of the global corporate events calendar, attracting more than 5 million visitors in 2008 (MyDSF 2010).

The B2B sector of the corporate events industry has seen the most significant growth over the last twenty-five years. Originating in North America's political and religious congresses in the nineteenth century, and in conventions of professional associations (Bowdin *et al*. 2011), Europe and North America witnessed the rise of planned business events, such as conferences and networking events, in the early twentieth century, but their growth has been most dramatic since the late 1980s in the Asia Pacific region (Weber and Ladkin 2003). This growth in the corporate events sector was influenced by a combination of internal and external factors, as set out in Table 12.1.

Internally, large companies are increasingly placing events within the mainstream of their activities, with some employing in-house event managers and the majority outsourcing event design and production to contractors (O'Toole and Mikolaitis 2002). This mainstreaming has come about as contemporary business models have begun to emphasise the importance of relationship-building between staff and with external partners and customers, as a key mechanism for improving profitability.

Externally, socio-economic pressures have also contributed to the growth of corporate events. Cities looking to maximise their income from visitors have invested heavily in conference centres and travel hubs to attract high-spending business tourists, enabling the staging of high-profile, global corporate events on a dramatic scale and introducing new competitive pressures into the market as corporations compete to produce the most high-impact events. Globalisation has also opened up new markets for companies, with those looking to achieve global competitiveness now obliged to attain visibility on new scales. Finally, the rapid pace of growth and technological development in the travel industry has meant that it has become both more practical and increasingly cost-effective for companies to support their staff to travel and network at greater distances.

Although corporate events have been the fastest-growing sector of the events industry (O'Toole and Mikolaitis 2002), as well as the sector with the highest yields, the Exhibition for the Incentive Business Travel and Meetings' (EIBTM) *Trends and Market Report 2015* confirms that such events have been hardest hit by continuing global economic uncertainty, because of a number of causes. As Davidson (2015) reported:

the world economy has been held back this year by slower growth in emerging markets. Most importantly, growth in China is slowing down. That country is expected to struggle to achieve its 2015 expansion target of around 7 percent. And of the other BRIC nations (Brazil, Russia and India), two are already in recession. The IMF expects the economy of Russia to shrink by 3.8 percent and 0.6 percent in 2015 and 2016 respectively, as a result of the dual blows of falling oil revenues and Western sanctions. This year, Brazil's economy will contract by 3 percent and then by 1 percent in 2016. For emerging economies as a whole, growth for 2015 is 4 percent, the weakest since 2009 and almost half of the growth rate of 7.5 percent recorded for emerging economies in 2010. The gap between growth rates of advanced economies and those of the emerging economies is narrowing.

The consequences of this include reduced demand within the corporate events market, which is likely to have a number of effects, including an excess of event venues and event production resources, reducing the profitability of the corporate events sector in the short to medium term as the purchasers of these products and services benefit from oversupply. In this climate, it is vital that future event managers are able to identify and respond confidently and flexibly to changes within the corporate events sector.

Many authors use the MICE acronym (Meetings, Incentives, Conferences and Exhibitions) to describe the various aspects of the corporate events industry (e.g. Bowdin *et al.* 2011), or place corporate events within a broader framework of 'organisational events' or 'business and trade events' (e.g. Shone and Parry 2010; Getz 2005). However, the MICE categorisation, which was developed in the business tourism literature of the 1980s, needs revisiting and updating to reflect changes in the nature of the contemporary marketplace. The overarching category of organisational events does not differentiate sufficiently between various organisational contexts, including party political conferences, charitable events, World Expos and business conferences. To address this issue, we have updated the MICE model below, and have provided a detailed description, with contemporary examples, for each category.

12.3 Categorisation

In order to gain a real insight into this key area of the events industry, it is necessary to analyse the specific events covered by the umbrella term 'corporate events' in more detail. These events are easily categorised as MINCE:

- Meetings and conferences
- Incentives
- Networking events
- Corporate hospitality
- Exhibitions and trade shows.

12.3.1 Meetings and conferences

12.3.1.1 Definition

Conferences and meetings bring together groups of people with commonalities of interests in order to interchange ideas (Shone and Parry 2014). These events are characterised by their focus on business, trade or politics, so they are B2B rather than B2C.

Study activity

Using the internet and trade publications, locate a recent event that relates to each of the five MINCE corporate event categories. Identify the suppliers and the target market for each event. Complete Table 12.2.

Table 12.2 **Categories of corporate events**

Category	Event name	Suppliers/Audience
Meetings and conferences		
Incentives		
Networking events		
Corporate hospitality		
Exhibitions and trade shows		

The conference and meeting market has traditionally been the most prolific sector of corporate events, with recent research by the MPI Foundation suggesting that more than 1.3 million meetings are held each year in more than 10,000 corporate event venues in the UK, with delegates spending almost £40 billion and contributing around 3 per cent of UK gross domestic product (MPI 2013). This market therefore makes a significant contribution to the overall UK economy, and it is equally significant in many other countries throughout the world.

12.3.1.2 Characteristics

According to the ICCA (International Congress and Convention Association), a conference is 'a participatory meeting designed for discussion, fact-finding, problem-solving and consultation, with a specific objective in mind' (ICCA 2010). Conferences vary in size, length and content, but they are typified by their focus on one particular topic, discussed during a plenary session of keynote presentations and panel discussions and often accompanied by breakout sessions and workshops. They are professionally organised and predominantly fee-charging, with a published programme of speakers and activities. Conferences are often supported by sponsors, and they can be either one-off events or held periodically.

There has been little research into what motivates audiences, or delegates, to attend conferences, because, as Getz (2007) suggests, it is widely assumed that people attend primarily to fulfil part of their business or job description. While this assumption is partially correct, the major motivation for attending conferences could be divided into 'content' (the information attendees are given) and 'networking' (the information and people they meet).

Meetings are less formal gatherings but they are still an important component of the corporate events industry. They are usually held off-site, with a chairperson and a specific agenda, focused on a very specific issue. They involve attendees from various organisations, all of whom share similar business interests. Meetings tend to be smaller in scale than conferences, which gives each attendee a greater opportunity to contribute to the agenda, debate or discussion.

Study activity

For the past thirty years, the Confederation of British Industry (CBI) has hosted an annual conference that attracts around 1,200 attendees, including senior government ministers, shadow ministers, global and UK business leaders and key principals from public bodies.

The Power-Gen Asia Annual Conference is an example of what Bauer *et al.* (2008) call a 'mega-business event'. It is run over three days and features a comprehensive conference programme with four dedicated tracks and over 8,000 delegates.

Look at the websites of both of these conferences – http://news.cbi.org.uk/events/annual-conference/ and www.asiapowerweek.com/en/power.html – and identify who organises the event, and what the key aims and objective might be. Identify five reasons why delegates attend these events. What lessons can you, as future event managers, learn from these successful events?

12.3.1.3 Key issues

There are four key components in the organisation of successful conferences and meetings, as outlined in Figure 12.1.

In order to deliver a successful meeting or conference, the organiser must first have a clearly defined concept and a robust programme. A conference programme includes details of the keynote speaker(s), a list of contributors with brief annotations of their subject areas, information on breakout sessions and workshops, plans for networking opportunities and full conference timings, including food and beverage breaks. The importance of getting the content of the programme right cannot be overstated – it is this content that provides one of the two key motivations for the target market to attend.

Once the programme has been established, finding a venue that suits the event becomes a priority. The importance of this aspect of corporate event planning is explored in more detail later in this chapter.

Another consideration is the target market – clearly identifying who will attend and why they should want to is pivotal to the success of any conference or meeting. As conferences are fee-generating, they are often deemed successful only in terms of their return on investment (ROI) and the income that they generate from delegate fees.

Creating and implementing an effective marketing plan is crucial to any event's success (see Chapter 7 for more information). Securing sponsorship is another vital component of conference delivery, as revenue from sponsorship often funds the event and drives budgeting (see Chapters 6 and 7).

12.3.1.4 Trends

As Bowdin *et al.* (2011) note, technological innovation affects many aspects of events management. However, some recent technological developments, especially in the fields of emerging technologies, such as video presence and mobile broadband and social media, have had a particularly significant impact on the design, marketing and delivery of corporate events. As the use of personal technology increases, conference and meeting organisers have to think creatively and offer something more than the traditional conference formula.

Figure 12.1 Key components for conference and meeting events
management

The industry has, therefore, seen a growth in webinars, teleconferencing and videoconferencing (Davidson 2010).

In addition to the increased opportunities offered by technology, external factors, such as environmental concerns (Getz 2005), and major international incidents, such as the terrorist attacks in Brussels and Paris and various conflicts and wars, have changed how, why and under what circumstances people are prepared to travel (Allen 2008). However, ultimately the conferences and meetings industry centres on face-to-face interaction, the sharing of ideas, and networking with like-minded individuals. Organisers have to work hard to ensure that the programming of their conference or meeting offers something that cannot be captured through technology alone. The programme has to convince the target market that they have to *be* there, or else they will miss out (Haug 2010).

Another innovation which is steadily growing in popularity is 'unconferencing'. This typically still involves face-to-face meetings and dialogue between attendees. Nonetheless, it differs from a traditional conference in terms of design. Wolf *et al.* (2011) have published a case study of an unconference held by a Swiss technical university – ETH Zurich. The event design included a general introduction from the university's vice-president; a structured process to ensure that each participant met at least five other participants; an 'ideas market', during which 50 ideas were proposed, examined and selected or abandoned by the entire audience; a reception and dinner that included external experts who helped to continue to shape these ideas; a panel of judges who watched the ideas being pitched; and a people's jury in which participants pitched ideas to each other.

Cvent CONNECT, Las Vegas, USA

Event name: Cvent CONNECT
Event type: conference
Venue: The Venetian, Las Vegas
Date: 26–30 June 2016
Attendance: over 2,000 planners, hoteliers and industry experts
Website: www.cventconnect.com/

Cvent CONNECT is an annual conference where group business, corporations and associations come together to connect, learn and engage with like-minded professionals from the meetings and events industries.

The event features 200+ exhibitors at the tradeshow, 100+ educational breakout sessions running alongside the full conference agenda, an award ceremony (the Plannies) and opportunities to undertake hospitality and event professional training. There is also a programme of delegate networking events, including drinks receptions, dinners and celebratory nights out. The event typically starts on a Sunday with a full conference programme of educational sessions followed by a sponsored dinner and reception. There are then three full days of conference programming, including a range of plenary and breakout sessions. Each day has a breakfast, lunch and dinner for all delegates.

The second to last day features the Plannies award luncheon and a celebratory night out. On the final day, there is a closing session and a number of breakout sessions, including classroom training and tech talks. The event ends at lunchtime with 'grab and go' box lunches.

The event features talks from 50+ globally recognised industry consultants, executives and influences, which are designed for delegates to learn best practice from peers and gain actionable insights into improving current processes. In addition, the event features an industry pavilion, which allows delegates to walk through the entire lifecycle of an event, learning how each piece of the platform helps you achieve your goals and create an ideal event experience. This includes hands-on training and question-and-answer sessions from the community of experienced customers and industry peers. The event also offers training and certification in event-related areas and offers excellent networking opportunities, as well as the chance to experience Las Vegas.

(Cvent 2016)

12.3.2 Incentives

12.3.2.1 Definition

The term 'incentives' covers a wide range of events, including trips and travel, training, away-days and team building. The incentives branch of the events industry has long been seen as a particularly lucrative one (Bowdin *et al.* 2011), and it continues to survive despite the global economic crisis that began in 2008, reflecting the key role that events of all kinds now play in corporate activities.

12.3.2.2 Characteristics

Incentive trips are defined by Davidson (2003) as exceptional travel trips that employees receive from their employer as prizes for winning a competition related to their jobs. The purpose of such trips is to encourage staff to meet certain business objectives. However, a more comprehensive view of the sector shows that, while incentive trips are still the largest component of incentive travel, the sector has grown to include a wider range of activities. A more relevant term, 'incentive travel', is becoming prevalent, as it relates to incentive trips *and* to destination management and exploration and familiarisation trips – journeys arranged by external agencies in order to allow stakeholders to experience specific destinations, activities or venues.

Other incentive events are event-based activities that focus on staff development. Training events, away-days and team-building activities all have motivational experiences for participants as their primary focus in order to achieve specific organisational goals or to increase performance levels (SITE 2010). This side of the industry is growing steadily, with a proliferation of such incentives as 'It's a Knockout' days – in which co-workers form teams and complete huge inflatable obstacle courses, often in fancy dress – or 'Olympiad' days – where colleagues compete in their own mini-Olympics. More often, incentive trips that work towards building the motivation of attendees take the form of cooking days, treasure hunts and quizzes.

As the economy grows and contracts, the incentives market usually follows suit. In boom times, spending tends to increase, with trips organised to more distant and exotic locations; during recessions, cost-cutting often leads to shorter trips to cheaper destinations (Davidson 2010).

12.3.2.3 Key issues

Incentive events are widely recognised as useful management tools since they are effective means of recognising and rewarding employees (Davidson 2003). However, offering incentive events is not the only way to reward employees: cash bonuses, promotions, gifts and profit-related pay are all frequently used by the corporate sector. Given the number of alternatives, and the high cost in financial and human resource terms that incentive events represent for organisations, the question is: why do companies continue to rely on such events? The answer lies in the reward economy and the motivational needs of potential attendees. In order for an incentive event to succeed, the venue, location and event programme must all be attractive to the potential attendees; organisers must also strive to communicate the offering effectively – building up awareness and anticipation is key (Severt and Breiter 2010).

An important consideration for organisers of incentive events is the demographic make-up of attendees. While there may be some commonalities, these are not necessarily related to age, sex, education or cultural background – the only real commonality is the sharing of a job or working for the same organisation. This makes planning for an incentive event that will appeal to a target market of various demographics both complicated and delicate.

In 2010, CMM Incentives organised Vie at Home's annual incentive trip to reward the cosmetic company's top performers. Seventy consultants and managers were taken on a four-day trip to Cape Town, where they stayed in the Table Bay Hotel. Activities included: a trip in a cable-car up Table Mountain, with drinks and canapés served at the top; a Winelands Discovery Adventure; whale-watching on a sunset cocktail cruise; a gala dinner at the Cape of Good Hope Castle; and a farewell picnic at the Kirstenbosch Gardens. The event manager had three key criteria for the selection of the destination: flight time, time difference and weather. But they also took into consideration the profile of the group – which was likely to be all-female and aged between 20 and 60 (Harwood 2010).

12.3.2.4 Trends

The EIBTM's *Trends and Market Report* (Davidson 2015) indicates that, although the economic downturn of 2009 affected incentive travel more than any other sector of the corporate events industry, this sector has recovered strongly, with incentive travel professionals expecting to increase the budgets from 1 per cent to 10 per cent in 2016. Although incentive travel trips *are* beginning to include international destinations again, predictions are that, during future periods of economic crisis, incentive groups will be smaller and incentive trips will visit less ostentatious destinations in order to reduce accusations of extravagance. Supporting this theory, *Conference and Incentive Travel* magazine reported that 'Axa Life has scaled down its incentive travel programme for the next two years in response to the fallout from the financial crisis. The insurance giant's UK division is cutting back on overseas trips, but will continue to run prize programmes and small rewards' (Henderson 2010).

12.3.3 Networking events

12.3.3.1 Description

In the past ten years, the focus of corporate events has shifted to a concentration of outcomes. Businesspeople have become more selective in the events they attend, and the motivation for attendance is no longer solely focused on the content of the event but also, and importantly, on the quality and relevance of the other attendees to the guests' corporate objectives. The importance of face-to-face meetings with colleagues, associates, consumers and/or potential clients has never been more strongly emphasised by event participants.

Many organisations see business networking as a low-cost marketing method to develop sales opportunities and contacts. Others see it as an environment in which they can share ideas and keep abreast of industry developments, or as an essential tool in career development that provides an opportunity to forge key business relationships through personal interaction. The events industry has responded to these developments by providing event spaces that facilitate opportunities to meet and greet interested and interesting parties in a networking-enabled environment.

These networking events include small-scale lunches and dinners, drinks receptions, product launches, conventions, congresses, awards ceremonies and symposia. The main focus is on providing networking opportunities – for sponsors to meet potential new clients; for large brands to raise awareness among a particular audience; for companies to demonstrate their new products to potential purchasers; and for association members to share ideas and innovations as well as to keep abreast of industry developments.

12.3.3.2 Characteristics

Association networking events are organised by trade bodies and professional/industry associations to communicate with their members. They provide opportunities for associations to discuss key issues and to share relevant information with their respective audiences (Allen *et al.* 2011). Since the late 1990s, these events have become central to the events industry, forming a key revenue stream for event professionals. They have continued to deliver throughout the financial crisis, with the EIBTM's 2010 report indicating that the association sector was less affected by the economic climate than the rest of the corporate sector (Davidson 2010).

Association networking events include conventions, congresses, symposia, summits and awards ceremonies. The first four of these are similar in form to conferences, but are usually larger in size and are often repeated annually. They can be held on a regional scale, such as the Regional Asthma Summit, held annually in Yorkshire and Humberside, UK; a national scale, such as the French Teachers Association Congress, held in the Gambia for the first time in January 2010; or an international scale, such as the G8 and G20 summits, held in Canada in 2010, which attracted 700 official delegates as well as a large number of accompanying guests. Many people will be familiar with the format of awards ceremonies, such as the internationally renowned Oscars. A large and robust industry specialises in corporate award ceremonies; usually (though not always), these are run by or for professional and industry associations. Examples include the Professional Beauty Awards, the Chemical Industry Association Awards and the Music Industry Association Awards.

Uniquely, these association networking events often have the same audience at each event. The priority is to ensure that audiences are kept abreast of developments in their professional fields and given ample time to network with colleagues and associates (Allen *et al.* 2011).

The other side of the networking events industry is typified by events run *by business for business* (B2B). The primary goal of these events is to encourage business networking or the promotion and marketing of a specific product or brand. They tend to be less formal than other corporate events, and often concentrate on the social side of networking. Examples include intimate lunches, dinners, drinks receptions, private members' clubs events and product launches. The Supper Club, founded in 2003 by the entrepreneur Duncan Cheatle, is attended by a group of UK entrepreneurs who share knowledge, contacts, best practice and experiences. Its primary function is to encourage peer-to-peer learning, and it actively excludes any organisation that may try to use the network for self-promotion. The Supper Club offers its members structured forums, social events and subject-specific dinners. By 2010, it had already hosted 560 events and its membership had increased significantly – unsurprisingly, as its members reported an average growth in sales of 26 per cent in 2009 (Supper Club 2010).

12.3.3.3 Key issues and trends

Networking event managers have to be forward-thinking, giving their participants new experiences and unique opportunities to meet colleagues and associates. The industry has recognised the need to drive networking forward as well as the reluctance of some participants to participate in traditional networking, which is often seen as a contrived and jaded concept. Successful organisers continue to devise new ways to ensure that target markets will want to attend their events and that participants will interact when they attend them. There is often a multitude of interests in one room, with guests from a variety of demographic backgrounds, though participants will usually share a common focus. This, coupled with the negative connotations of the word 'networking', has resulted in a need to try innovative ideas.

Digital media brand Mashable wanted to create networking events that were aligned with their image as a young, exciting company. To do this, they created an 'After-hours Speakeasy' at the Association of National Advertisers 'Masters of Marketing Conference' in Orlando, Florida, which was by invitation only and began at 11:30pm. The event also included an outdoor cigar lounge and live entertainment. All attendees received Mashable-branded 'Aviator' sunglasses (BizBash 2015).

In recent years, numerous organisations have emerged that utilise new technology at their networking events. One particularly popular tool is 5 Minute Networking software – an event facilitation system that fuses the concept of speed dating with the principles of business networking. The software seating programme initiates introductions while the database keeps track of who has met whom at previous events. The process continues after the event via the software company's website (5 Minute Networking 2010).

While there has been a move towards incorporating some innovation into networking events, the industry generally remains convinced that interpersonal relationships and face-to-face opportunities are still the best networking tools. This was confirmed by a survey of 600 executives conducted by Hilton Hotels, which found that face-to-face meetings are still considered more effective and productive than those utilising recent innovations in communications technology (Arvey 2009). Networking events therefore still tend to follow the formula of: a corporate objective (usually a brand, product or key issue that needs promoting or discussing); the participant's objective (to meet colleagues or associates, increase business interaction or gain awareness of new developments in their field of interest); and a networking opportunity (an event that allows all parties to interact face-to-face). These three segments can be viewed (as in Figure 12.2) as the base and centre of a pyramid, building towards the key motivation behind the event (the outcome).

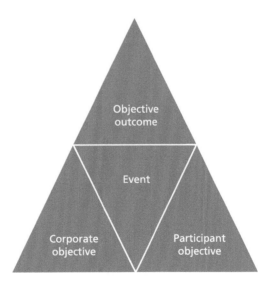

Figure 12.2 Achieving outcomes at networking events

Networking events are at their most successful when people with shared interests interact with each other face-to-face. With the continued advances in technology and the internet, how will this situation change? Using the internet, find one example of a networking event that embraces technology and requires guests to network in innovative ways.

12.3.4 Corporate hospitality

12.3.4.1 Definition

Corporate hospitality events have as their focus the entertainment of key clients in order to improve or cement business relationships. These events, therefore, involve an element of networking. However, they should not be confused with networking events – there is a clear difference between the two. A corporate hospitality event is a hosted event that forms part of another public live event; in essence, it is an event within an event. Key clients are invited, at no charge, to one event by a particular 'host' organisation. When they arrive at that event, the host organisation will have a hospitality suite for the private use of these invited guests. This suite will offer a premium view of the event itself, plus complimentary food and drinks.

12.3.4.2 Characteristics

In the past, corporate hospitality events happened mostly at sporting events, such as the Olympics, the French Open Tennis Championships and the Super Bowl. However, in recent years, there has been a move towards alternative corporate hospitality events, with an increasing number of cultural events providing opportunities to host key clients. Examples of these are boxes at large arenas to watch music concerts, premium seats at the theatre and movie premieres, tickets for opening days of flower shows and VIP areas at festivals. Corporate hospitality events are, by their very nature, one-offs, although corporate clients may well rent the same box at a sporting ground or return to the same festival with different clients every year. They usually last one day or less, and the hosting organisation covers all costs.

A typical corporate hospitality event involves a welcome drink, premium views of the event, usually from a box, complimentary drinks throughout the event and food – sometimes a seated meal, sometimes canapés. There is often a gift for guests to take away at the end of the event.

The corporate hospitality organiser Keith Prowse has various video clips of such events on its website.

12.3.4.3 Key issues

The corporate hospitality events industry places great importance on the guest experience. The success of a corporate hospitality event is largely dependent on the success of the hosting at the event itself, aided by a smooth invitation and acceptance process. The hosting at the event therefore has to be carefully planned and managed, with all of the guests' needs catered for by the event organiser so that the host can concentrate on cementing business relationships and potentially creating new opportunities. As Davidson (2003: n.p.) states:

'Relationship management' is the phrase used to describe the technique of forming close bonds with those people who are important to the competitiveness and profitability of a company . . . [C]orporate hospitality can be a highly effective method of establishing and maintaining a positive image for the company that invests in it, and ultimately improving their business performance.

The role of brand association is also important: the choice of event is informed by the impression that it will make on the host organisation's key clients. A brand such as Cartier hosts its key clients at various international polo events because it wishes to be associated with high-end experiences. (The relationship between sponsorship of events, corporate hospitality hosting and brand association is discussed in detail in Chapter 7.)

The Bureau of Investigative Journalism conducted an investigation into the effectiveness of corporate hospitality in 2010. This revealed that the UK's most senior civil servants were wined and dined by major corporations and interest groups on more than 3,100 occasions over a period of three years. The accountants PricewaterhouseCoopers and KPMG were the most active hospitality providers, although Fujitsu, BT, Deloitte and arms giant BAE were significant players, too. In an article about the investigation, Curtis and Evans (2010) noted that David Hartnett – the Permanent Secretary for Tax at HM Revenue & Customs (HMRC) – accepted invitations to eat and drink 107 times over the three-year period:

Hartnett sat down with representatives of the 'big four' accountancy firms 27 times . . . Corporate hospitality is part of Hartnett's approach to raising tax from big firms. Rather than confronting them, he has relied on persuading them to pay their share of tax.

HMRC defended Hartnett's activities by saying that he engaged with

people from all sectors of the economy in meetings which take place inside and outside office hours. The relationships that Dave has forged have enabled HMRC to transform its relationships with business and other taxpayers. This has made a significant contribution to the increased tax yield HMRC has achieved in the period.

(Curtis and Evans 2010)

12.3.4.4 Trends

The global economic crisis that began in 2008, and that has continued to produce economic uncertainty in all business sectors, has resulted in a move away from traditional, lavish corporate hospitality events as organisations cut their spending. Some of these changes have been relatively low key – sparkling wine has replaced champagne, and canapés have replaced dinner. Others changes have been more dramatic. There has been an increase in daytime events, and educational elements have been added to some corporate hospitality events. Such events are still seen as valid and successful marketing tools (Bell 2009), but organisations have increasingly realised that they need to be more of a justifiable business proposition in order to remain a viable option for guests.

12.3.5 Exhibitions and trade shows

12.3.5.1 Description

At the most basic level, exhibitions and trade shows involve a large number of manufacturers and retailers displaying a selection of their products to potential buyers and/or the general public. Exhibitions can therefore be for a consumer target market or for business purposes (the latter events are also known as trade shows). They take place in large, purpose-built venues – such as the ExCel Centre in London, the Vietnamese National Convention Centre or the San Diego Convention Center – are usually held on an annual basis and often attract an international audience.

It is important to note that the typologies 'fair', 'convention' and 'exposition' are sometimes used to describe exhibitions and trade shows (see, for example, Bowdin *et al.* 2011 and Allen *et al.* 2011). Conventions tend to be organised by associations or professional bodies for their members, and the term 'exposition' (expo) tends to be applied to larger-scale exhibitions. The primary difference between a fair and an exhibition is that fairs place more emphasis on entertainment by including live demonstrations related to the industry as well as live music, celebrity guest appearances and so on. Exhibitions, on the other hand, are likely to host accompanying conferences or seminars, which enable visitors to meet and speak to individuals from the companies and organisations in the relevant industry. This obviously increases opportunities for networking and allows influential figures from the industry to present their latest innovations and policies on a more intimate scale than at the exhibition itself.

In recent years, there has been increasing use of the term 'confex' to describe a conference and an exhibition taking place simultaneously at the same venue, with the same overall purpose and content. These events might prioritise the conference, with a small accompanying exhibition; or they might lead with the exhibition and run a small-scale conference alongside. International Confex is a leading UK event that delivers a comprehensive showcase of UK venues and event services and promotes the best of the international events industry during an exhibition that is attended by over 1,000 exhibitors. The 10,000 visitors to the exhibition are invited to attend the accompanying conference and delegates can also participate in an association events forum and the AEO sales conference. This features keynote addresses from industry specialists and seminar sessions that explore key areas of industry debate, marketing and business skills (International Confex 2016).

12.3.5.2 Characteristics

The key characteristic of any exhibition or trade show is that it is a marketing or communication tool. The benefits of these events are that they allow direct customer contact, provide a platform for products and services and create marketing opportunities by allowing the media to focus on companies or products (UFI 2011).

Exhibitions and trade shows can be divided into two categories: those that communicate primarily with a consumer target market (the general public); and those that focus on a specific business or trade. It is useful to explore these two areas separately, as the management of each kind of event requires significantly different approaches.

Consumer exhibitions and shows are open to the general public. They charge an entrance fee and are centred on such themes as cars, fashion and travel (Getz 2007). They sometimes move around the country, but, more often than not, they return to the same venue each year. Competition in this sector is fierce, and there are usually a number of exhibitions vying for the same target market.

Consumer-led exhibitions are seen as beneficial for all stakeholders as 'manufacturers test new products at shows, retailers try to sell and the consumer is searching for both ideas and entertainment' (Getz 2007: 40). An example of a large consumer exhibition is the Clothes Show Live, which takes place annually in Birmingham, UK, and regularly attracts 170,000 visitors and hundreds of exhibitors (Clothes Show Live 2016).

As Getz (2007) suggests, trade exhibitions and shows are invitation-based, and are usually staged for a specific business purpose or related to an association membership. Their primary function is, therefore, to promote or sell a product from a particular area of business. They allow visitors to evaluate products side-by-side, keep abreast of industry developments and meet suppliers directly.

The International Consumer Electronics Show is the largest trade show in America, hosting 2,500 exhibitors every year. It is not open to the general public, and visitors must work in the consumer electronics industry to attend. The event attracts 126,000 of these industry professionals annually. In addition to being invited to the exhibition, they can attend a conference that runs alongside it and enjoy numerous entertainment options, such as competitions, concerts and celebrity guests (International Consumer Electronics 2016).

A growing number of exhibitions and trade shows are now targeting a cross-sector market: these are known as hybrid shows. Their main target market may be the professionals from a specific industry, but they realise that their content will be of interest to the general public as well. In order to maximise their potential audience (and therefore their profit), they stage events that will appeal to both.

An example of a hybrid exhibition is Tattoo Jam, a three-day tattoo convention, which takes place annually at Doncaster Racecourse, UK. It features 300 working artists and traders in the Lazarus Exhibition Hall and has separate function rooms for workshops, seminars and live entertainment. Two days of the exhibition are open to the general public, while the third is reserved for registered tattooists, piercers, guests and associated traders. Tattoo Jam is run by the publishers of *Skin Deep* and other magazines and the organisers of other tattooing events, Tattoo Freeze and the Great British Tattoo Show (Tattoo Jam 2016).

12.3.5.3 Key issues

Staging an exhibition is a very complex events management skill. A daunting array of operational planning is required when dealing with such a large-scale event. In fact, lead times, from the original concept development through to delivery of the event, can be as long as two years. The exhibition event manager can be dealing with anything from 100 to 3,000 separate exhibitors as well as sponsors, caterers, venue, client, audiovisual providers and so on. The build-up and breakdown of an exhibition are particularly complex and need to be managed with tight control. At the same time, exhibition event managers must comply with a number of regulations, laws, permits and licences, including various Health and Safety Acts (1974, 1981, 1999), Electricity at Work Act 1998, Building Standards and Regulations, Lifting Operations and Lifting Regulations and so on (see AEO, BECA and EVA 2002 for a comprehensive list).

12.3.5.4 Trends

UFI, the Global Association of the Exhibition Industry, published its sixteenth Barometer Survey in January 2016 (UFI 2016). This report suggested that there would be an increase in turnover during 2016, a big improvement for Europe and the Americas following a period of very slow growth or shrinkage, a stable situation in the Asia Pacific Region and a slowdown for the Middle East–Africa region. Surveyed organisations identified the state of the home and global economies as the most important issue facing their business in 2016.

The report concludes that:
The most important business issues remain related to the general economic situation with the state of the economy in home market and global economic development

uncertainty consistently selected as among the three most important business issues for the last five years, together with competition from within the industry and internal challenges. The impact of digitalisation comes fifth globally, and fourth in Europe.

In terms of strategy, a large majority of companies intend to develop new activities, in either the classic range of exhibition industry activities (venue/organiser/services), other live events or virtual events, or in both: 75% in the Middle East & Africa, 86% in Asia/Pacific, 87% in Europe and 93% in the Americas. In terms of geographical expansion, only one to two companies out of ten on average in all regions, declare an intention to develop operations in new countries.

(UFI 2016: 30)

CASE STUDY 12.2

IBTM

Event name: IBTM Africa
Event type: exhibition
Venue: Cape Town, South Africa
Date: 8 April 2016
Sponsors: Gauteng, in partnership with SAACI, the South African Association for the Conference Industry
Website: www.ibtmafrica.com/

IBTM events consist of a range of exhibitions that take place on five continents around the world. Last year, these took place in Spain, the UAE, China, India, America and Latin America and this one in South Africa. The events vary in size but all aim to bring together meetings, events and incentive industry decision makers in order for them to connect together. Last year, the 8 events connected 5,000 suppliers from over 100 countries with 19,000 meetings and events planners.

IBTM Africa started off as a table top event but has now evolved into a high-quality content-driven education programme, focuses on future trends, procurement and consolidation. One of the key conversations at this event is around the benefits of Foreign Exchange, and the convergence of the travel and meeting industry, demonstrating how each IBTM provides content that is directly applicable to the area within which they are working.

This one-day event is markedly smaller than some of the other IBTM events (for example, IBTM World runs for four days and includes a full conference programme, and exhibition, a hosted buyers' programme and numerous networking opportunities). The single-day programme reflects the emerging nature of the meetings industry in Africa and there are no doubt plans to grow this IBTM Africa into a comparable size in the future.

(IBTM 2016)

12.4 Key logistical issues for corporate events

12.4.1 When do corporate events take place?

Corporate events have peak and off-peak seasons. Traditionally, few corporate events took place in December, July or August, as organisations' employees were often on long Christmas or summer holidays. However, as consumption and demand have grown over the past five years, and as the recession has resulted in a drive towards businesses working harder to attract and retain clients, the peaks and troughs have flattened out, with the peak season now stretching from the very start of February right into July and commencing again in the first week of September. Figure 12.3 illustrates the changes that have occurred in the peaks and troughs of a typical event season.

The day of the week on which a corporate event takes place is a key decision for the event manager. Choosing the wrong day impacts on the number of attendees registering and severely jeopardises the success of the event. With the notable exception of corporate hospitality, corporate events with businesses as their target market (B2B) tend to take place during the working week. Mondays and Fridays are less popular, as business guests are often away from the office (on long weekends) or are unwilling to attend an event that has elements of socialising at the start and end of the week. The majority of B2B corporate events therefore take place on Tuesday, Wednesday or Thursday. They are often run during business hours: attendees tend to view them as work, so they are usually unwilling to give up their free time to attend.

The notable exception to these unwritten rules of timings are corporate hospitality events, which take place throughout the year, on any day of the week, including weekends, and usually outside office hours. Attendees tend to view these events as entertainment and enjoyable, so they are willing to give up their free time to attend. Events run for members of associations or for consumers are also less stringent about avoiding Mondays and Fridays and often take place over weekends – the perception being that guests are interested enough in the product or in the activities of their association that they will happily invest their spare time in attending an event.

It is essential that corporate hospitality event managers check calendars for the relevant industry. For instance, there would be little point running an event aimed at university

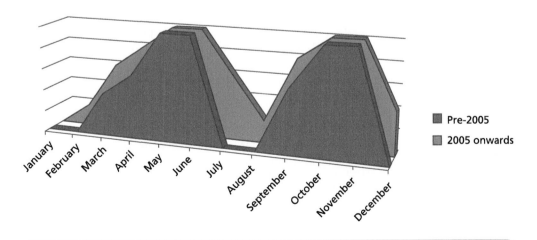

Figure 12.3 Peaks and troughs of an event season

academics in August, when they take time away from the office to write and prepare for the following year. Similarly, if possible, corporate events should not be scheduled to clash with major sporting events. Sometimes, however, this is unavoidable. One of the authors once held an event on FA Cup Final day. Three-quarters of the invited audience stated they would not attend if they could not watch the match, so screens were erected around the venue, and the entire programme was rearranged to ensure that guests could see the whole game, if they so desired.

Event managers should also keep track of national holidays. Bank holidays, school holidays, religious festivals and related holidays should all be avoided, unless the event has a specific and related theme.

The key is to choose a date that maximises the potential target market – event managers should identify the best date with the least number of obstacles for their invited guests.

12.4.2 Where do corporate events take place?

As we have seen earlier in this chapter, corporate events come in many shapes and sizes. They can be local, national or international, and while some of them (conferences, meetings, conventions, exhibitions and trade shows) take place in purpose-built conference and exhibition centres, many others (especially networking and incentive events) might be held in high-end restaurants, museums, art galleries, golf clubs, vineyards or hotels. There is an ever-increasing number of venue finders – organisations whose sole aim is to locate a venue that perfectly complements the event's content and objectives.

Of course, the venue must fit the general event requirements of size, capacity, location and so on (all of which are explored in detail in Chapter 4). However, beyond these logistical requirements, the corporate event manager will choose the venue on the basis of their perception of stakeholders and target market. The image that the venue projects and the message that it sends to the target market are key considerations in corporate events, where image is a large part of the whole event concept. A venue such as the Ritz Hotel in London gives an event an air of formality, wealth and top-class service with first-class food, whereas the Moulin Rouge in Paris is more risqué, with an image of informality, entertainment and fun. These images do not just reflect on the event itself, but send deeper messages about the organisers, their products and their work philosophies.

Moreover, the choice of venue often relates to the type of event that is being staged. Corporate events sometimes rotate around regions (or even countries), so the choice may be limited to a certain location. Similarly, they are often staged alongside other, more established events. For example, the number of corporate events will mushroom whenever a mega-event is in town, as skilful event managers attempt to exploit the sudden proximity of their target markets by inviting them to smaller-scale events. For instance, there is always a city- or nationwide peak in corporate events just before, during and immediately after the FIFA World Cup or the Olympics.

For these reasons, it is unwise to stick to a standardised, inflexible checklist of venue criteria. Each venue choice is so specific to the event that a new checklist should be devised every time a venue search is launched. Choosing the correct venue is the most important decision a corporate event manager can make.

> ### Study activity
>
> A key client has commissioned you to produce a corporate event. The client runs a high-level accountancy firm specifically for entrepreneurs turning over at least £1 million a year. The entrepreneurs all currently run their own businesses in a diverse range of industries. The brief is given below:
>
> - Event: evening networking drinks reception.
> - Attendees: 50 of our most important customers. They are all entrepreneurs and each of their companies generates over £1 million a year. They are mostly men in their forties and fifties.
> - Location: Central London.
> - Date: a Tuesday, Wednesday or Thursday in May.
> - Budget: £100 per head.
> - Additional notes:
>   - We would like a unique venue, preferably one that our customers will not have visited before.
>   - As our customers are high earners, the venue should be high-end and glamorous.
>   - We will require canapés and cocktails on arrival, plus drinks throughout the evening.
>   - There should be room for twenty-five staff members, in addition to the invited guests.
>   - We will need to be able to make speeches.
>
> Visit www.uniquevenuesoflondon.co.uk or www.venuefinder.com and identify the best venue for the event. In a small group, prepare a five-minute pitch for your venue proposal, clearly showing how your choice will add value to the event.

12.5 The corporate event customer

The term 'customer' can be confusing when applied to events. For corporate events, the customer can be either internal or external. Internal customers are people who work for the organisation arranging the event: for example, a meeting for a board of directors or a training day for a team from the shop floor. External customers come from outside the organisation. They are people with whom the organisation already does business, or with whom it would like to do business, or with whom it wishes to communicate in order to satisfy corporate objectives. This distinction between internal and external customers is important for the event manager, as they must identify the target market clearly in order to deliver an event successfully.

Uniquely in corporate events, the customer is not only the customer of the event (the delegate in a conference or the visitor to the trade show) but the customer of the corporation organising or hosting the event. In this sense, corporate events have a dual purpose: they must satisfy

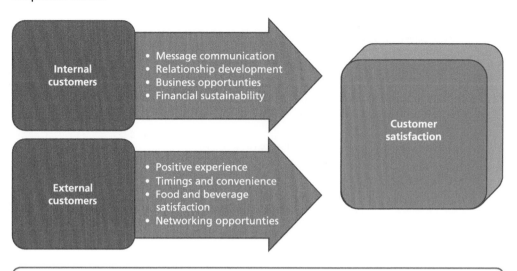

Figure 12.4 Corporate event customer satisfaction model

the wants, needs and demands of the *event* customer, but their primary purpose is to satisfy the wants, needs and demands of the *corporate* customer.

Corporate events allow organisations to maintain and develop business relationships, close deals and make sales, meet with competitors' clients and work towards the overall corporate objective. Corporate event managers therefore need to develop an understanding of the customer's desires in order to ensure that the event meets their expectations and perceptions from both event *and* corporate perspectives (see Figure 12.4).

These events focus on the recruitment and retention of corporate customers. Corporate events are designed to build, increase and protect corporate loyalty. This is a driving force in corporate events, which in turn form part of a wider continuum of business communication and marketing. The need to impress, entertain and get to know customers in order to build loyalty explains why corporate events place considerable emphasis on providing networking opportunities.

The hosts of corporate events are responsible for ensuring that the networking is effective, but it is the event manager's responsibility to ensure that the logistical and operational aspects are right. Everything that happens at these events is a direct reflection on the host organisation. Any impressions that are made will ultimately inform the customer's business decision. Will they want to do business with an organisation that serves bad food or allows an event to run over the advertised finish time?

These impressions also relate to the corporation's brand, product or message. As Allen *et al.* (2011) suggest, events aimed at external customers measure their success through, among other things, a change in attitude or perception. This is echoed by a study conducted by Nguyen and Leblanc (2001: 227), in which the authors discovered that 'the degree of customer loyalty has a tendency to be higher when perceptions of both corporate reputation and corporate image are strongly favourable'.

Consideration should also be given to another form of corporate event customer – the sponsors who are often involved in such events. Satisfying these people, along with other external stakeholders, such as associations and media partners, can be as important as pleasing the event customers, as they often provide the revenue and/or the promotion for the event. (Sponsorship is considered in more detail in Chapter 7.)

While the global economic downturn has resulted in a change in the corporate events sector – with lower budgets and less extravagance in evidence – the building of corporate loyalty through the perceptions that are created at events continues. As Kastelein (2010) reports, 'organisations continue to spend on such events to maintain healthy client/customer relationship. The desire for maintaining and strengthening customer or employee relationship is expected to drive companies to seek corporate hospitality services.' In fact, the UK corporate hospitality market is predicted to explode to £1.5 billion by 2015, partly fuelled by opportunities created by large-scale sporting events, such as the 2012 London Olympics (Kastelein 2010).

CASE STUDY 12.3

MIPIM Asia

Event name: MIPIM Asia
Event category: Global Summit
Venue: Grand Hyatt Hotel, Hong Kong
Date: 29-30 November 2016
Attendees: 812 CEOs and top executives and 89 speakers and keynotes
Sponsors: A range of sponsorship opportunities, with one platinum sponsor, five gold sponsors and six silver sponsors
Website: www.mipim-asia.com/

Image 12.1 MIPIM Asia
Credit: Bloomberg/Getty Images

MIPIM Asia is a two-day global leaders summit that explores Asia Pacific inbound and outbound investment flows, regional development opportunities and projects and retail real estate trends. It consists of the Asia Pacific Real Estate conference and tailor-made networking opportunities, including social events, topic-based luncheons, targeted breakfasts and the conference dinner and an awards ceremony.

Study activity

Comic-Con takes place in a large (460,000-square-foot) exhibition hall and features 5,445 exhibitors from comic-book and mainstream publishing, film studios, computer game companies and music companies. The first Comic-Con, in 1970, focused on comics and science-fiction novels and had a small, specialist audience. It is now the most visited exhibition-style event in the United States, reflecting the fact that comic-book characters have moved into the mainstream, with such films as the *Batman* and *Superman* franchises and the recent *X-Men* trilogy. The event combines a major exhibition with a range of conference sessions attended by movie stars, writers, film producers and artists. In addition, there are a number of interactive sessions where attendees can collect autographs, play games involving their favourite characters, attend workshops and buy products.

Explore the Comic-Con website at: www.comic-con.org.

1 List the main features of the event. How would you categorise it: as a conference, an exhibition or a confex? Is it primarily B2C or B2B? Explain your answer.
2 What features of the event make use of experiential marketing techniques? How important are these to the success of Comic-Con?
3 Who do you think are Comic-Con's key market? Name some ways that the organisers appear to be marketing to people outside their expected demographic.

12.6 Corporate event evaluation

As with all event typologies, evaluating the success of a corporate event is essential. Without measures in place that reveal the return on investment (ROI) and the satisfaction levels of internal and external stakeholders (often known as return on objectives (ROO)), the value of the event will remain undetermined and no lessons can be learned or advantages exploited.

Event evaluation for corporate events takes two forms. First, the 'hard' factors should be assessed. This mainly involves looking at the budget and final costings to decide if the event has been a financial success. However, the second form of evaluation is perhaps more important for a corporate event. This involves evaluating the 'soft' factors, such as enhancing loyalty among customers, aligning individual goals with corporate goals, and strengthening relationships (Hall 2009).

Corporate event evaluation typically begins with some form of financial modelling to ensure the 'hard' factors are assessed effectively, while a survey or questionnaire might be handed out for completion by delegates either at the event or immediately after it. Thereafter, focus groups might be held to evaluate success; reports might be carried out that can quantify increased business as a direct result of the event; 'wash-up' meetings with key stakeholders, such as sponsors, might be held; and in-depth monitoring of the level of PR or marketing for a set time after the event might be employed.

Some, or all, of these methods are used to create a final report that reflects the success (or failure) of the entire event in terms of how well it met the client's objectives and investment goals, and its legacy.

Industry voice

Thiago Ferreira, MICE Events Manager, co-founder of Talas Travel and TEMMS Consulting

As an events manager from Brazil who has been living and working in Serbia for over a half decade, I have often been faced with challenges. Before becoming one of the founders of two companies who have successfully developed the MICE industry in Serbia and the Balkans, I was born and raised in Rio de Janeiro, Brazil. When I left my hometown in the year of 2012, optimism ruled the country as it was getting ready to host two of the biggest events in the world – the 2014 FIFA World Cup and the 2016 Olympic Games. What would make a sane tourism and events manager leave Brazil and all its momentum to go to Serbia – a country of which most people are not even aware? Some people would call it a reckless move, but ever since I visited Serbia for the first time, I saw that there was a huge opportunity to develop its MICE industries.

Serbia is a landlocked country that suffered a lot in the nineties during the break-up of the former Yugoslavia. Nowadays, even though most of the visible consequences of the war are a thing of the past and the numbers of foreign visitors in the region has been growing every year, a significant number of people around the world still have prejudices about the country. In a scenario like this, those who are willing to work in the MICE industry need to be able to overlook the problems of the past and find ways to get over the poor image of the destination in order to attract delegates to their events or corporate clients to organize their events there.

One of the best things about the MICE industry is its dynamism and constant evolution. The change in the demands and expectations of event planners and delegates worldwide turned out to be useful for Belgrade and other off-the-beaten-path event destinations in the Balkans. As more and more people travel to attend corporate meetings, trade shows, conferences and other events worldwide, it is harder to organize an event that will impress them. *Increasingly*, the authenticity and uniqueness of a destination plays an important role in the process of choosing a destination for an event that will give delegates the 'Wow effect'. One of the best features of Belgrade that caught my attention when I started my business here is the fact that it is so close to the major European cities and, yet, so different from them. A delegate has the opportunity to visit a place where they will have a unique experience without having to waste too much of their valuable business time travelling to the event.

Authenticity and uniqueness are not only a crucial aspect of the destination, but also of the venue where an event will take place. The idea of organizing meetings in standardized, closed-up places with no windows so participants have no distractions is outdated. Belgrade might not have huge congress centers with the most modern technology, but it does have an increasing number of 'boutique' venues in old factories, warehouses and even in catacombs that date from the time of the Roman Empire. The added value that such a venue gives to an event is priceless, because they will keep the participants entertained and satisfied with the event, which will mean that they will spread the word about the event through the photos they have taken and posted on social media, and encourage them to stay in the venue and network with delegates after the main event has finished. Overall, the uniqueness of the venue will encourage them to share their good emotions online and offline, which will contribute to building a good general image of the event among participants and non-participants.

When starting my business in the competitive MICE industry, I knew I would need to keep innovating and follow the latest technology trends in order to succeed, but that was not all. It took me a while until I realized that the latest event apps and the best speakers do not mean much if there is no quality face-to-face interaction between people in the venue. When organizing a conference, leaving enough time for participants to network is essential, even if that means reducing the time of lectures or the number of speakers. Some delegates come from far-away countries to attend your event, just to exchange ideas and experiences with each other, so giving them time to do so is utterly important. Moreover, to multiply the networking possibilities, you should not forget the value of a social gathering after the main event – this could be a dinner or a party for the participants, for example. That interaction in a relaxed environment may be life-changing and can help them engage in deeper conversations without feeling pressure because of the limited time available in a formal event. For some people, that is the easiest and fastest way to get inspiration and meet new people who could be potential clients or partners with whom they could expand their businesses.

My job as a MICE event manager is to put all of these elements together to create the best possible event, but doing so in a developing destination like Belgrade sometimes requires me to look at the big picture and go beyond the Serbian border. In fact, international cooperation is one of the most powerful tools that we can use to increase the power of an event and that is a big opportunity for the Balkans. Every one of the Balkan countries have unique features that go from the buzzing cities, beautiful landscapes, warm hospitality and excellent cuisine. When combined, the result is diverse event or incentive trip that people cannot wait to experience. By engaging in international partnerships, we add value to our events or incentive trips, increasing the chances of attracting more people than we otherwise would.

The MICE industry has the power of changing the way people do business, but also the way people experience destinations they never thought they would visit. I learned valuable lessons in the time I spent in Serbia, but despite of how successful or not an event is, I am particularly proud of seeing participants of corporate events I organized coming back to Serbia on their vacations just because they loved it. My mission is complete.

12.7 Summary

This chapter has provided an overview of a diverse and dynamic sector of the events industry. It has focused on a broad sweep of corporate events, and noted the significance of technological and business developments for the sector. Corporate event managers face challenging times in the short to medium term as the world economy recovers from the financial crisis of 2008 and the recessions that have followed in Western countries. However, since the largest growth area for corporate events is Asia, it is likely that opportunities will continue to present themselves for entrepreneurial event managers and organisations to grow their businesses in an extremely competitive market. Events have become central to the way that many companies do business in the twenty-first century and this, along with innovations in emerging technologies, means that successful event managers need to keep pace with a vibrant and globalised industry.

Further reading

Bowdin, G., Allen, J., O'Toole, W., Harris, R. and McDonnell, I. (2011) *Events Management* (4th edn), Oxford: Butterworth-Heinemann. This textbook does not cover the particular intricacies of corporate events but it does include a brief discussion of them in Chapter 1.

Davidson, R. (2008) What Does Generation Y Want from Conferences and Incentive Programmes? Accessed at: www.fcb.fi/UserFiles/fcb/File/pdf/R_Davidson/RD_What_Does_Generation_Y_want_0from_Conferences_and_Incentive_Programmes.pdf. An investigation into the way in which conferences and incentive programmes can be designed in so that they appeal to members of the Y Generation – the youngest and fastest-growing consumers of conference and incentive events. The article examines these customers' particular motivations and needs.

Getz, D. (2012) *Event Studies* (2nd edn), Oxford: Butterworth-Heinemann. This text includes a rather complex dissection of the industry, but it is useful for the paragraph on various aspects of the exhibition industry and for its discussion on World Fairs in Chapter 2.

References

AEO, BECA and EVA (2002) *Guide to Managing Health and Safety at Exhibitions and Events*, London: AEO, BECA, EVA.

Allen, J. (2008) *Event Planning: The Ultimate Guide to Successful Meetings, Corporate Events, Fund-raising Galas, Conferences, Conventions, Incentives and Other Special Events*, Sydney: John Wiley & Sons.

Allen, J., O'Toole, W., Harris, R. and McDonnell, I. (2011) *Festivals and Special Events Management* (5th edn), Milton, Queensland: John Wiley & Sons.

Arvey, R. D. (2009) Why Face to Face Business Meetings Matter: The Hilton Family Group. Available at: http://newsroom.hilton.com/index.cfm/newsroom/detail/183. Accessed 24 June 2017.

Bauer, T., Law, R., Tse, T. and Weber, A. (2008) Motivation and Satisfaction of Mega-business Event Attendees: The Case of ITU Telecom World 2006 in Hong Kong, *International Journal of Contemporary Hospitality Management*, 20 (2): 228–234.

Bell, L. (2009) Corporates Question Value of Hospitality in Economic Climate. Available at: www.citmagazine.com/news/rss/902048/Corporates-question-valuehospitality-economic-climate/. Accessed 16 June 2017.

Big Tattoo Planet (2009) Tattoo Jam 2009. Available at: www.bigtattooplanet. com/features/convention/tattoo-jam-2009. Accessed 6 October 2011.

BizBash (2015) Why Mashable's Networking Event Started Close to Midnight. Available at: www.bizbash.com/why-mashables-networking-event-started-close-to-midnight/orlando/story/31235/#.V2GXRNeYInA. Accessed 6 February 2017.

Business Junction (2010) Home page. Available at: www.businessjuntion.co.uk. Accessed 9 August 2010.

Clothes Show Live (2010) Event Info. Available at: www.clothesshowlive.com/event-info. Accessed 10 August 2010.

Clothes Show (2016) *Clothes Show Live*. Available at: www.clothesshow.com/. Accessed 6 February 2017.

CVent (2016) Cvent Connect. Available at: www.cventconnect.com/. Accessed 6 February 2017.

Curtis, P. and Evans, R. (2010) Tax Boss Most Wined and Dined Mandarin, *Guardian*, 17 June.

Davidson, R. (2003) *Business Travel: Conferences, Incentive Travel, Exhibitions, Corporate Hospitality and Corporate Travel*, Harlow: Pearson.

Davidson, R. (2010) *Trends and Market Report*. Available at: www.eibtm.com/page.cfm/T=m/Action=Press/PressID=5. Accessed 5 August 2010.

Davidson, R. (2015) EIBTM Trends and Market Report, Barcelona: EIBTM.

Eventia (2009) *The UK Market Trends Survey*, n.p: Eventia.

5 Minute Networking (2010) Taking the Work out of Networking. Available at: www.5minutenetworking.com. Accessed 16 June 2017.

Getz, D. (2005) *Event Management and Event Tourism*, New York: Cognizant.

Getz, D (2007) *Event Studies*, Oxford: Butterworth-Heinemann.

Hall, A. (2009) ROI: Measured, Guaranteed, *Corporate Meetings and Incentives*, September: 19.

Harwood, S. (2010) Vie at Home's Cape Town Incentive. Available at: www. citmagazine.com/news/1009048/Vie-Homes-Cape-Town-incentive/. Accessed 31 July 2010.

Haug, L. (2010) Lift Lab. Available at: http://liftlab.com/. Accessed 28 July 2010.

Henderson, N. (2010) Axa Life Cuts back Incentive Travel Programme. Available at: www.citmagazine.com/news/search/965058/Axa-Life-cuts-back-incentive-travel-programme/. Accessed 31 July 2010.

IBTM Africa (2016) *IBTM Africa.* Available at: www.ibtmafrica.com/. Accessed 6 February 2017.

ICCA (2010) Events and Education. Available at: www.iccaworld.com/evps/. Accessed 4 October 2011.

IMEX (2010) Press Releases. Available at: www.imex-frankfurt.com/press.php?action=showstory&newsid=230. Accessed 7 August 2010.

International Conference on Consumer Electronics (2016) *ICCE 2016.* Available at: www.icce.org/. Accessed 6 February 2017.

International Confex (2016) Home. Available at: www.international-confex.com. Accessed 10 August 2010.

International Consumer Electronics (2016) Home. Available at: www.cesweb.org. Accessed 7 August 2010.

Intu (2016) *Sponsorship and Brand Immersion.* Available at: www.intugroup.co.uk/intu-experiences/sponsorship-and-brand-immersion/. Accessed 15 June 2016.

Kastelein, R. (2010) UK Corporate Hospitality Market to Explode to £1.5 Billion by 2015. Available at: www.euticketnews.com/20100708845/uk-corporate-hospitality-market-to-explode-to-p15-billion-by-2015.html. Accessed 5 August 2010.

Lift (2011) Lift10. Available at: liftconference.com/lift10. Accessed 4 October 2011.

Masterman, G. (2004) A Strategic Approach for the Use of Sponsorship in the Events Industry: In Search of a Return on Investment, in I. Yeoman, M. Robertson, J. Ali-Knight, S. Drummond and U. McMahon-Beattie (eds) *Festival and Events Management: An International Arts and Culture Perspective*, Oxford: Butterworth-Heinemann.

MBD (2009) UK Corporate Hospitality Market Report. Available at: www. mbdltd.co.uk/UK-Market-Research-Reports/Corporate-Hospitality.htm. Accessed 4 October 2011.

MIPIM Asia (2016) *MPIM Asia Summit.* Available at: www.mipim-asia.com/. Accessed 6 February 2017.

MPI (2013) *The Economic Impact of the UK Meeting and Event Industry,* London: MPI.

MyDSF (2010) Dubai Festival City. Available at: http://mydsf.ae. Accessed 5 August 2010.

Nguyen, N. and Leblanc, G. (2001) Corporate Image and Corporate Reputation in Customers' Retention Decisions in Services, *Journal of Retailing and Consumer Services*, 8 (4): 227–236.

O'Toole, W. and Mikolaitis, P. (2002) *Corporate Event Project Management*, New York: John Wiley & Sons.

Pine, B. J. and Gilmore, J. H. (1999) *The Experience Economy*, Cambridge, MA: Harvard Business Review.

Severt, K. and Breiter, D. (2010) The Anatomy of an Incentive Travel Program, Research Funded by the Incentive Research Foundation. Available at: www.incentivemotivate. com. Accessed 28 July 2010.

Shone, A. and Parry, B. (2014) *Successful Event Management: A Practical Guide* (4th edn), London: Cengage

SITE (2010) Home. Available at: www.siteglobal.com. Accessed 28 July 2010.

Supper Club (2010) The Story. Available at: www.supper-club.net/thestory. Accessed 10 August 2010.

Tattoo Jam (2016) Tattoo Jam 2016. Available at: www.tattoojam.com/. Accessed 6 February 2017.

UFI (2010) The Global Exhibition Barometer.

UFI (2011) UFI Mission & Figures.

UFI (2016): 30.

Vice (2014) *Smirnoff Experience Festival Case Study*. Available at: http://company.vice.com/en_us/casestudies/smirnoff-the-smirnoff-experience. Accessed 15 June 2016.

Weber, K. and Ladkin, A. (2003) The Convention Industry in Australia and the United Kingdom: Key Issues and Competitive Forces, *Journal of Travel Research*, 42: 125–132.

White, M. (2010) Comic-Con's Grown up Nerds Give Mattel, Hasbro New Toy Pitches. Available at: www.bloomberg.com/news/2010-07-22/comic-con-s-grownup-nerds-give-mattel-hasbro-new-way-to-pitch-girls-toys.html. Accessed 22 July 2010.

Wolf, P., Hansmann, R. and Troxler, P. (2011) Unconferencing as Method to Initiate Organisational Change: A Case Study on Reducing CO_2 Emissions of a University, *Journal of Organizational Change Management*, 24 (1): 112–142.

Chapter 13

Cultural events and festivals

Contents

13.1 Aims

By the end of this chapter, students will be able to:

- define the different categories of cultural events and festivals;
- explore key management issues for these types of events;
- analyse the challenges involved in marketing cultural events and festivals;
- discuss the ways in which cultural events and festivals can contribute to cultural and social change.

13.2 Introduction

Cultural events and festivals are major sectors of the events industry and are key drivers of the tourism and service economies in all the major developed economies and in most countries around the world. Cultural events are hugely diverse in nature, from a Justin Bieber tour to the Sundance Film Festival and celebrations of identity and nationality. The calendar of festivals within just one country will inevitably be crowded with religious, seasonal and community festival events.

This chapter provides an overview of the cultural events and festivals sector. The aim is to introduce the reader to the variety of different events and festivals in this category and to draw their attention to some key management processes involved in producing this diverse group of special events.

13.3 Cultural events

The word 'culture' is notoriously difficult to define (Ali-Knight and Robinson 2004). Some authors place cultural events under the more general category of 'special events' (Raj *et al.* 2013), while others include a separate category of 'cultural events' in their typologies of events, but separate these artistic events from other kinds of cultural expression, such as festivals of identity and community (Bowdin *et al.* 2010; Getz 2012). Sonder (2004) unites many of the kinds of events described in this chapter through the concept of 'entertainment', but elsewhere this term has been seen as separate, almost by definition, from the arts (Hughes 2006), which make up so much of our cultural practices. The term 'cultural events' takes a more holistic view of human activity and those events which emphasise the cultural, as opposed to other, aspects of our lives.

Any definition of cultural events needs to differentiate these events from others that are more easily defined as business events, sports events or mega-events, for example, while also remaining sufficiently open to cover the broad range of events that take place within the big tent of 'culture'. To resolve this, we can introduce two definitions of cultural events. The first, conceptual definition, allows us to incorporate a diversity of events within the framework of cultural events, while the second provides a stable base from which to move forward and discuss the management issues associated with staging these events.

13.3.1 Defining culture

Cultural events are associated with expressions of 'culture', but what does this term mean, if anything? The cultural economist Arvo Klamer (2002: 1) describes the diversities of culture and their significance:

> It may be a bridge, a piece of wood. Or a temple, a windmill, a painting, a piece of furniture, a mask, jewel, bead. It may even be a language, a ritual, or a practice. Whatever it is, it differs from other goods because people may consider it a symbol of something – a nation, a community, a tradition, a religion, a cultural episode.

To discuss the management of cultural events, it is necessary to elaborate on this list of cultural forms to produce one that resembles cultural forms as we experience them in the events marketplace; but even then the list is remarkably diverse. Within it, there are events in which culture is understood anthropologically – in Raymond Williams' (2010) terminology, as 'a way of life' – as well as events that are better understood as expressions of an aesthetic culture (see Table 13.1).

Terry Eagleton (2000: 1) sounds a note of caution here:

> It is hard to resist the conclusion that the word 'culture' is both too broad and too narrow to be greatly useful. Its anthropological meaning covers everything from hairstyles and drinking habits to how to address your husband's second cousin, while the aesthetic sense of the word includes Igor Stravinsky but not science fiction.

Although this overview of the diversity of culture as a concept gives us a framework for identifying cultural events, if we are to move on to a consideration of their management, there is a need for a more 'greatly useful' definition that event managers can operationalise.

13.3.2 Definition of cultural events

Getz (2012: 51) defines cultural celebrations as 'solemn or joyous events that have cultural meaning', but this anthropological definition does not capture the aesthetic components of

Table 13.1 Categorising cultural events

Anthropological		Aesthetic	
Type	Example	Type	Example
National cultural	St Patrick's Day in New York	Arts	Wagner Festival in Bayreuth
Religious	Divali in Bradford	Music	Bonnaroo Festival in Tennessee
Ethnicity	Mela in Oslo	Heritage	Festival of the Olive in New South Wales
Sexuality	Manchester LGBT Festival		
Community	Notting Hill Carnival in London		

culture, packaged together by many authors as 'merely' entertainment events. In response to this, and taking on board the conceptual framework of culture set out above, we can devise a more open definition of cultural events as those that either present a particular expression of culture or aim to represent the cultural expressions of specific groups.

13.4 Festivals

Festivals are extremely common forms of cultural practice and, although many have long histories, the majority have been founded much more recently (Getz 2012). The International Festivals and Events Association estimates that there are between 4 and 5 million recurring festivals worldwide each year (IFEA 2015: The Power of Celebration).

Festivals are both a particular kind of cultural event, each with its own history and tradition, and a specific celebratory form, with structural elements that can be used within a range of cultural traditions. Sonder (2004: 18) groups together parades, fairs and festivals as 'particular types of themed events that may simultaneously contain historical, cultural, ceremonial, religious, patriotic and social themes'.

The term 'festival' is used by event organisers to describe a broad range of event forms – from short celebrations of a particular place or culture to events that extend over weeks and can involve vast numbers of venues and performers.

> Every August, the Edinburgh International Festival transforms one of the world's most beautiful cities, presenting three exhilarating weeks of the finest creators and performers from the worlds of the arts – for everyone.
>
> Edinburgh's six major theatres and concert halls, a few smaller venues and often some unconventional ones too, come alive with the best music, theatre, opera and dance from around the globe.
>
> (Edinburgh International Festival 2015: About us)

> For the whole weekend commencing Saturday 4 September 2010 the town of Faversham will be home to the annual Faversham International Hop Festival. A traditional, fun festival set in the picturesque medieval town's square and surrounding streets, celebrating the olden days of hop picking in Kent. With music to suit eclectic tastes, children's entertainers, professional street theatre, stilt walkers, Morris dancing, craft fare, and ceilidh, it's a weekend for family and friends to enjoy!
>
> (Faversham Hop Festival 2010)

Bowdin *et al.* (2010) use South East Arts' categorisation to divide arts festivals into seven distinctive types:

1 High-profile celebrations of the arts.
2 Festivals that celebrate a particular location.
3 Art-form festivals.
4 Celebration of work by a community of interest.
5 Calendar.
6 Amateur arts festivals.
7 Commercial music festivals.

We can add to this list by reference to the conceptual framework for cultural events, above, to produce a more comprehensive list of festivals generally:

8   Celebrations of the expressions of specific cultural groups.

Getz (2013: 51) offers a simple, clear definition of festivals as 'themed, public celebrations', which he concedes does not 'do justice to the richness and diversity of meanings' attached to this kind of event. This difficulty stems from the historical and fundamental role that festivals have played in human culture – as celebratory, commemorative or ritualistic events. Perhaps the first festival took place in 534 BC in Greece in honour of the God Dionysus, and there are records of festivals playing important social and cultural roles from the twelfth century to the present day in Europe (Quinn 2005). Some writers even place the 'carnival-esque' experience of festivals at the heart of an understanding of how society manages itself and is governed. For theorists such as Bakhtin (1984), festivals offer a short period of time when we can rebel against, challenge and reimagine society, before we are obliged to return to an altered, but mainly preserved, social reality.

Because festivals and society are so intertwined, it can be very difficult to isolate the elements that define a 'festival', so it is perhaps useful to consider a loose arrangement of elements that combine to produce a festival event:

● themed content
● the presence of multiple individual events
● possibilities for participation
● extension in time and space
● celebratory or commemorative functions.

Each of these elements creates a set of management challenges that will be present to a greater or lesser degree in every festival.

CASE STUDY 13.1

La Tomatina – The tomato-throwing festival

Location: Buñol, Spain
Event type: festival
Attendees: 50,000

La Tomatina is an annual festival that takes place in the Valencian town of Buñol, in Eastern Spain, during which participants throw tomatoes at each other and at the crowds, in a giant food fight through the streets of the town. Buñol is a small town of around 9,000 inhabitants, which is surrounded by mountains and whose economy is based mainly on agriculture.

The event began in in 1945, during a traditional community festival at which giant papier mâché figures and giant heads were paraded through the town, in an example of a commonplace type of European festival, which can be seen most frequently in France and Northern Spain. In 1945, a group of young people joined the parade unofficially and caused a commotion because of their boisterous behaviour and loud music. An official float that was taking part in the parade was disturbed and its owners grabbed vegetables from a nearby stall to throw at the young people in anger. Over the following few years, local people began to bring tomatoes from home to throw at each other on the same date, the last Wednesday in August and, despite attempts to stop this by the local police, this became an annual event in its own right. In 1957, the festival was officially recognised by local government, who took responsibility for its management, and the supply of tomatoes, from 1980 onwards.

The festival today

2015 was the 70th anniversary of La Tomatina. It has grown from a small local festival to an annual tourism event, which attracts around 50,000 attendees every year from all over the world. As well as individuals throwing tomatoes, open trucks are driven through the town, filled with over 150,000 tonnes of imported

Image 13.1 **La Tomatina**
Credit: Anadolu Agency/Getty Images

tomatoes. Standing among the fruit, participants throw tomatoes out by the bucketload, onto spectators listening to bands and DJs in the streets.

The festival is organised by the Town Hall of Buñol, who work with a number of partners to deliver the event, including local, regional and national destination management organisations, ticketing agencies and a number of media partners. As well as La Tomatina itself, there are a number of satellite events associated with the main festival, including Tomatina Sound Festival (a music festival), Gastronmic at Tomatina (a food festival) and a junior Tomatina event, Tomatina for Kids. The festival generates an estimated €450,000 per year for the local economy during the event and additional income throughout the year associated with using La Tomatina for film and television locations, and in advertising, creating around €300,000 per year for the town. Google have featured La Tomatina in their advertising campaigns and Disney have produced a short film, *Al Rojo Vivo*, in which Mickey Mouse is pelted by tomatoes in the town.

Challenges

Two main challenges have been faced by the organisers of La Tomatina in recent years. First, as yearly numbers of attendees have continued to grow, it has become harder to manage the event in terms of health and safety, as well as to preserve the quality of the event experience and its significance for local people. Second, the costs associated with the event have become more significant. The economic crisis that has been affecting Spain since 2008 has made it difficult for the local authority to continue to fund the event. To keep growing the event in a sustainable way requires investment in marketing, events management and even in tomatoes – Buñol does not produce its own tomatoes and imports them from Extramadura, 500 miles away!

In response to this, the event was first ticketed in 2013. The organisers introduced tickets at a cost of €10 to be participant or bystander in the event, with higher-priced tickets available for attendees who wanted to take a more active part in the proceedings. For example, for €750 attendees could ride on one of the tomato trucks from which tomatoes were thrown. The aim of this ticketing approach was to limit numbers and to generate additional revenue. This had the benefit of making health and safety planning for the event more straightforward and generating revenue to fund police, security and medical staff for the festival. In addition, limiting the size of the event made it possible to maintain the quality of the event experience for ticket holders. The organisers hold back 5,000 tickets for local residents every year to ensure that the host community of the event continues to participate.

(Edwards 2015; Hamilos 2013; La Tomatina 2015)

Study activity

Many other cities around the world have copied La Tomatina to produce their own tomato-throwing events. What challenges would be faced by event managers where you live who wanted to recreate La Tomatina as a local festival?

In the following sections, we shall describe specific cultural event and festival forms in detail and then analyse the particular management functions that are associated with them.

13.5 Types of cultural events and festivals

13.5.1 Music events and festivals

Music events are by far the largest element of the whole events sector. In the United Kingdom, more than 60 million visits are made to music concerts each year, generating around £2.2 billion (Festival Insights 2013). They vary greatly in form and style, from individual performances in bars and community centres to multi-day touring music festivals. However, they can be categorised into four main types: the first two view music events from the perspective of the artist, while the second two take an organisational perspective.

13.5.1.1 Music concerts

Music concerts are one-off music events that attract an audience because of the presence of an individual performer or a small number of performers appearing together.

13.5.1.2 Music tours

Tours involve repeated performances by an individual performer or group of performers, moving between different venues. Touring occurs at three different scales: regional, national and international. Regional touring is usually carried out by artists with low national profiles, or artists working within local musical scenes. National tours take place when an artist's profile has developed to a level where they are gaining national media exposure. International touring is usually commercially viable only for the most successful artists.

13.5.1.3 Music programmes

Performance venues seek to design programmes (see the section on programming, below) that will attract event attendees to a venue throughout the year. These programmes can involve a succession of events featuring individual artists, or longer-term residencies where one artist or group of artists become a regular feature of a particular venue.

13.5.1.4 Music festivals

Music festivals are a growing phenomenon, with the British market for this categorisation alone including over 600 annual events. The outdoor rock and pop music festival market in

Britain has seen an increase of 71 per cent since 2003 (Anderton 2008). Although other music genres also make use of the festival form (for example, the annual Prague Spring Festival of classical music and JazzFest in Berlin), the rock and pop festival market is the most dynamic and attracts the largest audiences. These large events draw on a recent countercultural tradition in popular music and offer a packaged, multi-day experience that promises not only a procession of high-profile and credible musical entertainment but camping on site and a recreation of the glory days of the Woodstock era. One of the aspects of event design that separates festivals from other music events is the provision of non-music attractions, such as catering, accommodation, secondary events and retailing, all of which must be present in order to generate an 'authentic' festival experience (Bowen and Daniels 2005).

This phenomenon is not limited to Europe. As the events market matures in other regions, a similar growth in the outdoor festival market is occurring. In Taiwan, the Spring Scream Festival has grown from hosting 12 bands in 1994, when it began, to hosting 200 bands in 2014; across five stages over a four-day event that attracted more than 100,000 attendees each day.

13.5.2 Film events and festivals

Film events come in a number of forms, including screenings in cinemas or less unorthodox settings, promotional events and festivals. Screenings follow a standardised format that offers little scope for customisation by event managers, and promotional events can be best understood from a marketing perspective. This section will therefore concentrate on film festivals and the niche market for specialist screenings.

Film festivals can be analysed in two ways: the promotional services that they provide to the film industry; and the networking and development opportunities they provide to film professionals (see Table 13.2).

Film festivals vary enormously in size – from the Cannes Festival in France, with 350,000 attendees and an economic impact of $97 million (Grunwell and Ha 2008), to the Sundance Independent Film Festival in the US, with around 50,000 annual visitors, to small local and regional events.

Cannes is the world's most important film festival. It was launched in 1946 and takes place every year in the south of France. As well as bestowing a prestigious set of awards upon films entered in its competition, it generates promotional opportunities for films through screening opportunities and media exposure. In 2009, the festival's budget was £23 million, of which around half comes from the French state, and the rest from contributions from the film industry. In total, 299 feature films were shown at Cannes in 2009, along with 47 short films. These films were seen by 350,000 attendees, of whom 24,827 were accredited as professionals from the film sector. Reporting from Cannes were 3,469 accredited journalists.

Table 13.2 **Elements of a film festival**

Promotional services	Development opportunities
Film screenings	Technical exhibits
Marketing support	Networking events
Awards	Educational activities

Image 13.2 Bollywood actress Aishwarya Rai on the red carpet at the 64th International Cannes Film Festival
Credit: AFP/Getty Images

At the opposite end of the scale from the grandeur of Cannes are the 'Secret Cinema' events that have been running in London since 2008. Originally conceived by independent short-film producers Future Shorts, the events take place monthly and are announced just two days, or sometimes only a few hours, beforehand to members of an internet mailing list. Attendees have only vague ideas of the choice of film before it starts, gleaned from the instructions to act or dress in a particular way. The Secret Cinema events specialise in showing independent, arthouse and little-known films to a self-selecting audience of film fans, who expect an immersive experience that uses elements of event design to enhance the film experience through themed venues and supplementary performances. A recent review in *Empire* magazine gives an evocative description of the atmosphere at a screening of Wim Wenders' 1987 film, *Wings of Desire*:

> Inside, past the couple kissing at the bottom of the stalled escalator, the specially-designed posters . . . and the buzzing TVs was a rather cavernous upstairs, all black walls, decaying furniture and a pleasantly melancholy band playing at a cafe bit in the corner. A couple of small rooms were decorated like a child's room, and a small library (again, that should've helped me twig, but no) before we headed into the auditorium itself – where we were greeted by a circus. The Circus Alekan, in fact, which finally did give it away: it's going to be *Wings of Desire*!
>
> The floor of the theatre was set up with a mini sawdust ring, a juggler, a trapeze artist, ringmaster, knife-thrower and victim target. After a quick circus performance, a musical

interlude, short film *Splitting the Atom* and a bit more trapezery, the Wim Wenders film finally got underway. The reaction when the title card came up was interesting: hardly anyone left immediately, although about six people in my line of vision left during the running time, which is probably a good result for an arthouse film being shown to a general audience.

(O'Hara 2010)

These unorthodox events have proven so successful at generating a marketing buzz and media interest that they were produced 'in partnership' with Microsoft, which used them to promote its web technologies and smartphone software applications – an example of a synergetic partnership between a cultural and a business organisation, with both gaining from the relationship.

13.5.3 Community festivals and events

A community-themed festival or event is a 'public themed celebration which can act as a catalyst for demonstrating community values and culture' (Jepson *et al.* 2008: 2). A community represented through this process could be distinguished by its:

- nationality
- ethnicity
- sexuality
- interest
- place.

Festivals play an important role in helping to create and support community identities through celebration, preservation and renewal of the cultural identities and practices of a group of people. Huang *et al.* (2010: 254) define community-based festivals (CBF) more specifically as 'essentially small scale, bottom up, and run by one or more volunteers for the benefit of the locality. They take place in rural or semi-rural areas with the primary goal of providing cultural and entertainment benefits for locals and visitors.'

Although the majority of CBFs certainly are low-profile, small-scale events, many festivals and cultural events that have developed within specific communities now attract large audiences and have national and sometimes even international profiles. In some cases, transnational communities (Aksoy and Robins 2004) formed through diasporas and other migrations have generated international networks of cultural events and festivals, such as the annual Chinese New Year celebrations, held in China Towns in most of the world's major cities, or the festivals that are connected through the European Mela Network. The Mela was 'a festival tradition serving to celebrate ethnic community and folk cultures and identities in India, but increasingly becoming a showcase for global and hybridised cultural forms related to Indianness' (Carnegie and Smith 2006: 256).

13.5.4 Arts events and festivals

Arts events and festivals can focus on the performing arts, the visual arts, sonic art, or a combination of all three. They are the most common type of festival event (Allen *et al.* 2008)

The performing arts include, but are not limited to, dance, theatre and opera (Kotler and Scheff 1997). Often magical entertainment, circus arts and comedy are included within this framework, sharing common elements of performance, venue type and consumer. Performing arts events can take place on a one-off basis, as tours, as serial events or in festival format.

CASE STUDY 13.2

Pride in London

Location: London, UK
Event type: community festival
Attendees: 40,000

Pride in London is an example of a festival associated with a community of sexuality. Ammaturo (2015) explains that 'Gay Pride' events, including marches, festivals and parades are one very visible aspect of lesbian, gay, bisexual and transgender (LGBT) social movements that originated in the 1960s. Interpride, the international organisation for lLGBT festival events, has 196 member organisations, with a collective attendance at member events of more than 15 million people every year (Interpride 2015).

Pride in London has been held annually since 1972 and is held on the nearest Saturday to 28 June, the anniversary of the Stonewall riots in the USA, a key date in the history of the LGBT movement internationally. The event includes a main parade, which includes thousands of participants, as well as satellite events, talks and rallies. Pride is the only annual event to close Oxford Street, the iconic retail hub of London.

In 2015, more than 40,000 people took part in the event's largest ever parade. The participants included representatives from the following groups, demonstrating the wide base of support for the event:

- Charities [52.7%] including

    - [4.1%] HIV/AIDS charities
    - [14%] non-LGBT charities

- Non-LGBT charities [14%]
- Businesses [19.8%]
- Public sector [14%]
- Religious and faith [3.3%]
- Trade unions [3.3%]
- LGBT+ businesses [2.9%]
- Political [2.9%]
- Pride in London [1.2%]

Over the more than 40 years of its existence, the event has had a range of titles, including 'Gay Pride' and 'London Mardi Gras'. There have also been a number of organisations involved in managing the event. London Pride began as an event that was organised by a loose collection of groups working together, but as it has grown it has become more professional, and taken on more standardised events management practices. From 2004 to 2012, a charity called 'London Pride' ran the event, and more recently the Mayor of London supported the creation of the Community Interest Company 'Pride in London' as organisers. This new organisation is entirely run by volunteers and is supported by a large number of private and public-sector partners.

(Ammaturo 2016; Interpride 2015; Pride in London 2015)

Arts events that are in the fields of visual and sonic arts can include short-term exhibitions of art and opening events (Getz 2012), as well as festivals. Longer-term exhibitions of artworks are covered by the substantial literature in the field of museum and gallery management. Axelsen and Arcodia (2005) suggest that these short-term cultural events are little understood within the events management literature, despite their prominence within the visual arts field, with gallery managers increasingly using them to attract visitors and promote sales of specific artists and works. They suggest that these events are worthy of further exploration within the field of events management for three main reasons:

- They offer another perspective on events management as a subject and as a set of management techniques that can be incorporated into the development of subject knowledge and good practice in the industry.
- The art market is becoming less producer-led and more consumer-led, in common with the wider cultural industries, so understanding the art event consumer helps art event managers to meet the needs of the art market.
- Boundaries between high and low art have become blurred and there is a growing market of event consumers for art forms that have traditionally been seen as elitist, such as the visual arts.

An example of this kind of short-term event is Soundwalk – an annual one-day event that brings together international sound artists in Long Beach, California. The 2013 Soundwalk involved 50 artists from around the world, who collaborated to create a set of temporary sound art installations: 'The evening operates under the concept of a one-night multi-sensory experience as conveyed through sound art that is situated in various indoor and outdoor spaces throughout the East Village Arts District in Downtown Long Beach' (Soundwalk 2015). The Soundwalk events showcase the work of an emerging group of sound artists and introduce members of the public to a new artistic practice:

This year, FLOOD [the event organisers] will be exploring 'connectivity' by expanding both geographically and conceptually. The activation of 1st Street as a 'sound corridor' will connect the Arts District with Pine Avenue, thus offering both participants and attendees interesting new contexts in which to exhibit and to experience art set forth in sound.

It has been FLOOD's aim to raise awareness as well as engender an appreciation for alternative artistic practices by exposing audiences, along with the larger community, to aesthetic sensibilities and innovative approaches that exist outside those of the contemporary mainstream.

(Soundwalk 2010)

Serial events are unique to the performing arts. They involve repeated performances of the same event over an extended period and, in the case of contemporary mega-musicals, often simultaneously in several venues in different countries. The musical *Mamma Mia* has been seen by over 40 million people worldwide, grossing an estimated $2 billion at the box office in more than twenty countries. This is the serial reproduction of one 155-minute performance.

In many instances, a variety of art forms are programmed together in 'combined arts festivals' (CAFs) (Finkel 2006). The majority of these festivals are produced outside the commercial sector and are often produced and/or promoted by local authorities. Finkel profiles the Lichfield Festival, which has been running for 25 years in a small town near Birmingham, UK. It currently runs for ten days across 15 venues. A total of 61 events made up the programme for the 2003 festival, of which 27 (44 per cent) were music and 13 (21 per cent) were film. There were also seven drama and five visual arts events.

Finkel suggests that there is increasing local and regional competition between CAFs in the UK, as local authorities come to see them as key tools for enhancing destination image and boosting tourism.

13.5.5 Literary events and festivals

Literary events and festivals are a growing sector of the cultural events industry. They vary in size and scope, but include:

- commercial book launches
- book clubs and reading groups
- talks and readings given by authors
- literary festivals.

Commercial launch events are organised by book publishers and generally take place in bookshops for a small audience or at trade fairs (see Fenich 2005). The largest trade fair, in Frankfurt, attracted 257,791 visitors in 2015 (Albanese 2015).

Book clubs and reading groups are small, locally organised events that are usually informal in nature. However, Burwell (2007) notes that their increasing popularity, especially in the women's market, has led to them being targeted by publishing companies as an effective mechanism for generating word-of-mouth publicity for books. They have also become a feature of mass media and celebrity culture, with celebrity endorsements allied to publishers' more traditional marketing efforts. The most successful of these has been Oprah Winfrey's Book Club, with *Time* magazine reporting:

> It's the greatest force in publishing today, with the power to raise authors from the dead (Leo Tolstoy) or crucify them on the national stage (James Frey). The all-powerful Oprah's Book Club is not so much a club as a ruthlessly influential marketing vehicle, with the power to fundamentally alter best-seller lists, Amazon rankings and royalty payments. Sure, the 'club' has 2 million 'members' and a web site that provides a space for users to share thoughts on featured titles, read excerpts and get advice like, 'How to Read a Hard Book'. But in the 12 years Oprah's Book Club has existed, its significance has been – from the perspective of authors and editors, at least – not its sense of community, but its influence on sales, which has been known to increase a print run fivefold.
>
> (Pickert 2008)

Despite the commercial success of endorsed reading groups such as Oprah's, at the level of the individual event these book clubs are locally organised and, while they may make use of centrally (often publisher-) produced reading notes and supplementary material, they tend to involve no more than a dozen people at any one time. Literary festivals, by contrast, can attract thousands of times more visitors and are being developed in a number of countries, capitalising on the maturation of the festival market. These festivals combine authors' talks, catering, accommodation, retail and secondary events within the traditional festival spatial and temporal arrangements of a bounded site over multiple days.

The Hay Festival of Literature and the Arts is a charitable organisation that has promoted the Hay-on-Wye literary festival since 1988. Beginning as a small event that aimed to build on the tradition of bookselling in a small town in Wales, by 2010 it had set itself the target of attracting 100,000 people to a festival that Bill Clinton described as 'Woodstock for the mind' (BBC 2009). In that year, speakers included Pervez Musharraf, the former President of Pakistan, while previous headliners have included Archbishop Desmond Tutu and Paul McCartney, demonstrating that the original aims of promoting the book trade have widened to include a range of intellectual activities. The Hay Festival has also recently expanded internationally, to include parallel events in:

- Segovia, Spain
- Alhambra, Spain
- Cartagena, Colombia
- the Maldives
- Zacatecas, Mexico
- Nairobi, Kenya
- Beirut, Lebanon.

The festival in Kenya shows how literary festivals, as one kind of cultural event, can be developed to address broader social issues as well as being successful commercial events in their own right:

> The Storymoja Festival started out as a small gathering of 300 people in 2007, and has grown to a vibrant gathering of the greatest minds in Kenya and beyond, celebrating ideas and culture. The festival offerings are dynamic and diverse to cater for all age groups.
>
> Books are brought to life through poetry, storytelling, lively discussions with local and international artists, music, workshops, film and much more. In addition, topical issues such as health, careers, politics, technology, human rights, environment entrepreneurship and youth empowerment are presented in very interactive and stimulating sessions.
>
> (Storymoja Hay Festival Nairobi 2015)

Study activity

Visit the website for the Storymoja Hay Festival in Nairobi: http://storymojafestival.com/. Explore the programme for the event and answer the following questions:

- What are the various elements of the festival?
- How international is the festival?
- What are the aims of the festival?
- Who sponsored the event? Why do you think they wanted to be associated with it?

13.6 Programming cultural events and festivals

Although the idea of programming is used across the events industry, the term is used in a specific way for cultural events and festivals. In this instance, it describes the process of choosing and presenting a set of events that are joined together by venue, content or organisation. It is a central concept for understanding the management of cultural event organisations and cultural event venues, such as theatres and concert halls (Cuadrado-Garcia and Perez-Cabenero 2005). Programming in this manner should be distinguished from the concept of developing a programme for an event, which involves assembling the elements of event design for a single event within a theme (e.g. Getz 2012; Sonder 2004; Allen *et al.* 2012).

Castaner and Campos (2002) identify the factors involved in the programming decision-making process that event managers go through when designing a programme of cultural events. These can be divided into environmental and cultural factors that impact upon an organiser's ability to develop innovative programmes within a specified form.

13.6.1 Environmental factors

These can be divided into macro-, meso- and micro-level influences on the cultural organisation. Macro factors come from the external environment, such as changes in legislation, changes in society and the influence of other organisations. Micro factors are internal to the organisation and include its strengths and weaknesses, its level of available resources, and human resource issues. Meso factors refer to those influences that span the internal and external operating environments, such as relationships with particular funding bodies and sponsors, and organisations working in partnership (see Figure 13.1).

These environmental factors, taken together, form the practical horizons of what a cultural organisation will be able to programme within a venue or a festival.

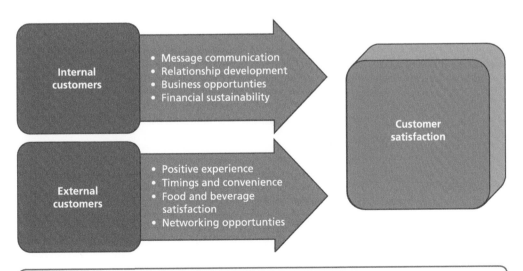

Figure 13.1 Determinants of cultural event programming

13.6.2 Cultural factors

In order to understand the programming process fully, it is necessary to examine cultural factors, too. These factors are both internal and external to an organisation and relate to the cultural orientations of the audience and to the orientations of the cultural programmers themselves. The influence of inherently conservative audiences or programmers will produce 'safe' programmes that avoid risk in order to consolidate existing audiences. Meanwhile, audiences and programmers who are enthusiastic about cultural innovation will exert pressure that produces more innovative, creative programming, even though this carries the risk of alienating the existing audience.

Successful programming works through a creative tension between conservative and innovative approaches to programming decision-making, within a set of environmental constraints that are specific to every cultural organisation.

Allen *et al.*'s (2012) discussion of the factors influencing the development of a programme for a *single* event shows that the process of event design and the development of multiple-event programmes operate under a similar set of constraints. The authors explain that the programme for a single event depends on:

- the expectations of the audience
- the constraints of the venue and the infrastructure
- the culture of the client and the main sponsors
- the availability of elements of the staging and their relationship to each other
- the logistics
- the creative intent of the event team.

Cultural programmes can be expressed according to four main stylistic conventions, as shown in Table 13.3.

Assassi (2005) carried out a study of French theatres to determine the characteristics of performing arts programming decision-making and discovered four elements of this process, as shown in Figure 13.2.

The *reactive component* of programming relates to the box-office potential of a cultural event, expressed either as an attendance figure or as an income stream. The *relational component* is a measure of how far the programme is designed as a response to feedback from and interaction

Table 13.3 Programming styles

Programming style	Example
Thematic	A concert season programmed in partnership with a scientific organisation, themed on the relationship between music and science
Temporal	A programme of outdoor theatre events during the summer in the grounds of a country estate
Disciplinary	A visual arts festival
Audience constituency	A festival of Kurdish music and poetry

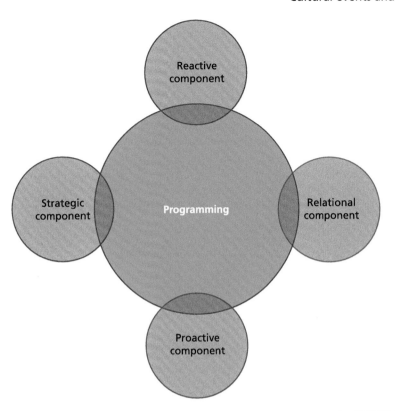

Figure 13.2 Components of programming
Source: Adapted from Assassi 2005

with cultural consumers. The *proactive component* describes how the programming decisions reflect the cultural objectives of the organisation. Finally, the *strategic component* refers to how far the programming decisions meet the broad strategic aims of the organisation.

According to this model, successful programming will be a mix of all four of these elements, with the split between the requirements of reactive and non-reactive elements determined by the financial situation and profit-driven motivation of the organisation involved.

Study activity

- Use the three models set out in this section to analyse the programming of a major national cultural venue or festival in your country.
- How useful do you find each model in understanding the programming decisions of the organisation?
- What information do you need to help you to carry out this analysis?
- What recommendations can you make for developing the programming strategy of your chosen organisation?

13.7 Marketing cultural events and festivals

Consumers are presented with an ever-increasing volume of marketing messages for cultural activities, due to the growth of the 'cultural industries' and the extension of the marketplace into their leisure time (Hesmondhalgh 2007). Cultural organisations are competing for consumers' attention, not only against other cultural organisations but with other 'agents of leisure', such as cinemas, leisure centres, digital broadcasters and shopping malls. In order to gain a competitive advantage, they now make use of sophisticated marketing techniques. This has been a relatively recent development, with the controversies over the commercialisation and commodification of culture now playing a less prominent role in cultural management discourse than when such concepts as 'arts marketing' first appeared in the 1980s. In 1986, in a rhetorical style that mirrored concerns about the pernicious role of money in the arts field, Hans Haacke wrote:

> Trained by prestigious business schools, they are convinced that art can and should be sold like the production and marketing of other goods. They make no apologies and have few romantic hang-ups.
>
> It is expected that the lack of delusions and aspirations among new arts administrators will have a notable impact on the state of the industry. Being trained primarily as technocrats, they are less likely to have an emotional attachment to the peculiar nature of the product they are promoting. And this attitude, in turn, will have an effect on the type of products they are promoting. And this attitude, in turn, will have an effect on the type of products we will soon begin to see.
>
> (Haacke, cited in Chong 2002: 2)

Thirty years later, Haacke's predictions have failed to materialise, and the field of cultural events is more diverse and widespread than ever. New technologies, innovative funding regimes and the growth of cultural sponsorship have all helped to support a global cultural sector that is recognised by most developed nations as fundamental to their economic success and cultural identity. This diverse group of cultural producers within the 'cultural industries' (Hesmondhalgh 2007) make use of the full repertoire of marketing strategies and techniques that were explored in Chapter 7. However, when considering cultural events specifically, we can make use of two models that help event managers to develop both their marketing strategies and the cultural form in which they are working. These models are the concept of the 'cultural consumer' and the group of social marketing techniques known as 'audience development'.

13.7.1 The cultural events consumer

Kolb (2013) sets out four core challenges facing cultural organisations in the competition for consumers:

1   Cultural marketers can no longer assume that they know what the consumer wants from the cultural experience.
2   Consumers living in a multi-media, cross-cultural environment will want more combinations of art forms and new delivery methods.
3   Cultural marketers must target packaged events to specific market segments.
4   These packaged events must provide multiple benefits to meet consumer needs, while fitting within consumers' time and budget constraints.

Bearing in mind these constraints, Kolb goes on to suggest that, when faced with this level of uncertainty within an organisation and the cross-cultural, multi-media competencies and expectations of cultural event attendees, there is a need for a specific cultural segmentation model for cultural consumers. This is in line with Getz's (2012) recommendation to use product-related variables when segmenting the market for an event. This model of the 'cultural consumer' can be used by cultural event managers to attract specific groups of attendees through the design and marketing processes. It first classifies the consumer in terms of their engagement with the cultural form or event (see Figure 13.3).

This model shows cultural consumers segmented into five groups, each of which is represented to a different degree for different cultural forms within a total population of cultural consumers. *Petty producers* have developed such a strong level of engagement with the culture that they have started to create it at an amateur level. They are looking for cultural experiences that allow them to participate in production or that offer opportunities for their advancement or development within their preferred cultural field.

Those within the *enthusiast* segment of the cultural consumer market place have an excellent knowledge of the cultural form that goes beyond mere attachment to a particular individual, group or venue. They are very knowledgeable about their chosen field and it is a significant element in their social and friendship networks. This group of event consumers will be attracted to cultural events and festivals that are innovative and have a clear relationship to the traditions associated with their cultural form.

Cultists are a heavily specialised segment of this market who have developed attachments to specific events, stars or groups. They are characterised by the lengths they will go to in order to indulge their interests, both financially and temporally. They will seek out events that are related to their particular interests and those that give them opportunities to meet like-minded consumers.

A *fan* is similar to a cultist, but will devote less time and money to pursuing their interest. This allows fans to have multiple allegiances and to be more open to developing new cultural

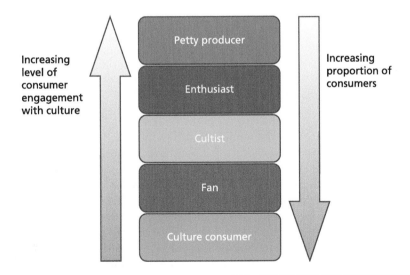

Figure 13.3 Cultural consumers
Source: Adapted from Kolb 2013

Table 13.4 Cultural consumer model applied to theatre events

Type of consumer	Example consumption activity	Value to the organisation
Petty producer	Begins to write and get involved in amateur theatre. Prepared to spend for 'important/exclusive' events.	Can generate new cultural workers and products. Audience for specific high-value events.
Enthusiast	Studies a course in theatre history.	Part of valuable networks that can be accessed for marketing purposes.
	Prepared to travel widely and invest in their interest.	Potentially a large attendee group, but often dispersed. Market for high-value events.
Cultist	Attends all events featuring a specific film star.	A reliable audience with patterns of repeat attendance.
		Likely to consume cult-related products, such as exclusive events and signings, and to purchase related merchandise.
		Part of valuable networks of cultists.
Fan	Excited by music, theatre and productions starring certain TV or film personalities.	A large audience group that can be targeted using specific events or programming.
Cultural consumer	Will attend the theatre as part of an evening out or in response to a marketing campaign that emphasises entertainment, price and/or convenience.	This is the mass audience for all culture. Theatres will need to attract these people to develop sustainable audiences to support wider programming aims and ensure financial survival.

interests. They are attracted by the familiarity of the form or content of the event, or the connection between the event and another that they have attended in the past.

The majority of the population – the mass audience for cultural events and festivals – can be classified as *cultural consumers*. They do not have specialist cultural event interests, but consume culture as part of day-to-day life. For these consumers, factors such as convenience and cost are key elements in their decision-making processes, as are the effects of reference groups.

Kolb's model is important for understanding the marketing of cultural events and festivals as it shows how different kinds of cultural consumers have specific, event-related expectations and desires, which will influence their value to a cultural organisation in terms of income or programming choices. However, cultural organisations seek to develop both the cultural forms in which they work and the audiences for their work. This idea of 'audience development' is fundamental to understanding the relationship between the marketing goals of a cultural event and its broader cultural mission.

Study activity

As the marketing manager of a contemporary pop music venue in a large city, how would you go about attracting the various segments of the cultural marketplace – as defined in Kolb's model – for your events?
Use the following questions as a guide:

- Which segment(s) would you focus on and why?
- How would you effectively market your event to your chosen segment(s)?
- How would your chosen segment(s) influence the event design process?

13.7.2 Developing audiences for cultural events and festivals

Audience development is an umbrella term for techniques and approaches that are designed to increase audiences for cultural events. While these have much in common with general marketing approaches, cultural organisations employ them in the hope of achieving broader goals. (In this sense, they are a form of social marketing.) These goals include cultural, financial and social objectives, and the innovative aspect of audience development is combining these within the field of cultural management, as is shown in Figure 13.4.

These objectives relate to the internal and external relationships of a cultural organisation. Some of these relationships are grounded in the mission of the cultural organisation, such as a commitment to develop a particular cultural form, while others focus on external factors, such as the requirements of funding bodies or a relationship with the local community.

Audience development aims to break down barriers to access and deliver new audiences for cultural events by changing perceptions and behaviours of potential and existing event attendees. These changes will then lead to attendees

- attending an unfamiliar cultural form
- attending more frequently
- attending new venues
- transforming from lapsed into regular attendees
- forming closer bonds with a cultural organisation
- becoming donors of time or money
- increasing their level of interaction within their social groups and the wider community.

Within cultural event and festival organisations, audience development is a cross-functional activity that requires the participation of the whole organisation. Successful audience development requires that cultural producers, marketers, educational professionals and strategists work together to align the activities of an event organisation with audience development plans. Kawashima (2006), having conducted a review of audience development practices in the cultural sector, shows the multiple benefits of pursuing such strategies:

- providing financial security
- increasing opportunities for cultural production and participation
- promoting individual development and fulfilment for audiences
- promoting social cohesion.

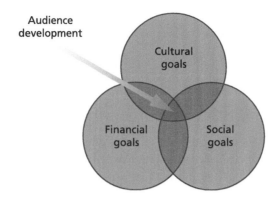

Figure 13.4 Audience development goals

Table 13.5 Audience development relationships and activities

Organisational goal	Relationship to organisation	Outcomes
Cultural	Internal	Enhancing understanding of a cultural form Building support for cultural innovation
	External	Developing dialogue with an audience
Financial	Internal	Increasing revenue Developing loyalty
	External	Meeting criteria of funding bodies
Social	Internal	Providing an educational experience
	External	Addressing issues of social exclusion Providing therapeutic benefits

All of these outcomes are dependent on increasing *participation* in cultural events. McCarthy and Jinnet (2001), in a study of arts organisations in the United States, found three ways in which participation can be increased:

- *Diversifying participation* involves attracting event attendees who would not normally attend a cultural event. Such people will need to be convinced of the benefits of attending, so this form of developing participation is the most time and resource-intensive.
- *Broadening participation* involves attracting more people to an event, from a pool of likely cultural event attendees. To broaden participation successfully, it is important to widen the scope of your marketing activities, providing information about your programmes and events to those who are already interested in your type of cultural event but who have not previously attended. Marketing messages that emphasise price and convenience are also appropriate for this strategy.

● *Deepening participation* involves strengthening the engagement of your existing audience. This can be accomplished through educational and special event programming, encouraging your existing audience to invest more in the organisation and to become increasingly loyal towards it.

Organising a variety of audience development techniques within these categories gives a useful overview of the diversity of audience development practices within the cultural sector (see Table 13.6).

Table 13.6 Audience development techniques

Participation strategy	Benefits to the organisation	Example techniques
Diversifying	Attracting new event attendees Developing new sources of revenue Generating support for cultural innovation	Producing new cultural forms: for example, staging performances of new musical forms or programming a season of films targeted at specific potential attendees
		Changing the environment, mood and/or tone of a venue or event
		Developing new customer service strategies
		Programming events that cross over cultural forms
Broadening	Increasing audience size Developing sustainable revenue streams Consolidating support for cultural innovation	Marketing development Pricing structure and incentives Communications Collaborative events with other providers
Deepening	Increasing audience loyalty Increasing audience spending Extending support for cultural innovation	Event interpretation: for example, pre- and post-event talks, access to rehearsals and/or venue tours
		Educational activity: for example, workshops, summer schools and/or master classes
		Increasing opportunities for feedback from and dialogue with event attendees

National Theatre Live

Location: London, UK
Venue type: arts venue
Attendees: various

The National Theatre was founded in 1963. It is the most prominent publically funded theatre in the United Kingdom and both receives and produces work of international quality. Since its inception, the National Theatre has produced more than 800 plays, ranging from traditional classics such as the works of Shakespeare to post-modern productions such as the opera written by Blur front man Damon Albarn, 'Wonder.land'. The current Director of the National Theatre, Nicholas Hyter, describes its mission: 'It's a great time to be a national theatre, and to rise to the challenge of living up to our name. We want to tell the stories that chart the way the nation is changing. We want to bring front-line reports from new communities and generations, and we want to see the present redefined in the context of the past.'

The National Theatre Live programme began in 2009, with a production of Phèdre, starring Dame Helen Mirren, which was screened live in 35 cinemas across the UK, while simultaneously being shown to an audience in the theatre itself. The aim of the programme is to create larger, more geographically diverse audiences for theatre productions and to engage new audiences with the theatre. The growth of digital projection in cinemas has made it possible for new kinds of content to be shown; the Metropolita Opera in New York pioneered this with a series of international live screenings and these opportunities have also been grasped by live music promoters. The National Theatre aimed to produce theatre events specifically for broadcast in this way.

The first National Theatre Live production had an audience of around 50,000 people and, in purely numerical terms, it is clear that the programme has been a success in *broadening participation* in these arts events. The evaluation carried out on the attendees at the cinema screening showed that a quarter of all attendees earned less than £20,000 per year and 50 per cent earned less than £50,000 per year, showing that the screenings were reaching different sections of the population than traditional theatre productions and that the programme was effective in *diversifying participation*.

(NESTA 2011; National Theatre 2015)

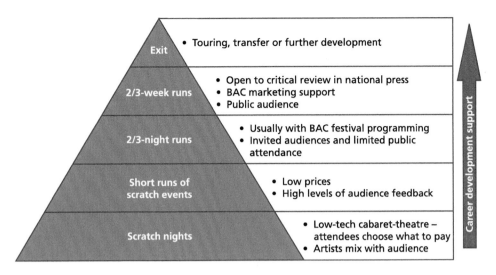

Figure 13.5 The BAC's Ladder of Development

13.8 The public role of cultural events and festivals

Cultural events and festivals are increasingly forming part of public sector strategy (Bowdin *et al.* 2010), usually linked to economic development through increased tourism, secondary spending or business development. Recently, they have also been promoted as vehicles for developing social capital and/or community cohesion through ideals of participation and the representation of excluded groups in the public sphere.

Hall and Rusher (2004) set out five perspectives from which the intersection of public policy and events can be studied:

- The political nature of the event policy-making process.
- Public participation in the event planning and policy process.
- The sources of power in event policy-making.
- The exercise of choice by public officials in complex policy environments.
- Perceptions as to the effectiveness of event policies.

Cultural events and festivals

Quinn (2005: 927) notes that there has been a 'reconceptualisation of the festival as a useful strategy for the contemporary city to adopt in the attempt to reposition and differentiate itself in an increasingly competitive world'. This new world for cities has been developed through new approaches to urban management that emphasise competitiveness and integration; structural changes in economic production that have seen Western cities deindustrialise and develop their service sectors, and the use of cultural industries to restructure wealth and job creation. All of this has taken place in a globalising system that has produced urban areas of incredible cultural diversity.

For example, the city of Manchester has seven designated 'pillar' events that together form a key part of the city's economic, tourism and community development strategies:

- Enchanted Evenings – combined arts festival
- Starbucks Manchester Jazz Festival
- D.Percussion – a music festival
- Manchester Pride
- Manchester Literature Festival
- Villa Espana Manchester Food and Drink Festival
- Manchester 'Smile' Comedy Festival.

These events contribute at least £49 million to the city's economy through direct and indirect event expenditure by 505,000 attendees (Jura Consultants 2006).

The European Festival Association (EFA 2010) states that festivals:

- Inspire citizens through the arts, challenge and offer them occasions to broaden their horizons.
- Help deconstruct stereotypes.
- Promote a creative society that sustains and develops quality of life, social well-being and equal opportunities for all.
- Boost geographic, social and generational solidarity by bringing people together through inventive and participatory initiatives.

However, one should not view these positive economic and social effects as inevitable. Hosting cultural events and festivals can have both positive and negative impacts, so the event manager must work hard to maximise the former while minimising the latter. Moscardo (2008) provides a useful summary of the range of negative and positive impacts that event hosting can have on a location (see Table 13.7).

In Serbia, the Exit Music Festival was held for the first time in 2000. This event demonstrates how the political and social potential of cultural festivals and events can be realised in a way that moves beyond the prevailing instrumental analyses of cultural events and festivals in the literature.

Table 13.7 Summary of event and festival impacts
Source: Moscardo 2008

Category	Positive	Negative
Economic	Direct income	Loss-making events
	Multiplier effect	Increased prices for locals
	Employment	Opportunity costs
Tourism	Enhanced destination image	Risk of reputation damage
	Extension of tourism season	

Category	Positive	Negative
Physical	New facilities and infrastructure Regeneration of rundown areas	Environmental damage Overcrowding Congestion
Socio-cultural	Social opportunities for locals Improved social networks	Commodification of culture Antisocial behaviour Dissatisfaction with event image
Psychological	Enhanced sense of community Excitement Pride	Conflict
Regional community development	Enhanced skills for volunteers and participants Support for other regional products and services	Conflict with other regional activities

CASE STUDY 13.4

EXIT 2015

Location: Novi Sad, Serbia
Event type: music festival
Attendees: 50,000

The first Exit Festival was held in the summer of 2000 and was conceived as a protest against the Milošević regime in Serbia, which was seen as illegitimate and repressive by many of the country's citizens. The tag line of this first event was 'Exit from ten years of madness' – in reference to the government – and it was held to coincide with the presidential elections as a way of mobilising young people to become more involved in politics.

> After 10 years of darkness, people who are not old enough to remember the good old days decided, since they couldn't move out of the country of darkness, to give themselves, their friends and their city some sort of happening to revive the cultural scene of Novi Sad . . . Free concerts, performances, parties, stands and film projections were frequented by the youth . . . from Novi Sad, but also many visitors came from the region, other cities and other countries. 34 large concerts were held that featured the biggest local bands, 12 theatrical performances, more than 120 films were shown (some were premiered in Novi Sad), 20 stands, 40 huge parties, 11 performances.
>
> (EXIT 2010)

After the overthrow of Milošević, the festival moved into the mainstream, and it has been funded and supported by a range of public bodies that see it as a key means of establishing national identity in the wake of two decades of conflict and of presenting a fresh destination image to the international tourism industry.

The festival today

The festival is held in the former fortress of Petrovaradin, a military fortification built in the seventeenth century and of immense cultural and symbolic significance as a relic of the former power of the region in European affairs. EXIT is now the largest music festival in South East Europe: in 2015 more than 200,000 people attended the four-day event. It takes place across twenty stages and features hundreds of music performers. In 2015, the line-up included The Prodigy, John Newman, Manu Chao and Motorhead.

As well as being a major event in the European festival circuit, comparable to Glastonbury in England and the Love Parade in Berlin, EXIT promotes peace, democracy, multiculturalism and human rights. This is a key element in the identity of the festival as a commercial brand and as an expression of contemporary Serbian culture and identity. The majority of attendees come from neighbouring former Yugoslavian states, and recent research has shown that most of them believe that EXIT has made a significant contribution to improving Serbia's image in the rest of the world.

(EXIT 2010; Lukic-Krstanovic 2008; Zakic *et al.* 2009; Wise and Mulec 2015)

Study activity

The Exit Festival shows how cultural events can have impacts that are more complicated than simply making an economic contribution to an area. Choose a music festival in your area and identify the range of impacts that are associated with it. Which of these do you think is the most significant and why?

Industry voice

Dee Ishani, Head of Digital, Marketing and Communications, Creative United, London, UK

 I've recently started as Head of Digital, Marketing and Communications at Creative United. This follows a 5½-year stint at digital agencies project managing website builds and digital campaigns for arts organisations, including theatres, galleries, art societies and museums, all of whom were involved in the cultural events and festival sectors. Before that, I spent 7 years freelancing in arts marketing. I worked with small producing companies, theatres, local authorities and unsubsidised arts charities. Having worked with a wide range of clients across the arts and creative sectors I have spotted several patterns when it comes to marketing cultural events.

It's still quite common for marketing to be brought on board quite late in the day with a project. It doesn't matter the scale of the project or whether the marketing team is internal, contracted or agency. Some companies value marketing and will bring their marketers on board early. This allows marketers to get involved early on and help finalise details of an event to maximise the opportunities to plan and produce great marketing collateral and solid campaigns.

Other companies still see marketing as an 'extra' which means that they only get it together late in the day – handing over to internal or external marketers when almost everything is set in stone. This can create a more challenging project. In many cases, marketers have their own approach to a campaign that gets rehashed again and again, simply because they're not involved early enough to be more creative. An uncomfortably large number of event venues, in my experience, have little to no marketing strategy and rely solely on campaigns. Branding can be patchy or nonexistent and this creates difficulties.

Every event will have a slightly different appeal and so the audience will vary slightly from the last event you did, even in the same venue. They might vary because of location, dates, times, cost, other events taking place, their interest in this specific event or activity. Marketers need to be able to work out who their audiences are, what it is about this show/event that will appeal to them and where the best place to reach them is.

When I worked at digital agencies, we frequently reminded our clients that their websites weren't for them – they were for their audiences. And the same applies to the show or event being promoted. You might know it's going to be great but the key to great marketing is convincing other people – who potentially don't know anything about you – to care about what you're doing. And to care enough that they will happily give up their time, money and social life to you.

Different audiences for your events may need different messages to entice them – don't be afraid to differentiate between them – some of the digital channels available today can be incredibly specific and allow you to test multiple messages without really incurring any additional cost. This really allows you to test your messages, see what works and run with the best solution within small budgets and timeframes. The channels you choose – whether print, press, digital, whatever – should be tailored to those audiences. Don't waste time and money setting up a digital channel and creating content specifically for it if your audience don't use it – use that energy elsewhere.

Once you've won them over you don't want to lose them. This is really why data is such a 'thing' at the moment. The more you know about your audiences, the easier it is to find them and promote the next event to them.

Some organisations will have some data about their audiences already. Some won't. Few events are one-offs so you should plan how you're going to build a picture of who actually comes to the event as part of your campaign. Make sure you understand what you can and can't do with data and that you honour terms and conditions and existing policies. I still come across organisations without any understanding of the Data Protection Act or its replacement the General Data Protection Regulation (in the UK) – and that's not good enough. It's a pet hate of mine. If you want your audiences to stick with you, to trust you and to develop with you then you have to treat them well. However amazing your event is, treating your audiences/customers badly will taint your reputation so it's best not to risk it.

People are at the heart of all of this. You need to be able to work with other people and to build relationships quickly. You need to have empathy – be able to put yourself in someone else's shoes and anticipate their needs so you can make it easy for them to show up on the day. The people you work with are just as important as the people you sell tickets to.

The small things matter. Pay attention to the detail. Because if you don't, then it'll be a customer who does and you never know who's attention they might get if they get angry!

13.9 Summary

This chapter has set out a framework within which one can identify a set of events and festivals that can be grouped together as 'cultural'. Bringing these events together is a response to the way in which the huge diversity of human cultural expressions has imploded under the pressures of globalisation and marketisation, forming the 'cultural industries' from which so many of our leisure and social experiences are drawn. Concepts such as the 'cultural consumer', 'audience development' and 'programming' unify the cultural events sector and help event managers to transfer knowledge between different events and festivals to produce successful events in an increasingly crowded cultural marketplace.

Further reading

Kolb, B. M. (2013) *Marketing for Cultural Organisations* (3rd edn), London: Thompson. A very useful, practical book that covers marketing from planning to evaluation, with a specific focus on the cultural sector.

Jepson, A. and Clarke, A. (2015) *Managing and Developing Communities, Festivals and Events* London: Palgrave MacMillan. Contains a range of case studies showing the social and cultural impacts of cultural events and festivals and the challenges involved in managing these types of events.

References

Albanese, A. (2015) *Frankfurt Book Fair 2015: In Surprise, Frankfurt Book Fair Attendance Rises.* Available at: www.publishersweekly.com/pw/by-topic/international/Frankfurt-

Book-Fair/article/68420-frankfurt-book-fair-2015-in-surprise-frankfurt-book-fair-attendance-rises.html. Accessed 6 January 2016.

Aksoy, A. and Robins, K. (2004) Parting from Phantoms: What is at Issue in the Development of Transnational Television from Turkey, in J. Friedman and S. Randeria (eds) *Worlds on the Move: Globalisation, Migration and Cultural Security*, London: I. B. Tauris.

Ali-Knight, J. and Robertson, M. (2004) Introduction to Arts, Culture and Leisure, in I. Yeoman, M. Robertson, J. Ali-Knight, S. Drummond and U. McMahon-Beattie (eds) *Festival and Events Management: An International Arts and Culture Perspective*, Oxford: Butterworth-Heinemann.

Allen, J., O'Toole, W., Harris, R. and McDonnell, I. (2012) *Festival and Special Event Management* (5th edn), Queensland: John Wiley & Sons.

Ammaturo, F.R. (2016) Spaces of Pride: A Visual Ethnography of Gay Pride Parades in Italy and the United Kingdom, *Social Movement Studies*, 15 (1): 19–40.

Anderton, C. (2008) Commercialising the Carnivalesque: The 'V' Festival and Image Risk Management, *Event Management*, 12: 39–51.

Arts Council England (2004) *Festivals and the Creative Region*, London: ACE.

Assassi, I. (2005) The Influence of Theaters' Programming Strategy on Their Relations with Artistic Production Companies: An Analysis Based on the French Experience, paper presented at the 8th International Conference on Arts and Cultural Management, 3–6 July, Montreal, Canada.

Axelsen, M. and Arcodia, C. (2005) Conceptualising Art Exhibitions as Special Events, *Journal of Convention and Event Tourism*, 6 (3): 63–80.

Bakhtin, M. (1984) *Rabelais and his World*, Indianapolis: Indiana University Press.

BBC (2009) Woodstock for the Mind is Belfast Bound. Available at: http://news.bbc.co. uk/1/hi/northern_ireland/8003768.stm. Accessed 26 October 2011.

Bowdin, G., Allen, J., O'Toole, W., Harris, R. and McDonnell, I. (2006) *Events Management* (2nd edn), Oxford: Butterworth-Heinemann.

Bowdin, G., Allen, J., O'Toole, W., Harris, R. and McDonnell, I. (2010) *Events Management* (3rd edn), Oxford: Butterworth-Heinemann.

Bowen, H. and Daniels, M. J. (2005) Does the Music Matter? Motivations for Attending a Music Festival, *Event Management*, 9 (3): 155–164.

Buchmesse (2010) Frankfurter Buchmesse 2010. Available at: www.buchmesse. de/. Accessed 9 May 2010.

Burwell, C. (2007) Reading *Lolita* in Times of War: Women's Book Clubs and the Politics of Reception, *Intercultural Education*, 18 (4): 281–296.

Carnegie, E. and Smith, M. (2006) Mobility, Diaspora and the Hybridization of Festivity, in D. Pickard and M. Robinson (eds) *Festivals, Tourism and Social Change*, Clevedon: Channel View Publications.

Castaner, X. and Campos, L. (2002) The Determinants of Artistic Innovation: Bringing in the Role of Organisations, *Journal of Cultural Economics*, 26: 29–52.

Chong, D. (2002) *Arts Management*, Abingdon: Routledge.

Cuadrado-Garcia, M. and Perez-Cabenero, C. (2005) The Process of Programming in the Performing Arts: An Empirical Research in Spain, paper presented at the 8th International Conference on Arts and Cultural Management, 3–6 July, Montreal, Canada.

Eagleton, T. (2000) *The Idea of Culture*, Oxford: Blackwell.

Edinburgh International Festival (2010) Home page. Available at: www.eif.co. uk/. Accessed 9 May 2010.

Edinburgh International Festival (2015) About us. Available at: www.eif.co.uk/about-us. Accessed 6 January 2016.

Edwards, P. (2015) *La Tomatina's 70th anniversary – and its big, messy secret*. Available at: www.vox.com/2015/8/26/9207787/la-tomatina. Accessed 6 January 2016.

EFA (2010) Home page. Available at: www.open-the-door.eu/. Accessed 10 May 2009.

EXIT (2010) Exit Festival. Available at: http://eng.exitfest.org/. Accessed 9 May 2010.

Faversham Hop Festival (2010) Home page. Available at: www.favershamhopfestival.org/. Accessed 6 July 2017.

Fenich, G. (2005) *Meetings, Expositions, Events and Conventions: An Introduction to the Industry*, New Jersey: Pearson Prentice Hall.

Festival Insights (2013) *Market Report 2013*, London: Festival Insights.

Finkel, R. (2006) Tensions between Ambition and Reality in UK Combined Arts Festival Programming: Case Study of the Lichfield Festival, *International Journal of Event Management Research*, 2 (1): 25–36.

Fox-Gotham, K. (2002) Marketing Mardi Gras: Comodification, Spectacle and the Political Economy of Tourism in New Orleans, *Urban Studies*, 39 (10): 1735–1756.

Fox-Gotham, K. (2005) Tourism from Above and Below: Globalisation, Localisation and New Orleans's Mardi Gras, in *International Journal of Urban and Regional Research*, 29 (2): 309–326.

Getz, D. (2005) *Event Management and Event Tourism*, New York: Cognizant Communication.

Getz, D. (2012) *Events Studies: Theory, Practice and Research for Planned Events*, Abingdon: Routledge.

Grunwell, S. and Ha, I. (2008) Film Festivals: An Empirical Study of Factors for Success, *Event Management*, 11: 201–210.

Hall, C. M. and Rusher, K. (2004) Politics, Public Policy and the Destination, in I. Yeoman, M. Robertson, J. Ali-Knight, S. Drummond and U. McMahon-Beattie (eds) *Festival and Events Management: An International Arts and Culture Perspective*, Oxford: Butterworth-Heinemann.

Hamilos, P. (2013) *Spain's Tomatina festival puts a price on tomatoes*. Available at: www.theguardian.com/world/2013/aug/28/spain-tomatina-festival-entry-fee-bunel. Accessed 6 January 2016.

Hesmondhalgh, D. (2007) *The Cultural Industries* (2nd edn), London: Sage.

Huang, J., Li, M. and Cai, L. (2010) A Model of Community-based Festival Image, *International Journal of Hospitality Management*, 29 (2): 254–260.

Hughes, H. L. (2006) Gay and Lesbian Festivals: Tourism in the Change from Politics to Party, in D. Pickard and M. Robinson (eds) *Festivals, Tourism and Social Change*, Clevedon: Channel View Publications.

IFEA (2015) *The Power of Celebration (Press Release)*. Available at: www.ifea.com/p/about/mediainformation/pressreleases. Accessed 6 January 2016.

Interpride (2015) Home page. Available at: www.interpride.org/. Accessed 6 January 2016.

Jepson, A., Wiltshier, P. and Clarke, A. (2008) Community Festivals: Involvement and Inclusion, paper presented at the CHME International Research Conference, Strathclyde Business School, University of Strathclyde, 14–16 May, Glasgow.

Jura Consultants (2006) *Economic Impact Assessment: The Pillar Events*, Edinburgh: Jura Consultants.

Kawashima, N. (2006) Audience Development and Social Inclusion in Britain, *International Journal of Cultural Policy*, 12 (1): 55–72.

Klamer, A. (2002) On the Economics of Arts and Culture. Available at: www. klmar.nl/art.htm. Accessed 26 July 2005.

Kolb, B.M. (2013) *Marketing for Cultural Organizations: New Strategies for Attracting Audiences*, London: Thompson.

Kotler, P. and Scheff, J. (1997) *Standing Room Only: Strategies for Marketing the Performing Arts*, Oxford: Blackwell.

La Tomatina (2015) *Home*. Available at: http://latomatina.info/en/. Accessed 6 January 2016.

Lukic-Krstanovic, M. (2008) The Festival Order: Music Stages of Power and Pleasure, *Issues in Ethnology and Anthropology*, 3 (3): 129–143.

McCarthy, K. and Jinnet, K. (2001) *A New Framework for Building Participation in the Arts*, New York: RAND.

Manchester Pride (2010) Who Are We. Available at: www.manchesterpride.com/aboutus/whoarewe. Accessed 19 May 2010.

Mardi Gras New Orleans (2010) Mardi Gras New Orleans. Available at: www.mardigrasneworleans.com/. Accessed 9 May 2010.

Mintel (2008) *Music Concert Events and Festivals*, London: Mintel Group.

Moscardo, G. (2008) Analysing the Role of Festivals and Events in Regional Development, *Event Management*, 11: 23–32.

National Theatre (2015) *About National Theatre Live*. Available at: www.nationaltheatre.org.uk/about-the-national-theatre/national-theatre-live. Accessed 6 January 2016.

NESTA – an innovation foundation, backing new ideas to tackle the big challenges of our time. Available at: www.nesta.org.uk. Accessed 7 July 2017.

O'Hara, H. (2010) Secret Cinema, the Experience. Available at: www. empireonline.com/empireblogs/empire-states/post/p783. Accessed 18 May 2010.

Pickard, D. and Robinson, M. (eds) (2006) *Festivals, Tourism and Social Change*, Clevedon: Channel View Publications.

Pickert, K. (2008) Oprah's Book Club. Available at: www.time.com/time/arts/article/0,8599,1844724,00.html. Accessed 19 May 2010.

Pride in London (2015) Home page. Available at: http://prideinlondon.org/. Accessed 6 July 2017.

Quinn, B. (2005) Arts Festivals and the City, *Urban Studies*, 42 (5/6): 927–943.

Raj, R., Walters, P. and Rashid, T. (2013) *Events Management: An Integrated and Practical Approach*, London: Sage.

Sonder, M. (2004) *Event Entertainment and Production*, Hoboken: John Wiley & Sons.

Soundwalk (2010) Home page. Available at: www.soundwalk.com/. Accessed 9 May 2010.

Soundwalk (2015) *Welcome to Soundwalk*. Available at: http://soundwalk.org/. Accessed 6 January 2016.

Storymoja Hay Festival Nairobi (2015) Home page. Available at: http://storymojafestival.com/. Accessed 6 January 2016.

Wang, Y. C. and Weng, A. (2008) Indies Music, Festivities and 'Spring Scream': A Taiwanese Case of Cultural Tourism, *Proceedings of the 19th Annual Conference of Chinese Management Educators*, Toronto, 24–26 July: 455–463.

Williams, M. and Bowdin, G. (2007) Festival Evaluation: An Exploration of Seven UK Arts Festivals, in *Managing Leisure*, 12 (2): 187–203.

Williams, R. (2010) *Keywords: A Vocabulary of Culture and Society*, London: Fontana Press.

Wise, N. and Mulec, I., 2015. Aesthetic Awareness and Spectacle: Communicated Images of Novi Sad (Serbia), the Exit Festival, and the Petrovaradin Fortress. *Tourism Review International*, 19 (4): 193–205.

Yeoman, I., Robertson, M., Ali-Knight, J., Drummond, S. and McMahon-Beattie, U. (eds) (2004) *Festival and Events Management: An International Arts and Culture Perspective*, Oxford: Butterworth-Heinemann.

Zakic, L., Ivkov-Dzigurski, A. and Curcic, N. (2009) Interaction of Foreign Visitors of the EXIT Music Festival with Domestic Visitors and Local Population, *Geographica Pannonica*, 13 (3): 97–104.

Chapter 14

Event impacts, sustainability and legacy

Contents

14.1 Aims

By the end of this chapter, students will be able to:

● evaluate the role of a range of impact measurements in evaluating events;
● evaluate the positive and negative impacts of a range of events;
● analyse and design sustainable events;
● explain the concept of event legacy.

14.2 Introduction

This chapter will provide an overview of a range of perspectives on the impacts of events. Different kinds of impacts will be explored, using examples, and the varied ways of measuring these impacts will be discussed.

It is through the measurement of event impacts, across a range of domains, that we can evaluate the sustainability of an event and begin to understand the place of green events within the events industry. Event sustainability is the measure of the contribution made by event impacts to positive change in external fields, including the environment, social justice and economic justice. The issue of event legacies will be introduced, along with a scale of event impacts, showing the important long-term and wide-ranging effects that are the hallmarks of a legacy scheme.

14.3 Event impacts

Event impacts can be split into three categories, as shown in Figure 14.1.

Figure 14.1 Event impacts

Personal impacts are covered in more detail in Chapter 3. Suffice to say here that they can include:

● Positive experiences, expressed as:

    ○ perceptions that the event met or exceeded expectations
    ○ satisfaction, happiness
    ○ attitude change (towards the events, sponsors, causes, or events in general)
    ○ fundamental personal change in terms of lifestyle, personality or values.

● Negative experiences, expressed as:

    ○ perceptions of poor value for money
    ○ no intent to repeat event experience
    ○ lack of satisfaction
    ○ failure to meet expectations. (Getz 2007)

Organisational impacts can include:

● Financial impacts – revenue generation, profit- and loss-making activity.
● Human resource impacts – recruitment and retention, motivation of staff, training opportunities.
● Impacts on organisational capacity – growth, skills development, client acquisition.
● Marketing impacts – profile-raising, word-of-mouth, media attention.

In this chapter, the focus will be on the *external impacts* of events and on the interactions between the events industry, the economy, the environment, society and culture.

14.3.1 Economic impacts of events

Economic impact assessments have been used to justify government support for events and in making decisions about investing in the events industry, including the construction of conference and exhibition venues as well as their supporting infrastructure, such as roads and hotels. For example, the Government of Kraków, Poland, invested €85 million to build the ICE Conference Centre, a facility with 36,000 square metres of conference space, including a 2,000-seat auditorium and capacity to host corporate events for 3,200 participants (ICE Kraków 2016). The venue was built to help attract high-level corporate events to a city that was already seeing the benefits of becoming a regionally important destination for meetings and events. The Mayor of Kraków, Jacek Majchrowski, explained that:

> Nearly 20% of the residents of Kraków make work in the tourism industry, including in the business tourist service field. There are significantly more business owners working directly and indirectly with the MICE industry in all of Małopolska region . . . The activities that will be undertaken by the ICE Kraków Congress Centre team in the next two years will therefore influence the entire sector of the meetings industry, which has been growing dynamically in Kraków for several years now. We need to maintain this trend in the coming years, as conferences and congresses affect the economic development of the whole region.
>
> (HQ 2016: The ICE Kraków Congress
> Centre is set to make a difference)

Morgan and Condliffe (2006) set out the three steps necessary to develop a methodology for assessing the economic impacts of an event:

1 Define the geographical area under study – this could be the town, city, district, region or country where an event takes place.
2 Identify the industries from which to collect data to assess direct impacts. For example, for investments in infrastructure and venues, you will need to collect construction industry data, while assessment of tourism impacts will need data from the leisure and hospitality sectors.
3 Collect data on or estimate the direct impacts of the event on the industrial sectors that have been identified.

Within this third point, a range of different approaches can be used to measure economic impact. It is important to be able to distinguish between the economic activity within an area independent of the presence of an event and when that area is influenced by an event. For this reason, it is always important to have baseline data of economic activity so that changes can be measured. Three of the most frequently used methods of calculating economic impacts are explained below.

14.3.1.1 Multiplier effects

Multiplier calculations are the most frequently used method for evaluating the economic impacts of events. Multipliers capture the direct and indirect spending associated with events by calculating the money spent by attendees on attending the event itself *and* the extra spending in the economy that is facilitated by this initial injection. The extent to which the initial attendee spend generates additional spending is known as the multiplier effect. As Carlsen (2004: 247) explains, 'The size of the multiplier effects will be determined by the extent to which the economy can retain the additional event-related expenditure in the local economy.' This relates to the concept of 'leakage' – the movement of event-related expenditure outside the geographical area within which impacts are being assessed. For example, a percentage of the revenue generated by a touring performance by the Rolling Stones at the O2 Arena in London will flow out of the event hosting area and return to the Netherlands, where the band members are registered for tax purposes. This is a leakage of money from the event area to another area, so it cannot be included in the local economic impact of an event and must be subtracted from a multiplier calculation.

A model setting out the various aspects of a multiplier calculation is given in Figure 14.2. By calculating the spending under each of the three categories in this figure, the total spending generated by an event can be worked out. This can then be used to produce a figure that demonstrates the impact of event spending on the local economy.

There are two ways of calculating a multiplier:

Direct spending + Indirect spending / Direct spending = Multiplier

or

Direct spending + Indirect spending + Induced spending / Direct spending = Multiplier

The more commonly used first type does not include induced spending as this is usually difficult to estimate.

For example, Hanly's (2012) research into the Irish market for association conferences showed that direct conference spending at these events totalled €131.1 million, which then in turn generated €235.8 million in additional output in the economy, €454.4 million in income, €101.6 million in value added, €52 million in imports and €9.3 million in product taxes, clearly

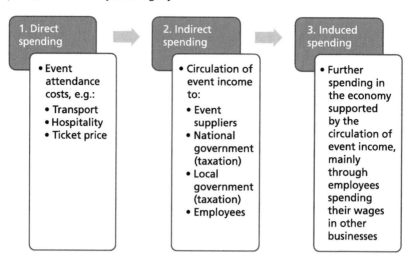

Figure 14.2 Aspects of multiplier calculations

showing the way in which multiplier effects transform the economic impacts of events in the economy.

Tribe (2005) shows the direct relationship between a multiplier value and leakage in the economic impacts of an event (Table 14.1).

14.3.1.2 Input–output analysis

Input–output modelling has a 'before and after' perspective on the economic impacts of events. The economic data used to carry out this form of analysis come from national-level statistical data that describe the economic relationships between various industrial sectors and regions. In the United Kingdom, these data are collected by the Office for National Statistics and are organised according to Standard Industrial Classification (SIC) codes, which categorise every business by industrial sector. The data show the contribution made by each industrial sector to the economy and give multiplier values that demonstrate how much an extra investment in any particular sector will contribute to the broader economy. By calculating the amount of income generated for each industrial sector by an event (for example, attendee spending on transport or hospitality), it is then possible to apply the multipliers given in the input–output table for that sector to calculate the value added to the economy by the event.

Table 14.1 **The multiplier–leakage relationship**
Source: Adapted from Tribe 2005: 271

Value of multiplier	Leakages from the local economy	Impact of expenditure on the local economy
High	Low	High
Low	High	Low

CASE STUDY 14.1

The Economic Impact of the Daejon Convention Centre in South Korea

Location: Daejon, South Korea
Event type: Corporate Events
Attendees: Up to 6,000
Website: www.dcckorea.or.kr/

Daejon is the fifth largest city in Korea, with a population of 1.5 million people. It houses a number of important government departments and private businesses and is one of the centres of the conference industry in the country. The Daejon Conference Centre was opened in April 2008 and offers 7,382 square metres of convention space and 2,520 square metres of exhibition space, including 24 meeting rooms. It has a capacity of more than 6,000 attendees spread across six multi-functional spaces. Also based in the venue is the Daejon-Chungcheong MICE Alliance, a public-private-partnership who promote the MICE industry in central Korea in partnership with local government, the events industry and universities.

Lee *et al.* (2013) measured the economic impact of this event venue, using an input–output methodology. To do this, they estimated spending at the venue by carrying out 1,370 surveys using a mixture of online and offline distribution, with five consumer groups at the venue: convention attendees, exhibition visitors, exhibitors, convention organisers and exhibition organisers. In the year of the study, US$254 million was spent. Exhibition visitors spent the largest amount, US$153 million, followed by convention attendees (US$48 million) and convention organisers (US$47 million). Exhibition organisers spent just US$3.3 million and exhibitors spent US$2.8 million. In addition to these headline figures, the researchers gathered data on individual items of expenditure by each category of attendee. The researchers then used input–output data for the regional economy, broken down by each industrial sector affected by spending at the event venue, thereby calculating the impact of each item of spending on the regional economy.

The results of applying this input–output methodology showed that the exhibition visitors generated the largest output impact of US$292.4 million followed by convention attendees (US$94.6 million) and convention organisers (US$89.6 million). Exhibition organisers and exhibitors had a much lower economic impact, when assessed in this way, of US$6.2 million and US$5.3 million, respectively. When looking at individual items of expenditure associated with attending events at the Daejon Conference Centre, spending at restaurants was found to generate the largest output impact (US$152.3 million) followed by transportation (US$78.4 million), accommodation (US$71.9 million) and culture/entertainment (US$60.1 million).

(Lee *et al.* 2013; Daejon Convention Centre 2016)

14.3.1.3 Cost–benefit analysis

This method of analysis places values on the costs associated with staging an event and the benefits that it generates. These two values are then compared and the event is deemed viable if the benefits outweigh the costs. This is a very simple method of calculating the economic impacts of an event and is often used as a starting point for economic analysis in the planning stages. It can, however, be used in a more sophisticated way by including the tangible and intangible aspects of event costs and benefits. Carlsen (2004) provides a description of the tangible and intangible elements of a cost–benefit calculation, as outlined in Tables 14.2 and 14.3.

The advantage of this method of analysis is that it allows for the incorporation of what economists call 'externalities'. These are aspects of the event that cannot be accounted for in direct economic terms; they appear in Carlsen's framework as the intangible costs and benefits. Traditionally, investment decisions have been made on the basis of return on investment (ROI) models, which make calculations such as those given above. However, contemporary events management takes into account these externalities in the production of sustainable events. The next two sections look at two categories of externality in event planning: environmental impacts and socio-cultural impacts.

14.3.2 Environmental impacts of events

The environment, in its natural or physical aspects, is a core part of the event product. The staging of an event in a particular country, region or locality implies a set of relationships to

Table 14.2 Tangible costs and benefits of events
Source: Carlsen 2004: 253

Tangible costs	Tangible benefits
Capital and construction costs	New facilities and venues
Wages and other employment costs	Employment for event employees
Additional essential services cost (e.g. police, sanitation, road maintenance)	Increased tourism expenditure before, during and after the event
Long-term event facilities maintenance	Positive media coverage and images

Table 14.3 Intangible costs and benefits of events
Source: Carlsen 2004: 253

Intangible costs	Intangible benefits
Crowding and inconvenience	Enhanced community pride
Noise and visual pollution	Cultural renewal
Personal crime and property damage	Increased interest and investment in host destination
Resident exodus and tourist avoidance of event area	Enhanced commercial and residential property values

the environment which are reciprocal in nature. The climate, landscape and setting of an event venue impact on the attractiveness and success of that event and are, in turn, acted on by the presence of the event.

In order to carry out an evaluation of the environmental impacts of an event, it is necessary to collect data in the following categories:

- Baseline environmental data for the location of the event, before the event takes place.
- The primary impacts of the event on the environment, such as the construction of facilities and infrastructure, waste management and the carbon footprint of the event itself.
- The secondary impacts of the event, such as congestion and pollution caused by travel to and from the venue and the use of accommodation by attendees.

No event will ever have zero environmental impacts, so it is incumbent upon event managers to develop management strategies that maximise positive impacts and minimise negative ones. Positive impacts can include the construction of zero-carbon facilities and the contribution that events can make to the physical improvement of town and cities. Negative environmental impacts associated with events include resource consumption, noise and the carbon footprint of the event itself and the travel associated with it. A number of festivals, especially music festivals, describe themselves as sustainable or 'green' events, and it is clear that the trend towards greater sustainability in festivals is a growing one that has benefits for both marketing to environmentally conscious young people and creating new, powerful event brands (Zifkos 2015).

David (2009) shows the energy consumption associated with the attendance of one consumer at an event, depending on their mode of travel (Table 14.4). For self-propelled travel, the energy needs are met through the consumption of foodstuffs, but for automated transport the energy comes from burning carbon in fuel.

Getz (2007: 315) suggests a number of techniques that can be used to minimise the negative impacts of events:

- *Impacts of event travel* – Support mass-transit travel solutions, concentrate multiple events in one location, stress small-scale events.
- *Investment in event infrastructure and venues* – Avoid sensitive areas, impose design standards, implement sustainable development practices.
- *Event activities* – Require green event practices, clean up after events, and educate visitors.

Table 14.4 **Transport energy intensity**
Source: David 2009

Means of transport	Energy consumption per passenger kilometre (KJ)
Aircraft	6000
Train	2100
Coach	2100
Car with 1–4 passengers	1900–7800
Cyclist	120
Pedestrian	250

CASE STUDY 14.2

Managing environmental impacts at the Bonnaroo Festival

Location: Tennessee, USA
Event type: music festival
Attendees: 70,000+

Bonnaroo is one of the largest music festivals in the US, taking place over four days each year in Manchester, rural Tennessee, sixty miles outside Nashville, and regularly attracting more than 70,000 attendees. This event has gained significant attention for its green policies, becoming one of only two US winners of the Greener Festival Award in 2008 and 2009, and marketing itself with messages of environmental responsibility and sustainability. The event is also highly regarded within the American music industry, described by *Rolling Stone* magazine as 'The American music festival to end all festivals' (cited in Arik and Penn 2005: 5).

> Bonnaroo is committed to investing the extensive time and resources necessary to be a leader in creating a sustainable festival. From our inception, the festival has strived to make the most sustainable choices while maintaining the ultimate experience for the fan, setting the standard in sustainability and greening practices for North American festivals.
>
> The Bonnaroo Music and Arts Festival is committed to partnering with the fans, other festivals, musicians, and artists to effect change. To take our sustainability practices to the next level, the festival is a proponent of behavior changes, long-term investments, and the ripple effect of education.
>
> Bonnaroo's overarching sustainability principle is: local is sustainable. We will use this principle to guide our decisions for 2009 and beyond.
>
> (Bonnaroo Music and Arts Festival 2009)

The main focus of sustainability efforts at Bonnaroo is on influencing the behaviour of event attendees. Kennell and Sitz (2010) investigated these efforts through micro-ethnographic research during the 2009 festival, when it was headlined by the Beastie Boys, Bruce Springsteen and Snoop Dogg.

One of the researchers gained access to all areas of the festival by interning for the Planet Roo eco-village coordinator. The researcher's job involved aiding the coordinator in all operational aspects of the eco village, including vendor management for environmental organisations, stage production and artist transportation. The researcher also worked alongside a group of volunteers who concentrated on environmental initiatives and the promotion of these among event attendees. This privileged access allowed for detailed observation of the event managers' efforts to minimise negative environmental impacts and the behaviour of attendees.

Image 14.1 Aerial view of the Bonnaroo Festival
Credit: Jeff Kravitz/Getty Images

The festival's environmental principles are translated into practice in three key ways:

- educational activities for volunteers and festivalgoers
- dedicated 'green' spaces
- embedding environmental concerns into the core values of the event.

Bonnaroo specifies education, outreach and activism as its primary greening policies; and, in an effort to maintain and improve its dedication to sustainability, it seeks to educate all parties involved in the festival. This begins with providing all Bonnaroo staff and volunteers with a 'greening handbook', distributed via email, which includes a list of festival purchasing policies and greening tips. Through this, it is hoped that Bonnaroo workers will 'make the most sustainable choices from their travel to the festival, to what they purchase while in Manchester, to how they treat the actual site'. The organisers also increase the educational aspect of the festival by: including the Bonnaroo environmental mission statement in all agreements and contracts with vendors, partners and sponsors; partnering with the Carbon Shredders organisation to encourage festivalgoers to pledge to reduce their carbon footprint by 10 per cent within the year; increasing sustainability signage throughout the festival grounds with the goal of educating attendees about the resources they are consuming (for example, signs about water conservation at each watering station); improving compost collection by increasing the number of manned recycling stations; and engaging a large number of volunteers to educate attendees on the proper disposal of rubbish.

Planet Roo is placed centrally within the festival grounds and acts as a promotional hub to educate attendees on both the festival's own greening programme and broader environmental and social issues. Various organisations have booths within Planet Roo to inform festival patrons about their issue of choice, while the village also acts as the home to 'ambassadors'. The organisations, ambassadors and festival itself host panel discussions, how-to sessions and documentaries in order to encourage interest and participation in environmental activities and education.

Discussions with managers revealed that they approach greening promotion subtly – through volunteer activism and attempts to influence behaviour – because they want Bonnaroo to continue to be a sustainable event, but they do not want that to become its sole purpose or focus.

Study activity

Based on your knowledge of large events like Bonnaroo, how effective do you think the organisers' efforts will be in reducing the environmental impacts of the event? What other measures could they implement to reduce the negative impacts of Bonnaroo on the local environment?

14.3.3 Social impacts of events

There has been a relatively small amount of research into the social impacts of events, when compared with the wealth of studies on economic and environmental impacts. However, all events, not just cultural events, take place in social and cultural contexts that differ from event to event and location to location. Understanding the social impacts of producing an event in a particular location is key to managing its impacts. Social impacts are 'the social outcomes that events create for particular communities of people and for society more generally' (Quinn 2013: 126).

Measurements of social impacts are usually constructed from resident perceptions of those impacts, rather than through an objective measure, due to the complexity of measuring subjective factors. This complexity makes it difficult for event managers to develop an objective social impact assessment methodology, but rather suggests that a conceptual approach is needed which identifies broad areas of impacts. Through genuine engagement with a host community, event managers might then identify particular areas of tension or positive impacts and concentrate their resources on those factors.

While most measurements of social impacts on a community assess the negative implications of hosting an event, Shone and Parry (2014) point out that events also serve an important positive function in contemporary Western society. The increasing demands of work, the

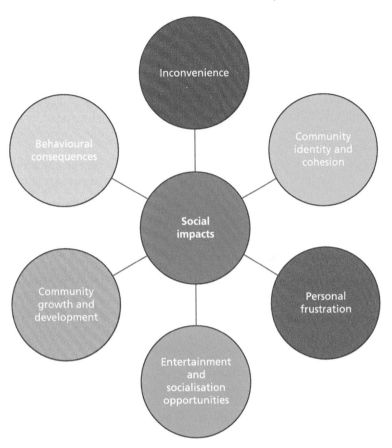

Figure 14.3 Small's social impact model
Source: Small 2007

isolating impacts of modern media and the changing of traditional family structures have all contributed to a reduction in opportunities for social interaction. Events at the community level, and those which involve communities in their planning and execution, can therefore fulfil important human needs for association and friendship.

Small (2007) conceptualises the social impacts of an event as shown in Figure 14.3.

- *Inconvenience* – This relates to the impact of hosting an event on the day-to-day lives of a community. It includes such factors as reduced parking availability, traffic congestion, increased queuing time in local shops, and extra noise and litter.
- *Community identity and cohesion* – This element is the extent to which an event increases feelings of togetherness and identity within a community. Events which are based on authentically local cultural practices, for example, will often increase residents' feelings of identity and cohesion.
- *Personal frustration* – This is the extent to which individual members of a community feel personally impacted by an event. Residents affected in this way feel that they are less important than event attendees during the event period and may therefore be resentful towards the event itself.

- *Entertainment and socialisation opportunities* – This identifies the extra opportunities for entertainment and social interaction that are available to residents due to the presence of an event. These opportunities can come from attending the event itself or from secondary effects in the community, such as increased numbers of tourists.
- *Community growth and development* – This element summarises the opportunities for skills development and other improving activities that become available to a community through hosting an event. This impact can be achieved through community involvement in the planning stages of an event as well as through participating in event-related activities, such as volunteering.
- *Behavioural consequences* – These are the new behaviours that can be introduced into a community through hosting an event. They can include increases in crime and vandalism, for example.

Olberding and Olberding (2014) provide an alternative model, which gives another categorisation of the social impacts of events that takes into account the non-economic aspects of place-marketing and community engagement associated with hosting events, some of which are social in nature:

Table 14.5 **Social Impacts of Events**
Source: Olberding and Olberding 2014

Place-marketing social impacts	Social welfare social impacts
Enhancing the destination image or brand	Building community
Increasing local pride	Strengthening social networks
	Supporting a social cause or causes

CASE STUDY 14.3

The social impacts of events: The Golden Boll Film Festival, Turkey

Location: Adana, Turkey
Event type: Cultural event

The Golden Boll Film Festival was first held in 1969 and continued intermittently until 1997 when it was cancelled due to the impacts of natural disasters and financial problems. In 2005, the festival was revived and has since been developed into an international film festival that brings together more than 700 filmmakers from Turkey and overseas and which attracts more than 1 million visitors each year. The Golden Boll Festival has become one of the most important national cultural events in Turkey and gives annual awards to Turkish films, with support from government and private sector funding.

Yolal *et al.* (2016) carried out research at the 2014 festival, through the collection of 452 self-administered questionnaires distributed to local residents who attended the festival. These were handed out at the entrances to movie theatres that were being used at the event. This research focused on the contribution that the event made to the well-being of attendees, an area of social impact research that does not easily fit into the standard models of social impacts used in events management. Subjective well-being considers how far an attendee feels that attending an event has positively affected their life.

The study found that when residents could see the community benefits of the festival, this positively affected their own subjective sense of well-being. For personal positive social impacts to take place, it was important that residents could see the positive social impacts on their wider community. Equally important, the research found that when the quality of life for members of the local community was affected through issues like vandalism, traffic congestion and noise, local people's perceptions of their own individual social benefits from the event were more negative. Both of these findings clearly show how the external social impacts of an event are crucial in terms of satisfying local resident attendees to a major event like the Golden Boll Festival, which has a significant range of impacts on its host community.

Study activity

Using Olberding and Olberding's social impact model, analyse the information in Case Study 14.3. How can you categorise the negative social impacts according to this model and how could you develop strategies to achieve more positive outcomes?

14.4 Measuring impacts and evaluating events

To understand the impacts of an event fully, it is necessary to carry out an evaluation. This is a process of checking performance against a set of predefined criteria. It is the method by which you measure the success of an event and is the first stage of the planning process for the next event. Getz (2005: 377) sets out seven practical reasons for investing management time and resources in the process of evaluation. It enables the event manager to:

- identify and solve problems
- find ways to improve management
- determine the worth of the event or its programmes
- measure success or failure

Event impacts, sustainability and legacy

- identify and measure impacts
- satisfy sponsors and other stakeholders
- gain acceptance, credibility and support.

Evaluation should be an ongoing process that is built into the management of an event, and it should draw on a number of quantitative and qualitative sources of data. Some areas of evaluation require both kinds of data in order to arrive at a holistic understanding of a particular set of impacts.

We can see from Table 14.6 that evaluation requires the synthesis of information from three perspectives, and it is only by combining these three perspectives that a systematic evaluation can be conducted (see Figure 14.4).

Table 14.6 Evaluation data sources
Source: Adapted from Shone and Parry 2014: 312

Quantitative data	Qualitative data
Attendee statistics, including market segmentation data	Attendee perceptions
Sales figures	Interviews with attendees and staff
Financial reports and accounts	Management notes and commentary
Economic impact analysis	Social impact analysis
Environmental impact analysis	Environmental impact analysis
Social impact analysis	

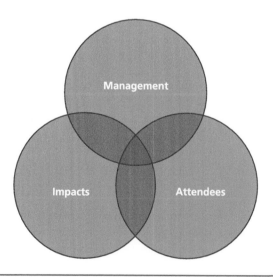

Figure 14.4 Perspectives in event evaluation

Table 14.7 **Evaluation data sets**

Evaluation perspective	Data sets	Suitable methodologies
Management	Financial information	Audit of financial records and accounts
	Attendee statistics, including market segmentation data	Analysis of booking data Attendee survey
	Management notes and commentary	Analysis of meeting records and staff communications Interviews with management staff
	Staff perceptions of the event	Interviews with staff Staff surveys
Attendees	Attendee perceptions of the event	Interviews Surveys Analysis of social media related to the event
Impacts	Economic impacts	Quantitative economic impact analysis
	Environmental impacts	Quantitative and qualitative environmental impact analysis
	Social impacts	Quantitative and qualitative social impact analysis

Table 14.7 categorises sets of data into each of these three perspectives and suggests methodologies for collecting this information.

14.5 Event sustainability

Event managers have ethical and, increasingly, legal responsibilities to produce events that are 'socially, culturally and environmentally responsible' (Getz 2005: 123). They also have responsibilities to their colleagues and stakeholders that relate to the health of their own organisation. Getz (2005: 123) goes on to state:

> Sustainable events are those which maximize benefits in each of these categories while minimizing negative impacts; sustainable events are those which can endure indefinitely without consuming or spoiling the resources upon which they depend, including the vital resource base of community goodwill and support.

Musgrave and Henderson (2015) distinguish between events which focus on the environment (often referred to as 'green' events) and events which take a more holistic approach to sustainable development, taking into account social, cultural and economic factors alongside environmental impacts.

The most widely quoted definition of 'sustainability' was set out by the United Nations World Commission on Environment and Development after the Rio Earth Summit in 1992: 'Sustainable development is development that meets the needs of the present without compromising the ability of future generations to meet their own needs' (UNCED 1992: 1.1). This overarching definition is now applied to many aspects of human activity, including business, urban planning, policy development and, progressively, events management. In recent years, growing acceptance of the probability of catastrophic climate change, as well as research into the social and cultural aspects of event impacts, has forced the events industry to reflect on its sustainability as a whole as well as the sustainability of individual events and event organisations. This reflection has prompted the development of new industry standards and awards, as well as the growth of a new kind of 'green event'.

Since 1992, the media, governments, interest groups and citizens have focused to a greater extent on issues of sustainability, and in particular on those issues associated with the environment and climate change. In these cases, most attention has been paid to the issue of resource use, especially the depletion of natural resources and the use of fossil fuels in transport and industry. To achieve the targets set by the Intergovernmental Panel on Climate Change, we need to reduce our global carbon emissions by 85 per cent by 2050, compared to 1990 levels. However, between 1990 and 2009, global carbon emissions actually *rose* by 40 per cent (Jackson 2009). This pessimistic outlook for the global climate places a moral obligation on everyone to act in a sustainable way, in order to allow future generations to live their lives in similarly favourable conditions to our own.

However, event managers work in resource-intensive economies, which place significant demands on them in terms of profitability and growth. Devoting resources to pursue what are sometimes seen as abstract moral objectives can generate difficulties in this regard, especially in a competitive operating environment. Nevertheless, there is certainly a growing sector of green events – defined by Laing and Frost (2010: 262) as an event that 'has a sustainability policy or incorporates sustainable practices into its management and operations' – with the events industry becoming more sustainable in response to external pressure from government and the broader society.

Although there is no international consensus on the relative national contributions to sustainable development and climate change reduction that should be made by each country, most governments have national policies on sustainable development. These policies relate to areas of government activity that directly impact on events management, such as transport policy, infrastructure development, energy and taxation. For instance, following the Stern Review of Climate Change Economics for the UK Treasury in 2006, the UK government passed a Climate Change Act that requires all businesses to report on their carbon emissions and sets new targets for businesses and local authorities in respect of their waste management (DECC 2008).

In addition to governments, two other external forces are driving the events industry towards greater sustainability: sponsors and consumers. Companies with a commitment to sustainability will seek to sponsor events that support this commitment and help them to broadcast it to a wider audience. The growth of corporate social responsibility (CSR) within corporations, and pressure from lobby groups, has meant that many large organisations now see sustainability as a core part of their brand and insist that this is reflected in the events they sponsor. Changing consumer preferences also have a direct impact on events management, with potential customers refusing to attend some events because of a perceived lack of sustainability.

CASE STUDY 14.4

The BS8901 standard for event sustainability

BS standards are British industrial standards that provide a guarantee to a consumer or service user that a product meets an agreed national benchmark for quality in its field. BS8901 was launched in 2007 as the standard for sustainable events. The standard is not for the event itself but for the management system through which it is produced. The aim of the standard is to provide a benchmarking process against which sustainable events management practices can be managed, giving the assurance that an event produced by a company that has been awarded BS8901 will have been produced to the highest standards of sustainability. The standard does not refer to any objective measures of sustainability, such as acceptable levels of carbon intensity for event processes or minimum standards for social impact assessment, but instead seeks to ensure rigour in sustainability planning and 'continuous improvements' in sustainable outcomes from these plans.

The awarding body, BSI Management Systems, identifies three 'tiers' of the events industry to which the standard can be applied: Tier 1 are event owners; Tier 2 are event managers; and Tier 3 are event suppliers. BSI claims that the standard can be applied equally to 'all types of events, from the local craft show to the London 2012 Olympics' (BSI 2009: 1), and, indeed the London Organising Committee of the Olympic Games has stated that it aims to be compliant with BS8901 and expects its suppliers to do the same.

BSI identifies three phases of sustainable events management:

- Phase 1 – Planning. The first phase is about planning the event and requires an organisation to define its policy and commitment to sustainable development. It requires you to identify key stakeholders, the sustainability issues and set key performance indicators for improved event sustainability.
- Phase 2 – Implementation. Phase 2 requires you to define responsibilities, ensure staff are sufficiently well trained and competent and provide sufficient resources to implement and operate your events management system. It also requires you to manage your supply chain.
- Phase 3. The final phase is about monitoring, measuring and evaluating the event in relation to the management system and the objectives set, and then taking action to continually improve event performance.

To gain BS8901 certification, an event organisation must be independently audited to ensure that its processes meet the standards set out in the detailed technical specification for the standard. Following a successful audit, the organisation can claim that it is BS8901 compliant and it is entitled to use this on its marketing material.

Study activity

As an event manager, what incentives would you have to book venues certified with BS8901 or similar standards for your events? Could you justify paying a premium rate to do so?

14.6 Event legacies

The concept of 'legacy' refers to those impacts of an event that continue to be felt long after the event has concluded. Elsewhere, these impacts are referred to as 'long-term effects' (for example, Bowdin *et al.* 2006). Typically, these are measured over years or even decades. When planning for very large and mega-events, the potential legacy benefits are often used to convince licensing authorities and investors to commit to the event. Gold and Gold (2009) note that in Olympic circles 'legacy' has acquired almost magical status in its ability to convince and persuade. Indeed, the majority of the supposed benefits of staging a mega-event tend to be expressed in terms of legacy. In 2007, the Olympic President Jacques Rogge said:

> Legacy is our *raison d'être*. It ensures that the Olympic Games are more than metres and medals . . . Values, partnership and legacy are all required to turn the Olympic Games into an enduring celebration of the human spirit. Once an Olympic City, always an Olympic City. Wherever the Games have appeared, cities are changed forever.
>
> (quoted in Gold and Gold 2009: 16)

It is tempting to view legacy in purely positive terms, but, of course, the impacts of any event can be positive or negative. Preuss (2007) sets out a series of positive and negative, tangible and intangible legacy effects associated with staging an event (see Table 14.8).

Table 14.8 **Legacy impacts**
Source: Preuss 2007

Legacy impact	Tangible	Intangible
Positive	New infrastructure	Destination image/reputation
	Urban realm improvements	Renewal in community spirit
	Increased tourism	Increased regional cooperation
	Urban regeneration	Formation of popular memories
	Additional employment	Educational opportunities
	Inward investment and company relocation	Production of new ideas and cultural forms
Negative	Debts from construction	Opportunity costs
	Debts from delivery	Socially unjust displacements
	Redundant infrastructure	Unjust distribution or resources
	Increases in property costs	

14.7 Events and the new economics

Following the economic crisis of 2008 and the global recession that followed, there has been an upsurge of interest in both new economic models and new ways of doing business, which will have a significant impact on the events industry in the future. The largest and fastest-growing sector of the industry has been the corporate sector (O'Toole and Mikolaitis 2002), but this has been hit hard by a global decline in business spending (EIBTM 2010). A period of economic restructuring in the advanced economies is now taking place, and the events industry of the future may play a different role in the public, private and third sectors from the one it does now.

The old economics is a way of thinking about the structure of society and economies from the start of the last major period of crisis and restructuring in the mid-1970s to the economic crisis of 2008. In this model, unrestrained globalisation and the individual pursuit of private profitability were seen as the preconditions for a period of endless economic growth. The measure of the success of this system was taken to be financial return, and a succession of policymakers in American and Western European governments believed that the benefits of this growth would trickle down to the less advantaged members of society, creating a situation where everyone benefited from the financial success of a few. In 2008, as a credit crunch and a banking crisis began to escalate, it became clear that this model was no longer functioning. The global connectedness of finance and the concentration on profitability above

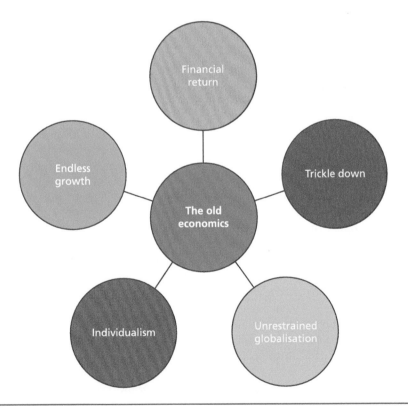

Figure 14.5 The old economics
Source: Adapted from Harvey 2007

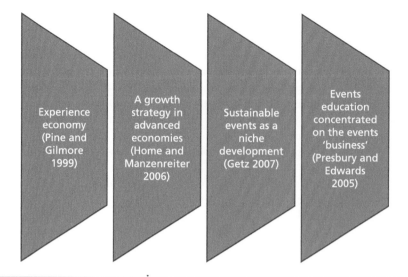

Figure 14.6 Events in the old economics

all other considerations had produced an economic system in which everyone was vulnerable to the poor judgement and mistakes of a few. During the subsequent period of public spending cuts, private sector job losses and economic contraction, increased attention has been paid to new ways of thinking about our economic system.

Under the old economics, events management was studied as a subject area that had its roots in profit-making service industries, especially tourism, and events management education was based on models from business education. Often, policymakers would look to event strategies and venue construction as forms of economic development to replace declining industries. The growth in the events sector was viewed as a consequence of the move towards the 'experience economy', in which commerce and consumption are based on participation in experiences rather than on traditional relationships of production and distribution. Until very recently, discussions of sustainability have been on the margins of events management – treated as an area of potential specialisation – in a way that has mirrored the role of sustainability within the wider economy.

The new economics (Boyle and Simms 2009) consists of a range of innovative methods for growing economies and implies a new set of relationships between the public and private sectors. Under the new economics, financial institutions and economic policy serve broader goals of increasing human welfare within limits that are ecological and social in nature. This model recognises that the old economics did not pay sufficient attention to its environmental and social impacts and seeks to address this through a concentration on localities, as opposed to global growth. It also appeals to the human capacity for cooperation, rather than individualism.

The new economics forces us to consider the future of the events industry in terms of impacts and sustainability in a much more profound way than has been the case up to now. The logic of the experience economy is now being extended beyond the business world, with some authors talking about the 'festivalisation' of everything, or the 'experience society' (Carmago 2007). In this way of thinking, events have a much greater role to play in the public and third sectors as well as the private sector. They provide the means to achieve a diverse range of social outcomes, including community cohesion, educational development, support for families and regional development. In this paradigm, sustainability has to be mainstreamed

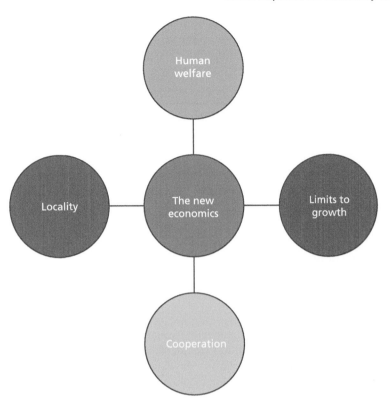

Figure 14.7 The new economics

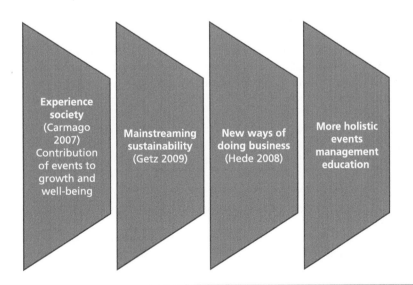

Figure 14.8 Events in the new economics

into organisations and event programmes, becoming a core element of business rather than something that can be incorporated on a piecemeal basis or merely as an attempt to gain market share with eco-conscious consumers.

Study activity

Choose a type of event (e.g. mega-event, community festival or sports event). Make the case for hosting the event in your region, first within the framework of the old economics and then within the framework of the new economics. Which of these frameworks would be more successful, and why, when presenting your proposal to:

- Local residents?
- Potential sponsors?
- Local politicians?

The new economics suggests that a more holistic approach to the study of events management is needed – one that places events within their social, economic and cultural contexts. It will also require event managers of the future to develop new skills and become aware of new business practices, two of which are outlined below.

14.7.1 Social return on investment (SROI) models

SROI is a modelling technique that accounts for broader aspects of the value created by investment than those produced by standard accounting models (Boyle and Simms 2009). It shares much with 'triple bottom line' (TBL) and 'social accounting' methods in that it considers the social and cultural impacts of spending, and it is increasingly being promoted within the fields of social enterprise and public policy.

SROI is based on principles that emphasise the specificity of the local socio-economic context of investment, and it is concerned with measuring the sustainable creation of social value. It can measure the value of the social impacts created by an event and provides a monetised indicator of this value:

SROI = value of event impacts / value of event spending

The value of the impacts is calculated by focusing on four areas (adapted from Rotheroe and Richards 2007: 34):

1 *Stakeholder engagement* – Event stakeholder objectives are identified and made central to the process.
2 *Materiality* – Focusing the analysis of impacts on those areas determined as important to the event stakeholders, who will be both within and outside an events management organisation: for example, local residents and sponsors.
3 *Impact map* – Using a cause-and-effect chain from inputs through to outputs, outcomes and impacts. Develops a pathway to understand how the event causes changes in its external environment.

Table 14.9 Event stakeholders
Source: Hede 2008

Individual level	Organisational level
Residents	Community groups
Shareholders	Government
Tourists and attendees	Sponsors
Volunteers	Media
Event employees	Business

---

4 *Appreciation of deadweight* – Calculating the proportion of outcomes that would have occurred regardless of the presence of the event.

This approach to placing a financial value on event impacts has much in common with TBL accountancy practices. It places ecological and social impacts alongside financial information to report on event performance in three categories, rather than the traditionally dominant 'bottom line' of profit and loss. Hede (2008) discusses the TBL model as reflecting the three interests of event stakeholders:

- economic interests
- social interests
- environmental interests.

Hede identifies two overarching groups of event stakeholders whose interests should be taken into account in this reckoning of event impacts (see Table 14.9).

14.7.2 Social enterprise

Social enterprises are businesses that exist to fulfil a social or environmental purpose. They generate profits, but invest those profits back into the business or into the communities in which they are based. In the UK alone, there were more than 70,000 social enterprises, employing almost a million people and generating more than £24 billion for the economy (Social Enterprise UK 2015).

Social enterprises are alternative forms of business to conventional profit-making organisations, but more entrepreneurial and less bureaucratic than registered charities. This new form of organisation is a fast-growing sector, offering opportunities to develop new businesses within the new economics model. As the events industry restructures to meet the needs of the post-financial crisis economy, social enterprise will become a more common model for events businesses to adopt. An example of an events social enterprise is Fuse Events agency, a full-service events company who have delivered events in more than 40 countries for a range of clients and who explain their social goals by saying that:

> Fuse exists to create positive social change by producing events with people and organisations with world changing ideas. We're a social enterprise, and in order to fulfil

our ambitions we provide a high quality, day-to-day service to our clients, culminating in a seamless, professional event experience.

(Fuse Events 2016: The difference)

Industry voice

Zoë Turner, Deputy Events Manager, Trinity House, London, UK

When I started working in the hospitality and events industry 20 years ago, hardly anyone knew what 'sustainability' meant. The word was never used. That said, the concept has always been there, for example: if a business was not making a profit, it simply closed down. Nowadays we would explain it by saying that the business was 'not financially sustainable'.

Sustainability as a four-pronged concept makes logical sense. By using local suppliers prices can be kept down, carbon footprints reduced and local traders are supported. The historic venue I work in has been sustainable for over 200 years. Management of it has evolved with the changing times. It wasn't always an events venue – that has happened within the last 30 years in a bid to maintain *financial* sustainability. In doing so, the *cultural* and *social* history of it have been celebrated as characteristics of the venue. The challenge is to make it and other historic houses *greener*. In order to do this, more environmentally friendly heating and air-conditioning systems (among other things) need to be installed. This will involve countless emails, letters, face-to-face meetings and site visits, which can be extremely costly. It is not always possible to achieve both alongside each other. Or, at best, it is an arduous and ongoing process.

Twenty years ago sustainability certainly didn't factor into event bookers' decision-making. Even now, sustainability is still mainly thought of in terms of environmental issues. However, in the events industry some progress has been made and there is the occasional mention now of financial sustainability, too. A lot of clients now expect the food and drinks served at their events to be ethically and locally sourced (feel free to let us know where we can find locally sourced orange juice in London!), and more attention is given to recycling and maintaining resources. But, the word 'sustainability' is still all too often used as a marketing tool in the events industry, and lip service is paid to the 'importance of sustainability', rather than a sincere all-round approach towards *social* sustainability and *cultural* sustainability, as well as *financial* and *environmental* sustainability.

Like many historic venue and event managers, I feel duty-bound to preserve the building I work in to ensure that its history is preserved for future generations to enjoy and learn from. Environmental, financial, social and cultural sustainability play a massive role in this. If it weren't for sustainability measures, in particular cultural sustainability, there would be little justification for maintaining such buildings, and then we would have significantly fewer visual reminders of our own history as a society.

By utilising so many historic buildings as event spaces, jobs are created, and the passion shown by those who work in these buildings is infectious. There is so much to benefit from maintaining them and it is vital that sustainability is thought of from all four angles. In short, sustainability should not be treated as a marketing tool. The concept of sustainability has always been there, just under a different buzz word. Event managers of all kinds should support, encourage and incorporate sustainable measures into every aspect of their events because *it is the right thing to do.*

14.8 Summary

In this chapter, a range of perspectives on the impacts of events has been covered. First, three different techniques for calculating economic impacts were explained. Second, the environmental impacts of events were explored. Finally, the social impacts of events were identified. In each of these sections, a case study was included to help readers see how these concepts can be applied in practice, while study activities gave readers the opportunity to develop their own expertise in these areas. The sections on sustainability and legacy put these individual impacts into a broader context.

The events industry, like all other industrial sectors, will have to change and adapt as the consequences of the economic crisis play out over the next ten years. The last section of this chapter dealt with some of the new economic ideas that are currently influencing business and government policy, and offered two examples of the new business practices that are emerging in the present period. It is clear that the event managers of the future will have to possess skills in impact assessment and will need to be able to apply these in an environment of increasing ecological and social change.

Further reading

Boyle, D. and Simms, A. (2009) *The New Economics: A Bigger Picture*, London: Earthscan. Begins by setting out the conditions leading up to the economic crisis of 2008 and goes on to sketch out the principles of the new economics in a practical, clear way.

Holmes, K., Hughes, M, Mair, J. and Carlsen J. (2015) *Events and Sustainability*, Clevedon: Channel View Publications. Offers an introduction to a wide range of topics, covering every aspect of sustainable development of relevance to students of events management.

Jones, M. (2014) *Sustainable Event Management: A Practical Guide*, Oxford: CABI. A text that can be used by students, researchers and events managers to understand, create and manage sustainable events.

References

Allen, J., O'Toole, W., Harris, R. and McDonnell, I. (2008) *Festival and Special Event Management*, Milton: John Wiley & Sons.

Arik, M. and Penn, D. (2005) *Economic Impact of Bonnaroo Music Festival on Coffee County: Report Prepared for Axis Ventures*, Knoxville: Axis Ventures.

Morgan, T. (2001) Cypriot's Club Culture Fear. Available at: news.bbc.co.uk/1/hi/world/europe/1417977.stm. Accessed 19 September 2010.

Bonnaroo Music and Arts Festival (2009) Home page. Available at: www. bonnaroo.com/. Accessed 12 May 2009.

Bowdin, G., Allen, J., O'Toole, W., Harris, R. and McDonnell, I. (2006) *Events Management* (2nd edn), Oxford: Butterworth-Heinemann.

Brundtland Commission (1987) Report of the World Commission on Environment and Development: Our Common Future. Available at: www.un-documents.net/wced-ocf.htm. Accessed 20 October 2010.

BSi (2009) *Make Your Event Sustainable*, London: BSi.

Carlsen, J. (2004) The Economics and Evaluation of Festivals and Events, in I. Yeoman, M. Robertson, J. Ali-Knight, S. Dummond and U. McMahon-Beattie (eds) *Festival and Events Management: An International Arts and Culture Perspective*, Oxford: Butterworth-Heinemann.

Carmago, P. (2007) Using Tourist Resources as Tools for Teaching and Creating Awareness of Heritage in a Local Community, in G. Richards (ed.) *Cultural Tourism: Global and Local Perspectives*, New York: Howarth Press.

Conference Consortium (2010) About Consortium. Available at: www. conferenceconsortium. org/about-consortium.html. Accessed 10 October 2010.

David, L. (2009) Environmental Impacts of Events, in R. Raj and J. Musgrave (eds) *Event Management and Sustainability*, Oxford: CABI.

Daejon Convention Centre (2016) *About DCC*. Available at: www.dcckorea.or.kr/. Accessed 15 December 2016.

DC Convention (2007) Washington Convention Centre Authority Concludes Bond Sale: Press Release. Available at: www.dcconvention.com/PressRoom/PressReleases/PressReleasePages.aspx?id=93&year=2007. Accessed 20 October 2010.

Department for Energy and Climate Change (DECC) (2008) Climate Change Act 2008. Available at: www.legislation.gov.uk/ukpga/2008/27/contents. Accessed 1 November 2010.

Derrett, R. (2003) Making Sense of How Festivals Demonstrate a Community's Sense of Place, *Event Management*, 8: 49–58.

Dwyer, L., Mellor, R., Mistilis, N. and Mules, T. (2000) Forecasting the Economic Impacts of Events and Conventions, *Event Management*, 6: 191–204.

EIBTM (2010) Trends and Market Report. Available at: www.eibtm.com/page. cfm/T=m/ Action=Press/PressID=5. Accessed 5 August 2010.

Fuse Events (2016) *The Difference*. Available at: http://fuseevents.org/about/the-difference/. Accessed 15 December 2016.

Getz, D. (2005) *Event Management and Event Tourism*, New York: Cognizant Communication.

Getz, D. (2007) *Event Studies*, Oxford: Butterworth-Heinemann.

Getz, D. (2009) Policy for Sustainable and Responsible Festivals and Events: Institutionalisation of a New Paradigm, *Journal of Policy Research in Tourism, Leisure and Events*, 1 (1): 61–78.

Getz, D. and Andersson, T. (2008) Sustainable Festivals: On Becoming an Institution, *Event Management*, 12: 1–17.

Gold, J. and Gold, M. (2009) Riding the Mexican Wave: Deciphering the Meaning of Olympic Legacy, in J. Kennell, E. Booth and C. Bladen (eds) *People, Place, Enterprise: Proceedings of the First Annual Conference on Olympic Legacy*, London: GUP.

Hanly, P. A. (2012) Measuring the economic contribution of the international association conference market: An Irish case study. *Tourism Management*, 33 (6), 1574–1582.

HQ (2016) *The ICE Kraków Congress Centre is set to make a difference*. Available at: www. meetingmediagroup.com/article/the-ice-krak-w-congress-centre-is-set-to-make-a-difference. Accessed 15 December 2016.

Harvey, D. (2007) *A Brief History of Neoliberalism*, Oxford: Oxford University Press.

Hede, A.-M. (2008) Managing Special Events in the New Era of the Triple Bottom Line, *Event Management*, 11: 13–22.

Horne, J. and Mazenreiter, W. (2006) An Introduction to the Sociology of Sports Mega-events, *Sociological Review*, 54 (2): 1–24.

ICE Kraków (2016) *About ICE*. Available at: www.icekrakow.com/information/about-ice. Accessed 15 December 2016.

Jackson, T. (2009) *Prosperity without Growth: Economics for a Finite Planet*, London: Earthscan.

Kennell, J. and Sitz, R. (2010) Greening Bonnaroo: Exploring the Rhetoric and Reality of a Sustainable Festival through Micro-ethnographic Methods, paper presented at the Global Events Congress IV, Leeds, 14–16 July.

Laing, J. and Frost, W. (2010) How Green Was My Festival: Exploring Challenges and Opportunities Associated with Staging Green Events, *International Journal of Hospitality Management*, 29: 261–267.

Lee, C. K., Lee, M. and Yoon, S. H. (2013) Estimating the Economic Impact of Convention and Exhibition Businesses, Using a Regional Input–Output Model: A Case Study of the Daejeon Convention Center in South Korea. *Asia Pacific Journal of Tourism Research*, 18 (4), 330–353.

Morgan, A. and Condliffe, S. (2006) Measuring the Economic Impacts of Convention Centre and Event Tourism: A Discussion of the Key Issues, *Journal of Convention and Event Tourism*, 8 (4): 81–100.

Morgan, T. (2001) Cypriots' Club Culture Fear. Available at: http://news.bbc.co.uk/1/hi/world/europe/1417977.stm. Accessed 19 September 2010.

Musgrave, J. and Henderson, S. (2015) A Pathway to Sustainable Event Management, in C.M. Hall, S. Gössling and D. Scott (eds) *The Routledge Handbook of Tourism and Sustainability*, Abingdon: Routledge.

Olberding, J. C. and Olberding, D. J. (2014) The Social Impacts of a Special Event on the Host City: A Conceptual Framework and a Case Study of the Cincinnati Flying Pig Marathon, *International Journal of Hospitality and Event Management*, 1 (1), 44–61.

O'Toole, W. and Mikolaitis, P. (2002) *Corporate Event Project Management*, New York: John Wiley & Sons.

Pine, B. J. and Gilmore, J. H. (1999) *The Experience Economy*, Cambridge, MA: Harvard Business Review.

Presbury, R. and Edwards, D. (2005) Incorporating Sustainability in Meetings and Event Management Education, *International Journal of Event Management Research*, 1 (1): 30–45.

Preuss, H. (2007) The Conceptualisation and Measurement of Mega Sport Event Legacies, *Journal of Sport and Tourism*, 12 (3–4): 207–227.

Quinn, B. (2013) *Key Concepts in Event Management*, London: Sage.

Raj, R., Walters, P. and Rashid, T. (2009) *Events Management: An Integrated and Practical Approach*, London: Sage.

Rotheroe, N. and Richards, A. (2007) Social Return on Investment and Social Enterprise: Transparent Accountability for Sustainable Development, *Social Enterprise Journal*, 3 (1): 31–48.

Saveriades, A. (2007) A Sociometric Examination of Perceptions of the Impact of Contemporary Tourism on Society in the Tourist Resort of 'Ayia Napa', Cyprus: A Qualitative Approach, *Society and Leisure – Montreal*, 30 (1): 177–195.

Shone, A. and Parry, B. (2014) *Successful Event Management: A Practical Handbook* (4th edn), Andover: Cengage Learning.

Small, K. (2007) Social Dimensions of Community Festivals: An Application of Factor Analysis in the Development of the Social Impact Perception (SIP) Scale, *Event Management*, 11: 45–55.

Social Enterprise Coalition (2010) About Social Enterprise. Available at: www.socialenterprise. org.uk/pages/about-social-enterprise.html. Accessed 9 November 2010.

Social Entreprise UK (2015) *State of Social Enterprise Survey 2015*, London: Social Enterprise UK.

Tohmo, T. (2005) Economic Impacts of Cultural Events on Local Economies: An Input–Output Analysis of the Kaustinen Folk Music Festival, *Tourism Economics*, 11 (3): 431–451.

Tribe, J. (2005) *The Economics of Recreation, Leisure and Tourism* (3rd edn), Oxford: Butterworth-Heinemann.

United Nations Commission on Environment and Development (UNCED) (1992) Our Common Future. Available at: www.un-documents.net/ocf-02.htm. Accessed 1 November 2010.

Yolal, M., Gursoy, D., Uysal, M., Kim, H. L. and Karacaoğlu, S. (2016) Impacts of Festivals and Events on Residents' Well-being. *Annals of Tourism Research*, 61, 1–18.

Zifkos, G. (2015) Sustainability Everywhere: Problematising the 'Sustainable Festival' Phenomenon, *Tourism Planning & Development*, 12 (1), 6–19.

Chapter 15

Events and the media

Contents

15.1 Aims

By the end of this chapter, students will be able to:

- define event media;
- understand the role of the media in modern events;
- identify what is required to manage media coverage of events;
- predict the challenges inherent in modern coverage of events.

15.2 Introduction

This chapter focuses on media coverage as a mediated reality between those directly involved in an event and its wider stakeholders. Media coverage has been responsible for revitalising certain events and even re-engineering how events are organised and delivered. Media coverage not only increases sponsorship exposure among a much wider audience but significantly shapes international perceptions of events, resulting in important new challenges to their planning, management, delivery and legacies. In some cases, it can overshadow the main event objectives, and even 'hijack' the impact of their planned outcomes. However, many of the challenges that event planners face in obtaining media coverage, whatever the size of the event, can be overcome, and an attempt to understand how the media operates might well contribute to a more successful event.

Event managers face an increasingly challenging media environment, irrespective of geographical location, and they cannot ignore the importance of being effective managers of the media. Like it or not, the media plays an important role in our lives generally and we have no option but to work closely with the media, and to learn how they operate. There has been a proliferation of media training courses, many of them run by former journalists and broadcasters. The increased fragmentation of the media in general means that there are many more points of contact for event planners to consider. They must also come to terms with social media platforms, such as Facebook, Instagram, Twitter and YouTube, which present fresh opportunities and challenges. They must bear in mind that the media have the potential to make or break an event, so they should understand how to make best use of this influence, while at the same time ensuring that it does not destroy the reputation of an event.

The media, while very powerful and hungry for stories, works in a particular way, so an understanding of its rituals and procedures should lead to a much stronger mutual working relationship. It is therefore vital to understand all aspects of the media, its key players and the roles they occupy. The event team should make informing the media an important part of its overall tasks, in an attempt to maintain interest in the run-up to an event and during its staging, and should even consider employing a media specialist if the budget allows. There should also be a plan to deal with any stories that might damage the reputation and standing of the event, with crisis management built into the overall event planning process.

15.3 What is the media?

The media can be defined as any communication medium that is designed and managed by an owner with the aim of informing or entertaining an audience (Katz 2007). Also referred to as the mass media, it is a form of communication that operates on a large scale, reaching and involving most people in society. Originally, the written word was the most effective way of communicating with an audience, but this was superseded by the arrival of radio and television. Distinctions were then made between print and electronic media. However, given the introduction of web-based technology, a newspaper can now be in print format and/or in an electronic version on a website (Katz 2007). Such is the rise of the web as a means of obtaining news that many newspapers globally have closed and many more are now facing closure as their sales plummet. Others have skillfully managed the transition from hard copies to web-based and can offer both versions to their readers. Those that have embraced new technology are thriving and the immediacy of the web means that they often require more copy since they constantly update their stories.

There is much discussion about what the media is, and the elements shown in Table 15.1 (adapted from Katz 2007) are somewhat different from those itemised by McQuail (2002), who suggests that the media consists of newspapers, magazines, film, radio, television and recorded music. To this, we must add social media, such as Facebook, Instagram, Pin and Twitter, which offer opportunities to events managers to pass information on to their stakeholders, as will be discussed in more detail later in this chapter.

Newspapers and TV stations, in particular, invest heavily in their websites as they are an important platform, which require a constant supply of stories and regular updating. For many people, the media fills a large part of their social and leisure time, so the stories and images relayed can be highly influential. It is the role of the media to convey information and entertainment to a variety of audiences, ranging from individuals to companies and other organisations (Katz 2007). While the media is not always seen as a positive force in advanced societies, and it is often considered too powerful, it cannot be ignored. It communicates with millions of people (Williams 2003), and it has the potential to change their attitudes towards specific events. It is worth considering the various components of the media in order to establish which represents the best choice when looking to communicate with an event audience.

15.3.1 Television

Television is possibly the most powerful of all media, given the size of the audience it can reach and the fact that it can be viewed on demand not only on television sets, but also on portable devices and mobile phones. Some television stations are owned by the state, and as a general rule they do not attract advertising revenue, whereas others are owned by private companies and usually generate income from advertising and sponsorship. The majority of these stations are viewed predominantly in their countries of origin, so they usually target the domestic market, although some programmes can be viewed in more than one country.

Table 15.1 **Components of the media**
Source: Adapted from Katz 2007

Print media	Electronic media	Social media
Newspapers	Television	Facebook/LinkedIn
Magazines	Radio	Twitter/Pin
Outdoor billboards	Internet	Blogs
Direct mail	Podcasts	Instagram

Satellite television companies are generally multi-country and may specialise in specific areas, such as music and sports. Event managers can send information to television news programmes or specialist programmes in order to publicise their events. In some cases, they might secure a television interview, although this is advisable only if they are competent and feel confident that they will be able to hold their own with the interviewer (Baines *et al.* 2005).

It is perhaps harder to gain publicity on television than in any other media, but that should not put off the ambitious event manager, as the sheer size of the audience means that the event may well receive a significant and instant boost if it *is* covered on TV. Where an event receives coverage in the media, it is possible that their website will receive a dramatic increase in the number of visits.

15.3.2 Radio

The number of radio stations has grown significantly over the past twenty-five years, primarily through the proliferation of new private stations, where the advancement of technology means that it is much easier and possibly cheaper to set up new radio channels. Most countries also have national radio stations that are usually aimed at specific target markets. A private commercial station tends to look for news items to fit into its hourly bulletins, with local stations concentrating on local events. Event managers should look to establish links with their local stations, and even target specific programmes or presenters, because they offer a targeted audience and can deliver instant news. This can be especially useful if attendees need to be given last-minute information, for instance, about traffic delays or congestion near the event.

15.3.3 Newspapers

There are significant differences in the availability of national and local newspapers, depending on the country. For instance, in the USA, there are many regional newspapers; whereas in the UK, national tabloids enjoy much wider circulations than local newspapers. All newspapers attempt to inform and entertain their readers through print and photographs. While they generate some revenue through direct sales, their main income comes from advertising, so they cannot afford to offend the companies and organisations that buy advertising space.

15.3.4 Magazines

It is important to recognise the two broad categories of magazine: consumer magazines, aimed predominantly at individuals; and trade magazines, which are read mainly by people who work in a particular business area. Event managers tend to make use of both categories to promote their events: for instance, details of a music festival might appear in both the *NME* and in trade magazines aimed at the catering industry. All magazines produce reader data and media packs on their websites to encourage companies to buy advertising space, and these are useful for the event manager to check whether the attendee profile of their event matches that of some of the magazine readers.

15.3.5 Social networking sites

The proliferation of social media opportunities presents a number of challenges for event managers and it is imperative to be an innovator and embrace social media. Social networking sites – such as Facebook, LinkedIn, Pin, Instagram and Twitter – offer new ways of communicating with stakeholder groups and are now essential. According to the Sports Business Group report in 2015, Manchester United FC had just over 4 million Twitter followers, whereas Real Madrid and FC Barcelona had 14.4 million and 13.8 million. These sites bring together like-minded people and allow them to maintain dialogue with family, friends or business associates. Companies are increasingly using these sites to build contact lists of people who are interested in particular events or products. Glastonbury Festival also has around 580,000 Twitter followers and 700,000 followers on its official Facebook page.

15.4 The role of the media in events management

When considering the media and events management, we must first look at the media's impact on society as a whole. A news story has the potential to reach millions of people within a very short period of time. A video on a social network site can reach millions in just a few days. Such is the power of the media that political groups are increasingly using it to inform the public of their activities. In terms of events management, the media plays a significant role in informing stakeholder groups about the importance of events, while at the same time making some events the focus of their stories. The 2010 Commonwealth Games in Delhi were dominated by media stories of poor facilities and problems with stadium management, even though, in reality, this was a relatively successful event in a developing country.

It might be argued that event managers are in competition with each other in pursuit of media coverage to increase interest in, or encourage people to attend, their events. The fact is that the events industry needs the media to help make events more prominent and increase awareness levels. With heightened awareness, there is a greater chance of enhanced ticket sales. Given the increase in satellite communication, the media is able to transfer information about events instantly all around the world to media partners in other countries. Bowdin *et al.* (2010) even suggest that some events may be created for media consumption, and that a TV audience may dwarf the number of attendees. They then suggest that 'integration of the event with the media provides greater exposure to the event' (Bowdin *et al.* 2010: 638), which means that if the event organisers treat the media as potential partners, the latter will be more likely to be supportive.

The goal of developing relationships with the media is, therefore, to generate publicity, which Kitchen (1997: 7) states is 'information from an outside source used by the news media based on its news value or information perceived by the media as relevant to its audiences'. When the media endorses information in this way, it improves the event's relationship with its target audience. Even murderous regimes have understood the importance of utilising the power of the media: for instance, in 1978, the Argentinian military dictatorship hired a leading US public relations agency to improve its public image in the run-up to the FIFA World Cup.

15.4.1 Media events

A media event is either planned specifically to appeal to the media or simply receives extensive coverage because various media outlets feel it will be of interest to their audiences. While it is difficult to manufacture a media event, recognising when this happens is critical and might even form part of an overall plan for dealing with the media. These events are usually significant, sometimes on a global scale. They have been called 'a unique media genre that results when television's visual and narrative power taps into public fascination with a story that transcends daily experience' (Rivenburgh 2002: 32). People feel compelled to watch such an event, and in many cases broadcasters will adjust their schedules in order to cover it and audiences will adjust theirs in order to see it. One example is when a national sports team progresses into the final of a major tournament. Even though the rights to broadcast the match might be owned by one key media supplier, others will still cover the story in depth.

15.4.2 Media rights

Media companies often pay a premium to secure the rights for a particular event and compete with their rivals to secure these exclusive rights. The value of these broadcasting agreements is based on the amount of interest that such events generate among a television audience (which, for many major events, is likely to be a global audience). In the case of a major music festival, the media company that pays for exclusive broadcasting coverage will also invest heavily in promoting its involvement in the event and producing additional programmes in order to maximise the return on their investment. For instance, it might make a programme about setting up the event or one that shows its history. This programme might then hold a competition in which audience members can win tickets for the event or meet performers. This means that event organisers must be open to collaboration and see these extra events as important for improving awareness.

When a media company pays for exclusivity, it is important that the event manager does not breach the conditions of their agreement and allow rival broadcasters too much access. So, for instance, they should be careful not to leak stories to rival media groups or even answer every question that they receive about the event.

In order to improve the ratings for its main coverage of an event, a television company might include features in its main news programming. This reflects the importance of the event to the broadcasting organisation, rather than its importance to a wider audience, but it can serve to increase the event's popularity.

Study activity

For the following day-long events, suggest news stories that you think will be covered by the media. You should focus on participants, sponsors, attendees and spectators, and should suggest which media outlets might be interested in the stories.

1 A local music festival, with 50 acts, whose aim is to promote multi-culturalism in the community.
2 An international trade fair for food and drink companies, with at least forty countries represented.
3 A 5-kilometre fun run in fancy dress to raise money for disadvantaged children.

15.5 The media and links to stakeholders

Table 15.2 identifies stakeholder groups that are important to event managers. Each of these stakeholders can influence the outcome of an event, so the event manager must attempt to communicate with all of them. As it is difficult and resource-intensive for the event manager to contact such a wide range of stakeholders individually, they can provide information to the media in the hope that this will then be shared with the wider stakeholder group. While the media is listed as just one of a number of stakeholder groups in the table, it is a crucial resource for event managers as it can be used to influence all of the other groups. Event managers must also be aware of the credibility of the media outlets that they use and ensure that the media audience is not too different from their own target audience. Arts events are very careful about their choice of media partners as they have to protect the image of their events.

Event organisers have access to a range of communication tools with which they can reach the most important stakeholder groups. It may well be impossible to communicate directly with all of the stakeholder groups listed in Table 15.2, perhaps due to budget or time constraints, so it is essential to prioritise them on the basis of their importance to the event. For large groups (such as attendees), media with a broad reach (such as television and newspapers) may be most effective, and these media might also communicate a message to other stakeholder groups.

However, event managers need to ensure that they always communicate with particular stakeholder groups in the most appropriate way, which means tailoring messages to specific audiences. For instance, it is probably advisable to contact government departments personally – through letters and an invitation for face-to-face meetings. Many media organisations – especially local radio stations and newspapers – are increasingly reliant on receiving news rather than using their own journalists to find it, so they are more likely to reproduce press releases. One way of engaging the media with a new event or a mass participation event, is to invite members of the media to take part in the event. Journalists who are offered a place in a celebrity golf or football day or invited to take part in a festival or carnival are more likely to cover the event, which will usually lead to more media coverage.

Table 15.2 Stakeholder groups and communication tools

Stakeholder groups	Communication tools
Attendees at the event (past, present or future)	Television, social media
	Radio
Event suppliers/agents	Newspapers
Community (location of event)	Magazines
Media	Specialist publications
Financial community/investors	Website
Sponsors	Social media (Facebook, Twitter, etc.)
National/local government	Personal letters
Employees/volunteers	Meetings
Potential employees/volunteers	Newsletter
Opinion leaders or formers	Direct mail and social media

Study activity

What are the key messages that an event organiser should be trying to get across to their stakeholders? For an event of your choice, identify the most important stakeholders and show which messages you should target at each stakeholder group.

CASE STUDY 15.1

Working effectively with the media: lessons from the Rugby World Cup, 2015

Location: Australia, 2015
Event type: sporting event
Attendees: 1 million, TV audience 75 million

When a major sponsor for the Rugby World Cup threw a beach party for the hundreds of journalists, broadcasters and media professionals who had gathered to cover the event, the world's press embraced the event and took part in the activities that had been organised for them. This event would give the media access to the players in the England team in a more relaxed environment, but to what extent did they realise that the party was part of the sponsor's elaborate PR plan and that their principal aim was to gain minutes of TV coverage and pages of free write-ups in leading magazines, newspapers and websites? Not only were the press and England players invited, the sponsor also took the opportunity to include a number of their customers who had entered competitions as part of the sales promotion campaigns.

Given the relaxed nature of the event, the sponsor was able to use a number of innovative ways to maximise coverage of their logo, including a number of flags on the beach and a sand sculpture of a rugby ball and shirt that featured the logo of the sponsor. All players were also kitted out in beachwear that was covered in their name, meaning that virtually any picture taken of a player was likely to feature the sponsor's logo, which would again be featured in the photographs that made their way into the media. Inviting the press to play small games of beach rugby with key players meant that the event received a number of dedicated pages of coverage with journalists and broadcasters keen to show their audiences that they were playing rugby with the players who were rapidly becoming heroes back at home as a result of securing a place in the final. The players themselves had been well-briefed by the Public Relations Agency that represented the sponsor, who understood that extra media coverage would also improve their value as a brand, and so gave several interviews and featured in many photographs taken with members of the media.

The key to this success was that the beach party was a much-needed event for the media, many of whom had spent the entire three weeks away from family and friends at home and needed an opportunity to relax. While the events took part on a Sydney beach, the sponsor also made sure that they provided facilities for the media to carry out their jobs effectively with tents set up with internet access and secretaries on hand to provide admin support. The cost of setting up this beach party is estimated to have been £20,000 but the amount of media coverage gained from the event more than justified this outlay, and once the media had carried out their interviews and taken photographs they were then able to relax and enjoy the party. All parties were pleased with the outcome of the event and the sponsor had shown how to work closely with the media, develop better relationships and gain more publicity for the event, as well as showing other event organisers that creative ideas can help to maximise publicity by working closely with the media.

15.5.1 Working with journalists

Many event managers do not have experience of working closely with journalists. However, along with many other people, they may have preconceived ideas of what journalists are like. Many commentators talk of a new breed of journalist who could not be more different from the traditional reporter, who was forever in pursuit of a lead, knocking on doors and interviewing members of the public. These new journalists spend most of their time at their desks, trawling the internet and looking at Twitter leads to find the latest information that they need for their stories. This phenomenon presents new opportunities for any event organiser who is willing to provide the media with consistently good copy. Given the value of achieving widespread media coverage for events, event managers should do everything in their power to make the journalist's job as easy as possible by supplying them with high-quality material, and in some cases, aiming to be a friend of the press. Once a journalist starts to trust a particular source of information, he or she is likely to keep going back for more stories.

Since newspapers are still often produced both digitally and in print, there is an even greater demand for stories. Events are perfectly equipped to meet this demand, and frequently provide great news stories that are usually well received by the journalists' audiences. Developing effective long-term relationships with the media should, therefore, be the goal of every event manager.

15.5.2 Working with the media at an event

Given the importance of the media to the event organisers, it is vital to ensure that their needs are catered for at events. It is important to designate specific media areas where the reporters can produce the material that is needed for their particular medium. This usually entails setting up a press room with refreshments and perhaps even offering administrative support – all of which should make it easier for the journalists to write their (hopefully favourable) copy. Elsewhere, the media should be provided with photo opportunities and press passes that enable them to move around the venue with ease. Key features of new stadiums is their investment in the media, with a main press area and even space for the many photographers who attend an event. Good Wi-Fi access is a must for the media at your event.

15.6 Media management

Getz and Fairley (2004) considered the management of media at four different sporting events in Australia. Their paper contained interesting observations about the means employed by event organisers to develop their relationships with the media, and these can serve as guidelines for other event managers:

1 Employ a media relations officer to feed stories to the media and create media interest.
2 Advertise in local magazines or newspapers, and especially in special interest magazines, to promote the event.
3 Develop an event website to provide information to the media and other stakeholders.
4 Host media-familiarising tours of the event.
5 Organise media events to involve the media more closely with the event.
6 Monitor all media coverage, possibly through an agency.
7 Keep sponsors regularly informed of media coverage.
8 Employ a professional camera operator to capture images.
9 Create video 'postcards' and stories to send to the media.
10 Employ a photographer to develop digital images to send to the media.
11 Develop long-term media relationships.

This is a crucial checklist for event managers and highlights areas where new skills or additional resources might be required because a number of these options may stretch the budgets of smaller events. It is important to recruit the right people for these tasks, since dealing with the media demands considerable experience and understanding of how the system works. Employing a media relations officer will probably represent a new cost for the event, but hiring such a specialist, such as a former journalist – someone who is comfortable dealing with the media and knows how to create stories – should show a return on the investment. There might even be an experienced media person who might volunteer for this role, in return for access to the event.

Study activity

How would you suggest an event manager might maximise coverage of their event in the media? Use Getz and Fairley's framework to help develop your answers.

15.6.1 Creating news stories

It is important to understand the relationship between the media and advertisers when submitting information to the former. Advertising revenue usually represents the largest income stream for a media organisation, especially a small-scale one, so placing an advert for an event in the local paper will not only provide information for the target audience but will help to build up a close, mutually beneficial relationship with the newspaper as well. Some publications also feature 'advertorials' – combined adverts and news stories. These can be a useful way of increasing the column inches devoted to an event. After all, the newspaper's editor might decide that an event is worth only four lines and no photo on an inside page, rather than the front-page splash that the event organiser had expected. Nevertheless, an experienced media relations officer should understand that any amount of coverage is valuable and should also know how to measure its impact.

There will be several opportunities to work closely with the media during larger events, including tours to the venue to give journalists more insight into the event. The media also now make extensive use of websites to gather information, so setting one up should be a priority for any event manager. Obviously, the website should be carefully managed to ensure that it releases only the appropriate information to the media and other stakeholders.

The event organiser must collect and monitor data about all the media coverage that has been generated, either by members of the media themselves or through press releases. While this research can be carried out by the event team itself, it might be better managed by a specialist agency that has the resources to monitor global media coverage as well as local stories. Remember that an event such as the annual Nuremberg Toy Fair can receive media attention in around 100 different countries and it would be difficult to monitor global coverage from their base in Germany. It is also important for sponsors to be kept informed of any coverage that they have received, since sponsorship deals can sometimes be improved on the basis of early positive coverage.

To reiterate a valid point: event organisers should try to help the media as much as possible. For instance, an event is much more likely to receive a favourable write-up if the journalist is sent a pin-sharp digital image rather than a poor-quality photo (Getz and Fairley 2004). Video 'postcards' and stories are also useful tools for publicising an event. Some event managers might think that the media should incur the costs of producing such material, as they will be using it to fill their pages or their news bulletins. However, the initial outlay will be recouped many times over if the material forms the basis of a five-minute segment on a local news programme or a half-page feature in a newspaper.

The event manager should strive to produce media kits and press packs that give more information than a simple press release, and they should present it in a format that the media can use immediately (Shone and Parry 2010). This means employing people who can provide good content and who understand the media business.

15.6.2 Media and sponsorship

As we saw in Chapter 7, sponsorship is an important element in events management. While media organisations sometimes sponsor events and promote their links to them, they are not always willing to promote other event sponsors in their coverage. They will usually mention a title sponsor – if the event officially carries the name of that sponsor – but at other times they will instruct their camera operators to avoid showing a sponsor's name, particularly during interviews that take place with sponsors' names and logos in the background. Consequently, many sponsors' logos are only partially shown or are out of focus during TV coverage of events.

Why do the broadcasters go to such lengths to keep the sponsors' names out of shot? The answer is simply that they are trying to protect their own advertisers (if they are a commercial station) or are trying to prevent sponsors from gaining free air time and name awareness (if they are state-owned). When the NFL cover events at Wembley Stadium in London, the stadium managers have to cover any location outside the stadium that might feature the name of a sponsor from a previous event. Nevertheless, sponsors will pay heavily for events that receive wide media coverage, as these give them golden opportunities to expose their names to a large audience.

There is clearly a link between the media and sponsorship, and the event manager must be aware of its importance. The aim of the event manager should be to gain widespread media coverage for their event and then to use that coverage to leverage better sponsorship deals. Having secured these deals, they should work with the sponsors to devise a plan for maximum media presence during the event. Of course, television coverage of an event like a music festival might also generate more interest in the event itself and encourage viewers to attend the following year.

15.6.3 Media and logistics

One important consideration for an event manager is the area that is assigned to the media, because, as Bowdin *et al.* (2010) suggest, their presence might well be disruptive. This is particularly true when the arena has limited space, as is the case at many sporting events. How much space will be needed for technical support staff, and where will they stay if they need to be present at the event for more than one day? At mega-events, such as the Olympics, as many as 8,000 journalists might cover an event with only 2,000 participants (Horne 2007).

Specialist press areas are created for many major events. In the case of major sporting events, such as the FIFA World Cup Final, journalists tend to occupy areas that are converted back to seating areas for spectators once the main event has concluded. In the case of the London Olympics the Media Centre was housed in the Orbit, a huge tower that was converted into a visitor centre after the Olympic Games with panoramic views across London.

CASE STUDY 15.2

NBA and European football television contracts

Many sporting events receive significant income through the sale of media rights. In most cases, the largest figure comes from television rights. Clearly, many events make for excellent television programmes that generate high viewing figures, so media companies are prepared to pay much more than the event organisers could possibly generate in ticket sales. Such is the value of these media deals that the broadcasters wield significant influence over the event organisers and even dictate when some events take place. For instance, Monday night football games – which are now so common in television schedules around the world – were initiated by media companies looking to fill a previously little-watched slot. Many events are now timed to suit the largest global TV audiences, rather than the live attendees or even the local TV audience. This has certainly had an impact: several studies have shown that attendance at the event itself usually falls when a game is shown live on television (Borland and Macdonald 2003; Forrest *et al.* 2006; Buraimo *et al.* 2010).

The figures in Table 15.3 show that the television rights for the NBA were around $500,000 a year in 1980, but this has now risen to beyond $1 billion per year. This deal allows media companies to televise all of the games, and to show live action on internet channels or through mobile technology. It is around 20 per cent higher than the previous deal and four times higher than the deal struck in 2001. It was unclear if the value of these deals would continue to rise or if media companies had reached their limits, but the latest round has shown another significant increase.

In 2008, the new TV deal for the English Premier Football League began. It was worth £1.7 billion over three years, covered 138 live matches, and was granted to Sky and Setanta, although the latter went bankrupt not long after the

Table 15.3 NBA cable television contracts
Source: Inside Hoops 2011

Year	Broadcaster(s)	Value of contract
1979–80 to 1981–82	USA	$1.5 million/3 years
1982–83 to 1983–84	USA/ESPN	$11 million/2 years
1984–85 to 1985–86	TBS	$20 million/2 years
1986–87 to 1987–88	TBS	$25 million/2 years
1988–89 to 1989–90	TBS/TNT	$50 million/2 years
1990–91 to 1993–94	TNT	$275 million/4 years
1994–95 to 1997–98	TNT/TBS	$397 million/4 years
1998–99 to 2001–02	TNT/TBS	$840 million/4 years
2002–03 to 2007–08	TNT	$2.2 billion/6 years
2008–09 to 2015–16	ABC/ESPN/TNT	$7.4 billion/8 years
2016–17 to 2025–26	ESPN/Turner	$2.6 billion annually

deal had been signed. While this deal is the highest for any football league in the world, it is still dwarfed by those negotiated by American sports. However, the new deal is now worth about £5.1 billion over three years, which puts it at a similar level to sports in the USA.

Like the NBA, the Premier League negotiates deals on behalf of all the clubs in the league. However, Spanish football clubs negotiate their own deals. This means that the two biggest clubs – Real Madrid and FC Barcelona – account for 43 per cent of all football TV revenue in Spain, with the remaining 57 per cent split between the other 16 clubs in the top division. This has recently been challenged by the Spanish Government who feel that the revenue should be split more equitably and are attempting to pass legislation.

Perhaps the key question, given the annual increase in payments for media rights, is just how high media companies might be prepared to go to secure exclusive rights to these major sporting events in the future. The fact that the media are now prepared to pay such huge amounts suggests that rights used to be sold far too cheaply, to the benefit of the media companies and the detriment of the clubs, so the price might well continue to rise. On the other hand, if TV deals have now peaked and start to decline, this will obviously have a significant impact on sporting events organisers, who have perhaps become too reliant on the media to finance their events. Certainly, organisers should not under-estimate the importance of negotiating media deals and should have a clear idea of the value of their product to the media.

Study activity

What do you think are the key developments in events media coverage over the past twenty years in your country, as well as globally?

15.7 The impact of media coverage on events

Media coverage – be it positive or negative – invariably has some impact on an event. Getz *et al.* (2007) found that many festival organisers in Australia and Sweden believed that the media had more impact than any other group of stakeholders. They also learned that the local media in Sweden was the most effective means of changing people's perception of a music festival (from negative to positive). The importance of generating goodwill for an event through the media is also a priority when local government has pledged its financial support to an event and needs positive feedback from the local community. In this case, communication with the community is almost entirely facilitated through media coverage.

15.7.1 Valuing media coverage

Carlsen *et al.* (2001) highlight frequent criticism of the Australian government by rival political parties and the media, who often claim that events have lost money and have had negative rather than positive impacts. By contrast, positive media coverage can certainly contribute to the success of an event, and there are a number of ways of evaluating this. Such evaluation will help the event planner to understand the impact of media coverage and will provide data that can then be used for setting objectives in future event plans.

Perhaps the most commonly held view is that any story about an event in the media is free publicity and therefore promotes the event (Dwyer *et al.* 2001). The simplest way to evaluate this impact is to time the length of the report (if it is broadcast media) or to calculate the number of column inches (if the story appears in print). However, this technique has its critics, and it is certainly the crudest way of evaluating impact. The number of tweets about an event can also be measured as well as visits to a website and these present further evaluation tools for event managers.

Cutlip and Center suggest that the first stage in assessing impact should be to compare the number of messages sent to the media with how many of those messages subsequently appear in print or on TV (Broom 2012). The next stage uses general viewing or readership figures to calculate how many people were likely to have seen the messages. Finally, more targeted research is undertaken to ascertain how the messages influenced people's attitudes to the event.

McNamara (2005) suggests that various forms of research – surveys, interviews and focus groups – should be carried out before, during and after an event to assess its impact. However, perhaps the most frequently used method for evaluating coverage in the media is advertising equivalency (see Chapter 7 for details of this technique). This is of limited use, though, because it does not take into account the quality of the coverage and the extent to which it reaches the event's target group and stakeholders. Coverage in a specialist publication about music festivals with a readership of only 20,000 might impact on many more potential attendees than an article in a regional newspaper with a readership of 100,000. Here, it is vital to understand who the key event stakeholders are and how they might best be reached through the media.

Brassington and Pettitt (2003) suggest that media coverage should be monitored for its 'tone'. While this is a subjective way of measuring coverage, the main emphasis is on trying to gauge whether the coverage is 'favourable' and/or 'prominent'. The most effective means of testing the impact of this type of coverage is to undertake attitude research before and after an event to monitor any changes in attitude. A clear example of attitude measurement was the IPSOS survey (IPSOS 2010), which showed that Londoners' attitudes to hosting the 2012 Olympic Games had changed: by July 2010, 73 per cent were in favour, compared with 69 per cent four years earlier.

15.7.2 Working with the events media

Anyone writing press or media releases must remember that the media are only interested in news stories: that is, any story that editors or producers believe will be of interest to their audiences. This can be frustrating for event managers. Their primary goal might be to inform potential attendees of the start date for a festival, but the media will only be interested in a quirky detail relating to a group of volunteers or the venue. While this generates some publicity for the event, it does not contain the main message that the organisers wish to get across. It is also important to understand that there is never enough space to cover every aspect of every story, and the media are usually inundated with stories that they generate themselves or have been given via press releases.

Media coverage is very competitive, and a newspaper might not publish an article on an event if its leading competitor has already broken the story. The quality of information sent to the media may also result in a story not being published or broadcast. Unfortunately, many press releases are simply not newsworthy as they tend to read more like adverts for the event. If we consider trying to generate coverage for a music festival, then the story might not necessarily be the festival itself, but the fact that one of the groups consists of a group of high-profile actors. The story of the festival should flow naturally from this story, but the main emphasis will remain on the group. The fact that you have reduced the event's carbon footprint might not be considered newsworthy by a major newspaper, but a specialist publication might find it fascinating. The event manager must therefore understand the priorities and interests of various media in order to increase the chances of the story being covered and reaching the target audience.

15.7.3 How to write a news or press release

A news release is sent to TV and radio stations, while press releases provide information for newspapers and magazines and social media groups. It is important to follow certain principles when sending information to the media. The event manager should research all of the specialist publications that are likely to feature events, and should consider their exact requirements and the main points of contact.

The event team should be familiar with how a newsroom operates. A local radio station that broadcasts a news bulletin every hour usually employs only a handful of staff, so they are highly unlikely to answer phones minutes before the bulletin goes out on air. The newsroom is a busy, hectic place as deadlines approach, and, as ever, event managers should do everything in their power to make the journalists' lives easier. They should not pressurise editors to cover their stories, because in the media – in contrast to other business sectors – persistence usually does not pay off and it can create the wrong impression. If the editorial team do not think a story should be covered, then that is the end of the road for that story – at least until the next opportunity to publicise it arises.

If an event manager manages to secure coverage on radio or television, obviously they should make every effort to comply with the broadcaster's wishes. For instance, if a radio station wants to conduct an interview on its breakfast show and asks the event manager to be at the studio by 6am, it would be unwise for the event manager to ask if this could be changed to 8am. Attempting to dictate the schedule to a programme editor in this way will often result in the item being dropped altogether, meaning that the event manager loses precious free publicity as well as the opportunity to communicate information to key stakeholders.

Holden and Wilde (2007) devised a template that is generally suitable for press and news releases (but always make sure that you follow publications' and broadcasters' individual guidelines for press releases, if they have them):

TODAY'S DATE

This allows the department receiving the press/news release to assess its newsworthiness. Never send out a release that was dated some time ago.

FOR IMMEDIATE RELEASE

It goes without saying that you have sent this at the right time for it to be used. If the story is not ready to be released, do not send it.

HEADING OR HEADLINE

Your target publications will probably be better at writing headlines than you are, so anything you write here is likely to be changed, but it is still worth putting down something. Practise writing headlines of fewer than ten words, and *always* include the most important and interesting points.

FIRST PARAGRAPH

Remember that the rest of the press release might not be used (or even read), so it is important that the main facts of the story are included in the first paragraph. It might read like a summary of the rest of the press release.

You should include the 5Ws: who, what, why, when and where:

- Who is the story about? (In this case the event, the team and/or the participants.)
- What are you going to do?
- Why are you going to do this?
- When will it happen? (It is important to provide dates and times.)
- Where will this event take place? (If the release is about an event that has already taken place, make this clear.)

SUBSEQUENT PARAGRAPHS

These expand on the basic information given in the first paragraph. However, try to limit the whole text to about one side of A4. If the publication/broadcaster needs more information, the editorial team will contact you. Remember that good communication is possible in very few words.

INCLUDE QUOTATIONS

Try to include a quotation in the release. This could come from a participant at the event or from a member of the management team, but you should always ensure that the journalists who receive the press release are in no doubt about who is being quoted.

'ENDS'

Centre this word at the end of the press release so that the journalist can see where it finishes.

NOTES FOR EDITORS

Here you can include some additional background information for the editor. You might re-emphasise the name of the event or its website address at this point.

CONTACT DETAILS

Make sure that the journalists can get hold of you easily if they need to follow up the story. Ensure that your phone is always switched on: if an editor needs to check something and is unable to get hold of you, the chances are that they will drop the story. Include details of your website and politely suggest that the editor can find additional information there.

PHOTOGRAPHS

Digital technology has made it much easier for everyone to produce professional-looking photographs. It is often worth including a photograph, but only if it is appropriate for your press release. Check with each publication which format they prefer. A recurring criticism is that photographs do not have sufficiently high resolution for print purposes. Remember that if the story is interesting, the publication might well send its own photographer to get a picture.

15.7.4 Avoiding problems with press and news releases

Compiling and sending out a press/news release is time consuming, so it is important to get it right. The following points should help the event manager to avoid some common mistakes when producing and distributing their releases.

15.7.4.1 An advert disguised as a release

It is natural for an event manager to want to advertise their event in the media, especially if they believe they can do so for a fraction of the cost of buying conventional advertising space. Consequently, the news release is often seen as a way of gaining maximum publicity for very little outlay. However, editorial staff will immediately throw such obviously self-serving releases straight in the bin or send the file to trash. The key to a successful release is to create a story that will be of interest to the publication's target audience while still containing a clear link to and information about the event itself.

15.7.4.2 Poorly constructed media releases

Event managers sometimes send out releases that contain mistakes, miss the publication's or broadcaster's deadline, or lack key information. Journalists are busy people, and they always have alternative stories to cover, so they will not accept these errors. Again, the release will be discarded.

15.7.4.3 Contact details are missing or incorrect

A significant amount of work goes into producing press and news releases, so it would be a terrible shame if all your effort succeeded in arousing the interest of an editorial team, only for them to be unable to get hold of you to follow up the story. Journalists work to tight deadlines, so if they cannot contact you easily and quickly, they will move on to something else.

15.7.4.4 The story has been used elsewhere

In an attempt to gain maximum coverage, many see it as standard practice to send the release to as many media contacts as possible. However, it is important to remember that some major publications will not cover a story that has already featured in the pages of a rival as it loses any feel of exclusivity and ceases to be a new story.

15.7.5 Holding a press conference

A press conference enables the event planner to assemble important members of the press, television and newspapers and facilitates a two-way flow of information. Imagine all of the most important media people in one place, all fighting to ask the key question before relaying the answer back to their readers, listeners or viewers. They will generate interest in the event and awareness levels will rise dramatically. It is a straightforward process and merely requires a venue that can comfortably accommodate all of the invited journalists, with a stage area for the event representatives.

However, we should not underestimate the amount of time that will need to be devoted to organising such an event, nor the skills and time required to answer all of the journalists' questions at the conference itself. Also, remember such conferences do impose costs on the media companies that agree to attend – they will have to dispatch camera crews, technicians and recording equipment, as well as their reporters – so it is vital not to waste their time with a poor presentation. If the ultimate goal is to persuade the general public that you are staging an important and professionally run event, then the first people you have to convince are the reporters. Thus, you should only ever arrange a press conference when you have something important to say – something that cannot be communicated in a press release.

You must also be realistic and objective about the importance of your event before arranging a press conference. They are usually worthwhile only for big, significant events. The media are likely to attend only if they believe they are going to come away with a major news story that will be of interest to their readers and viewers – so holding a press conference simply to announce the dates of an annual festival, for instance, will generally be a waste of time.

In some cases, such as when an event has received negative publicity, the event team might be desperate to call a press conference to give their side of the story. But you should always remember that you can never force the media to attend, so the story you have to tell must be of interest to them, too.

15.8 Crisis management for event managers

The one thing that any event manager dreads is that something happens at their event that impacts on the safety of spectators and participants. While in most cases events run without problems, we must be aware of the damage to our reputation should a serious incident occur and there not be a contingency for dealing with it. Crisis management (CM) planning begins with identifying crises – or 'known knowns' (Regester 2008; Horne 2007) – that might impact on an event. The next stage is to prepare a response, which will enable the event team to be ready for action should the worst happen. Crises will obviously be of interest to the media, and to other stakeholders, so the CM plan must contain key media outlets' contact details and draft press releases that, with some modifications, could be used immediately. These crisis communication plans will enable the event manager to 'deal with the media in a demanding situation' (Jefkins 1994: 52) and will hopefully prevent that 'demanding situation' from becoming a major controversy. If there is crowd disorder at a music festival, the event organisers should immediately inform the media that procedures are in place to deal with the situation and avoid injury to attendees. Of course, crowd disorder at a major festival is a great news story for the media, so they will not ignore it, but they cannot be allowed to think that it has occurred because of the organisers' negligence, as that could have disastrous consequences for the event owners. Feeding key information to the media might kill off the story before it has a chance to develop, and it also allows the event organisers to communicate with a wider audience to show that their event is professionally managed.

Regester (2008) suggests that an event organiser who reacts positively and decisively to a crisis situation might even be viewed in a more positive light once it is over. The message is quite simple for all event managers: make yourself accessible to the media and put your side of the story, as this will reduce the risk of journalists going to other sources for their information.

Study activity

There are crowd problems at the entrance to your event and ten people have been injured and taken to hospital. Thankfully, they are not seriously injured, but the press have picked up on the story and they are trying to blame your organisation for the incident. Some journalists are suggesting that you could have done more to prevent the overcrowding and a rumour is circulating that excessive drinking might have exacerbated the problem. The reputation of your event is clearly at stake, and you need to show that you are a responsible event organiser.

Produce a 100-word report in the form of a press release to show that you took all possible steps to prevent the overcrowding and address all of the accusations that are being made against you.

Case Study 15.3 illustrates the problems encountered by the media in state-controlled countries like China, and how the Western media attempt to expose government interference in events. In the case study, while the Chinese government appears to be hiding any problems from the press, the Western press are doing everything in their power to highlight any weaknesses. The lessons for event managers are that they must be aware of political intervention and indeed must be conscious of the need of governments that host mega-events, like the Olympic Games, to run them successfully. There is usually some indication of potential issues prior to an event taking place, so event organisers should monitor press coverage carefully and identify any areas that might become problematic later.

CASE STUDY 15.3

The media representation of Beijing 2008 Olympic volunteers

Location: Beijing, China
Event type: mega-event
Attendees: 7 million

Many events now rely heavily on the goodwill of volunteers to provide professional assistance and reduce their overall operating costs. Among other reasons, people volunteer simply to be part of a memorable event, to have a chance of getting close to their heroes, to meet and develop friendships with other volunteers, and to gain work experience that might enhance their chances of gaining full-time employment in the future.

Wilson (2000) defines volunteering as any activity in which time is given freely to benefit another person, group or organisation, whereas Stebbins (1996) classifies it as a leisure pursuit. The cost savings to an event organiser can be considerable: as many as 70,000 largely unpaid volunteers assisted at the 2008 Beijing Olympics.

Analysis of the media representation of volunteers at the Beijing Olympics in 2008 identified two main themes. The first was that the volunteers were mainly Chinese, altruistic and friendly, having overcome intense competition in order to participate in the event. By contrast, the second theme, mainly originating in foreign online reports, suggested that these volunteers were ineffective in their roles because they lacked essential skills and instead functioned covertly as tools of the Chinese state to promote fakery. For instance, some stories suggested that they were used as seat-fillers to make events look more successful and also acted as plain-clothes security personnel. Other reports stated that they were mistreated by the organisers and consequently did not enjoy the volunteering experience.

The foreign press also criticised the number of volunteers, their lack of training and their poor language skills. By contrast, many articles in the Chinese press emphasised that the volunteers were making huge sacrifices, but ultimately increasing their chances of future employment. It was apparent that the foreign media tended to report the negative aspects of the volunteers, while the Chinese press countered this with praise for the hard work that they were doing on behalf of the nation.

This case study shows that the international media were suspicious of China's attempts to conceal any weaknesses in its delivery of the Games, so they accused the government of using excessive numbers of volunteers to ensure that the event ran smoothly. The implication was that these volunteers were not treated as well as those at Western events, and that many of them were unhappy with their volunteer experience.

(Bladen 2010)

Industry voice

Neil Silver, Journalist and Broadcaster at major sporting events

Neil Silver is an experienced journalist and has over 20 years' experience of covering major sporting events. He now combines this role with his job as Head of the School of Media at UCFB, a private higher education institution where he delivers courses on sports media, broadcasting and journalism to students from around the world. He has written degrees in sports broadcasting, journalism and media and is highly regarded in the higher education sector for his innovative approach to teaching and learning. Neil responded to the following questions:

Tell us a little about the events that you have covered as a journalist during your career to date.

The biggest global sporting event that I covered is the Olympic Games, and in 2004 I covered the Games in Athens as the Athletics Correspondent for the Press Association. This included the training camp for Team GB in Cyprus, which provided a great opportunity to get to know the athletes before the competition started. So, for example, when Kelly Holmes won a historic double-Gold in the 800m and 1500m, she was happy to stop right in front of me in the Mixed Zone to share her joy.

I saw the other side of the coin when I worked at the London 2012 Olympics, this time as part of the Press Operations team. I was employed as a football specialist and, as well as writing match reports and articles for the Games' official wire service, my role included supervising the volunteers in the Mixed Zone and at press conferences who were writing for the news feed we supplied on a daily basis. On the subject of athletics, I also covered the Commonwealth Games in Edmonton, Canada, and then in Manchester.

Another massive global event is football's World Cup, and I covered the finals in Japan and Korea in 2002, as the Press Association's Republic of Ireland correspondent. This also started with a pre-tournament training camp, on the tiny island of Saipan, where I was involved in breaking the biggest story of the whole tournament – when the Republic's high-profile captain was sent home before a ball had been kicked. On the domestic front, I have covered a number of FA Cup finals.

In terms of major UK sporting events, I used to cover the Open Golf Championship on an annual basis, at venues ranging from Kent in the south to Scotland in the north. The biggest team event in golf is the Ryder Cup, and I covered the competition which took place at The Belfry. Tennis is a sport which takes over the headlines in the UK for a fortnight every summer with the Wimbledon Championships, and this is an event I also covered on an annual basis.

I have turned my hand to many sports, and covered events ranging from boxing world title fights, to the World Darts Championships.

In the events that you have covered, which have treated the media best? Can you tell us what an event organiser should do to help journalists who cover their events?

The best events for a journalist to cover are in the world of golf and tennis. This is because the organisers provide full transcripts of all interviews that take place with the sportsmen and women, meaning you never miss a quote.

These events will have a Helpdesk in the media centre, staffed with people who will try to answer any questions you may have.

It is a similar situation at any major event, such as the Olympics. As well as the main media centre, there will be dedicated press officers for each event, who are based at that sport's venue, and they are usually specialists in that sport who can offer a great deal of help. Compare this to a football mixed zone, which is a lottery, and the difference can be huge. In a football mixed zone you take your chances and hope that the player you want to speak to will stop and oblige. However, in an age of overpaid stars with oversized egos, it is not easy to get your preferred player to stop and talk. A friendly press officer from the club may try and steer a player to you, but beware that it may not be your first-choice player.

Do you have any examples of where journalists have been treated badly at events? You can disguise the name of the event if necessary!

Most of the worst treatment for journalists happens at football matches. The problem is, too many football clubs employ press officers who have never been journalists, and therefore do not fully understand the needs of the journalist. As a result, instead of being proactive and having a chance to control the media spin, these press officers just end up blocking genuine attempts to get a fair and accurate story, and the journalist ends up looking for alternative ways to get the story.

A recent example I can give is when I covered a midweek football match for a national newspaper which featured Doncaster Rovers visiting a London club. Doncaster had picked up a rare victory on their travels and after listening to the home manager's press conference we sat waiting for the visiting manager, Darren Ferguson (yes, the son of Sir Alex) to come upstairs and talk to the assembled media. It got to the point when I knew he just wasn't going to come, and as I needed quotes from him and was close to deadline I went down to where he would exit the stadium. A friendly home press officer gave me permission to stand by the door of the team bus (yes, I needed permission) and wait for Mr Ferguson. Yet when he came out, he told me he had already spoken to a local Doncaster journalist (while the rest of us were upstairs listening to the home manager) and I had 'missed my chance'. I pointed out that I simply wanted to ask him one or two questions about his team's important victory, yet he just brushed past me and boarded the coach. Nice. When I tried to speak to the club press officer, I discovered he had already left the stadium as he had to catch a train back to Doncaster. I will never understand why this manager could not spare me two minutes of his time to help create some positive publicity for the club and talk about some 'good' news.

Part of the blame lies with club press officers, and a particularly unhelpful one has overseen the media at Crystal Palace for a number of years. He is so bad that he does not even respond to your polite requests for interviews or information. I doubt the chairman knows that this key employee is preventing the club from attracting some positive publicity. Fortunately for me, the manager of the club is a good friend, so now I go directly to him if I have a question and I miss out the pointless press officer.

How has Twitter affected media coverage of events? Is this a medium that journalists are good at using?

Twitter has helped turn some journalists into celebrities. Henry Winter spent 20 years writing for the *Daily Telegraph* before being poached by *The Times*. While Henry is indeed one of the finest football writers in the business, I am sure his move was helped by the fact that he is the sports writer with the biggest Twitter following, of more than a million. Twitter has also given more of the spotlight to controversial journalist Piers Morgan. Although Piers is not a sports journalist, he is known for his tweets about his favourite football club, Arsenal. This, and the fact that he likes to provoke his followers, has helped him accumulate nearly 5 million followers.

Another well-followed personality is Gary Lineker. The former England striker was a truly world-class striker, and moved into television after his playing days ended. Does this mean that the popular presenter can be classed as a 'sports journalist'? Certainly, he did not have the same training and background as the likes of Henry or Piers. However, it has not stopped Gary from amassing 4.5 million followers on Twitter. I do not think that Twitter has affected media coverage of events. However, football clubs, PRs and journalists do use it to break stories and to add their opinions, so it certainly helps to shape coverage at times.

If you were advising an event manager, what advice would you give him/her if they are trying to build up a good relationship with the media?

Journalists just want to be loved. The best thing an event manager can do is to have a regular dialogue with a journalist. Talk to them, give them an insight into the event they are covering, and maybe even give them some off-the-record titbits. Make them feel part of it, and if possible give them access to the people who matter at the event. An element of trust will be required, but if the journalist doesn't let down the event manager (and there is no reason why they should), then everyone will go away happy. On a technical issue, the best thing an event organiser can do is ensure that the journalist has access to a good internet connection, whether by Wi-Fi or a hard-wired connection.

Thanks to the pressure of deadlines, a journalist wants to be able to file his or her copy on time, and having a good internet connection makes all the difference. It also allows the journalist to carry out additional research during the event. A journalist will also be happy if they are given plenty of working space, and a power point for their laptop.

15.9 Summary

The events industry is coming to terms with the importance of the media and the need to develop very strong relationships with media companies, but there is still a long way to go. The media thrive on the news stories that events present to them, which they need in order to keep their audiences entertained. Event managers and the media are entering a new area where greater emphasis is being placed on developing mutually beneficial relationships. The fragmentation of the media, and the introduction of new, digital media, such as Facebook and Twitter, also means that the event manager has to work hard to understand the changing needs of the media, and to develop new skills for working within it.

New television deals for leading sporting events are driving these events forward, and they now provide the largest revenue streams for many individual sports clubs. The case studies in this chapter have shown how the media have been largely successful in developing top-quality events by providing income for those events in return for media coverage. Obviously, event managers need to keep abreast of current deals, and they should keep a careful eye on how they develop in the future.

The media's role is changing at a rapid rate, so event managers must be prepared to devote time, energy and money to developing their relationships with the press and broadcasters. They must have a good understanding of how publicity is generated, and must be able to calculate the value of the extra awareness that this creates. Finally, they should develop an appreciation of how media organisations work, which will enable them to send out the most appropriate information at the right time.

Further reading

Broom, G. M. (2012) *Cutlip and Center's effective public relations* (11th edn), Prentice Hall. This book covers the tasks that a PR manager has to undertake.

Getz, D., Andersson, T. and Larson, M. (2007) Festival Stakeholder Roles: Concepts and Case Studies, *Events Management*, 10: 103–122. This article considers the role of stakeholders at festivals. It is one of the leading papers in this research area.

Horne, J. (2007) The Four 'Knowns' of Sports Mega-Events, *Leisure Studies*, 26 (1): 81–96. This article looks at the under-researched area of crisis management and discusses the key factors that might threaten a major sporting event.

References

Baines, P., Egan, J. and Jefkins, F. (2005) *Public Relations: Contemporary Issues and Techniques*, Oxford: Elsevier.

Bladen, C. R. (2010) Media Representation of Volunteers at the Beijing Olympics, *Sport in Society*, 13 (5): 784–796.

Borland, J. and Macdonald, R. (2003) Demand for Sport, *Oxford Review of Economic Policy*, 19 (4): 478–502.

Bowdin, G., Allen, J., O'Toole, W., Harris, R. and McDonnell, I. (2010) *Events Management* (3rd edn), Oxford: Butterworth-Heinemann.

Brassington, F. and Pettitt, S. (2003) *Principles of Marketing*, New Jersey: Prentice Hall.

Buraimo, B., Paramio, J. L. and Campos, C. (2010) The Impact of Televised Football on Stadium Attendances in English and Spanish League Football, *Soccer and Society*, 11 (4): 461–474.

Carlsen, J., Getz, D. and Soutar, G. (2001) Event Evaluation Research, *Events Management*, 6: 247–257.

Chalip, L., Green, B. and Hill, B. (2003) Effects of Sport Event Media on Destination Image and Intention to Visit, *Journal of Sport Management*, 17: 214–234.

Deloitte and Touche (2008) Football Money League Report. Available at: www.deloitte.com/view/en_GB/uk/industries/sportsbusinessgroup/b54ae8e99defd110 VgnVCM100000ba42 f00aRCRD.htm. Accessed 4 November 2011.

Dwyer, L., Mellor, R., Mistilis, N. and Mules, T. (2001) A Framework for Assessing 'Tangible' and 'Intangible' Impacts of Events and Conventions, *Events Management*, 6, 175–189.

Football Marketing (2011) Home Page. Available at: www.football-marketing. com. Accessed 2 June 2011.

Forrest, D., Simmons, R. and Buraimo, B. (2006) Broadcaster and Audience Demand for Premier League Football, in C. Jeanrenaud and S. Késenne (eds) *The Economics of Sport and Media*, Gloucester: Edward Elgar.

Getz, D. and Fairley, S. (2004) Media Management at Sport Events for Destination Promotion: Case Studies and Concepts, *Events Management*, 8: 127–139.

Holden, P. and Wilde, N. (2007) *Marketing and PR*, London: A&C Black.

Inside Hoops (2011) NBA TV Contracts. Available at: www.insidehoops.com/nba-tv-contracts. shtml. Accessed 31 October 2011.

IPSOS (2010) Survey. Available at: www.ipsos-mori.com/Assets/Docs/Polls/olympics-2012-survey-for-bbc-london-july-2010-topline.pdf. Accessed 1 June 2011.

Jefkins, F. (1994) *Public Relations*, London: Macdonald & Evans.

Kitchen, P. J. (1997) Integrated Marketing Communications in US Advertising Agencies: An Exploratory Study, *Journal of Advertising Research*, September–October: 7–16.

Katz, H. (2007) *The Media Handbook*, New Jersey LEA.

McNamara, J. (2005) *Public Relations Handbook*, Australia: Archipelago Press.

McQuail, D. (2002) *McQuail's Mass Communication Theory*, London: Sage.

Paraskevas, A. (2000) Dream on but Realise the Basics: Insights from Visitor Satisfaction, the Case of the Millenium Dome, paper presented at the 1st International Conference on Tourism, Recreation and Leisure, Athens, Greece, 24–26 August.

Regester, M. (2008) *Risk Issues and Crisis Management in Public Relations*, London: Kogan Page.

Rivenburgh, N. (2002) The Olympic Games: Twenty-first Century Challenges as a Global Media Event, *Sport in Society*, 5 (3): 32–50.

Shone, A. and Parry, B. (2010) *Successful Event Management: A Practical Handbook* (3rd edn), Andover: Cengage.

Stebbins, R. A. (1996) Volunteering: A Serious Leisure Perspective, *Non-Profit and Voluntary Sector Quarterly*, 25 (2): 211–224.

Williams, K. (2003) *Understanding Media Theory*, London: Arnold Publications.

Wilson, J. (2000) Volunteering, *Annual Review of Sociology*, 26: 215–240.

Index